Committees of Influence

Sarah Moulds

Committees of Influence

Parliamentary Rights Scrutiny and Counter-Terrorism Lawmaking in Australia

Springer

Sarah Moulds
Justice and Society
University of South Australia
Adelaide, SA, Australia

ISBN 978-981-15-4349-4 ISBN 978-981-15-4350-0 (eBook)
https://doi.org/10.1007/978-981-15-4350-0

This Springer imprint is published by the registered company Springer Nature Singapore Pte Ltd.
The registered company address is: 152 Beach Road, #21-01/04 Gateway East, Singapore 189721, Singapore

Foreword[1]

The role of Parliamentary committees in the promotion and protection of human rights is a topic that has gained considerable attention from both human rights law and public law scholars in countries such as Australia, the United Kingdom and New Zealand in recent years.[2] While none of those jurisdictions has a constitutionally entrenched bill of rights with broad-ranging protections, each of them has adopted legislative measures and enhanced Parliamentary human rights procedures to strengthen the role of Parliaments in more effectively protecting against encroachments on rights.

In some instances the reforms have involved the establishment of a new Parliamentary Committee with the specific mandate of scrutinising draft or existing laws against explicit human rights standards derived from international law or a domestic human rights statute based on international norms. In others an explicit human rights scrutiny mandate has been added to the functions of existing committees, often the committee that scrutinises draft legislation or subordinate legislation against 'common law rights and freedoms'. The contribution that these human rights scrutiny committees have made to preventing the enactment of laws that violate human rights has been the object of widespread and intense study by legal scholars in particular over the last two decades or so and there have been a flourishing of literature on the topic in Australia and elsewhere in the last 5 years.

Those new committees or committees with an expanded scrutiny role are not the only Parliamentary bodies that have the opportunity to assess the human rights consistency of proposed legislation and policies: they exist alongside a range of other Parliamentary committees in individual legislatures. These other bodies include standing committees responsible for particular portfolios or sectors such as defence, national security, economics or social affairs, as well as ad hoc committees set up to inquire into particular pieces of legislation. These deliberations and the views of

---

[1] Andrew Byrnes: External legal adviser, Australian Joint Parliamentary Committee on Human Rights (2012–2014)

[2] See, in particular, Julie Debeljak and Laura Grenfell (eds), *Law Making and Human Rights: Executive and Parliamentary Scrutiny across Australian Jurisdictions* (Thomson Reuters, 2020). See also Murray Hunt (ed), *Parliaments and Human Rights: Redressing the Democratic Deficit* (Hart Publishing, 2017).

these committees can critically influence the fate and content of legislation (including on human rights grounds), and in some cases carry greater political weight and persuasive force than the findings of a human rights scrutiny committee, and are sometime in competition with each other for influence.

In this book Dr Moulds makes a significant contribution to the literature on the role of Parliaments in the protection of human rights in Australia, and more generally. In addition to its contribution to developing new methodology for assessing the impact of Parliamentary committees at the federal level, her study makes a persuasive, well-documented argument that previous studies have focused too narrowly on the role that individual committees play and that a full assessment needs to take into account how the overall system of Parliamentary committees operates. It contributes original research findings based on extensive documentary research and interviews with various actors engaged in Parliamentary process, both within the Parliament and outside of it (including the public service and civil society). Finally, it proposes a wide range of recommendations for action that the thesis argues will improve the overall functioning of the Parliamentary committee system in the Commonwealth Parliament, recommendations that may also be equally applicable to other Parliaments in Australia and elsewhere.

The book engages with the existing body of Australian and overseas research examining the effectiveness of Parliamentary scrutiny committees in Westminster systems in ensuring that laws enacted by legislatures conform with human rights standards and fundamental principles of good governance and administration. Much of that literature has to date focused on the work of traditional common law scrutiny committee such as the Senate Standing Committees on the Scrutiny of Bills and on the Scrutiny of Regulations and Ordinances and their State or Territory equivalents, committees with explicit human rights mandates such as the Australian Parliamentary Joint Committee on Human Rights (PJCHR), or on committees which combine those two mandates such as the scrutiny committees of the Victorian and ACT legislatures.

As Dr Moulds points out, much of that literature, especially the more recent literature, focuses on whether the work of such committees, especially those applying an explicit human rights mandate such as the PJCHR, have had a positive impact on legislative compliance with the applicable human rights standards. These analyses focus primarily on the work of an individual committee – the PJCHR has drawn a good deal of attention because of its recent establishment and novel mandate, but recent studies have examined the work of other committees. In their evaluations, these analyses tend to place priority on the existence of evidence of legislative amendments that can be identified as stimulated by the work of the relevant committee, as well as looking to Parliamentary citation of the work of these committees, particularly citation in Parliamentary debates. They also tend to note the importance of the potential impact of the scrutiny procedures on those developing and proposing legislation, that is, developing a 'culture of human rights' in the public service, but generally limit their assessment of progress by examining statements of compatibility that accompany legislative proposals without qualitative empirical work such as interviews with those involved in the process of developing legislation.

A significant number of those analyses also engage with the issue of whether the protection afforded through the policymaking and legislative processes would be bolstered if there were a statutory charter of rights in place that would permit external judicial review of laws and executive actions. They generally conclude that a bill of rights would enhance protection.

This book builds on but extends these approaches in ways that are both original and significant and draws on some of the more developed ways of assessing the effectiveness of Parliamentary scrutiny such as the Dickson Poon Law School's effectiveness framework.[3] The most important innovation is the way in which Dr Moulds' examination does not limit itself to focusing on an individual committee and its success or failure in relation to a particular statute or series of laws. Rather it explores how the Parliamentary committee system as a whole performs both in explicit recognition of human rights compatibility issues and substantive amendments of laws that temper or remove excesses whether or not they are responding to specific human rights issues within the rights listed in the mandate of the technical scrutiny committees such as the PJCHR.

The book approaches this inquiry by examining the work of four Commonwealth Parliamentary committees, the PJCHR, the SSCSB, the Legislation and Constitutional Affairs Committees and the Parliamentary Joint Committee on Intelligence and Security (and its predecessors). The choice of the two thematic committees is influenced by the subject-matter of the legislation chosen for the case studies, namely counter-terrorism legislation. Drawing on Stephenson's work,[4] Dr Moulds emphasises the importance of seeing that Parliamentary review may involve 'multi-stage review', over a period of time and by different actors, sometimes revisiting similar issues that were not resolved at an earlier stage.

The book also sets out a series of indicators of potential impact – an approach shared by a number of other studies – including an impact on Parliamentary debate and deliberation, impact in the media, and the hidden impact in the policymaking and legislative process. In the last case the findings based on interviews provide a significant addition to efforts to document what many commentators consider to be a critical component of any assessment of these legislative scrutiny processes.

The book addresses the questions it poses by examining a series of statutes in the broad field of counter-terrorism that were proposed or enacted since 2001 by the Commonwealth Parliament. Many of these represented significant intrusions on and in some cases violations of internationally accepted human rights. Most of these statutes and the Parliamentary record of intensive and continuing legislative activity in this area have been the subject of detailed analysis by academic commentators, and for the most part, Parliamentary scrutiny and civil society engagement with those procedures has been significant, resulting in (or at least contributing to)

---

[3] Philippa Webb and Kirsten Roberts, *Effective Parliamentary Oversight of Human Rights: A Framework for Designing and Determining Effectiveness* (June 2014). https://www.kcl.ac.uk/law/research/parliamentshr/assets/outcome-document---advance-copy-5-june-2014.pdf.

[4] Scott Stephenson, *From Dialogue to Disagreement in Comparative Rights Constitutionalism* (Federation Press, 2016).

amendments to many of the proposed laws. Most of those amendments have been what Dr Moulds describes as 'rights-remedying' – removing the worst excesses – rather than 'rights-enhancing' – eliminating provisions which are clearly or probably violations of human rights norms.

Both the documentary and empirical research offer different insights into the impacts of scrutiny frameworks. One of the important findings of the book is that the general and specific guidance that emerges from the scrutiny committees in their practice, annual or thematic reports and the underutilised device of Guidance Notes is of practical importance to how public servants go about the business of developing legislative proposals and that this is in some respects a diffuse and hard to document process in many cases.

In this book Dr Moulds offers a detailed menu of recommendations for improvements to the present system of committees. They are deliberately designed to be incremental and not require legislative amendment. Many of them make eminent sense; some would require additional resources, while others would not. Whether already overstretched Parliamentarians of their secretariats would feel able to take up all the recommendations relating to their own activities remains to be seen.

One of the real challenges that Parliamentary committees examining draft legislation face is that it is hard to shift legislative proposals once they have been introduced into the legislature. Informal consultation between public servants and the relevant scrutiny committees, and increased opportunities to examine exposure or draft bills, obviously avoids some of the rigidity that often is a feature of an introduced legislative proposal.

The book argues that what can be achieved within even an improved committee system is largely an increase in 'rights-enhancing' actions rather than 'rights [violation]-remedying' ones. In any case, improving the committee system is not seen as the exclusive path to reform, and Dr Moulds accepts that there may be other parallel routes to improve human rights compliance.

Dr Moulds' study is a stimulating, extensively researched and extremely valuable contribution to the field. Its principled and pragmatic approach drawing on a sound understanding of political theory and human rights norms combined with the practicalities of political life is convincing account of what can be achieved within existing committee systems and what cannot, and what may need to be pursued by other means.

Faculty of Law
University of New South Wales,
Sydney, NSW, Australia
March 2020

Andrew Byrnes

Preface

This book is designed to provide a new, evidence-based perspective on Australia's parliamentary model of rights protection and on the experience of counter-terrorism lawmaking in Australia since 2011. By focusing on the hidden, public and legislative impact of the federal parliamentary committee *system*, it offers a fresh standpoint from which to consider the contemporary legal debate on the best legal mechanism for rights protection in Australia. By using counter-terrorism laws as a detailed case study, it also contributes in a timely, authoritative way to the debate on balancing individual liberties with national security.

Uniquely in the Western world, Australia relies on an 'exclusively parliamentary' model of rights protection at the federal level, which relies heavily on Parliament rather than the courts to protect and promote rights. Central to this model of rights protection is the system of parliamentary committees that inquire into and scrutinise proposed laws. This book tests the limits of the parliamentary model of rights protection, using a case study that includes 15 counter-terrorism-related Acts and explores whether parliamentary committees have had a rights-enhancing impact on these laws and whether the rights-enhancing impact of parliamentary committees can be improved.

The methodology employed in this research considers a range of evidence to provide a holistic account of the impact of the parliamentary committee system on the case study Acts. This includes consideration of the legislative impact of parliamentary committees on the content of the Acts, evidenced by legislative amendments attributed to the work of committees in parliamentary debates or Explanatory Memoranda. This research also considers the role parliamentary committees play in the public and parliamentary debate on the case study Acts, for example, by considering references to individual committees in Hansard debates and media articles. In addition, this research investigates the hidden impact parliamentary committees may be having on policy development and legislative drafting, considering both documentary materials such as guidelines and manuals as well as material obtained from interviews with key participants in the lawmaking process. This material is then considered against the backdrop of a broader analysis of the multiple stages of rights review that occur within the Australian Parliament, in the context of counter-terrorism lawmaking at the federal level.

The results are surprising. This book finds that parliamentary committees have had a rights-enhancing (although rarely rights-remedying) impact on the case study Acts, and that the nature of this impact varies across the different committees studied. Further, this book finds that the hidden or behind-the-scenes impact of parliamentary committees on the development of proposed laws provides a particularly fertile ground for improving the rights-protecting capacity of the committee system. Most significantly, this book finds that the rights-enhancing impact of parliamentary committees is most strongly felt when individual parliamentary committees work together as a *system*. This has important implications for the types of reforms that should be pursued to improve the rights-protecting capacity of the Australian Parliament.

This book concludes by offering a range of practical recommendations designed to improve the rights-enhancing capacity of the parliamentary committee system, while also solidifying the system's respected and valued place with the Australian Parliament. These system-wide recommendations are complemented by proposed committee-specific changes that aim to build upon the strengths of individual committees and maximise the potential for multiple committees to work collaboratively.

When taken together, this research shows that the parliamentary committee system is worth investing in when seeking to improve the current parliamentary model of rights protection, and when exploring alternative models of rights protection at the federal level. As a result, this work has broad implications for rights scholars and rights advocates contemplating new models of rights protection in Australia. It also offers important practical insights to other jurisdictions grappling with the challenges posed by ensuring robust rights protection whilst responding to the threat of terrorism.

Adelaide, SA, Australia Sarah Moulds

Acknowledgements

My research is inspired by the people working in the parliamentary committee system and, in particular, the people I interviewed for this book. I wish to thank all interviewees for their thoughtful insights and generous contributions to my research. Thank you also to the many other participants in the committee system that spoke to me off the record about their experiences. Your experiences have shaped my thinking and challenged my assumptions about the parliamentary committee system at the federal level.

A very big thank you to Associate Professor Laura Grenfell, Dr Anna Olijnyk and Dr Adam Webster who supervised my Doctor of Philosophy research with enthusiasm, patience and care. Thank you also to my professional mentors, the Honourable Thomas Gray QC and Dianne Gray, Professor John Williams and Penny Wright, who have provided wise guidance at key stages of this research and at other important moments in my legal career. I am also grateful for the encouragement, guidance and friendship provided by my colleagues at the University of Adelaide and University of South Australia, and for the Australian Postgraduate Award and Zelling Gray Postgraduate Scholarship that I received during 2015–2018.

I am sincerely grateful for the support of my family, in particular my parents Carla and Bryan for their unwavering love and support. My children Astrid and Jarvis have showed much patience throughout this project and developed an unusually strong interest in all things parliamentary, and Otis had an in-utero introduction to the committee system. Most importantly I thank my partner Jonah. This book represents your hard work as much as mine. Thank you for everything you do for me and our family.

Contents

List of Acronyms and Abbreviations

ACT	Australian Capital Territory
Citizenship Act	*Australian Citizenship Amendment (Allegiance to Australia) Act 2015* (Cth)
AHRC	Australian Human Rights Commission
AFP	Australian Federal Police
ALRC	Australian Law Reform Commission
ASIO Bill 2002	Australian Security Intelligence Organisation Legislation Amendment (Terrorism) Bill 2002 (Cth)
ASIO Bill 2003	Australian Security Intelligence Organisation Legislation Amendment (Terrorism) Bill 2003 (Cth)
Control Orders Act	*Anti-terrorism Act (No 2) 2005* (Cth)
COAG	Council of Australian Governments
Data Retention Act	*Telecommunications (Interception and Access) Amendment (Data Retention) Act 2015* (Cth)
Foreign Fighters Act	*Counter-Terrorism Legislation Amendment (Foreign Fighters) Act 2014* (Cth)
IGIS	Inspector General of Intelligence and Security
INSLM	Independent National Security Legislation Monitor
Haneef Inquiry	Inquiry by the Hon John Clarke QC into the Case of Dr Mohamed Haneef
National Consultation	National Consultation on Human Rights (2009)
NZ	New Zealand
OIL	Office for International Law
OPC	Office of Parliamentary Counsel
PJC on ASIO, ASIS and DSD	Parliamentary Joint Committee on the Australian Security and Intelligence Organisation, Australian Secret Intelligence Service and Defence Signals Directorate

PJCIS	Parliamentary Joint Committee on Intelligence and Security
PJCHR	Parliamentary Joint Committee on Human Rights
Parliamentary Scrutiny Act	*Human Rights (Parliamentary Scrutiny) Act 2011* (Cth)
SoCs	Statements of Compatibility
Sheller Committee	Security Legislation Review Committee
SLAT Acts	*Security Legislation Amendment (Terrorism) Act 2002* (Cth) (and related Acts)
LCA Legislation Committee	Senate Legal and Constitutional Affairs Legislation Committee
LCA References Committee	Senate Legal and Constitutional Affairs References Committee
SFPAC	Senate Standing Committee on Finance and Public Administration
SSCSB	Senate Standing Committee on the Scrutiny of Bills
SSCRO	Senate Standing Committee on Regulations and Ordinances
TEO Act	*Counter-Terrorism (Temporary Exclusion Orders) Act 2019 (Cth)*
UN	United Nations
UK	United Kingdom

List of Tables

Part I
Parliamentary Committees and Rights Protection in Australia

Chapter 1
Introduction

Abstract This chapter introduces the key themes of the book and underscores its relevance for public law scholars and students, and those engaged in the parliamentary system, for example as public servants or parliamentary counsel. It introduces themes such as the role of parliamentary committees in rights protection in Australia and addresses the conventional scepticism of the parliamentary model of rights protection. It also sets out the structure of the book.

In introducing these key themes, this chapter also foreshadows the key findings arising from this research. This includes the finding that when different parliamentary committees work together, important rights-enhancing results can emerge, even in the context of politically-popular counter-terrorism policies. This suggests that carefully examining the role parliamentary committees play in rights protection should be of interest to all rights scholars, including those considering what reforms could be made to strengthen Australia's parliamentary model of rights protection.

1.1 Why Study Parliamentary Committees?

At the heart of Australia's constitutional character is the Australian Parliament. This is the institution that is entrusted with protecting and promoting individual rights and balancing competing public interests. This is the body the public relies upon to protect us from majoritarian rule, to scrutinise proposed laws and to guard us from the exercise of unbridled executive power. Parliament is also the place we look to for representation, deliberation, and engagement with the law-making process. Even when it disappoints us, Parliament is the forum for democratic expression in Australia, and the sovereign law-making institution under our Constitution.

It is in this context that the structures and practices within the Australian Parliament take on significance for anyone interested in rights protection or improving the quality of the law-making process in Australia (see e.g. Debeljak and Grenfell 2020a, pp. 2–28). Among these structures and practices are parliamentary committees, which in many ways epitomise the values of representation,

S. Moulds, *Committees of Influence*, https://doi.org/10.1007/978-981-15-4350-0_1

deliberation and scrutiny the public expect from this parliamentary model of rights protection.

The goal of this book is to recognise and evaluate the role parliamentary committees play in Australia's parliamentary model of rights protection, and to identify practical options for improving the rights-enhancing capacity of the parliamentary committee system. In this way, my work helps to signpost the type of rights-enhancing legislative or policy impact that can be achieved within the existing committee system, and what may need to be pursued by other means. In short, it is a study of the work and role of federal parliamentary committees.

My research uses the experience of developing, debating and enacting counter-terrorism laws in the period from 2001 to 2019 as a canvas to investigate the rights-enhancing impact of parliamentary committees. It focuses on four committees that have been particularly prominent in scrutinising Australia's counter-terrorism laws. These are the Senate Standing Committee for the Scrutiny of Bills (SSCSB), the Senate Standing Committee on Legal and Constitutional Affairs Legislation and References Committees (LCA Committees), the Parliamentary Joint Committee on Intelligence and Security (PJCIS) and the Parliamentary Joint Committee on Human Rights (PJCHR). Using documentary and interview-based material, I argue that only by considering parliamentary committees working together as a system can we develop realistic proposals for substantive improvement in the parliamentary model of rights protection.

For many, parliamentary committees conjure banal images of bored parliamentarians drudging through piles of paperwork or harried public servants forced to answer seemingly never-ending questions about stationary purchases or office furnishings. The Senate Estimates process, which has left many a public servant shaking in their boots (Tatz 2015), is perhaps the most well recognised committee activity by those not intimately involved in the legislative process. However, a closer look at parliamentary committees reveal that they both reflect and feed into the fundamental features and values of our federal Parliament. They provide a forum for all parliamentarians to play a role in the legislative process. They analyse proposed laws and policies and produce vital, independent information about their purpose, effectiveness and impact. They also provide a forum for experts and members of the community to share their views on a proposed law and document the views of a wide range of individuals and organisations on matters critical to the lives and rights of Australians. In this way, parliamentary committees have both *deliberative* attributes (such as facilitating forums for the public to engage in the law-making process) and *authoritative* attributes (such as the power to publicly scrutinise the government's spending, or proposed laws or policies). These attributes can be present within individual committees, and across the committee system, and help explain the challenges and opportunities presented by parliamentary committees undertaking a rights-protecting role.

As a rights advocate and law reformer, this makes parliamentary committees particularly interesting to me. Like many other rights scholars (e.g. Fletcher 2018; Evans and Evans 2006a; Stellios and Palfrey 2012; Kinley and Ernst 2012; Dixon 2012; Mannreitz 2012; Horrigan 2012; Burton and Williams 2013a), when I started this research I was sceptical of the extent to which Australia's exclusively parliamentary model of rights protection could deliver meaningful outcomes for Australians (Colmar Brunton Social Research 2009; Lynch 2010). I shared the orthodox view that within a system of representative and responsible government like Australia's, which provides ideal conditions for executive dominance, parliamentary committees have very little influence on the legislative process and limited means of providing rights protection unless backed up by judicial intervention (Debeljak and Grenfell 2020a, pp. 3 and 7; Banfield and Knopff 2009). Having participated in many parliamentary committee proceedings from a range of standpoints, I was sceptical of the extent to which parliamentary committees could improve the overall effectiveness of the parliamentary model of rights protection.

However, after undertaking this research, and, having spoken to a broad range of key participants in the committee system, I have changed my view. I am convinced that parliamentary committees can and do have a significant rights-enhancing impact on the development and content of our laws and, when considered as a system, provide fertile ground for improving the overall capacity of the parliamentary model of rights protection to deliver real results for the Australian community.

As discussed below, this does not mean I am advocating the retention of the status quo when it comes to rights protection in Australia. Important changes must be made to the way individual parliamentary committees go about their work, and to the way committees interact as a system. In addition, it is important to note the limits of the rights impact shown by research. My research suggests that parliamentary committees can have an important rights-*enhancing* impact on the development and content of counter-terrorism laws that is different in character and scope to the rights-*remedying* changes that would be necessary to ensure that Australia complies with its full range of international human rights obligations. For example, a proposed law may include a provision investing an intelligence agency with coercive questioning powers that interfere with a person's fair trial rights or common law privileges. A rights-*remedying* change could be an amendment that repeals the provision, removing the coercive powers and remedying the rights concerns with the proposed law. A rights-*enhancing* change may include limiting the circumstances in which the coercive powers can be used, or subjecting the use of such powers to external oversight, or incorporating safeguards such as use-immunity privilege. These changes would not completely resolve the potential rights concerns with the provision, but they would enhance its rights compliance, by removing the worst excesses of the provision and limiting its practical implications.

As a result, my findings, with their focus on rights-*enhancing* impact, do not go so far as to suggest that investing in the committee-system *alone* has the capacity to provide comprehensive rights protection at the federal level in Australia. Broader structural reforms, such as the introduction of a more explicit role for the judiciary in rights protection, may still be necessary in addition to investment in the parliamentary committee system to guarantee comprehensive rights protection in Australia. However, as explored in Part III of this book, my research suggests that understanding the rights-enhancing impact of the parliamentary committee system is fundamental for any rights advocates developing or evaluating options for improving or replacing Australia's parliamentary model of rights protection, and may in fact offer new opportunities for structural or cultural change.

For these reasons, I suggest that studying parliamentary committees is particularly important for any scholar interested in rights protection, as well as any lawyer seeking to understand how laws are made at the federal level. Studying parliamentary committees tells us something useful about how the Parliament balances competing public interests and rights, and how the legislature approaches its task of giving legal effect to public policy (Castan and Galloway 2015; Spigelman 2010). Looking at how parliamentary committees operate, as well as how policy makers and parliamentary counsel interact with these committees, also allows lawyers to gain important perspectives about the extent to which the legal principles they take for granted are reflected in the legislative process at the federal level. This is particularly relevant in counter-terrorism law, which comprises the central case study for this book, as is evident by the robust public law scholarship on these laws (Rajanayagam 2020; Dalla-Pozza 2016, 2020; Appleby 2014; Reilly and Lynch 2007), which has included a sustained focus on legislative scrutiny and reform (Security Legislation Review Committee 2006; Council of Australian Governments 2013; Walker 2011).

Although my research focuses on the role parliamentary committees play in scrutinising and developing legislation, these committees are involved in a range of other important roles in the parliamentary system, including as forums to hold the executive to account for public spending and to investigate and resolve transgressions in parliamentary rules and procedures. This means that there is a clear public interest in ensuring that parliamentary committees are performing efficiently and effectively in each of these roles, and a need to understand how individual committees perform their various functions within the broader committee system.

Improving the effectiveness of parliamentary committees is also of interest to those who spend a large proportion of their time engaged in committee work. Interviews with parliamentarians suggest that for opposition Senators and government backbenchers, committee work represents the *major* aspect of their parliamentary life. For some submission makers, engagement with parliamentary committees is a key plank of their advocacy strategy, and entire units of public servants are dedicated to ensuring effective engagement with these committees (Commonwealth Department of Parliamentary Services 2017). Some of these people have expressed views about how to improve the parliamentary committee system. By listening carefully to their views, and reflecting on other sources of evidence of how the committee system works, I can identify practical options for improving the impact and efficiency of the committee system.

1.1.1 Why Is This Research Unique?

The scope, methodology and findings of this book are unique, primarily because this research evaluates the rights-protecting role of parliamentary committees working together *as a system* and considers the full range of impacts of this system on law making, including those hidden from public view. In other words, my research takes a 'total parliament' approach, rather than focusing on the effectiveness of a particular committee (cf. Fletcher 2018, 2020; Williams and Burton 2015; Williams and Reynolds 2016; Reynolds and Williams 2020; Argument 2011). This is achieved by looking for evidence of three different types of impact the system of parliamentary committees have on proposed laws (hidden, public and legislative) through a specifically developed, transparent assessment framework that addresses the challenges identified in previous attempts to evaluate parliamentary committees. This allows my research to transcend the typical inquiry into whether parliamentary committees influence the content of the law (Holland, 2009). I look 'behind the scenes' to uncover whether parliamentary committees have an influence on the development of proposed laws at the pre-introduction phase. To do this, I use evidence obtained from interviews with those responsible for developing Australia's counter-terrorism laws, and those who support and advise parliamentary committees, in addition to public sources such as the Office of Parliamentary Counsel's Drafting Directions and the Department of the Prime Minister and Cabinet's *Legislation Handbook*. The interview material also shapes the recommendations made in Part III and provides a unique source of information against which to test findings derived from my analysis of Hansard debates, committee transcripts and reports. This aspect of my work allows rights scholars to reflect on how the parliamentary system *actually operates* and gives insights into what legal reforms may hold the genuine potential to impact practice. In this way, my work has parallels with the extensive studies of the United Kingdom parliamentary committee system undertaken by Russell and Benton (2009), and the international expert group facilitated by the Dickson Poon School of Law, Kings College, London (Webb and Roberts, 2014).

My book also explicitly recognises that individual committees have distinct functions and goals, which influence their potential to have a strong rights-enhancing impact, and allow them to contribute in different ways to the parliamentary committee system. As Chap. 3 explains, understanding how committees contribute to the broader functions of Parliament helps to elucidate realistic options for improving the capacity of the system to contribute to Australia's parliamentary model of rights protection.

1.1.2 Why Use Counter-Terrorism Law as a Case Study?

My research does not aim to evaluate *every* experience of formal parliamentary scrutiny at the federal level. This would be a near impossible task. Rather, I focus on one particularly powerful case study, comprised of 15 counter-terrorism Acts, to demonstrate how multiple committees work together, and to highlight the circumstances in which these committees have a particularly strong rights-enhancing impact. The 15 case study Acts are the:

- *Security Legislation Amendment (Terrorism) Act 2002* (Cth) (and related Acts) (SLAT Acts, CSA 1).
- Australian Security Intelligence Organisation Legislation Amendment (Terrorism) Bill 2002 (Cth) (CSA 2);
- *Australian Security Intelligence Organisation Legislation Amendment (Terrorism) Act 2003* (Cth) (CSA 3);
- *Anti-terrorism Act 2004* (Cth) (CSA 4);
- *National Security Information (Criminal Proceedings) Act 2004* (Cth) (CSA 5);
- *Anti-Terrorism Act (No 2) 2005* (Cth) (Control Orders Act, CSA 6);
- *Independent National Security Legislation Monitor Act 2010* (Cth) (INSLM Act, CSA 7);
- *National Security Legislation Amendment Act 2010* (Cth) (CSA 8);
- *Telecommunications (Interception and Access) Amendment (Data Retention) Act 2015* (Cth) (Data Retention Act, CSA 9);
- *Counter-Terrorism Legislation Amendment Act (No 1) 2014* (Cth) (CSA 10);
- *Counter-Terrorism Legislation Amendment (Foreign Fighters) Act 2014* (Cth) (Foreign Fighters Act, CSA 11);
- *Australian Citizenship Amendment (Allegiance to Australia) Act 2015* (Cth) (Citizenship Act, CSA 12);
- *Criminal Code Amendment (High Risk Terrorist Offenders) Act 2016* (Cth) (High Risk Offenders Act, CSA 13); and
- *Telecommunications and Other Legislation Amendment (Assistance and Access) Act 2018* (Cth) (Encryption Act, CSA 14)
- *Counter-Terrorism (Temporary Exclusion Orders) Act 2019* (Cth) (TEO Act, CSA 15)

I selected the counter-terrorism case study following a careful review of past efforts to evaluate parliamentary committees in Australia and elsewhere (set out in Chap. 2). While no consistent criteria for selecting case studies emerges from these past evaluations, it is clear that the most useful case studies are those that provide the maximum opportunity to gather a diverse range of information relating to the evaluation criteria being applied (Smookler 2006). Past studies (Aldons 2000, 2003; Benton and Russell 2013; Evans and Evans 2006b; Feldman 2004; Griffith 2005; Halligan 2008; Marsh 2004; Monk 2010) also suggest that, in order to offer a sufficiently robust evaluation, it is necessary to select a case study that:

- is appropriate for the jurisdiction being considered (in this case, federal);

- has a predominantly legislative, rather than regulatory, character;
- addresses subject matter that generates strong parliamentary attention, evokes public discussion and engages a broad range of individual rights and freedoms;
- engages a range of government department and agencies, as well as non-government organisations and community groups; and
- extends across a range of governments, parliaments and individual political personalities.

Unlike other examples of prolific legislative activity over the past two decades, the counter-terrorism case study easily meets the full range of criteria necessary to undertake a robust and systematic evaluation of the parliamentary scrutiny system in action (discussed further in Chap. 2).

Some have suggested that selecting case studies that involve the implementation of popularist, bipartisan policies, or that respond to particularly significant domestic or international events, may present risks when seeking to analyse or assess formal parliamentary scrutiny (Evans and Evans 2006b, c; Benton and Russell 2013; Williams and Burton 2015; Williams and Reynolds 2016). There may be an assumption, for example, that the strong bipartisan support for 'tough on terror' policies sidelines or excludes any meaningful parliamentary scrutiny. However, the analysis undertaken in this book suggests that this is not the case in practice. In fact, as Part II demonstrates, the impact of parliamentary committee scrutiny on the case study Acts was significant and multi-faceted, despite – and in some cases because of – the legal and socio-political characteristics of the case study Acts.

The 15 Acts comprising this case study have some exceptional features. For example, many of the Acts were introduced in response to extraordinary international or domestic events or particular threats to Australia's national security (such as the Security Legislation Amendment (Terrorism) Bill 2002 (Cth)), and propose novel powers for intelligence and law enforcement agencies, and/or new criminal offences (such as the Anti-Terrorism Bill (No. 2) 2005 (Cth)). The majority of these laws remove or at least limit a large number of individual rights and freedoms, change the parameters of criminal liability and extend the powers of law enforcement and intelligence agencies. They have also been introduced against an international context where it is important that a 'state of trust' exists between the Australian community and the national security agencies charged with protecting them from the threat of terrorism (Commonwealth Department of Prime Minister and Cabinet 2017; Omand 2010). Taken together, the 15 case study Acts represent one of the most significant and rights-engaging areas of federal legislative activity over the last two decades, making it a particularly important subject area for detailed legal analysis.

Australia's counter-terrorism laws also provide the perfect canvas for evaluating the rights-protecting role of parliamentary committees. In the absence of a charter or bill of rights at the federal level, scrutiny by parliamentary committees is one of the only practical means by which the rights-intrusive scope of these laws can be curtailed and the state of trust between the community and the national security agencies preserved. This makes studying the impact of parliamentary committees on the content and development of counter-terrorism laws not just interesting, but also critically important. As Evans and Evans (2006b) observe:

> Around the world the commitment of legislatures to human rights is being tested as they respond to terrorism, national security concerns and natural disasters. It is essential to develop strong, credible methodologies that will assist in assessing and strengthening the capacity of legislatures to protect rights and in assessing the need for other institutions to supplement or oversee legislatures in carrying out this role (p. 569).

To maximise the potential for my findings to have broader application, I have chosen Acts with a diversity of content and contextual background. For example, many of the Acts studied attracted the scrutiny of multiple parliamentary committees despite short time frames between introduction and enactment (for example the *Counter-Terrorism Legislation Amendment (Foreign Fighters) Act 2014* (Cth)). Many of these Acts also attracted large numbers of public submissions, gave rise to multiple days of public hearings and generated large numbers of second reading speeches in Parliament. Other Acts in the case study (such as the *National Security Legislation Amendment Act 2010* (Cth) and *Independent National Security Legislation Monitor Act 2010* (Cth)) reflect longer-term efforts to review and reform Australia's counter-terrorism framework, to improve its effectiveness, or to improve its rights compliance. The case study Acts also include examples of proposed laws that are more technical in character, which attract less public attention, but still undergo robust parliamentary scrutiny and substantive legislative change (such as *National Security Information (Criminal Proceedings) Act 2004* (Cth) and *Anti-terrorism Act 2004* (Cth)). This diversity of scrutiny experiences contributes to the strength of this case study for examining the work of parliamentary committees.

As outlined in Chap. 2, I have also employed a range of methodological strategies to ensure that the exceptional legal and socio-political character of my case study does not unduly restrict the broader applicability of my research. For example, my methodology incorporates interview and documentary material that contains reflections on the workings of the committee system more broadly, not just limited to the counter-terrorism experience. In addition, Part III sets out a range of recommendations designed to facilitate further research to confirm the broader applicability of my, including focusing on other case study examples. My own research extends to the experience of marriage equality reform in Australia (Moulds 2020), which has further underpinned and refined the broader application of the findings made in the book.

1.1.3 What 'Rights' Are Considered?

My research focuses on the rights-enhancing impact of parliamentary committees. I use the term 'rights' inclusively to span those human rights recognised under the international conventions to which Australia is a party, such as the *Universal Declaration of Human Rights*, the *International Covenant on Civil and Political*

Rights (ICCPR), and the *International Covenant on Economic, Social and Cultural Rights* (ICESCR).

It also includes those rights recognised under the *Australian Constitution* and the common law (Hume and Williams 2013). This includes the implied freedom of communication (*Australian Capital Television v Commonwealth* (1992) 1777 CLR 106; *Lange v Australian Broadcasting Corporation* (1997) 189 CLR 250), the right to vote and equality of voting power (*Constitution* ss 7, 24, 41); religious rights (*Constitution* ss 116, 117; *Street v Queensland Bar Association* (1989) 168 CLR 461); economic rights such as the right to be compensated for the acquisition of property (*Constitution* s 51(xxxi); *Trade Practices Commission v Tooth & Co Ltd* (1979) 142 CLR 397); and the right to trial by jury (*Constitution* s 80; *Cole v Whitfield* (1988) 165 CLR 360).

This is important because, as will be discussed further in Part II, the Australian Parliament uses a range of language to describe individual rights and freedoms, some of which draws on common law and constitutional concepts. These articulations of rights form part of what Spigelman has described as the Common Law Bill of Rights (Spigelman 2008; French 2009; Goldsworthy 2010, p. 17; Australian Law Reform Commission 2016). They commonly include:

- legal professional privilege;
- the privilege against self-incrimination;
- the right to access legal counsel when accused of a serious crime;
- the right to procedural fairness when affected by the exercise of public power;
- freedom from retrospective operation of criminal laws; and
- the principle that the prosecution should bear the onus of proof in criminal matters.

A similar list of rights is regularly included in the 'principle of legality', which can be applied by the courts as a tool for interpreting ambiguous legislation (*Re Bolton; Ex parte Beane* (1987) 162 CLR 514, 523; *Coco v The Queen* (1994) 179 CLR 427, 437 (Mason CJ, Brennan, Gaudron and McHugh JJ) Spigelman 2005; Lim 2013; Meagher and Groves 2017; Westbury 2008).

In this book I also use the phrase 'rule of law', a phrase that is commonplace in Australian political and legal discourse, but one rarely clearly articulated or unpacked into discrete, accessible components (Dicey 1959, pp. 187–195). According to the orthodox view, summarised below by Sawer, Abjorensen and Larkin (2009), the notion of 'rule of law' generally contains the following key features:

> No one should be above the law, and all are equal before it, whatever their position or standing.
> All public officials should be subject to the law, and act within the terms of legally prescribed duties, powers and procedures.
> Parliamentary law-making should conform to constitutionally defined procedures and limits.
> The judiciary should be clearly independent of both executive and parliament in order to interpret and enforce the law without fear or favour.
> All law should be certain and its provision and penalties known in advance.

> No one should be held or punished without a specific charge and a fair hearing before a duly constituted court (p. 25).

A range of scholars have considered whether this view is too narrow in the context of modern parliamentary democracies (e.g. Radin 2017; Chesterman 2008; Fallon 1997). These arguments provide important context for how Australians conceptualise the rule of law, and how it is applied in practice. However, as explored further in Chap. 6, the above description of the 'rule of law' is an important starting point for this book because of its relatively linear relationship with the scrutiny criteria applied by several federal parliamentary committees.

As will be discussed further in Chaps. 6 and 7, cultural familiarity with this orthodox notion of the rule of law has infused the way Australian parliamentarians talk about individual rights and liberties, and the types of rights issues they focus on most closely when undertaking their scrutiny role. Parliamentary committees remain heavily influenced by this notion of the rule of law, as is evident both in the language used and findings made by the committees examined below. Rule of law principles also feature prominently in the prescribed terms of reference for several scrutiny committees, including the SSCSB.

While my evaluation framework aims to be as inclusive as possible when it comes to what 'rights' are considered, I am conscious that the counter-terrorism case study gives rise to a strong focus on civil and political rights contained in the ICCPR, with less occasion to consider the equally important economic, social and cultural rights listed in the ICESCR. This has two important implications that are explored further in Part III of the book. The first relates to the need to engage in further case study research to ascertain the broader applicability of the findings in this book to other contexts, particularly those engaging economic, social and cultural rights. I have commenced this process by examining the role and impact of the federal parliamentary committee system in the context of marriage equality reform in Australia (Moulds 2020), with findings that mirror those presented in this book. Other scholars have also turned their mind to the role of parliamentary committees and the protection of economic, social and cultural rights, including Fletcher (2018), Goldblatt (2017), and Williams and Reynolds (2016), whose work focuses primarily on the impact of the Parliamentary Joint Committee on Human Rights. Byrne's 2020 consideration of the role of the Parliamentary Joint Committee on Human Rights in the context of economic and social rights is particularly instructive, and highlights the important differences when it comes to scrutinising proposed and existing laws for compliance with rights standards that are relatively static (civil and political rights) compared with those that are designed to be achieved through progressive realisation (economic and social rights). The work of these scholars is considered further in Part III. The second implication of the focus on civil and political rights is the question of whether these rights are particularly well suited to effective parliamentary scrutiny, including by the parliamentary committee system. This implication is considered further in Chap. 6 of the book, which investigates the question of whether a set of common rights scrutiny principles is emerging at the federal level, and what this may mean for rights advocates and scholars contemplating broader structural reform.

1.2 Parliamentary Committees and Rights Protection in Australia

At the federal level Australia has an 'exclusively' parliamentary model of rights protection (Williams and Burton 2015), which exists within a constitutional framework that limits the law-making powers of the Commonwealth, but is in sharp contrast to most other Western nations which have constitutional or statutory bills of rights. In other words, Australia recognises the Parliament as the *only* legitimate arbiter of human rights. The judicial contribution to the conversation on rights is restricted to the resolution of particular disputes, the application of established rules of statutory interpretation (such as the principle of legality discussed above and the presumption of compliance with treaty obligations, see *Minister of State for Immigration & Ethnic Affairs v Teoh* (1995) 183 CLR 273), and the determination of a more limited range of constitutional or common law rights (such as those described above with reference to Spigelman 2008). While these constitutional and common law rights may cross over with the list of rights contained in international human rights instruments, they are nonetheless considered quite separate in both a legal and normative sense. As Davis (2016) observes:

> [A]n historic commitment to parliamentary sovereignty has resulted in the Federal Parliament rejecting judicial oversight of human rights. Instead Australia has a firm commitment to political rights review. Federal Parliament is empowered … to act as the sole body responsible for the scrutiny of legislation to ensure compliance with human rights standards (pp. 213–4).

Parliamentary committees – whether specifically assigned a rights-protecting role, or performing another scrutiny or inquiry function – are central to this parliamentary model as they provide the most practical forum for detailed consideration of the purpose, content and rights impact of proposed new laws. They also provide a source of concrete recommendations for legislative or policy change that regularly improve the rights compliance of proposed federal laws. In other words, parliamentary committees are the core place where legislation is scrutinised for rights compliance and for impact on individual rights. For these reasons, studying the impact of parliamentary committees is crucial to any evaluation of the parliamentary model of rights protection, and the only way to identify the types of changes or reforms that are likely to have practical utility for those working within and engaging with the federal parliamentary system.

1.3 Scepticism About the Parliamentary Model of Rights Protection

While Australia's human rights record is relatively strong from an international perspective (Castan and Gerber 2019, pp. 1, 15), many rights advocates in Australia and elsewhere have expressed scepticism about the extent to which parliamentary committees can have a rights-enhancing impact on the development and content of laws and questioned the capacity of a parliamentary model of rights protection to deliver meaningful rights outcomes (see e.g. Reynolds and Williams 2020 ; Fletcher 2018, pp. 289–296; Debeljak 2013; Evans and Evans 2006a; Stellios and Palfrey 2012; Kinley and Ernst 2012; Dixon 2012; Mannreitz 2012; Horrigan 2012; Burton and Williams 2013a).

At the heart of this scepticism is the fact that the parliamentary model of rights protection depends largely on the executive, via the Parliament, determining rights disputes and addressing gaps in rights protection. In practice, the executive government can be focused strongly on electoral outcomes, and may be particularly poor at promoting and protecting the rights of unpopular minorities (Charlesworth 2002, pp. 74–5; 2008, p. 127). According to this argument, parliamentary committees, public servants and human rights commissions cannot hope to exert the type of political influence necessary to control the executive government, and thus constitute weak forms of rights protection. For example, Debeljak (2013) explains that, under the current parliamentary model, there is an 'under-enforcement' of rights at the federal level and those seeking redress are 'denied an effective rights-focussed, non-majoritarian forum within which their human rights claims can be assessed' (p. 57).

This has led many scholars to call for broader structural reform at the federal level that would see the judiciary invested with an explicit rights-protecting or rights-oversight role (see e.g. (Williams and Williams 2016; Reynolds and Williams 2017; Davis and Williams 2002; Tate 2009; Williams 2003; Debeljak 2013; Fletcher 2018). In other words, many rights advocates want to move from the current model, where Parliament has a monopoly on rights protection, to one where each branch of government is involved in 'institutional dialogue' about the content, scope and limits of human rights (Rice 2020; Debeljak 2013, p. 59). This push for reform has also been reflected in community views, including during the 2008–09 National Consultation on Human Rights, following which the Human Rights Consultation Committee (2009) reported that:

> Most of the people who attended the community roundtables and presented written submissions to the [National Consultation] Committee wanted to see greater protection and promotion of human rights and responsibilities. Only a minority believed that our current protections are adequate (at p. 15).

Rights advocates in favour of structural reform at the federal level have often been divided on whether a constitutional or statutory statement of rights is preferable, depending on whether they support the courts or the Parliament having the final say on rights disputes or the rights compatibility of laws. For example, those that prefer the constitutionally entrenched model argue that giving the courts the final say on the rights compatibility of a law is the only way to successfully guard against unjustified legislative or executive interference with fundamental rights, particularly those of minorities (Burdekin 1994, p. v). In contrast, those in favour of the statutory model (e.g. Chappell et al. 2009; Webber 2006; Charlesworth 2002; Alston 1994) often describe it as addressing the 'democratic deficit' inherent in a constitutional bill of rights because, under many statutory models, the courts have a role in assessing and interpreting the rights compatibility of laws but the Parliament has the final say on whether rights-intrusive legislative provisions can be enacted (e.g. Williams and Burton 2015; Webber 2006). Hiebert (2012) also argues that the statutory model ensures that the focus of those involved in policy development is on utilising rights standards to improve the quality of the proposed law, rather than avoiding potential constitutional litigation. As explored in Part II of this book, my findings suggests that similar benefits arise from the work of parliamentary committees in the Australian parliamentary model of rights protection, particularly when the hidden impact of the committee system is considered and explored.

At least until 2010, proposals for statutory statements of rights generated support in several Australian jurisdictions and dominated the debate on rights protection at the federal level. Several unsuccessful efforts were made to introduce human rights Acts at the federal level (e.g. Chappell et al. 2009, pp. 72–73; Williams 1999, 2000), and in 2004 the *Human Rights Act* was introduced in the Australian Capital Territory (ACT), followed by the introduction of the Victorian *Charter of Rights and Responsibilities Act 2006* (Vic) (the Victorian Charter) in 2006. Over a decade later, Queensland followed suit with its *Human Rights Act 2019* (Qld), which commenced operation on 1 January 2020, and which also establishes a Parliamentary Committee on Human Rights.

Despite these state-level developments, forward momentum behind the push for a federal human rights Act was stymied by two key events. The first was the decision of the Rudd Government not to implement a federal human rights Act following the National Consultation (Human Rights Consultation Committee 2009). The second was the High Court's decision in *Momcilovic v The Queen* (2011) 245 CLR 1 (*Momcilovic*), which involved consideration of a number of key features in the *Charter of Rights and Responsibilities Act 2006* (Vic) and sounded a warning for rights advocates keen to implement similar legislation at the federal level. In *Momcilovic*, the majority of the High Court upheld the constitutional validity of the relevant provisions of the Victorian Charter, but took a conservative approach to the courts' role in relying upon these provisions to 'remedy' rights-infringing laws, and displayed a clear deference to Parliament when it comes to interpreting statutory provisions (Debeljak 2011, 2014, 2020; Victorian Government Solicitors Office 2011). Debeljak (2011) has described the *Momcilovic* decision as sanctioning a 'rights-reductionist' approach to giving effect to the key statutory interpretation provisions in the Charter mechanisms and 'muting' the institutional dialogue between the courts and the legislature (p. 16), particularly in so far as it limits the remedial reach of the obligation in the Charter to interpret statutory provisions in a manner consistent with international human rights. Other commentators agree that the High Court's decision is likely to have a restrictive impact on the design of any future statutory model of rights protection in Australia (e.g. Zhou 2012; Bateman and Stellios 2012).

In light of this stalled momentum behind the push for a federal human rights Act, some rights advocates have turned their focus to the package of reforms introduced by the Rudd Government in response to the National Consultation, including the establishment of the Parliamentary Joint Committee on Human Rights (PJCHR). These reforms were introduced by the *Human Rights (Parliamentary Scrutiny) Act 2011* (Cth). Many (e.g. Campbell and Morris 2015) hoped that the PJCHR, and related mechanisms such as the requirement to introduce laws with statements of rights compatibility, would help overcome some of the weaknesses identified in past studies of the parliamentary model of rights protection at the federal level (e.g.. Evans and Evans 2006b). However, a number of studies of the PJCHR and the requirement to table Statements of Compatibility (SoCs) suggest that these reforms have largely failed to live up to expectations (e.g. Fletcher 2018, 2020; Reynolds and Williams 2016, 2020; Rajanayagam 2015, 2020; Williams and Burton 2015). For example, in their 2016 study of the post-PJCHR parliamentary model of rights protection, Williams and Reynolds found that, when it comes to improving the content of proposed laws, the PJCHR's findings had a minimal impact (p. 490). The authors also found that the PJCHR's 'deliberative impact' on rights protection in Australia was also minimal, reflecting a 'slow improvement from a low base', and that much of this improvement was attributable to a 'few outspoken advocates for the human rights scrutiny regime' (p. 488). The authors also found that judicial use of the rights scrutiny regime has been extremely limited (pp. 494–5) and public awareness was low (pp. 496–7). Responding to these findings, Williams and Reynolds observed that the executive dominated House of Representatives largely obfuscated the possibility of any parliamentary based human rights regime producing substantive legislative changes or amendments. For these authors, it was simply 'not realistic' (p. 507) to expect that a parliamentary committee could assert any meaningful influence over a dominant Executive Government – at least in the absence of any judicial supervision or enforcement by the courts. In a 2019 reconsideration of their earlier evaluative work, Williams and Reynolds largely confirmed these findings, concluding that factors such as variable and poor quality statements of compatibility with human rights, the timing of PJCHR reports and responsiveness of Minister's to questions and requests for further information greatly reduced the overall deliberative, legislative or judicial impact of the Committee (Reynolds and Williams 2020).

These findings echo earlier warnings about the limits of Australia's parliamentary model of rights protection (e.g. Williams and Burton 2015; Palfrey 2012; Santow 2010; Stellios and Palfrey 2012; Hiebert 2011). This experience has also solidified the scepticism of many rights advocates about the capacity of the parliamentary model to deliver real rights outcomes for Australians. As will be discussed below, my research challenges several findings made in these studies, and suggests that there is value in overcoming this scepticism at least when it comes to understanding the rights-enhancing impact of the parliamentary committee system.

1.4 Overcoming Scepticism About the Parliamentary Model of Rights Protection

As noted above, when commencing this research, I shared the views of many of the scholars discussed above. The rights-abrogating content and operation of many federal laws, including counter-terrorism laws (see e.g. Lynch 2006; Lynch and McGarrity 2008; Appleby 2015; Williams 2015; Hocking 2004), seemed proof enough that the parliamentary model of rights protection simply was not working, and would be nearly impossible to fix. However, after undertaking a careful analysis of the three tiers of impact parliamentary committees have had on the development of Australia's counter-terrorism laws, and listening to those with direct experience working within the committee system, I changed my view. It became clear that individual committees have had a significant rights-enhancing (although rarely rights-remedying) impact on these laws and, more interestingly, when multiple committees worked together this impact was stronger and longer lasting. In other words, these findings suggest that the work of parliamentary committees removed the worst excesses of proposed provisions that would otherwise have abrogated individual rights, or subjected these provisions to important safeguards or oversight mechanisms even if they were not always able to remove the potential for some negative impact on individual rights to occur. It also became clear that the way parliamentary committees operate (including how they engage key participants and the way they talk about rights) is making a discernible contribution to Australia's parliamentary model of rights protection.

My analysis directly challenges findings made by past studies of Australian parliamentary committees and rights protection or, at the very least, presents a different picture of their overall rights-enhancing impact. For example, unlike the 2006 findings made by Evans and Evans, Part II of the book presents evidence that the scrutiny criteria applied by some parliamentary committees are deeply entrenched in policy making and parliamentary drafting practice, and that this has tangible rights-enhancing results.[1] Part III of this book also finds that some committees have the capacity to make a long-term contribution to the development of proposed laws and provide a deliberative forum to debate rights-related issues. This book also documents instances of consistently strong rights-enhancing legislative impact by particular committees in the system. Key among my findings is that, when different committees work together as a system, the rights-enhancing impacts can be particularly strong. This suggests that, rather than looking exclusively at the rights-protecting capacity of one committee, such as the PJCHR, many committees in the system may be well placed to play an active role in rights protection.

These findings are important as they point to the need to consider the parliamentary committee system carefully when evaluating options for improving rights

[1] Fletcher also considers the 'behind the scenes' impact of the work of parliamentary committees, but with an explicit and exclusive focus on the Parliamentary Joint Committee on Human Rights see Fletcher (2018 particularly pp. 290–291).

protection in Australia. They also highlight the merit in some of the arguments made by scholars who claim that the existing parliamentary model of rights protection has distinct advantages over constitutionally entrenched or statutory enshrined charters of rights (see e.g. Campbell 2006; Goldsworthy 2001; Stone 2001; Chappell et al. 2009). For example, prior to the introduction of the PJCHR, Campbell advocated the establishment of a 'democratic' human rights committee at the federal level, with wide-ranging inquiry powers and the capacity to proactively generate rights-protecting legislation, in addition to the power to scrutinise proposed laws for compliance with human rights standards (Campbell 2006, p. 333). Such a committee would have constitutional backing, not in the form of a prescribed bill of rights, but to entrench its place in the Parliament and preserve its procedural integrity, regardless of the views of the executive government (Campbell 2006, pp. 333–4; Stone 2009). The rights standards to be applied by such a committee would be generated by the committee itself and popularly endorsed (Campbell 2006, p. 334). The proposed committee would also have the power to delay legislation to ensure that human rights considerations are addressed and to require rights-protecting legislation to be brought forward within a specific time frame (Campbell 2006, p. 334). While the proposed committee would have no power to block legislation, it would be able to require ministers to respond to its requests for information, call witnesses, conduct inquiries and obtain expert advice (Campbell 2006, pp. 334–5). For Campbell, a committee-based approach to rights protection, where the rights standards to be applied are generated and articulated by the committee itself, 'avoids overly legalistic formulations of rights' and gives rise to 'superior democratic legitimacy' than other models of rights protection (Campbell 2006, pp. 336–7). These ideas are reflected in other efforts to articulate the appropriate 'democratic' role of parliaments in rights protection, including the draft *Principles and Guidelines on the Role of Parliaments in the Protection and Realisation of the Rule of Law and Human Rights* reproduced in Hunt, Hooper and Yowell (2015, pp. 485–99) and discussed in detail by Fletcher (2018).

While my recommendations depart from those made by Campbell in important respects (see in particular the discussion in Chap. 10), my findings on the role parliamentary committees can play in enhancing the deliberative quality (considered in detail by Levy and Orr 2016 and discussed further below) of the law-making process align with many of Campbell's arguments. The findings in Part II demonstrate the ways in which the parliamentary committee system aims to resolve difficult decisions about 'balancing rights' (see e.g. Craven 2004; Campbell 2006, pp. 326–7; Allan 2002; cf. Levy and Orr 2016, pp. 76–80) and to encourage public participation in rights discussions (see e.g. Campbell 2006; Stone 2003; Allan 2003; Galligan and Morton 2003). The material I present in Part II suggests that alternative, less rights-intrusive options are often identified through committee processes and later adopted as successful legislative amendments to proposed laws. This suggests that the way rights issues are debated between the executive and the Parliament can be nuanced and meaningful, even in the context of strong bipartisan support for 'tough on terror' policies. As discussed further in Part III, this organically developing dialogue may have advantages over other rights-protecting models where the judiciary enters this dialogue in a more explicit way, such as under statutory or constitutional models where the courts declare a law to be inconsistent with a list of protected rights without offering policy alternatives.

In this way, my findings share similarities with scholars such as Kinley, who support models of rights protection that focus on developing a culture of rights compliance at the pre-legislative phase, rather than rights-protection models that include remedial, post-introduction judicial determination of rights disputes (Kinley 1999; Kinley and Ernst 2012, p. 69). For Kinley, these pre-legislative scrutiny models of rights protection are preferable because they are more 'democratic' than constitutional or statutory charters of rights: they work to exert 'electoral pressure' upon problematic legislation by drawing public attention to the key features of proposed laws and their potential impact on human rights (Kinley 1999, p. 162). Morris and Campbell share this perspective, as is evident from their 2015 evaluation of the PJCHR, where the authors found that during its first few years of operation the PJCHR had 'improved Australia's human rights institutional performance' and created the chance for a wide range of actors, including parliamentarians, commentators and non-government organisations, to be part of a rights scrutiny framework (Campbell and Morris 2015, p. 27). My research builds upon this finding by suggesting that when parliamentary committees, including the PJCHR, work together as a system their capacity to contribute to a pre-legislative culture of rights compliance at the federal level is considerably enhanced. This has the distinct advantage of engaging the public in the human rights discourse rather than reserving the question of rights compliance to party room to consider behind closed doors, or for the judiciary to determine in a post-enactment environment. As explored further in Part III, engagement with the parliamentary committee system means that individual Australians and individual parliamentarians are part of the democratic conversation on rights, regardless of the broader 'institutional dialogue' that may derive from the current parliamentary model of rights protection, or other statutory or constitutional forms of rights protection that have been proposed at the federal level.

My research can also be considered within the analytical framework of 'multistage rights review' employed by Stephenson (2016) in his comparative analysis of different common law jurisdictions' approaches to rights protection. Unlike many other scholars, Stephenson (2016) rejects the idea of analysing models of rights protection with reference to institutional *dialogue* on rights (where the system is categorised as either one of legislative supremacy or judicial supremacy) in favour of focusing on the direct and indirect *disagreements* that occur between different institutions of government on rights issues (where systems are understood as involving multiple stages of rights review by different institutions of government). This approach helps to reveal similarities and differences across models of rights protection that may not be visible under the 'dialogue' approach. For example, applying the 'dialogue' analytical approach to the Australian federal experience, the Parliament (and not the courts) has the final say on rights issues or rights-abrogating laws. However, this can mask the contribution other branches of government may make along the way to the final resolution of the rights issue by Parliament. As Stephenson (2016) explains:

> A legislature that resolves rights issues in an informal manner with little interference from other institutions is in a markedly different position from a legislature that resolves rights issues only after the executive, a specialist legislative committee and the courts have offered their views and placed pressure on the legislature to heed them (at p.5).

Stephenson's approach highlights the importance of identifying and analysing both *direct* and *indirect* inter-institutional disagreement on rights that occur in different jurisdictions (Stephenson 2016, pp. 6–7). Although, like other scholars, I continue to describe the Australian model of rights protection as 'parliamentary', my research helps to illustrate the multi-stage rights review that occurs at the federal level, by documenting the important direct and indirect contribution parliamentary committees make to resolving rights issues within this system. In addition, my research provides an example of some of the 'points of tension between forms of institutional disagreement' that Stephenson discusses in his comparative analysis (Stephenson 2016, pp. 11–12). For example, the analysis undertaken in Part II of my research exposes how the bureaucracy anticipates rights scrutiny when providing advice to Ministers, and how the rights-intrusive nature of proposed provisions can be removed by the legislative implementation of recommendations made by parliamentary committees. Like Stephenson, my research suggests that these tensions between or within the institutions of government on rights issues provide an *opportunity* for improving the quality of rights review in Australia, rather than pointing to a fundamental flaw in the rights dialogue between these institutions (Stephenson 2016, pp. 210–219).

This more nuanced approach to analysing the way institutions of government engage in rights review also provides an important context for examining whether an organically emerging rights-scrutiny culture may exist within a particular jurisdiction, which in turn has important implications for what types of rights reforms may be accepted or rejected by that culture. For example, the material set out in Part III suggests that there are a range of common rights-scrutiny principles that appear to be consistently applied by the federal Parliament and the public service when formulating and scrutinising counter-terrorism laws that may have application beyond the case study examined in this book. In this way, my research also builds upon the 2019 observations of Byrnes, Rice and Dalla-Pozza, who share my interest in understanding how parliamentary scrutiny bodies (such as committees) interact with the Executive and with non-parliamentary actors (such as the Independent National Security Legislation Monitor) when undertaking their legislative scrutiny role. These authors have also offered views on what these interactions might tell us about the rights scrutiny culture that may exist at the federal level, and each highlight the importance of reflecting on Australia's particular relationship with internationally articulated human rights standards, and to the centrality of Parliament as the (sole) legitimate arbiter on rights issues. This is also considered by Debeljak and Grenfell (2020, pp. 789–818) in the context of what the authors describe as a 'culture of justification' when it comes to law making and protection of human rights in Australia.

If substantiated by further research, in particular research that considers the role of parliamentary committees in protecting and promoting economic, social and cultural rights (e.g. Byrnes 2020; Goldblatt 2017, p. 183), this emerging rights-scrutiny culture may be particularly important for those seeking to articulate an Australian list or statement of rights or for those seeking to engage the full range of political decision makers in rights protection. In summary, by focusing on the way multiple committees work together as a system, my research explores the Australian parliamentary model of rights protection in a deep and nuanced way, and reveals important new perspectives on the current and future capacity of this model to deliver meaningful rights protection at the federal level.

I want to be clear that the findings made in this book do not obviate the need to consider other rights-protecting mechanisms at the federal level. Indeed, the rights-abrogating content of Australia's counter-terrorism laws is a stark reminder that the current system is not producing consistent rights-protecting results. A number of domestic and international scholars have undertaken detailed analysis of the extent to which Australia's counter-terrorism laws comply with the international human rights obligations Australia has voluntarily assumed, and the principles of established Australian criminal or constitutional law (see e.g. Lynch and McGarrity 2008; Scheinin 2006; Hocking 2004; Lynch et al. 2007; Michaelsen 2006). These scholars have overwhelmingly found Australia's counter-terrorism laws to be non-compliant with a large range of these rights and principles.

In addition, scholars such as Roach (2011), Golder and Williams (2006), Joseph (2004), Zifcak (2013) and Lumina (2007) have compared Australia's counter-terrorism laws to those in comparative jurisdictions, such as the United Kingdom (UK), New Zealand (NZ) and Canada, and found that Australia's counter-terrorism framework is broader in scope and more rights-intrusive (e.g. Roach 2011, p. 309). For example, as Williams and Burton (2015) note, Australia's control order regime is based on a regime introduced in the UK in 2005 via the *Prevention of Terrorism Act 2005* (UK) that was later 'heavily criticised and found to violate the European Convention on Human Rights', including on the basis that it unjustifiably interfered with the right to liberty, the right to a fair trial and freedom from discrimination (Burton and Williams 2013b; Bates 2009, p. 100; Fenwick and Phillipson 2012; Carlile 2006, pp. 13, 15–6). The UK control orders regime was abolished in 2011 and replaced with a new regime of terrorism prevention and investigation measures; however, as discussed further in Chap. 3, the Australian control order regime remains in force, and has been extended on multiple occasions since 2011. Burton and Williams (2013b) note that this is just one example of an Australian counter-terrorism law with serious rights defects (at p. 205). These scholars demand that Australia do something more than improve its parliamentary committee system if it is serious about protecting rights, pointing to comparable jurisdictions with statutory and constitutional statements of rights, such as the UK, NZ and Canada.

This research has a different focus. It seeks to understand the multi-stage rights protection system currently in place at the federal level, and to identify its strengths and weaknesses. It asks whether or not parliamentary committees have had an impact on the case study Acts and, if so, whether this impact was rights-enhancing. In so doing, it seeks evidence-based findings about what is working well, and what reforms could be made to improve the rights-enhancing impact of the parliamentary committee system.

My research also uncovers important features of the rights-scrutiny culture that appear to be developing organically at the federal level, which may have implications for those considering broader structural reform. As Stephenson has noted, each model of rights protection – whether 'exclusively parliamentary', statutorily prescribed or constitutionally entrenched – generates its own particular rights-scrutiny culture, and exists within its own particular institutional context (Stephenson 2016, p. 211). This can make each system resistant to broader structural change, or inclined to revert back to its 'original' rights culture even when structural change occurs (Stephenson 2016, p. 8; Hiebert 2012). My research suggests that there is value in understanding the cultural and contextual features of the current Australian model of rights protection, including by understanding the hidden or behind-the-scenes impact of the parliamentary committee system. As Part III explores, this helps to identify how the rights-enhancing capacity of the committee system can be improved, and highlights what types of considerations should be kept in mind by those advocating more radical reform.

1.5 Structure and Overview of Chapters

This book is comprised of three parts, organised around the central task of recognising, evaluating and improving the role parliamentary committees play in the Australian parliamentary model of rights protection. Part I sets out the assessment framework employed in this book (Chap. 2), and introduces the case study Acts and particular committees studied, having regard to the parliamentary landscape in which laws are developed, debated and enacted (Chap. 3). The focus of Part I is on *recognising* the role parliamentary committees play in the federal Parliament, and in counter-terrorism law making in Australia.

Part II of the book is focused on *evaluating* the role parliamentary committees play in the Australian parliamentary model of rights protection, using counter-terrorism law making as a case study and applying the assessment framework set out in Chap. 2. This Part of the book presents evidence with respect to each component of the assessment framework, allowing findings to be made about the overall impact of parliamentary committees on the case study Acts. Chapter 4 identifies the key *participants* in the four committees studied, and looks for evidence of whether these participants consider these committees to be *legitimate* or respected, effective and authoritative part of the federal Parliament (Peter 2017). Chapter 5 sets out evidence of the *legislative impact* of the four parliamentary committees on the case study Acts, providing a powerful indicator of their overall influence. Chapter 6 sets out evidence of the *public impact* of the four parliamentary committees on the case study Acts, including evidence that committees influenced or were considered in public or parliamentary debate or post-enactment review. Chapter 7 considers evidence of the *hidden* or '*behind-the-scenes*' impact of the four parliamentary committees on the case study Acts, including whether the work of these committees influenced or was considered in the pre-introduction phase.

Part III of the book is focused on identifying ways to *improve* the role of the federal committee system in Australia's parliamentary model of rights protection. It uses the evidence presented in Part II to substantiate the central finding of this book. It argues that only by considering parliamentary committees working together as a system can we propose realistic substantive improvements in the parliamentary model of rights protection. It demonstrates that making changes to the processes, mandates or powers of individual committees provides only limited scope to improve the committee's rights-protecting capacity. Instead, it is the system of parliamentary committees that provides the most realistic and practical options for meaningful, short-term reform. Part III concludes by setting out a range of practical options for improving the capacity of the parliamentary committee system to contribute to rights protection in Australia.

References

Legal Materials

Cases

Australian Capital Television v Commonwealth (1992) 1777 CLR 106.
Coco v The Queen (1994) 179 CLR 427.
Cole v Whitfield (1988) 165 CLR 360.
Lange v Australian Broadcasting Corporation (1997) 189 CLR 250.
Minister of State for Immigration & Ethnic Affairs v Teoh (1995) 183 CLR 273.
Re Bolton; Ex parte Beane (1987) 162 CLR 514.
Street v Queensland Bar Association (1989) 168 CLR 461.
Trade Practices Commission v Tooth & Co Ltd (1979) 142 CLR 397.

Legislation

Anti-terrorism Act (No 2) 2005 (Cth).
Anti-terrorism Act 2004 (Cth).
Australian Citizenship Amendment (Allegiance to Australia) Act 2015 (Cth).
Australian Security Intelligence Organisation Legislation Amendment (Terrorism) Act 2003 (Cth).
Australian Security Intelligence Organisation Legislation Amendment (Terrorism) Bill 2002 (Cth).
Counter-Terrorism (Temporary Exclusion Orders) Act 2019 (Cth).
Counter-Terrorism Legislation Amendment (Foreign Fighters) Act 2014 (Cth).
Counter-Terrorism Legislation Amendment Act (No 1) 2014 (Cth).
Criminal Code Amendment (High Risk Terrorist Offenders) Act 2016 (Cth).
Independent National Security Legislation Monitor Act 2010 (Cth).
National Security Information (Criminal Proceedings) Act 2004 (Cth).
National Security Legislation Amendment Act 2010 (Cth).

Security Legislation Amendment (Terrorism) Act 2002 (Cth).
Telecommunications (Interception and Access) Amendment (Data Retention) Act 2015 (Cth).
Telecommunications and Other Legislation Amendment (Assistance and Access) Act 2018 (Cth).

International Law Materials

International Covenant on Civil and Political Rights, opened for signature 16 December 1966, [1980] ATS 23.
International Covenant on Economic, Social and Cultural Rights, opened for signature 16 December 1966, [1976] ATS 5.

Books/Articles/Reports/Speeches

Aldons, A. (2000). Rating the effectiveness of parliamentary committee reports: The methodology. *Legislative Studies, 15*(1), 22–32.
Aldons, M. (2003). Problems with parliamentary committee evaluation: Light at the end of the tunnel? *Australasian Parliamentary Review, 18*(1), 79–86.
Allan, J. (2002). Oh that I were made judge in the land. *Federal Law Review, 30*(3), 566.
Allan, J. (2003). A defence of the status quo. In T. Campbell, J. Goldsworthy, & A. Stone (Eds.), *Protecting human rights: Instruments and institutions* (pp. 173–192). Oxford: Oxford University Press.
Alston, P. (Ed.). (1994). *Towards an Australian bill of rights* (pp. 88–93). Canberra: Australian National University Press.
Appleby, G. (2015). The 2014 counter-terrorism reforms in review. *Public Law Review, 26*(1), 4–7.
Appleby, G., Grenfell, L., & Reilly, A. (Eds.). (2014). *Australian Public Law* (2nd ed). Oxford: Oxford University Press.
Argument, S. (2011, July 21–22). *Of parliament, pigs and lipstick (slight return): A defence of the work of legislative scrutiny committees in human rights protection*. Paper presented at the Australian Institute of Administrative Law Forum, Canberra.
Australian Law Reform Commission. (2016). *Traditional rights and freedoms – Encroachments by commonwealth laws*. Report No. 129 (2016). Retrieved from https://www.alrc.gov.au/publication/traditional-rights-and-freedoms-encroachments-by-commonwealth-laws-alrc-report-129/. Accessed 7 Jan 2020.
Banfield, A. C., & Knopff, R. (2009). Legislative versus judicial checks and balances: Comparing rights policies across regimes. *Australian Journal of Political Science, 44*(1), 13–27. https://doi.org/10.1080/10361140802654968.
Bateman, W., & Stellios, J. (2012). Chapter III of the constitution, federal jurisdiction and dialogue charters of human rights. *Melbourne University Law Review, 36*(1), 1–40.
Bates, E. (2009). Anti-terrorism control orders: Liberty and security still in the balance 29 Legal Studies *29*, 99–130.
Benton, M., & Russell, M. (2013). Assessing the impact of parliamentary oversight committees: The select committees in the British House of Commons. *Parliamentary Affairs, 66*, 772–797.
Burdekin, B. (1994). Foreword. In P. Alston (Ed.), *Towards an Australian bill of rights* (p. a). Canberra: Australian National University Press, v.
Burton, L., & Williams, G. (2013a). Australia's exclusive parliamentary model of rights protection. *Statute Law Review, 34*, 58–94. https://doi.org/10.1093/slr/hms048.
Burton, L., & Williams, G. (2013b). What future for Australia's control order regime. *Public Law Review, 24*, 182–208.
Byrnes, A. (2020). Economic and social rights in the Australian parliamentary human rights scrutiny process. In J. Debeljak & L. Grenfell (Eds.), *Law-making and human rights* (pp. 135–171). Sydney: Thompson Reuters.

Campbell, T. (2006). Human rights strategies: An Australian alternative. In T. Campbell, J. Goldsworthy, & A. Stone (Eds.), *Protecting rights without a bill of rights* (pp. 319–334). London: Ashgate.

Campbell, T., & Morris, S. (2015). Human rights for democracies: A provisional assessment of the Australian Human Rights (Parliamentary Scrutiny) Act 2011. *University of Queensland Law Journal, 34*(1), 7–27.

Carlile, A. (2006). *Final report of the independent reviewer pursuant to Section 14(3) of the Prevention of Terrorism Act 2005 (UK)*. London: Stationary Office.

Castan, M., & Galloway, K. (2015). Extending public law: Digital engagement, education and academic identity. *Legal Education Review, 25*, 331–348.

Castan, M., & Gerber, P. (2019). Human rights landscape in Australia. In M. Castan & P. Gerber (Eds.), *Contemporary perspectives on human rights in Australia* (pp. 1–18). Sydney: Lawbook.

Chappell, L., Chesterman, J., & Hill, L. (2009). *The politics of human rights in Australia*. Cambridge: Cambridge University Press.

Charlesworth, H. (2002). *Writing in rights: Australia and the protection of human rights*. Sydney: UNSW Press.

Charlesworth, H. (2008). Democratic objections to bills of rights. *Sydney Papers, 20*(3), 124–134.

Chesterman, S. (2008). An international rule of law? *The American Journal of Comparative Law, 56*(2), 331–362.

Colmar Brunton Social Research. (2009). *Final report, national human rights consultation – community research phase*. Retrieved from http://www.jca.asn.au/wp-content/uploads/2013/11/P01_13_02_28-Brennan-paper.docx.pdf. Accessed 7 Jan 2020.

Commonwealth Department of Parliamentary Services. (2017). *Employment: Department of Parliamentary Services*. Retrieved from http://www.aph.gov.au/About_Parliament/Employment/Department_of_Parliamentary_Services. Accessed 7 Jan 2020.

Commonwealth Department of Prime Minister and Cabinet. (2017). *Independent intelligence review*. Retrieved from https://pmc.gov.au/national-security/2017-independent-intelligence-review. Accessed 7 Jan 2020.

Council of Australian Governments Counter-Terrorism Review Committee. (2013). *Review of counter-terrorism legislation*. Retrieved from https://www.ag.gov.au/Consultations/Pages/COAGReviewofCounter-TerrorismLegislation.aspx. Accessed 7 Jan 2020.

Craven, G. (2004). *Conversations with the constitution: Not just a piece of paper*. Sydney: Sydney University Press.

Dalla-Pozza, D. (2016). Refining the Australian counter-terrorism legislative framework: How deliberative has parliament been? *Public Law Review, 27*(4), 271.

Dalla-Pozza, D. (2020). A dual scrutiny mechanism for Australia's counter-terrorism law landscape: The INSLM and the PJCIS. In J. Debeljak & L. Grenfell (Eds.), *Law-making and human rights* (pp. 673–700). Sydney: Thompson Reuters.

Davis, F. F. (2016). Political rights review and political party cohesion. *Parliamentary Affairs, 69*, 213–221.

Davis, M., & Williams, G. (2002). A statutory bill of rights for Australia? Lessons from the United Kingdom. *University of Queensland Law Journal, 22*(1), 1–29.

Debeljak, J. (2011). Who is sovereign now? The Momcilovic court hands back power over human rights that parliament intended it to have. *Public Law Review, 22*(1), 15–52.

Debeljak, J. (2013). Does Australia need a bill of rights? In M. Castan & P. Gerber (Eds.), *Contemporary perspectives on human rights in Australia* (pp. 37–70). Sydney: Lawbook.

Debeljak, J. (2014). Proportionality, rights-consistent interpretation and declarations under the Victorian Charter of Human Rights and Responsibilities: The Momcilovic litigation and beyond. *Monash University Law Review, 40*(2), 340–388.

Debeljak, J. (2020). Rights dialogue where there is disagreement under the Victorian Charter. In J. Debeljak & L. Grenfell (Eds.), *Law-making and human rights* (pp. 267–320). Sydney: Thompson Reuters.

Debeljak, J., & Grenfell, L. (2020a). Contextualising law- making and human rights. In J. Debeljak & L. Grenfell (Eds.), *Law-making and human rights* (pp. 2–28). Sydney: Thompson Reuters.

Debeljak, J., & Grenfell, L. (2020b). Future directions for engaging with human rights in law-making: Is a culture of justification emerging across Australian jurisdictions? In J. Debeljak & L. Grenfell (Eds.), *Law-making and human rights* (pp. 789–818). Sydney: Thompson Reuters.

Dicey, A. V. (1959). *Introduction to the study of the law of the constitution* (10th ed.). London: Macmillan.

Dixon, R. (2012). A new (inter)national human rights experiment for Australia. *Public Law Review, 23*, 75–80.

Evans, C., & Evans, S. (2006a). *Australian parliaments and the protection of human rights*. Paper presented in the Department of the Senate Occasional Lecture Series, Canberra, 8 December 2006.

Evans, C., & Evans, S. (2006b). Evaluating the human rights performance of legislatures. *Human Rights Law Review, 6*, 545–569. https://doi.org/10.1093/hrlr/ngl012.

Evans, C., & Evans, S. (2006c). Legislative scrutiny committees and parliamentary conceptions of human rights. *Public Law, 785*.

Fallon, R., Jr. (1997). The rule of law as a concept in constitutional discourse. *Columbia Law Review, 97*, 1–56.

Feldman, D. (2004). The impact of human rights on the UK legislative process. *Statute Law Review, 25*, 91–115. https://doi.org/10.1093/slr/25.2.91.

Fenwick, H., & Phillipson, G. (2012). UK Counter-terror Law Post-9/11: Initial acceptance of extraordinary measures and the partial return to human rights norms. In V. Ramraj, M. Hor, K. Roach, & G. Williams (Eds.), *Global anti-terrorism law and policy* (p. 481). Cambridge: Cambridge University Press.

Fletcher, A. (2018). *Australia's human rights scrutiny regime*. Melbourne: Melbourne University Press.

Fletcher, A. (2020). Human rights scrutiny in the Federal Parliament: Smokescreen or democratic solution? In J. Debeljak & L. Grenfell (Eds.), *Law making and human rights: Executive and parliamentary scrutiny across Australian jurisdictions* (pp. 31–66). Sydney: Thompson Reuters.

French, R. (2009, September 4). *The common law and the protection of human rights*. Speech delivered at the Anglo-Australasian Lawyers Society, Sydney, 4 September 2009. Retrieved from https://www.hcourt.gov.au/assets/publications/speeches/current-justices/frenchcj/frenchcj4sep09.pdf. Accessed 7 Jan 2020.

Galligan, B., & Morton, F. L. (2003). Australian exceptionalism: Rights protection without a bill of rights. In T. Campbell, J. Goldsworthy, & A. Stone (Eds.), *Protecting human rights: Instruments and institutions* (pp. 19–34). Oxford: Oxford University Press.

Goldblatt, G. (2017). Social (in)security and inequality in Australia: The limited role of human rights in the policy debate. In A. Durbach & B. Edgeworth (Eds.), *Law and poverty in Australia: 40 years after the Poverty Commission* (pp. 183–198). Sydney: Federation Press.

Golder, B., & Williams, G. (2006). Balancing national security and human rights: Assessing the legal response of common law nations to the threat of terrorism. *Journal of Comparative Policy Analysis, 8*, 43–62. https://doi.org/10.1080/13876980500513335.

Goldsworthy, J. (2001). Legislative sovereignty and the rule of law. In T. Campbell, K. Ewing, & A. Tomkins (Eds.), *Sceptical essays on human rights* (pp. 69–81). Oxford: Oxford University Press.

Goldsworthy, J. (2010). *Parliamentary sovereignty: Contemporary debates*. Cambridge: Cambridge University Press.

Griffith, G. (2005). Parliament and accountability: The role of parliamentary oversight committees. Briefing Paper No. 12/05. Parliamentary Library Research Service, New South Wales.

Halligan, J. (2008). Parliamentary committee roles in facilitating public policy at the commonwealth level. *Australasian Parliamentary Review, 23*(2), 135–156.

Hiebert, J. L. (2011). Governing like judges? In T. Campbell, K. D. Ewing, & A. Tomkins (Eds.), *The legal protection of human rights: Sceptical essays* (pp. 40–65). Oxford: Oxford University Press.

Hiebert, J. L. (2012). Parliamentary engagement with the charter: Rethinking the idea of legislative rights review. *The Supreme Court Law Review: Osgoode's Annual Constitutional Cases Conference, 58*, 87–107. http://digitalcommons.osgoode.yorku.ca/sclr/vol58/iss1/3.

Hocking, J. (2004). *Terror laws: ASIO, counter-terrorism and the threat to democracy*. Sydney: University of New South Wales Press.

Holland, I. (2009). *Senate committees and the legislative process*. (Parliamentary Studies Paper No. 7). Retrieved from http://www.aph.gov.au/~/media/05%20About%20Parliament/52%20Sen/524%20Research%20and%20education/Other%20Publications/PSP07_Holland.ashx. Accessed 7 Jan 2020.

Horrigan, B. (2012). Reforming rights-based scrutiny and interpretation of legislation. *Alternative Law Journal, 37*, 228–232. https://doi.org/10.1177/1037969X1203700403.

Human Rights Consultation Committee (2009) *National Human Rights Consultation report*. Retrieved from https://trove.nla.gov.au/work/35853626?selectedversion=NBD44855144. Accessed 7 Jan 2020.

Hume, D., & Williams, G. (2013). *Human rights under the Australian constitution* (2nd ed.). Oxford: Oxford University Press.

Hunt, M., Hooper, H. J., & Yowell, P. (Eds.). (2015). *Parliaments and human rights: Redressing the democratic deficit*. Oxford: Hart Publishing.

Joseph, S. (2004). Australian counter-terrorism legislation and the international human rights framework. *University of New South Wales Law Journal, 27*, 428–543.

Kinley, D. (1999). Parliamentary scrutiny of human rights: A duty neglected. In P. Alston (Ed.), *Promoting human rights through bills of rights: Comparative perspectives* (pp. 158–172). Oxford: Oxford University Press.

Kinley, D., & Ernst, C. (2012). Exile on main street: Australia's legislative agenda for human rights. *European Human Rights Law Review, 1*, 58–70.

Levy, R., & Orr, G. (2016). *The law of deliberative democracy*. London: Routledge.

Lim, B. (2013). The normativity of the principle of legality. *Melbourne University Law Review, 37*, 372–400.

Lumina, C. (2007). Counter-terrorism legislation and the protection of human rights: A survey of selected international practice. *African Human Rights Law Journal, 7*, 35–67.

Lynch, A. (2006). Legislating with urgency – The enactment of the Anti-Terrorism Act (No. 1) 2005. *Melbourne University Law Review, 30*(3), 747–781.

Lynch, P. (2010, March 1). Rights bill is long overdue. *Sydney Morning Herald* (online). https://www.smh.com.au/politics/federal/rights-bill-is-long-overdue-20100228-pb4s.html. Accessed 7 Jan 2020.

Lynch, A., & McGarrity, N. (2008). Counter-terrorism laws: How neutral laws create fear and anxiety in Australia's Muslim communities. *Alternative Law Journal, 33*(4), 225–228.

Lynch, A., McDonald, E., & Williams, G. (Eds.). (2007). *Law and liberty in the war on terror*. Sydney: Federation Press.

Mannreitz, H. (2012). Commonwealth statements of compatibility – Small steps, early days. *Human Rights Law Centre Bulletin, 71*, 8.

Marsh, I. (2004, November 26). *Australia's representation gap: A role for parliamentary committees?* Speech delivered at the Department of the Senate Occasional Lecture Series, Parliament House, Canberra.

Meagher, D., & Groves, M. (Eds.). (2017). *The principle of legality in Australia and New Zealand*. Sydney: Federation Press.

Michaelsen, C. (2006). Balancing liberties against national security? A critique of counter-terrorism rhetoric. *University of New South Wales Law Journal, 29*(2), 1–21.

Monk, D. (2010). A framework for evaluating the performance of committees in Westminster parliaments. *Journal of Legislative Studies, 16*, 1–13. https://doi.org/10.1080/13572330903541904.

Moulds, S. P. (2020). Parliamentary committees facilitating parliamentary deliberation: A case study of marriage equality reform. In J. Debeljak & L. Grenfell (Eds.), *Law making and human rights* (pp. 745–786). Sydney: Thompson Reuters.

Omand, D. (2010). *Securing the state*. Oxford: Hart Publishing.

Palfrey, M. (2012). A new federal scheme for the protection of human rights. *Australian Institute of Administrative Law Forum, 69*, 13.

Peter, F. (2017). Political legitimacy. In E. N. Zalta (Ed.), *The Stanford encyclopedia of philosophy*. (online, last updated 24 April 2017) https://plato.stanford.edu/entries/legitimacy/.

Radin, M. (2017). Reconsidering the rule of law. In R. Bellamy (Ed.), *The rule of law and the separation of powers* (pp. 37–76). London: Routledge.

Rajanayagam, S. (2015). Does parliament do enough? Evaluating statements of compatibility under the Human Rights (Parliamentary Scrutiny) Act. *University of New South Wales Law Journal, 38*(3), 1046–1077.

Rajanayagam, S. (2020). Urgent Law-Making and the Human Rights (Parliamentary Scrutiny) Act. In J. Debeljak & L. Grenfell (Eds.), *Law-making and human rights* (pp. 647–672). Sydney: Thompson Reuters.

Reilly, A., & Lynch, A. (2007). The constitutional validity of terrorism orders of control and preventative detention. *Flinders Journal of Law Reform, 10*, 105–129.

Reynolds, D., & Williams, G. (2017). A Charter of rights for Australia. Sydney: NewSouth Books, 4th ed.

Reynolds, D., & Williams, G. (2020). Evaluating the impact of Australia's federal human rights scrutiny regime. In J. Debeljak & L. Grenfell (Eds.), *Law-making and human rights* (pp. 67–96). Sydney: Thompson Reuters.

Rice, S. (2020). Allowing for dissent: Opening up human rights dialogue in the Australian parliament. In J. Debeljak & L. Grenfell (Eds.), *Law-making and human rights* (pp. 99–134). Sydney: Thompson Reuters.

Roach, K. (2011). *The 9/11 effect: Comparative counter-terrorism*. Cambridge: Cambridge University Press.

Russell, M., & Benton, M. (2009, June 24). *Assessing the policy impact of parliament: Methodological challenges and possible future approaches*. Paper presented at the Public Service Association Legislative Studies Specialist Group Conference, London. Retrieved from https://www.academia.edu/2069151/Assessing_the_policy_impact_of_Parliament_Methodological_challenges_and_possible_future_approaches. Accessed 7 Jan 2020.

Santow, E. (2010). The act that dares not speak its name: The National Human Rights Consultation report's parallel roads to human rights reform. *University of New South Wales Law Journal, 33*(1), 8–33.

Sawer, M., Abjorensen, N., & Larkin, P. (2009). *Australia: The state of democracy*. Sydney: Federation Press.

Scheinin, M. (2006). *Report of the special rapporteur on the promotion and protection of human rights and fundamental freedoms while countering terrorism, Australia: study on human rights compliance while countering terrorism*. UN Doc A/HRC/4/26/Add.3 (14 December 2006).

Security Legislation Review Committee. (2006). *Report of the Security Legislation Review Committee*. Retrieved from https://www.ag.gov.au/NationalSecurity/Counterterrorismlaw/Documents/Report%20of%20the%20Security%20Legislation%20Review%20Committee.pdf. Accessed 7 Jan 2020.

Smookler, J. (2006). Making a difference? The effectiveness of pre-legislative scrutiny. *Parliamentary Affairs, 59*, 522–533.

Spigelman, J. (2005). The principle of legality and the clear statement principle. *Australian Law Journal, 79*, 769–775.

Spigelman, J. (2008, March 10). *The Common Law Bill of Rights*. Speech delivered at the University of Queensland, Brisbane, 10 March 2008. Retrieved from http://www.aph.gov.au/DocumentStore.ashx?id=c190ac6b-aa39-4bab-97a4-c2aab8b899f9. Accessed 8 Jan 2020.

Spigelman, J. (2010). Public law and the executive. *Australian Bar Review, 34*, 10–14.

Stellios, J., & Palfrey, M. (2012). A new federal scheme for the protection of human rights. *Australian Institute of Administrative Law Forum, 69*, 13–19.

Stephenson, S. (2016). *From dialogue to disagreement in comparative rights constitutionalism*. Sydney: Federation Press.

Stone, A. (2001). The Australian free speech experiment and scepticism about the UK Human Rights Act. In T. Campbell, K. Ewing, & A. Tomkins (Eds.), *Sceptical essays on human rights* (pp. 391–430). Oxford: Oxford University Press.
Stone, A. (2003). Australia's constitutional rights and the problem of interpretative disagreement. In T. Campbell, J. Goldsworthy, & A. Stone (Eds.), *Protecting human rights: Instruments and institutions*. Oxford: Oxford University Press.
Stone, A. (2009). Tom Campbell's proposal for a democratic bill of rights. *Australian Journal of Legal Philosophy, 34*. University of Melbourne Legal Studies Research Paper No. 495. Available at SSRN: https://ssrn.com/abstract=1669065
Tate, P. (2009). Human rights in Australia: What would a federal charter of rights look like? *Southern Cross University Law Review, 13*, 1–24.
Tatz, S. (2015, December 19). Senate estimates: We're all losers in this game of "gotcha". *The Drum* (online). http://www.abc.net.au/news/2015-10-19/tatz-senate-estimates:-were-all-losers-in-this-game-of-gotcha/6860784. Accessed 7 Jan 2020.
Victorian Government Solicitors Office. (2011, September). *Case note: Momcilovic v The Queen*. Retrieved from http://vgso.vic.gov.au/news-events/news/case-note-momcilovic-v-queen-2011-hca-34-8-september-2011. Accessed 8 Jan 2020.
Walker, B. (2011). *Independent national security legislation monitor, annual report*. Retrieved from http://www.dpmc.gov.au/publications/INSLM/index.cfm. Accessed 7 Jan 2020.
Webb, P., & Roberts, K. (2014). *Effective parliamentary oversight of human rights: A framework for designing and determining effectiveness*. Paper presented at the Dickson Poon School of Law, King's College London, University of London. Retrieved from https://www.kcl.ac.uk/sspp/policy-institute/projects/government/assets/Human-Rights-Policy-DocumentV5.pdf. Accessed 7 Jan 2020.
Webber, J. (2006). A modest (but robust) defence of statutory bills of rights. In T. Campbell, J. Goldsworthy, & A. Stone (Eds.), *Protecting human rights: Instruments and institutions* (pp. 266–276). Oxford: Oxford University Press.
Westbury, D. (2018). The *principle of legality as a reflection of the constitutional relationship between parliament and the courts*. AUSPUBLAW Blog. https://auspublaw.org/2018/2/the-principle-of-legality. Accessed 7 Jan 2020.
Williams, G. (1999). *The Federal Parliament and the protection of human rights*. Parliamentary Research Paper No. 20 of 1998–99, Parliamentary Library, Parliament of Australia, 11 May 1999. Retrieved from https://www.aph.gov.au/About_Parliament/Parliamentary_Departments/Parliamentary_Library/pubs/rp/rp9899/99rp20. Accessed 7 Jan 2020.
Williams, G. (2000). *A bill of rights for Australia*. Sydney: UNSW Press.
Williams, G. (2003). Constructing a community-based bill of rights. In T. Campbell, J. Goldsworthy, & A. Stone (Eds.), *Protecting human rights: Instruments and institutions* (pp. 247–254). Oxford: Oxford University Press.
Williams, G. (2015). The legal assault on Australian democracy: The annual Blackburn lecture. *Ethos, 236*, 18–23.
Williams, G., & Burton, L. (2015). Australia's parliamentary scrutiny act: An exclusive parliamentary model of rights protection. In M. Hunt, H. J. Hooper, & P. Yowell (Eds.), *Parliaments and human rights: Redressing the democratic deficit* (pp. 258–279). Oxford: Hart Publishing.
Williams, G., & Reynolds, D. (2016). The operation and impact of Australia's parliamentary scrutiny regime for human rights. *Monash University Law Review, 41*(2), 469–508.
Williams, A., & Williams, G. (2016). The British bill of rights debate: Lessons from Australia. *Public Law*, 471–490.
Zhou, S. (2012). *Momcilovic v. the Queen: Implications for a federal human rights charter*. Working paper, Social Science Research Network, 2012. Retrieved from https://papers.ssrn.com/sol3/papers.cfm?abstract_id=2128005 Accessed. 8 Jan 2020.
Zifcak, S. (2013). Counter-terrorism laws and human rights. In P. Gerber & M. Castan (Eds.), *Contemporary perspectives on human rights in Australia* (pp. 418–433). Sydney: Lawbook.

Chapter 2
Methodology

Abstract This chapter sets out the unique methodology employed in this research, which seeks to measure three 'tiers' of impact: legislative (whether the content of proposed laws changes as a result of parliamentary committee activity); public (whether the public or parliamentary debate on proposed laws is influenced by the work of parliamentary committees); and hidden (whether the work of parliamentary committees has an impact on how proposed laws are developed prior to introduction into Parliament). This chapter also includes an overview of past evaluations of parliamentary committees and describes how the assessment framework used this research is designed to overcome weaknesses and challenges previously encountered.

2.1 Assessing Parliamentary Committees

Given that the Parliament is the sovereign, constitutional law-maker in the Australian system, measuring the *influence* or *impact* of the Parliament on the content of legislation or the law making process can seem an paradoxical task: its influence seems at once obvious and illusive, both all consuming, but then somehow in the background to the roles of other branches of government. The challenges associated with measuring the impact of parliaments and their many individual components has been recognised by scholars across the world including Russell and Benton (2009) who warn that given the complex and dynamic nature of parliamentary committees, evaluating their performance is not always straightforward. As discussed further in Part II, the membership alone of Australian parliamentary committees can be highly changeable and politically charged, particularly when Senators are involved as either regular or participating members, against a backdrop of party politics that regularly includes minor parties or independents holding the balance of power in the Senate. In this context, it can be difficult to define precisely what a high-performing committee looks like and there is a risk that the assessor's approach will influence what a 'good' committee means (Webb and Roberts 2014 p. 3). However, these challenges should not diminish the importance of understanding how these

S. Moulds, *Committees of Influence*, https://doi.org/10.1007/978-981-15-4350-0_2

committees work, particularly when they have the potential to have a real and significant impact on people's rights and lives (Larkin et al. 2009).

Many scholars have grappled with these challenges when seeking to evaluate the performance of parliamentary committees in a range of different areas (Kavanagh 2015; Russell and Benton 2009; Griffith 2005; Tolley 2009; Evans and Evans 2006b; Smookler 2006). For example, some scholars point to the challenge of overcoming the perceived structural weakness in the Australian Westminster system, derived from the dominance of the executive government over the legislature (Hiebert 2015 at p. 41; Monk 2010 at p. 7). As Feldman (2015) explains, governments generally seek to avoid scrutiny because they are keen to articulate (and control) a policy and legislative agenda free from compromise or complexity, maximising the political capital that comes from their party's majority in the Parliament (at p. 98). This executive control can dominate the outcomes generated by parliamentary committees, particularly when combined with the very strong party political discipline exerted by political parties in Australia, described by Hirst as stronger than that experienced by analogous political parties in the UK, Canada and New Zealand (Hirst 2010; Stone 1998). This can lead to findings that parliamentary committees in Australia generally enjoy a low level of influence and generate relatively few legislative amendments (Willams and Reynolds 2016). It can also lead some to query the viability and desirably of measuring the impact of parliamentary committees at all (Lindell 2005).

In my research, I accept the reality of executive-dominated Australian parliaments, but this does not deter my investigation into the impact parliamentary committees have on the development and content of federal laws, or the contribution such committees make to rights protection in Australia. Rather, I seek to factor the executive-centric nature of the Australian landscape into my assessment framework, for example by outlining the institutional context in which the parliamentary committee system operates, identifying the key participants involved in the parliamentary committee system and documenting their views on the variations in legitimacy afforded to the four committees studied, and assessing three tiers of impact – legislative, public and hidden – of parliamentary scrutiny on counter-terrorism laws. Having analysed the impact of the parliamentary committee system on the case study Acts, my research suggests that there is reason to take a slightly optimistic view of the Parliament's capacity to resist the will of the executive, even when dealing with policy issues attracting broad bipartisan support. Indeed, as discussed in Part III, it is this sometimes surprising capacity of the Parliament to push back against the will of the executive in counter-terrorism laws that makes this case study so pertinent when seeking to evaluate the role the committee system plays in rights protection in Australia.

Several scholars who have examined parliamentary committees in Australia and elsewhere have also pointed to the difficulties associated with attributing executive or parliamentary action (including legislative amendments) to parliamentary scrutiny (Feldman 2015; Hiebert 2002, 2015; Hunt 2010). Others have noted that executive acceptance of parliamentary committees' recommendations cannot always be taken at face value and may not in fact translate into legislative or policy change (e.g. Hawes 1992).

The assessment framework employed in this book incorporates features that address these salient warnings. Most significantly, this book tests findings relating to the legislative impact of parliamentary committees against empirical evidence obtained through interviews with public servants, parliamentary staff, parliamentary counsel, committee members and Chairs, submission makers and parliamentarians. This is in line with the approach endorsed by Tolley (2009), Aldons (2000), and Benton and Russell (2013), who suggest that this kind of qualitative approach is crucial to making an objective and holistic assessment of a committee's impact. As former Committee Secretary to the SSCSB Stephen Argument has noted (2011), these behind-the-scenes perspectives on the parliamentary scrutiny system can be critical both to determining how parliamentary committees work in practice and to evaluating their impact and effectiveness (see also Uhr 2006 at p. 54). As noted above, this also aligns with Stephenson's approach to analysing models of rights protection (Stephenson 2016 pp. 8, 211), as it prompts an investigation into both the direct and indirect contributions parliamentary committees make to rights review at the federal level in Australia.

Some scholars also have lamented the lack of a clear or consistently applied methodological approach to evaluating the effectiveness of parliamentary committees (Aldons 2003; Holland 2009). In this context, my research provides a unique opportunity to articulate a methodical, transparent template for evaluating parliamentary committees that responds to the challenges posed by past scholars and is capable of being adapted to apply in comparable jurisdictions. The key features of the assessment framework employed in my research are outlined below.

2.2 The Assessment Framework Adopted in This Book

As noted above, in this book I adopt an assessment framework specifically designed to evaluate the impact of parliamentary committees on the development and content of federal laws. Like Stephenson, my research recognises the multi-stage rights review that occurs at the federal level in Australia, and the assessment framework actively looks for direct and indirect contributions to resolving disagreements on rights between and within institutions of government (Stephenson 2016 pp. 6–7). My assessment framework also shares features with the approach adopted by Evans and Evans in their 2006 research investigating the Australian Parliament's role in rights protection. Like the Evans and Evans (2006a) model, my assessment framework is multi-staged and specifically designed to take account of the 'particular conceptual complexities of rights and the institutional peculiarities of legislatures' (2006 Human Rights Law Review at p. 569). By building on the qualitative strategies employed by Evans and Evans (2006a) and adopting an explicit three-tiered impact analysis (van Ham and Chappell 2017; Fletcher 2017, 2018 and 2020; Reynolds and Williams 2020), my methodology identifies the strengths and weaknesses of the parliamentary model of rights protection and uncovers new opportunities for the model to be improved. The contextualised features of my assessment framework (such as inquiries into a committee's legitimacy or political authority among key participants) also allows for considerations of what Campbell and Morris (2015) have described as the 'political approach' (at p. 10) to human rights, where value is attributed to the political protection and promotion of human rights, as an alternative to, or in addition to, specific legislative or judicial protection of legally enforceable rights (see also Kinley and Ernst 2012; Kinley 1999). As discussed below, my methodology has also been developed with close regard to the international rights-mechanism evaluation model developed by the Dickson Poon School of Law (Webb and Roberts 2014).

2.3 Key Steps in the Assessment Framework

As discussed above, the first step in any successful evaluation of the effectiveness of parliamentary models of rights protection is to understand the institutional context in which such models operate. The Australian federal parliamentary landscape is set out in Chap. 3, along with the Australian experience of enacting counter-terrorism laws since 2001. Chapter 3 also briefly outlines the history of federal parliamentary committees, providing important contextual information about why and when particular committees were established and the role the committee system plays within Australia's federal parliamentary model of rights protection.

The counter-terrorism case study used in this book necessitates a focus on the following four parliamentary committees that are regularly involved in scrutinising or inquiring into Australia's counter-terrorism laws: the SSCSB, the Senate Standing Committees on Legal and Constitutional Affairs (the LCA Committees), the PJCIS and the PJCHR. The history, functions and legal frameworks governing these committees are outlined in detail in Chap. 3. This is important as it demonstrates that not all of the four parliamentary committees are specifically designed to consider the rights compatibility of proposed laws. Some committees have other less rights-explicit functions and objectives, such as improving the operational effectiveness of the proposed law (in the case of the PJCIS) or providing a deliberative forum for the public to express their views on a proposed law (in the case of the LCA Committees). As discussed in Part III, these other roles can offer important opportunities for individual committees to contribute to Australia's parliamentary model of rights protection, particularly when they are undertaken in conjunction with the work of rights-specific scrutiny committees such as the PJCHR and the SSCSB.

The next step in the assessment framework identifies the *key participants* in the parliamentary committee system and looks for evidence of whether particular committees are seen as *legitimate* by some or all of these participants. The key participants in the parliamentary committee system include parliamentarians, elected members of the executive government, submission makers and witnesses to parliamentary committee inquiries, public servants and government officers, independent oversight bodies and the media. As Chap. 4 explains, rates of participation and diversity of participants differ across the committees studied, as does the level of legitimacy attributed to each body. This provides important insights into how each committee contributes to the parliamentary model of rights protection.

In this book, as in the Dickson Poon Framework (Webb and Roberts 2014), 'legitimacy' refers to 'political legitimacy', which generally denotes a quality of political institutions, political actors and the laws and policies that they make. A wealth of literature exists on the topic of political legitimacy and the meaning attributed to this term has been contested and developed over time (see e.g. Beetham 1991; Buchanan 2002). Some scholars, such as Weber, interpret political legitimacy *descriptively*, using it to describe how people feel about political authority and/or their political obligations (such as whether they accept the authority of a particular political institution, and the need to obey its commands) (Weber 1918). Others, such as Rawls (2007) and Ripstein (2004), see political legitimacy as a *normative* concept: a way to measure whether the exercise of political power or authority is accepted or seen as justified by the community it serves. Political legitimacy has also been discussed in the context of representative democracy and deliberative democracy theories, connecting the *process* of political decision making with the notion of legitimacy, as well as (or sometimes instead of) the substance of the political decision itself (see e.g. Manin 1987; Pettit 2001; Levy and Orr 2016). It is beyond the scope of this book to explore these different articulations of 'political legitimacy'; however, the use of the term in this book is infused with both descriptive and normative aspects and, as discussed further in Chap. 4, has a clear connection to deliberative democracy theory, particularly in so far as it intersects with the above discussion relating to rates of participation.

One of the additional benefits of explicitly considering rates of participation and views on legitimacy is to guard against some of the methodological challenges identified above, particularly those relating to the structural power dynamic occurring between the Parliament and the executive and within the executive itself. The level of legitimacy attributed to a particular committee can both indicate and reflect a shift in this structural power dynamic that will be relevant to evaluating the impact of the committee, and its capacity to play a rights-enhancing role. For example, the evidence presented in Part II suggests that, when submission makers consistently prioritise one parliamentary committee over another (extending it greater legitimacy), the preferred committee has a much stronger legislative impact, and important rights-enhancing changes can be made to the laws it scrutinises or reviews.

The final step is the most intensive and detailed step in the assessment framework. It aims to determine what impact a particular committee, and the committee system more broadly, is having on the proposed law. This step, which is addressed in Chaps. 5, 6 and 7, examines the three levels of impact across the 15 Acts in the counter-terrorism case study.

2.3.1 Legislative Impact

Legislative impact focuses on whether a committee, or the committee system, has done something that has directly changed the content of a law. There are many reasons why legislative impact is an attractive basis for evaluating the effectiveness of parliamentary committees. Chief among these is the fact that legislative impact can be expressed in quantitative terms. For example, it is possible to look at the recommendations made by a parliamentary committee and compare these to any amendments made to a Bill prior to enactment and reach a conclusion on whether the committee has had an impact. However, as discussed above, if legislative change is the sole impact measured, the evaluation may be blind to other, potentially more significant, impacts of the parliamentary committee system. For these reasons, the assessment framework adopted in this book also considers public impact and impacts largely hidden from public view.

2.3.2 Public Impact

My research looks for evidence that the work of the parliamentary committee has influenced or been considered in public or parliamentary debate on a case study Bill, or in subsequent commentary or review of a case study Act. For example, evidence of public impact could include:

- unsuccessful amendments introduced to address parliamentary committee recommendations;
- changes to an Explanatory Memorandum accompanying the Bill because of a committee recommendation; and
- reference to the findings or recommendations of a committee in parliamentary and public debates on the Bill, reports or transcripts of other parliamentary committees, or reports of other relevant oversight bodies or non-parliamentary review mechanisms.

'Public impact' also considers the capacity of the parliamentary committees to gather and disperse information, or bring new voices into the public debate (Shaw 1998; Griffith 2005). As discussed in Chap. 6, there is a strong relationship between evidence of 'public impact' and parliamentary committees' role in providing a deliberative forum for the consideration of a wide range of views on a proposed law (Dalla-Pozza 2016 at p. 274; Uhr 2006 p. 25). When considered in concert with Step 2 (relating to legitimacy), evidence of 'public impact' can also be used to demonstrate what Aldons (2003) has described as the 'power' or 'influence' of the committee in its institutional context.

2.3.3 *Hidden Impact*

The most unique and arguably most valuable aspect of the assessment framework employed in this book is the use of empirical evidence gained from targeted interviews with participants to uncover the 'hidden impact' of parliamentary committees on the content and development of the case study Acts.[1] This part of the framework asks whether those at the coalface of developing and drafting counter-terrorism laws turn their mind to the work of parliamentary committees when undertaking their tasks, and considers whether this has a rights-enhancing impact.

The 'hidden impact' of the parliamentary committee system, and particular components of that system, is considered in detail in Chap. 7. Evidence of 'hidden impact' includes evidence of:

- improved or growing 'rights literacy' among those directly involved in the legislative and policy development process;
- scrutiny principles or criteria, or past committee findings, being considered or anticipated in the legislative and policy development process; and/or
- scrutiny principles or criteria, or past committee findings, being incorporated into public servant training manuals or guidelines.

As discussed above, collecting evidence of the hidden impact of parliamentary committees can be challenging due to the need to look beyond documentary sources and consider more subjective material including interviews but, as Evans and Evans (2006a) and Benton and Russell (2013) have shown in their empirical-based work, it is not impossible. Much publicly available material exists that points to the hidden impacts of scrutiny, including training manuals, published guidelines, information in annual reports, and submissions and oral evidence given at parliamentary and other public inquiries and hearings. This material can then be tested against a range of targeted individual interviews I conducted with key participants in this process.

References

Books/Articles/Reports/Speeches

Aldons, A. (2000). Rating the effectiveness of parliamentary committee reports: The methodology. *Legislative Studies, 15*(1), 22–32.

Aldons, M. (2003). Problems with parliamentary committee evaluation: Light at the end of the tunnel? *Australasian Parliamentary Review, 18*(1), 79–86.

Argument, S. (2011, July 21–22). *Of parliament, pigs and lipstick (Slight Return): A defence of the work of legislative scrutiny committees in human rights protection*. Paper presented at the Australian Institute of Administrative Law Forum, Canberra.

[1] Details about the process for selecting interviewees and how interviews were conducted is available in Moulds 2018 Appendix A.

Beetham, D. (1991). *The legitimation of power*. Basingstoke: Palgrave.
Benton, M., & Russell, M. (2013). Assessing the impact of parliamentary oversight committees: The select committees in the British house of commons. *Parliamentary Affairs, 66*, 772–797.
Buchanan, A. (2002). Political legitimacy and democracy. *Ethics, 112*(4), 689–719.
Campbell, T., & Morris, S. (2015). Human rights for democracies: A provisional assessment of the Australian Human Rights (Parliamentary Scrutiny) Act 2011. *University of Queensland Law Journal, 34*(1), 7–27.
Dalla-Pozza, D. (2016). Refining the Australian counter-terrorism legislative framework: How deliberative has parliament been? *Public Law Review, 27*(4), 271.
Evans, C., & Evans, S. (2006a). Evaluating the human rights performance of legislatures. *Human Rights Law Review, 6*, 545–569. https://doi.org/10.1093/hrlr/ngl012.
Evans, C., & Evans, S. (2006b). Legislative scrutiny committees and parliamentary conceptions of human rights. *Public Law, 785*.
Feldman, D. (2015). Democracy, law and human rights: Politics as challenge and opportunity. In Hunt, M. Hooper, H. J & Yowell, P. (Eds.), Parliaments and human rights: Redressing the democratic deficit (pp. 95–117). Oxford: Hart Publishing.
Fletcher, A. (2017, November 1). *Human rights scrutiny in the Australian parliament*. Paper presented at 'Evaluating inquests, commissions and inquiries' symposium, La Trobe University, Melbourne.
Fletcher, A. (2018). *Australia's human rights scrutiny regime*. Melbourne: Melbourne University Press.
Fletcher, A. (2020). Human rights scrutiny in the Federal Parliament: Smokescreen or democratic solution? In J. Debeljak & L. Grenfell (Eds.), *Law- making and human rights* (pp. 31–63). Sydney: Thompson Reuters.
Griffith, G. (2005). *Parliament and accountability: The role of parliamentary oversight committees* (Briefing paper no 12/05). Sydney: Parliamentary Library Research Service.
Hawes, D. (1992). Parliamentary select committees: Some case studies in contingent influence. *Policy & Politics, 20*, 227–236.
Hiebert, J. L. (2002). *Charter conflicts: What is parliament's role?* Montreal: McGill-Queen's University Press.
Hiebert, J. L. (2015). Legislative rights review: Addressing the gap between ideals and constraints. In Hunt, M. Hooper, H. J & Yowell, P. (Eds.), Parliaments and human rights: Redressing the democratic deficit (pp. 39–52). Oxford: Hart Publishing.
Hirst, J. (2010, August 25). A chance to end the mindless allegiance of party discipline. *The Sydney Morning Herald* (online) https://www.smh.com.au/politics/federal/a-chance-to-end-the-mindless-allegiance-of-party-discipline-20100824-13q9b.html. Accessed 8 Jan 2020.
Holland, I. (2009). *Senate committees and the legislative process* (Parliamentary studies paper no 7). Retrieved from http://www.aph.gov.au/~/media/05%20About%20Parliament/52%20Sen/524%20Research%20and%20education/Other%20Publications/PSP07_Holland.ashx. Accessed 7 Jan 2020.
Hunt, M. (2010). The impact of the human rights act on the legislature: A diminution of democracy or a new voice for parliament? *European Human Rights Law Review, 6*, 601–629.
Kavanagh, A. (2015). In M. Hunt, H. J. Hooper, & P. Yowell (Eds.), *Parliaments and human rights: Redressing the democratic deficit* (pp. 111–134). Oxford: Hart Publishing.
Kinley, D. (1999). Parliamentary scrutiny of human rights: A duty neglected. In P. Alston (Ed.), *Promoting human rights through bills of rights: Comparative perspectives* (pp. 158–172). Oxford: Oxford University Press.
Kinley, D., & Ernst, C. (2012). Exile on main street: Australia's legislative agenda for human rights. *European Human Rights Law Review, 1*, 58–70.
Larkin, P., Hindmoor, A., & Kenyon, A. (2009). Assessing the influence of select committees in the UK: The education and skills committee 1997–2005. *Journal of Legislative Studies, 15*, 71–89. https://doi.org/10.1080/13572330802666844.
Levy, R., & Orr, G. (2016). *The law of deliberative democracy*. London: Routledge.

Lindell, G. (2005, August). How (and whether?) to evaluate parliamentary committees – From a Lawyer's perspective. *About the House* (pp. 55–58).

Manin, B. (1987). On legitimacy and political deliberation. *Political Theory, 15*, 338–368.

Monk, D. (2010). A framework for evaluating the performance of committees in Westminster parliaments. *Journal of Legislative Studies, 16*, 1–13. https://doi.org/10.1080/13572330903541904.

Moulds, S. P. (2018). *The rights protecting role of parliamentary committees: The case of Australia's counter-terrorism laws* (Doctoral thesis). University of Adelaide, Adelaide, South Australia, Australia. https://digital.library.adelaide.edu.au/dspace/handle/2440/115212

Pettit, P. (2001). Deliberative democracy and the discursive dilemma. *Philosophical Issues, 11*, 268–299.

Rawls, J. (2007). *Lectures on the history of political philosophy*. Cambridge: Harvard University Press.

Reynolds, D., & Williams, G. (2020). Evaluating the impact of Australia's federal human rights scrutiny regime. In J. Debeljak & L. Grenfell (Eds.), *Law- making and human rights* (pp. 67–96). Sydney: Thompson Reuters.

Ripstein, A. (2004). Authority and coercion. *Philosophy and Public Affairs, 32*(1), 2–35.

Russell, M., & Benton, M. (2009, June 24). *Assessing the policy impact of parliament: Methodological challenges and possible future approaches*. Paper presented at the Public Service Association Legislative Studies Specialist Group Conference, London. Retrieved from https://www.academia.edu/2069151/Assessing_the_policy_impact_of_Parliament_Methodological_challenges_and_possible_future_approaches. Accessed 7 Jan 2020.

Shaw, M. (1998). Parliamentary committees: A global perspective. *Journal of Legislative Studies, 4*(1), 225–251. https://doi.org/10.1080/13572339808420547.

Smookler, J. (2006). Making a difference? The effectiveness of pre-legislative scrutiny. *Parliamentary Affairs, 59*, 522–533.

Stephenson, S. (2016). *From dialogue to disagreement in comparative rights constitutionalism*. Sydney: Federation Press.

Stone, B. (1998). Size and executive-legislative relations in Australian parliaments. *Australian Journal of Political Science, 33*(1), 37–55.

Tolley, M. C. (2009). Parliamentary scrutiny of rights in the United Kingdom: Assessing the work of the Joint committee on human rights. *Australian Journal of Political Science, 44*(1), 41–55. https://doi.org/10.1080/10361140802656922.

Uhr, J. (2006). The role of Australian legislatures in protecting rights. In T. Campbell, J. Goldsworthy, & A. Stone (Eds.), *Protecting rights without a bill of rights* (pp. 41–62). London: Ashgate.

van Ham, C., & Chappell. (2017). L. Democracy and human rights: A tripartite conceptual framework. *Australian Journal of Human Rights, 23*(2), 143–167. https://doi.org/10.1080/1323238X.2017.1371927.

Webb, P. & Roberts, K. (2014). *Effective parliamentary oversight of human rights: A framework for designing and determining effectiveness*. Paper presented at the Dickson poon School of law, King's College London, University of London. Retrieved from https://www.kcl.ac.uk/sspp/policy-institute/projects/government/assets/Human-Rights-Policy-DocumentV5.pdf. Accessed 7 Jan 2020.

Weber, M. (1918). Politics as a vocation. In H. H. Gerth & C. Wright Mills (Eds.), *From Max Weber: Essays in sociology*. London: Routledge. 1991.

Willams, G., & Reynolds, D. (2016). The operation and impact of Australia's parliamentary scrutiny regime for human rights. *Monash University Law Review, 41*(2), 469–508.

Chapter 3
The Australian Landscape and the Making of Counter-Terrorism Laws

Abstract Understanding the institutional context of Australia's parliamentary committee system is critical when evaluating the impact of this system on the case study Acts and identifying options to improve its rights-enhancing capacity. This chapter introduces the Australian parliamentary committee system, with a focus on the four committees studied and how they fit within the broader parliamentary landscape.

This chapter also provides a broader overview of counter-terrorism law making in Australia since September 2011, sketching some of the domestic and international circumstances in which Australia's modern counter terrorism framework was developed and introduced. This chapter lays the foundation for a more detailed exploration of how parliamentary committees interact with the different law-making institutions at the federal level and the role they played in directly and indirectly identifying and addressing rights issues within the case study Acts.

3.1 The Parliamentary Committee System and the Australian Parliament

3.1.1 The Constitutional Understanding of the Role of Parliament

Understanding the key features of the Australian Parliament and its constitutional basis is the crucial first step in understanding how and why the parliamentary committee system came about. As many constitutional scholars remind us, the Australian Constitution is a document designed to lay the basis for effective power sharing between colonies and a tool for negotiating improved prosperity and security for the new federation (Quick and Garran 2014; Dicey 1959). Unlike its American counterpart, it was not drafted to encapsulate a statement of shared national identity or to settle a claim of individual rights against the state (see e.g. *Theophanous v Herald and Weekly Times Ltd* (1994) 182 CLR 104, 171-173 per Deane J; Clark 1997).

S. Moulds, *Committees of Influence*, https://doi.org/10.1007/978-981-15-4350-0_3

However, the American constitutional experience was highly influential in the design of the Australian version, with the drafters embracing the *doctrine of separation of powers* to clearly delineate the relationship between of each branch of government, and diffusing power *horizontally*, across the executive, legislature and the courts (see e.g. *R v Kirby; Ex parte Boilermakers' Society of Australia* (1956) 94 CLR 254 (*Boilermakers Case*), *Waterside Workers' Federation of Australia v J W Alexander* (1918) 25 CLR 434; Mason 1996; French 1996).

The Australian constitutional drafters also embraced the American concept of federalism (through bicameralism) diffusing power *vertically* between the States and the federal Parliament (Odgers 2012 at pp. 4–5; Shell 2001; Bennett 2004). The *bicameral, federal* nature of Australia's constitutional structure is particularly vital to understanding the federal parliamentary committee system that has given rise to the deeply entrenched notion of the Senate as the 'House of Review'. While this label may be contested (Mulgan 1996), it provides both the structural and cultural genesis of the parliamentary committee system (Odgers 2012 at pp. 4–5).

These doctrines are reflected in the structure of the *Australian Constitution*, which contains a separate Chapter for the Parliament (Chap. 1), and invests legislative power exclusively within the Parliament, which consists of the Queen, a Senate, and a House of Representatives. Separate Chapters are also dedicated to the Executive (Chap. 2) and the Judiciary (Chap. 3), giving effect to the horizontal separation of law-making power, and legislative power is further defined by prescribing the subject areas with respect to which the federal Parliament can make laws, and attributing the States with residual law making power (*Australian Constitution* s51). These explicit structural features of the *Constitution* provide the context against which the parliamentary committee system operates.

The doctrine of *responsible government* (see e.g. *Commonwealth v Kreglinger & Fernau Ltd* (1926) 37 CLR 393, 413) is also a defining feature of the *Constitution* and informs the character of the parliamentary committees considered in this book (see e.g. Galligan 1990). Generally speaking, 'responsible government' means that the constitutionally enshrined Head of State (in Australia's case the Queen represented by the Governor-General) acts on the advice of his or her Ministers who are directly responsible for their actions to the Parliament, and the people. For example, by subjecting government legislative proposals to public scrutiny and by providing a forum for Ministers and their delegates to be questioned, the system provides a 'fairly direct line of accountability' between the electorate and their elected members of parliament (Galligan 1990; Quick and Garran 2014 p. 704; Menzies 1967 at p. 54). The doctrine of responsible government also helps to explains why the parliamentary committee system is seen by some as an attractive form of rights protection, when compared with other models that incorporate specific roles for the judiciary in the determination of rights disputes (Goldsworthy 2001; Stone 2001; Chappell et al. 2012 at pp. 67–9).

The principle of *parliamentary sovereignty* (Dicey 1959 at pp. 39–40; *R (Jackson) v Attorney General* [2006] 1 AC 262, 302 (Lord Steyn)) is also at the heart of Australia's exclusively parliamentary model of rights protection, and provides an important legitimising basis for the parliamentary committee system. This principle was the primary practical and normative focus of the framers of the *Constitution*, and it remains at the centre of modern democratic discourse in Australia (Goldsworthy 1999 at p. 1; *McGinty v Western Australia* (1996) 186 CLR 140). As Goldsworthy (2010) explains, the doctrine of parliamentary sovereignty invests a single law-making body elected by the people with the power to respond to emerging issues and needs, and to modify outdated laws (at p. 17). A sovereign parliament also forms part of what Hart has described as a 'rule of recognition' (Hart 1994 at p. 92; Goldsworthy 1999 at pp. 1 and 239), providing the criteria for determining the validity of other laws, and seen as binding by the most senior participants in the system (Goldsworthy 2010 at p. 17).

The final feature of the Australian Parliament that is particularly relevant to the committee system is the role and dominance of *political parties* (Goldsworthy 1999 at p. 185; Reid and Forrest 1989; Hirst 2010). Australia's strong party-political culture, often exerted through Cabinet or Party Room meetings wherein policy is solidified and members bound to follow the 'party line', can mean that the law-making functions of the House are regularly synonymous with the will of the executive, and the scrutiny functions of the major party Opposition are prescribed by the 'party line'. In other words, when one or both major parties adopt a 'tough on terror' policy at the Cabinet or Party Room level, the orthodox view is that individual parliamentarians will be at best reluctant and at worst prohibited from advocating an alternative policy position or questioning their own party's policy rationale (Halligan 2007; Siaroff 2003). As discussed in Parts II and III of this book, my findings challenge this orthodox view and suggest that parliamentary committees can provide the deliberative space and political incentives for individual parliamentarians to engage in rights scrutiny and change aspects of their party's counter-terrorism policy or proposed legislation. In fact, my research suggests that engagement with the parliamentary committee system empowers backbenchers and Ministers to engage in a meaningful and reflective way with policy decision making at the Party Room level, as well as providing alternative options for influencing policy and legislation, for example by building cross-party coalitions and generating strong community support for rights-enhancing change.

The role of party politics in the Australian Parliament is also important to understanding the critical role of the Senate, and the Senate Committee system, as providing a central (and sometimes exclusive) public parliamentary forum for debating laws and contesting policy (Sawer et al. 2009 at pp. 153–4; Stone 2005). This is because the Senate is much more likely to be comprised of candidates who are not aligned with the major political parties, such as minor parties or independents, leading to a 'hung Parliament' (where neither major party holds a clear majority in the House), or a scenario where a minor party or a group of independents holds the balance of power in the Senate. This provides political incentives for the Senate, and its committee system, to rigorously scrutinise proposed Government Bills beyond the parameters set by the major party Opposition 'party line'. For example, independent Senators and minor party Senators may be able to refer a Government Bill to a Senate committee for inquiry and report, setting broad terms of reference for scrutiny that transcend the boundaries of either major political party policy platforms.

Despite this potentially powerful Senate structure, some take the view that, as the dominance of political parties rises, the potential for the carefully designed Australian parliamentary system to offer robust scrutiny of executive action decreases (Feldman 2015 at p. 98). However, like all of the features of the Parliament discussed in this chapter, the rise and dominance of political parties is a dynamic rather than static phenomenon. As will be explored further in Part III, party politics is thus crucial to understanding how the Parliament and its subsidiary bodies work, but it too can be contested and subject to change.

3.1.2 Parliamentary Committees and Parliamentary Lawmaking

As noted above, under the *Constitution,* the Parliament has exclusive power to make and pass legislation. The exclusive nature of this power reflects the founders' intention to protect the rights of citizens from the unbridled will of the executive. It is in this context that the parliamentary committee system plays a crucial role (Evans and Evans 2006). In practice, both Houses regularly rely on the committee system to fulfil their law-making function. This is because, as Griffith and Ryle note, both Houses spend most of their time responding to the policy initiatives or legislative proposals of the government of the day (Griffith and Ryle 1989 at p. 5). In this way, Parliament's law-making function can be described as a *scrutiny function.* It is a forum to debate the content, effect and policy merits of laws proposed by the executive government. The committee system allows the Parliament to 'outsource' this legislative scrutiny function at key points in the process, by referring a Bill to a particular Senate, House or joint committee for inquiry and report. As Marinac (2003) has observed, the committee system provides the practical forum for the Senate to manage its very large workload[1] without abandoning the type of considered scrutiny of government-proposed legislation that lies at the heart of the notion of the Senate as the 'house of review' (at p. 129).

The Parliament also relies heavily on the committee system to give meaning to its constitutional commitment to representative democracy by providing a forum for members to hear directly from the people they represent (Thompson 1998). The committee system offers all members the opportunity to contribute to the law-making process, regardless of their ministerial or shadow ministerial status. In this way, the committee system can also be described as a means of facilitating *deliberative democracy* (Uhr 2006 at p. 10–11; Levy and Orr 2016), which is based on the notion that democracies should provide for informed, reflective and cooperative decision making and policy development (Levy and Orr 2016 at pp. 22–23). As Levy and Orr (2016) explain, ideally deliberative law making should be inclusive,

[1] For example, in the year 2015, the Senate sat for a total of 60 days and passed 177 separate Acts. In 2010, the Senate sat for only 46 days and passed 150 Acts.

and open-minded, where key participants speak as well as listen and seek to extend beyond the notion of majoritarian rule, and give life to other shared, democratic values (at p. 4). Dalla-Pozza (2006) suggests that there are two primary ways in which the parliamentary committee system helps the Parliament to achieve its deliberative function. (at pp. 20–1). The first is through the practical capacity of committees to 'reach out' to the community by inviting written submissions and holding public hearings. This ensures that a wider range of interests are consulted (Paxman 1998 at p. 76) and also provides what Odgers (2012) has described as 'a chance for those with different perspectives or positions to find common ground' (at p. 129). This also has similarities to what Marsh (2006) has described as a shared understanding of policy issues among key participants, including parliamentarians, public servants, commentators, non-government organisations and the broader community (at p. 1). The second is through the act of scrutiny itself, which Uhr describes as 'at the heart of the work of a deliberative assembly' (Uhr 1998 at p. 149–50).

The parliamentary committee system also allows the Parliament to fulfil its constitutional role of holding the executive government to account for its exercise of legislative power (Appleby et al. 2014 at pp. 103–4). Senate committees play a particularly important role in holding the executive to account and have developed procedural features that guard against the type of executive dominance that often infects the House committee system (Reid and Forrest 1989 p. 190). Among these are the standing 'technical' scrutiny committees that inquire into every Bill and regulation (rather than waiting for a referral from one of the Houses of Parliament) and the powers of Senate committees to hold hearings into estimates of government expenditure (Appleby et al. 2014 at p. 16).

Finally, as discussed in Chap. 1, the parliamentary committee system also makes a central contribution to Parliament's rights-protecting function. Committees are tasked with alerting the Parliament to executive actions that unduly interfere with individual rights or freedoms, or abrogate certain rule of law principles (Galligan 1990). As described in Chap. 6, committees also arm members of the public, including sophisticated submission makers, with the information they need to challenge or question the merits of proposed law or policy that may have particular rights implications for groups within the Australian community. As discussed in Chap. 1, many scholars have questioned both the effectiveness of the committee system at performing this function, and the appropriateness of relying on this form of rights protection in Australia (e.g. Evans and Evans 2006; Stellios and Palfrey 2012; Kinley and Ernst 2012; Dixon 2012). However, regardless of whether Australia's parliamentary model of rights protection is viewed as strong or weak, the committee system is an undisputed and central component of Australia's parliamentary model of rights protection. This makes evaluating the impact of parliamentary committees on rights-engaging laws particularly important.

3.2 The Emergence of the Australian Parliamentary Committee System

From the above discussion, it may be tempting to think that committees have always been a part of the Australian Parliament; however, in reality it took many years to establish the sophisticated system of committees that operates today (Odgers 2012, especially Chap. 16). The first Standing Committee[2] to be established was the Senate Standing Committee on Regulations and Ordinances (SSCRO) in 1930 (Grenfell 2015 at p. 21). It was tasked with scrutinising proposed regulations to ensure that they are:

(a) in accordance with the statute;
(b) do not unduly trespass on personal rights and liberties;
(c) do not unduly make the rights and liberties of citizens dependent upon administrative and not upon judicial decisions; and
(d) do not contain matter more appropriate for parliamentary enactment (SSCRO 1930 at p. 23).

As Grenfell (2015) documents, these scrutiny principles initially attracted criticism, including on the basis that they invited inquiries of a political nature that some Committee members considered would be better dealt with by the Senate as a whole (at p. 44). However, over time the SSCRO has emerged as 'a pioneering chapter' in the development of legislative scrutiny practices across Westminster Parliaments (Uhr 2006 at p. 51; Halligan et al. 2007 at p. 44) and proven influential in the development of future committees, including those considered in my research (Debeljak and Grenfell 2020).

The next significant development in the history of the federal committee system occurred in the late 1950s when the well-respected Clerk of the Senate, James Odgers, travelled to the United States to study the American committee system (Reid and Forrest 1989 at p. 373). Upon his return, he provided a *Report on the United States* (1956) to the Senate recommending the introduction of a system of Senate Standing Committees to document and scrutinise the implementation and administration of federal laws and to inform the public about the government's operations (see also Millar 1991 at p. vi). No action was taken for many years, until parliamentary committees made a cameo appearance in Gough Whitlam's 1967 federal election campaign, with the Labor Party promising to establish a Senate committee system if elected to office (Millar 1991 at p. vii).

Following the election, Senator Lionel Murphy became Leader of the Opposition in the Senate and, with the support of Odgers and a band of backbenchers, began a robust campaign to establish a strong Senate committee system (Millar 1991 at p. vii). Proposals were put for both Estimates and General Purpose committees, and in

[2] Select Committees of the Senate emerged as the first parliamentary committees on the Commonwealth scene, followed by the establishment of two joint committees (Public Accounts and Public Works) in 1913. Subsequently, a third category, Standing Committees, was introduced to provide for committees with more permanent membership and powers. See Reid and Forrest 1989 at pp. 368–70; Odgers 2012 Chap. 16.

a single night in 1970 (with the help of the Queensland Liberal dissident Ian Wood who crossed the floor) seven Legislative General Purpose Committees and five Estimates Committees were established in the Senate (Millar 1991 at p. vii). Each of these committees had six members, three chosen by the government and three nominated by the Leader of the Opposition in the Senate in consultation with any minority group or groups, or independent Senators or Senator (Reid and Forrest 1989 at p. 375). This system was later reflected in the Standing Orders, and the Senate's Legislative and General Purpose Standing Committees became an entrenched part of the Australian parliamentary culture, particularly in the Senate (Reid and Forrest 1989 at p. 467).

The next important landmark occurred in 1981, with the establishment of the SSCSB. The SSCSB's origins are intrinsically linked to the work of the SSCRO, which had become increasingly active in its scrutiny of delegated legislation. It became clear to some parliamentarians that legislative provisions were being enacted that, had they been in the form of regulations, would have certainly attracted the attention of the SSCRO (Pearce 1991 at p. 4). This led some Senators, including Senator Alan Mission who was Chair of the Senate Constitutional and Legal Affairs Committee at that time, to call for the establishment of a specific committee tasked with scrutinising Bills against a similar set of criteria as the SSCRO (Pearce 1991 at p. 4). This was reflected in a recommendation made by the Senate Constitutional and Legal Affairs Committee in 1978 that a new Joint Committee on Scrutiny of Bills be established (Pearce 1991 at p. 4). The initial scrutiny criteria recommended for the proposed joint committee were ambitious in scope and the recommendation was not well received at the time (Grenfell 2015 at p. 25). Despite this, support began to build for the new committee and sometime later a compromise proposal was put. It involved the Senate Constitutional and Legal Affairs Committee undertaking the work of the proposed SSCSB for a six-month probationary period, applying a narrower range of scrutiny to mirror that of the SSCRO. This was accepted by the Parliament, and the scrutiny of Bills work commenced (Pearce 1991). The early SSCSB was able to survive its probationary period, and became a separate committee. It also began to produce one of its most valued outputs, the Alert Digest.

The late 1980s saw the beginning of a number of procedural reforms to the committee system, including changes in 1989 to provide for a systematic approach to the process of referring bills to legislative and general purpose committees through what became the Senate Standing Committee on the Selection of Bills (Paxman 1998 at p. 76; Childs 1992). The implementation of these reforms saw a rapid increase in the number of Bills referred to Senate Standing Committees for inquiry and report, up from 30 Bills in the period 1970–1980 to 279 Bills during the time between 1990 and 1996 (Odgers 2012 at pp. 446–7). Then, in 1994, the previously separate Estimates and Senate General Purpose Standing Committees amalgamated. This gave rise to the system of 'paired' committees that we see today. Under this system, committees are allocated 'portfolios' or thematic subject areas (such as finance and administration or legal and constitutional affairs) and undertake both the scrutiny and estimate functions of the legislative committees, as well as the broader or thematic policy inquiries previously undertaken by the general-purpose committees. These pairs of committees include one with responsibilities for reviewing legislation (with government Chairs and government majorities) and the other for reference inquiries (with non-government Chairs and non-government majorities) (Odgers 2012 at pp. 446–7).[3] As discussed below with respect to the Senate Standing Committees on Legal and Constitutional Affairs, these pairs of committees are also supported by professional secretariat staff and sometimes external expert advisors.

By the time the Howard Government won the 2004 federal election, the paired standing committee system had resulted in dozens of public hearings and numerous reports each year, compared with the much smaller handful of reports the committee system had procedure prior to the pairing reforms. For example, during the period 2002–2004 the Senate Standing Committees on Legal and Constitutional Affairs conducted a total of 23 inquiries (nine conducted by the References Committee and 14 by the Legislation Committee) compared with a total of 17 inquiries that were conducted by the committee during the entire period between 1987 and 1996. Bills were regularly referred to standing committees for inquiry – including at times to references committees, who often took a more critical approach to review and scrutiny. For example, from 1996 to 2005 legislation was referred to references committees on 146 occasions instead of legislation committees (Minchin and Moore 2010). The Howard Government responded by making changes to the system that would effectively revert to the pre-1994 arrangements. Instead of a system of 'pairs' of committees, each standing committee would resume both legislative and general purpose functions and be chaired exclusively by a government member, effectively providing each committee with a government majority (Minchin and Moore 2010). Unsurprisingly, this change was strongly opposed by the Labor opposition and the minor parties, who accused the government of 'completely trashing' the committee system and undermining governmental accountability to the Senate (Minchin and Moore 2010). However the move did not appear to lead to a substantive decrease in committee inquiries into government Bills. For example, under the 'paired' system, the Senate Standing Committees on Legal and Constitutional Affairs conducted 28 inquiries during the period December 2004 until March 2006. The 'unpaired' Legislation Committee then conducted 23 inquiries from September 2006 until October 2007. By 2009, the Rudd Government had reversed the relevant changes (Senate Standing Committee on Procedure 2008) and the refreshed 'paired' committee system was reflected in the Senate Standing Orders 17–39. This remains the broad structure for the Senate standing committees operating today.

[3]Each committee was comprised of six Senators: three appointed by government, and the other three by the Leader of the Opposition in the Senate in consultation with independents and minor parties. The legislation committees had government-appointed Chairs with casting votes, assuring a government majority. In contrast, the references committees had non-government Chairs, and thus non-government majorities.

3.3 Committees Examined in Detail in this Book

3.3.1 Senate Scrutiny of Bills Committee

3.3.1.1 Membership, Scrutiny Mandate and Outputs

The modern SSCSB is established under Senate Standing Order 24, and comprises six Senators, three nominated by the government, and three members nominated by the opposition in consultation with any minor parties or independent senators. The Chair of the SSCSB is appointed on the nomination of the Leader of the Opposition in the Senate and enjoys a casting vote (SSCSB 2012 at para [2.5]). The SSCSB is supported by a secretary, secretariat staff and an external legal advisor. Standing Order 24 also sets out the committee's scrutiny mandate. It requires the SSCSB to consider whether Bills or Acts:

- trespass unduly on personal rights and liberties;
- make rights, liberties or obligations unduly dependent upon insufficiently defined administrative powers;
- make rights, liberties or obligations unduly dependent upon non-reviewable decisions;
- inappropriately delegate legislative powers, or
- insufficiently subject the exercise of legislative power to parliamentary scrutiny.

The SSCSB has described its five scrutiny principles as broadly reflecting 'themes of good governance; administrative fairness and accountability; and parliamentary propriety (maintaining appropriate parliamentary engagement with the legislative process)' (SSCSB 2014). While the committee exercises its discretion when it comes to articulating the detail of its scrutiny criteria (SSCSB 2014), it has recently provided examples of some of the issues it has commented on with respect to the scrutiny principle relating to personal rights and liberties. These include the use of coercive powers; breaches of the privacy of individuals; the right to vote; the use of strict liability provisions; and the abrogation of the privilege against self-incrimination (SSCSB 2012 at para [3.5]). As will be discussed further in Parts II and III, the types of rights the SSCSB focuses on, and the way it talks about rights, gives the committee particular advantages when it comes to having a strong hidden impact on counter-terrorism laws, and in contributing Australia's parliamentary model of rights protection.

When conducting its scrutiny work, the SSCSB employs a 'dialogue model' in which the committee and ministers exchange formal correspondence which is then published in the committee's Digests and Reports (Cooney 1991; ALRC 2016 at para [2.23]; SSCSB 2012). This is supported by the provision of swift legal analysis by the legal advisor to the committee, which forms the basis of the SSCSB's Alert Digest on the Bill.[4] This short summary report alerts the reader to the key issues or

[4] In 2017, the SSCSB began publishing its scrutiny comments on recently introduced Bills (including responses received on matters previously considered by the committee) in one report, the *Scrutiny Digest*. However, the *Scrutiny Digest* continues to be divided into initial reports on the

questions arising from the Bill relevant to the SSCSB's scrutiny criteria. This is then followed by a final report, which contains the committee's conclusions, having considered any responses it may have received from questions posed to the proponent Minister. The SSCSB's conclusions are generally couched in terms of 'raising scrutiny concerns with particular provisions of a Bill', and the committee regularly leaves the question of whether and how the provision should be amended 'to the Senate as a whole to consider' (SSCSB 2014). It very rarely recommends specific legislative amendments.

The requirement to scrutinise all Bills and legislative instruments gives rise to a heavy workload for the committee.[5] This means it can be difficult for the SSCSB to table its final report on a Bill prior to the completion of parliamentary debate. As discussed in Chap. 6, this often depends on the SSCSB receiving a timely response from the relevant Minister to its requests for further information. To address these challenges, the SSCSB pushed for Standing Order 24 to be amended to empower the committee to 'maintain on its website a list of bills in relation to which the committee has sought advice from the responsible minister and not yet received a response' (Senate Standing Order 24(1)(d)). The Standing Order was amended in November 2017 and also provides that, where the SSCSB has not been able to complete a final report on the Bill because a ministerial response has not been received, then any senator may ask the Minister for an explanation why a response was not received (24(1)(e)), which can be followed by a motion without notice, recording the Minister's response or failure to respond (24(1)(f)-(g)).

In addition to producing and tabling Alert Digests and reports, the SSCSB also reports on matters which have been referred to it by the Senate, such as the 2006 *Inquiry into Entry, Search and Seizure Provisions in Commonwealth Legislation, and produces a regular 'scrutiny news' newsletter on key issues arising from its scrutiny work (SSCSB* 2017*).*

As discussed further in Part III, one of the particular strengths of the SSCSB is the way it provides accessible analysis of a Bill to other committees, and to submission makers to inquiry-based committees. Since 2012, the SSCSB has been actively seeking to increase its communication with other parliamentary committees to ensure that they are alerted to issues raised by the SSCSB in a timely manner (SSCSB 2012 at para [7.8]; SSCSB 2014). For example, since 2012 Standing Order 24 has provided that the SSCSB's comments on Bills 'stand referred to legislation committees inquiring into those bills'. The SSCSB also has informal communication channels to the SSCRO and the PJCHR, primarily through the use of a 'shared secretariat' (SSCSB 2014) and, as will be explored further in Part II, the work of the SSCSB features frequently in the submissions to and reports of the other committees.

Bill (previously called 'Alert Digests', now called 'Initial Scrutiny') and concluding reports on the Bill (previously called 'Reports' now called 'Commentary on Ministerial Responses').

[5] For example, the SSCSB reported that: '[f]rom 2001 to 2011 the committee considered a total of 2524 bills and commented on 1144 or 45.3 per cent of these bills. During the same period 574 bills or 22.7 per cent of all bills were amended. Of the amended bills the committee commented on 125 amendments or 21.8 per cent.' SSCSB 2014at para [2.25].

3.3.1.2 A Technical Scrutiny Committee?

The SSCSB has consistently seen its role as providing 'technical scrutiny' of proposed laws rather than an evaluation of the policy merits of each Bill (SSCSB 2012 at para [2.11]; SSCSB 2014). As discussed further below, the SSCSB's 'technical scrutiny' character gives it broad legitimacy in the eyes of a range of key participants in the committee system and important strengths when it comes to influencing the pre-introduction development of laws. However, it is important to keep in mind that this 'technical scrutiny' role is self-imposed, rather than prescribed by Standing Order 24.

Some key participants have debated whether the SSCSB's role should be confined to 'technical scrutiny', or whether it should serve a broader, social justice objective by preventing undue legislative interference with personal rights and liberties (SSCSB 2012 at para [3.26]). For example, when speaking at the tenth anniversary of the SSCSB, Uhr suggested that the committee could build upon its current role of contributing to the information adding to the available to the Senate about a Bill by developing legislative options to improve the problems or shortcomings identified in its scrutiny reports (Uhr 1991 at p. 79). For Uhr, this would be a legitimate role for the SSCSB and necessary for the committee to maintain a relevant and respected role in Parliament (Uhr 1991 at pp. 81–2).

The technical scrutiny character of the SSCSB is considered in further detail in Parts II and III of my book, and is directly relevant to both the overall impact the committee system has on the development and content of case study Acts and rights protection in Australia.

3.3.2 Parliamentary Joint Committee on Intelligence and Security

The PJCIS is a statutory committee with origins that trace back to the 1970s. Since the establishment of ASIO, successive parliaments have been keen to ensure specific parliamentary oversight of the workings of Australia's key national security agencies, and the country's national security laws (Royal Commission on Intelligence and Security 1977). The need for parliamentary oversight became even more acute following the terrorist attacks in the United States on 11 September 2001 (Flood 2004 at p. 51), and a number of specialist oversight bodies have since been established at the federal level, including the Parliamentary Joint Committee on the Australian Security and Intelligence Organisation, Australian Secret Intelligence Service and Defence Signals Directorate (the PJC on ASIO, ASIS and DSD), which was introduced to review and report on how intelligence agencies use their powers.[6] In 2004 the powers of this committee were expanded to keep pace with legislative developments and in 2005, the PJC on ASIO, ASIS and DSD was renamed the PJCIS (Flood 2004 at p. 51).

The functions of the PJCIS are prescribed by Part 4 and Schedule 1 of the *Intelligence Services* and have changed regularly since the committee's establishment. They broadly relate to reviewing the administration, expenditure and performance of the 'Australian Intelligence Community'[7] and reviewing the operation, effectiveness and implications of a number of specific national security laws. The PJCIS does not have the power to initiate its own inquiries but it can ask the responsible Minister to refer a particular matter to it for review. *Intelligence Services Act 2001* (Cth) s29 also sets out matters beyond the scope of the PJCIS, including reviewing the intelligence gathering and assessment priorities of the intelligence agencies.

The PCJIS's membership is also prescribed and comprises 11 members (five Senators and six members of the House) with a government Chair and a majority of government members (*Intelligence Services Act 2001* (Cth) s28(2) and Schedule 1). Ministers, Speakers and Presidents of the Senate are not eligible to become members of the PJCIS. House members of the committee must be approved by the House following a recommendation from the Prime Minister. Senate members of the committee are approved by the Senate, following recommendations from the Leader of the Government in the Senate. Although regard must be had to the 'desirability' of ensuring that the membership of the PJCIS largely reflects the 'representation of recognised political parties in the Parliament' (Schedule 1, 14(5)), as at 2018 the membership of the PJCIS has been limited to Members and Senators from the major political parties. A secretary and professional secretariat staff support the PJCIS, including on occasion 'secondee' staff from law enforcement and intelligence agencies who provide technical assistance to the secretariat. Each member of the secretariat staff must receive a high level security clearance (Schedule 1, 14(5), 21). As discussed in Part II, this tightly controlled membership and access to specialist staff gives the PJCIS particular strengths when it comes to influencing key legislative decision makers and receiving government support for its recommendations. It has also given rise to concerns about the nature of the PJCIS's relationship with law enforcement and intelligence agencies.

Like the LCA Committees, the PJCIS is an inquiry-based committee and has powers to call for witnesses and hold public and private hearings (*Intelligence Services Act 2001* (Cth) Schedule 1 Part 1). The PJCIS regularly makes direct contact with potential submission makers, including relevant government departments,

---

[6]In March 2002, the Parliamentary Joint Committee on the Australian Security and Intelligence Organisation, Australian Secret Intelligence Service and Defence Signals Directorate (the PJC ASIO, ASIS and DSD) was established, replacing the former Parliamentary Joint Committee on ASIO, which was provided for under the *Australian Security Intelligence Organisation Act 1979.*

[7]The Australian Intelligence Community is comprised of ASIO, ASIS, Australian Geospatial-Intelligence Organisation (AGO), Defence Intelligence organisation (DIO), Australian Signals Directorate (ASD) and Office of National Assessments (ONA).

law enforcement and intelligence agencies, independent statutory offices such as the Inspector General of Intelligence and Security (IGIS) and the Independent National Security Legislation Monitor (INSLM). However, unlike the other committees studied, the PJCIS has a specialist national security focus and a range of special powers that enable it to provide secure forums for the consideration of classified national security information (*Intelligence Services Act 2001* (Cth) Schedule 1 Part 1). In addition, the PJCIS must not include any operationally sensitive information in its reports or risk the disclosure of any information that might prejudice Australia's national security (*Intelligence Services Act 2001* (Cth) Schedule 1, 7). These powers are supported by a range of offences for unauthorised disclosure of national security or operationally sensitive information (Schedule 1, 9-13). There are also a range of secrecy provisions that apply specifically to the members and staff of the PJCIS (Schedule 1, 12). As discussed in Part II, these special powers contribute to the PJCIS's strong legitimacy among government departments and agencies, and help explain its comparatively strong impact on the content of the case study Acts (Moulds 2016, 2020; Dalla-Pozza 2020).

The unique and influential features of the PJCIS have been noted by many parliamentarians, including by ALP Senator Kristina Keneally who said, in the context of debate on the TEO Bill in 2019, that the PJCIS is unlike every other parliamentary committee and holds a special place within the Parliament.

> Since 2013, the government has not explicitly rejected a recommendation of the PJCIS. And it is not like every other committee; this committee is set up by its own legislation. This committee has always sought to improve and better the national security legislation in this country (24 July 2019, p. 772).

Like the LCA Committees, the PJCIS regularly cites the work of the SSCSB and the PJCHR in its reports and refers to the work of other parliamentary committees. There are also many instances where the PJCIS has carefully considered the work of other independent reviews of counter-terrorism laws or national security agencies. As discussed below, improving the collaborative capacity of the PJCIS is a focus of the reforms discussed in Part III of this research.

3.3.3 Senate Standing Committees on Legal and Constitutional Affairs

The LCA Committees were established in 1970 pursuant to Senate Standing Order 25 and take the form of a pair of committees – the Senate Legal and Constitutional Affairs *Legislation* Committee (the LCA Legislation Committee) and the Senate Legal and Constitutional Affairs *References* Committee (the LCA References Committee) – each with a related but different mandate and membership. Both LCA Committees have six members and contain at least one member nominated by minority parties and/or independent senators (Senate Standing Order 25. The LCA Legislation Committee has a government Chair with a casting vote (and therefore a government majority) and the LCA References Committee is chaired by a non-government Senator (providing it with a non-government majority) (Senate Standing Order 25(10)). Standing Order 25(7) also provides that other Senators can be appointed to the LCA Committees as substitutes for existing committee members or as 'participating members' for particular inquiries. As discussed further in Chap. 4, this gives the LCA Committees particular strengths when it comes to engaging a diverse range of Senators, who in turn help to encourage a broad range of submission makers and witnesses to the committees' public inquiries. A secretary and professional secretariat staff support the LCA Committees, generally without an external legal advisor.

Unlike the SSCSB, the LCA Committees are not required to review every Bill introduced into Parliament. Instead, the LCA Committees inquire into matters *referred to them* by the Senate. The LCA Legislation Committee is responsible for consideration of Bills, estimates processes, and departmental matters. The LCA References Committee deals with thematic or issues-based references from the Senate, which since 2008 generally do not include consideration of the provisions of particular Bills (Senate Standing Order 25(2)). Both LCA Committees receive guidance from the Senate about the focus of its inquiry and reporting times. This means that, in practice, it is the Senate Standing Committee for the Selection of Bills that determines the workload of the LCA Legislation Committee (Paxman 1998 at pp. 76–8).

The Selection of Bills Committee was set up in 1988 pursuant to Senate, Standing Order 24A and is effectively a committee of whips with members including the Government Whip, the Opposition Whip and the whips of any minority groups. A member of the Selection of Bills Committee, typically a non-government Senator, proposes that a bill be referred to another Senate committee (such as one of the LCA Committees), giving reasons for referral, nominating a committee and a possible reporting date. The Selection of Bills Committee then presents this referral recommendation to the Senate as a whole to endorse (or reject). Most commonly, the Selection of Bills Committee referrals are endorsed by the Senate, and the Bill is then referred to the other committee (such as the LCA Legislation Committee) for inquiry and report.

One of the key strengths of the LCA Committees is their ability to conduct public inquiries into the Bills or issues referred to them by the Senate (Senate Standing Order 25(1); Odgers 2012 at pp. 491–3). The first step in the inquiry process is to call for written submissions through advertising its inquiry in national newspapers and online, as well as by directly approaching a range of potentially interested parties, including legal bodies, government departments and independent statutory bodies (sometimes described as the 'usual suspects' eg by Marinac 2003 and discussed further in Chap. 4). The LCA Committees then select a range of submission makers to attend a public or private hearing and provide further oral evidence and answer the committee members' questions. As a report marking the first 20 years of the LCA Committees observed:

> Because they can travel around Australia in the course of their inquiries, the Legislative and General Purpose Standing Committees literally take Parliament to the people. In this way they gather information from interested members of the public and from experts and specialists (Senate Legislative and General Purpose Standing Committees 1990).

After the inquiry process is complete, the LCA Committees prepare a report to be tabled in the Senate typically containing a number of specific recommendations for amendments to the Bill or policy proposal, as well as an overview of the key issues raised during the inquiry. Unlike the SSCSB, whose reports are almost invariably consensus reports, the LCA Committees' reports regularly include dissenting or additional comments by opposition or minor party committee members.

Unlike the SSCSB or the PJCHR, the LCA Committees are not required to apply any particular analytical framework or rights-scrutiny criteria when undertaking an inquiry into a Bill or other matter. Despite this, common themes are evident in the approach of the LCA Committees, and in particular the LCA Legislation Committee. These themes are largely informed by the approach adopted by the most regular and influential submission makers to the LCA Committees, and commonly involve rights issues, even if they are not always expressed with reference to international human rights law (Evans and Evans 2006). As explored further in Chap. 6, the themes commonly explored by the LCA Committees when reviewing the case study Acts include: consideration of relevant constitutional doctrines, particularly the doctrine of separation of powers; the preservation of a meaningful oversight role for Parliament over the exercise of executive power; consideration of relevant 'rule of law' principles; and the need to justify any significant departure from established criminal law and common law principles.

The LCA Committees have a number of informal ways of liaising with other parliamentary committees, particularly those who share responsibilities for scrutinising Bills, such as the SSCBC and the PJCHR. However, the LCA Committees' relationship with other inquiry-based committees can be complex. Since the procedural reforms in the 2000s, efforts have been made to reduce the potential for more than one parliamentary committee to consider the same Bill or reference at the same time (Senate Standing Order 25(13)). In addition, since 2013, there has been a strong tendency among government Chairs of the LCA Legislation Committee to decline to inquire into counter-terrorism or national security Bills that are also subject to inquiry by the PJCIS. The evidence presented in Part II of this book suggests that, while this is understandable, these efforts to avoid multi-committee inquiries into national security laws may dilute the potential for the committee system to have a rights-enhancing impact. For these reasons, Part III explores options for improving the opportunities for the inquiry-based committees to work efficiently and collaboratively when it comes to reviewing rights-engaging laws such as those relating to counter-terrorism.

3.3.4 Parliamentary Joint Committee on Human Rights

3.3.4.1 Membership, Mandate and Outputs

The newest parliamentary committee evaluated in this book is the PJCHR, and unlike many other committees within the federal system, it has been subject to sustained academic evaluation and critique since its establishment in 2011 (Rice 2020; Byrnes 2020; Fletcher 2018, 2020; Williams and Reynolds 2016; Reynolds and Williams 2020; Rajanayagam 2020). As noted in Chap. 1, this committee was established by the *Human Rights (Parliamentary Scrutiny) Act 2011* (the Parliamentary Scrutiny Act) as part of the Rudd Government's response to the 2008–2009 National Consultation (Australian Human Rights Framework 2010). Under the Parliamentary Scrutiny Act s4, the PJCHR must examine Acts, Bills and legislative instruments for compatibility with human rights and inquire into any matter relating to human rights which is referred to it by the Attorney-General (s7). The Parliamentary Scrutiny Act also introduced the requirement for all Bills and disallowable instruments to be introduced with a Statement of Compatibility with Human Rights.

The PJCHR's membership is also prescribed and comprises 10 members, five appointed by the Senate and five appointed by the House. The PJCHR has a government Chair with a casting vote (Parliamentary Scrutiny Act s5). A secretary, professional secretariat staff and an external legal adviser assist the committee.

In practice, the most frequent role of the PJCHR is to table reports on the human rights compatibility of a proposed Bill or legislative instrument. The 'human rights' referred to in the Parliamentary Scrutiny Act s3 are those rights listed in the following seven core human rights conventions to which Australia is a party:

- *International Convention on the Elimination of all Forms of Racial Discrimination*,
- *International Covenant on Economic, Social and Cultural Rights*,
- *International Covenant on Civil and Political Rights*,
- *Convention on the Elimination of All Forms of Discrimination Against Women*,
- *Convention Against Torture and Other Cruel, Inhuman or Degrading Treatment or Punishment*,
- *Convention on the Rights of the Child*
- *Convention on the Rights of Persons with Disabilities*

These rights total over 100 in number, which posed a challenge for the new committee. However, having operated for a number of years, it appears that a smaller handful of rights consistently make up the majority of the PJCHR's detailed scrutiny work (see e.g. PJHCR Annual Report 2013–2014 at [3.5]–[3.6]). As Byrnes (2020) has observed, the fact that the PJHCR's mandate extends beyond civil and political rights to encompass the 'progressively realised' economic and social rights has presented particular challenges when it comes to the process of articulating and applying clear rights 'standards' or 'tests' to apply to proposed laws, and distinguishes the PJCHR from its New Zealand and UK counterparts.

Like the SSCSB, it is common for the PJCHR to express a view on a Bill's compatibility with its scrutiny criteria but leave the question of amending or removing a particular provision to Parliament as a whole to consider. Less frequently, the PJCHR makes specific recommendations for amendment to ensure the compatibility of the legislation with Australia's human rights obligations (PJHCR Annual Report 2013–2014 at [2.11]). Like the SSCSB, the PJCHR considers *all* Bills and legislative instruments introduced to Parliament and faces a heavy and unrelenting workload (Jenkins 2012).

In order to manage its heavy workload and maximise its capacity to table its reports prior to the conclusion of parliamentary debate or the requisite disallowance period, the PJCHR has developed strategies for prioritising its work that centre around categorising Bills and legislative instruments on the basis of the significance of the human rights issues they raise (see e.g. PJHCR Annual Report 2013–2014 at [1.19], [2.15]–[2.17]). However, despite these strategies, the PJCHR is not always able to table its scrutiny reports prior to the conclusion of the second reading debate on the relevant Bill.

As discussed in Chap. 6, two factors contribute to the occasional delay in tabling PJCHR reports. The first is procedural and arises from the fact that the PJCHR is a *joint* committee. This means that the PJCHR typically meets when both the House and the Senate are sitting, and the Chair tables the committee's reports after each of these meetings (PJHCR Annual Report 2013–2014 at [2.2]). This means that PJCHR scrutiny reports may not be tabled in weeks when the Senate alone is sitting and debating Bills.[8] The second factor relates to the PJCHR's general practice of waiting to receive a response to its requests for further information from the proponent Minister before tabling its reports. Unlike the SSCSB, which sets out its preliminary concerns with a Bill in the form of a short Alert Digest, at least until recently the PJCHR has typically only issued a concluded scrutiny report on a Bill that includes excerpts from any response received from the proponent Minister to requests for further information. Under this approach, the PJCHR sets out its concerns with respect to a Bill in correspondence to the proponent Minister and allows the Minister to respond *before* the PJCHR tables its report. This 'behind-closed-doors' exchange of correspondence between the committee and the proponent of the Bill on issues arising from the SoC is seen by some as central to the human rights 'dialogue' the committee is tasked with creating (see e.g. PJCHR Chairs Tabling Statement 11 Oct 2016). However, unless the proponent Ministers respond swiftly to the PJCHR's correspondence, this approach can leave the Parliament without the benefit of the PJCHR's analysis of a Bill during the critical second reading stage.

As discussed further below, my research suggests that this delay in the publication of the PJCHR's analysis of a Bill is having a negative impact on the committee's capacity to influence legislative outcomes. This is also in line with findings made by Rajanayagam (2020), Fletcher (2018, 2020), Williams and Reynolds

---

[8] For example in 2012 there were 3 weeks when the House of Representatives was sitting when the Senate was not and 2 weeks when the Senate was sitting when the House was not (out of a total of 20 sitting weeks).

(2016) and Reynolds and Williams (2020). For this reason, in Part III I recommend that the PJCHR consider adopting Alert Digest style reporting, such as that used by the SSCSB, along with a number of other strategies to improve the timeliness and accessibility of its reports.

In addition to tabling reports on Bills and legislative instruments, the PJCHR has also published a *Guide to Human Rights* (2015) and two Guidance Notes: *Drafting statements of compatibility* (2014), and *Offence provisions, civil penalties and human rights* (2014). These materials reflect the PJCHR's approach to assessing human rights compliance, which, although drawn from international law principles, aims to be 'practical' and contextualised for the Australian experience (Stephens 2013). These Guidance Notes are directed primarily at public servants responsible for drafting and preparing SoCs and, as discussed further in Part III, provide a foundation on which to improve the PJCHR's overall impact on the content and development of proposed laws. Some commentators, such as Fletcher (2018), have raised concerns that these guidance materials, produced in close consultation with the Attorney-General's Department, may have the effect of diluting the quality of rights scrutiny undertaken by the PJCHR, particularly if they represent a 'conflation' or 'compromise' in approaches between the PJCHR and the Government of the day. However, as discussed in Part III, my research suggests that there is great value in fostering positive working relationships between policy makers and parliamentary committees when it comes to improving the overall rights-impact of the parliamentary committee system.

3.3.4.2 A 'Dialogue-Creating' Committee?

Although it has the power to hold public inquiries and receive private briefings (Parliamentary Scrutiny Act s7(c)), in its work practices the PJCHR has generally based itself on the 'technical scrutiny' approach of the SSCSB and rarely actively requests written submissions on the Bills it considers. The PJCHR has also been particularly keen to foster a close working relationship with the SSCSB and the SSCRO and this has evolved to include 'sharing' certain secretariat staff and functions (Fletcher 2017, 2018; Campbell and Morris 2015).

Successive PJCHR Chairs have also underscored the 'technical' character of the committee (see e.g. PJCHR Annual Report 2013–2014; PJCHR Annual Report 2015–2016) and in its 2015 *Guide to Human Rights* (2015) publication, the PJCHR clearly states that it undertakes a 'technical' scrutiny function concerning compliance with Australia's international human rights obligations and 'does not consider the broader policy merits of legislation' (at p. ii). On this view, the human rights 'dialogue' the PJCHR seeks to create with the executive is based on the preparation and consideration of SoCs and the correspondence exchanged between the committee and the proponent of the Bill or instrument being scrutinised.

However, some commentators suggest that the PJCHR should play a more active role in directly engaging the Australian community on human rights issues (see e.g. Rice 2020; Burton and Williams 2013; Dixon 2012; Stellios and Palfrey 2012). These commentators often point to the legislation establishing the PJCHR, which clearly provides that the committee has the power to hold public inquiries into human rights matters referred to it and into existing Acts or proposed Bills (Parliamentary Scrutiny Act s7(c)). This broader community engagement role is also said to be reflected in the second reading speech of the proponent of the Parliamentary Scrutiny Act, the then Attorney-General, the Hon Robert McClelland MP, who said:

> [T]he new parliamentary committee will establish a dialogue between the parliament and its citizens whereby the members of the committee can canvass the views of the public, including affected groups, as to how they will be affected by proposed legislation.
>
> In that sense, these measures incrementally advance the concept of participatory democracy by providing additional means for citizens to have input into the legislative process (30 September 2010 at p. 271).

For some scholars, the PJCHR's lack of broader public engagement when undertaking its Bills scrutiny is a sign of its lack of effectiveness as a rights-protecting mechanism (see e.g. Williams and Reynolds 2016). Others, such as Rice (2020) call for a reconsideration of the type of 'technical scrutiny' that is being undertaken by the PJCHR, suggesting that 'opening up' the scrutiny process being applied to proposed federal laws by the PJCHR to dissenting views and to more 'contestable' standards of rights compliance would improve the quality of the dialogue occurring between the PJCHR and the executive, and provide new opportunities for public engagement with the Committee. These issues are explored further in Part II and Part III of the book, where I argue in favour of the PJCHR retaining its 'technical' as opposed to 'inquiry' character, but share Rice's (2020) and Evans and Evans' (2006) thoughts on the value of reflecting a more contestable, 'Australian' set of human rights standards when it comes to determining the rights compatibility of proposed laws.

3.3.5 Non-Parliamentary Scrutiny Bodies

Although my research evaluates the rights-enhancing impact of parliamentary committees, a number of non-parliamentary review mechanisms also played an influential role in the development of the case study Acts and contribute in direct and indirect ways to Australia's parliamentary model of rights protection (see e.g. Dalla-Pozza 2020; Appleby 2017). They include:

- the INSLM established in 2011 to review and report on the operation, effectiveness and implications of Australia's counter-terrorism and national security legislation on an ongoing basis, including the impact of these laws on individual rights. (*Independent Monitor of National Security Information Act 2010* (Cth) Part II). When carrying out his or her functions, the INSLM is required to have regard to Australia's obligations under international agreements, including human rights obligations (s8).
- the IGIS, an independent statutory office holder who is authorised to review the activities of the Australian Intelligence Community 'to ensure that the agencies act legally and with propriety, comply with ministerial guidelines and directives and respect human rights' (*Inspector-General of Intelligence and Security Act 1986* (Cth) ss 8, 9, 9A).

- the Australian Human Rights Commission (AHRC), with an explicit statutory mandate to provide advice about the human rights compliance of Australia's federal laws, including counter-terrorism laws (*Australian Human Rights Commission Act 1986* (Cth)).
- the Commonwealth Ombudsman who is tasked with investigating complaints about the administrative actions of federal departments and agencies, including the Australian Federal Police (without an explicit human rights mandate) (*Ombudsman Act 1976* (Cth)).
- the Council of Australian Governments (COAG), which has played an important role in the development and review of Australia's counter-terrorism laws, particularly in the context of considerations of the referral of state powers and the enactment of complementary state and territory laws. COAG has members from each Australian government, including the Prime Minister, state and territory Premiers and Chief Ministers and the President of the Australian Local Government Association. The decisions of COAG are reflected in communiqués or sometimes including National Agreements and National Partnership Agreements. COAG invests its specialist committees with specific mandates which can include the consideration of the human rights implications of proposed or existing counter-terrorism laws.

In addition to these bodies, a number of inquiries have been specifically established to examine, review and report on various aspects of Australia's counter-terrorism laws. The relationship between these review bodies and the parliamentary committee system is discussed in Chap. 6 and considered by Dalla-Pozza in her 2019 examination of the 'dual scrutiny' experience of counter-terrorism law making in Australia.

3.4 Counter-Terrorism Law Making in Australia

During the period from 2001 to 2019 Australia has faced the exceedingly complex task of protecting its people from the threat of terrorism, and has sought to engage in local, regional and international efforts to prevent terrorism and extremism and respond to acts of politically motivated violence. The nature of this threat has changed over time to include a wide range of activities and platforms. In response to this threat, Australia has enacted over 70 laws and invested significant resources in intelligence gathering, law enforcement and counter-extremism activities (Renwick 2018 at p. 14). By mid 2018, more than 50 people had been convicted of terrorism offences, with 40 matters still before the courts (Renwick 2018 Appendix 1). This period has also seen a number of terrorist-related attacks on Australia and Australians, as well as countless terrorist incidences around the world and all indications are that terrorist-related threats to Australia's national security are unlikely to dissipate any time soon (Renwick 2018 at pp. 14–15).

The next part of this chapter describes the key tranches of counter-terrorism law making between the period 2001 to 2019, setting the scene for the evaluation in Part II of the legislative, public and hidden impact of the parliamentary committees described above. Summarising the experience of counter-terrorism law making in Australia is a daunting task (see eg. Williams et al. 2015, 2010; Williams and Lynch 2006; Williams 2011), and I do not aim to provide a comprehensive overview of even the most significant domestic and international developments that have given rise to one of the most prolific areas of federal legislative activity in recent decades. Rather, I introduce the case study Acts within the context of six key tranches of counter-terrorism law making in order to provide some context for why these Acts were introduced, and why they make particularly compelling case studies. These Acts are:

- *Security Legislation Amendment (Terrorism) Act 2002* (Cth) (and related Acts) (SLAT Acts, CSA 1).
- Australian Security Intelligence Organisation Legislation Amendment (Terrorism) Bill 2002 (Cth) (CSA 2);
- *Australian Security Intelligence Organisation Legislation Amendment (Terrorism) Act 2003* (Cth) (CSA 3);
- *Anti-terrorism Act 2004* (Cth) (CSA 4);
- *National Security Information (Criminal Proceedings) Act 2004* (Cth) (CSA 5);
- *Anti-Terrorism Act (No 2) 2005* (Cth) (Control Orders Act, CSA 6);
- *Independent National Security Legislation Monitor Act 2010* (Cth) (INSLM Act, CSA 7);
- *National Security Legislation Amendment Act 2010* (Cth) (CSA 8);
- *Telecommunications (Interception and Access) Amendment (Data Retention) Act 2015* (Cth) (Data Retention Act, CSA 9);
- *Counter-Terrorism Legislation Amendment Act (No 1) 2014* (Cth) (CSA 10);
- *Counter-Terrorism Legislation Amendment (Foreign Fighters) Act 2014* (Cth) (Foreign Fighters Act, CSA 11);
- *Australian Citizenship Amendment (Allegiance to Australia) Act 2015* (Cth) (Citizenship Act, CSA 12);
- *Criminal Code Amendment (High Risk Terrorist Offenders) Act 2016* (Cth) (High Risk Offenders Act, CSA 13); and
- *Telecommunications and Other Legislation Amendment (Assistance and Access) Act 2018* (Cth) (Encryption Act, CSA 14)
- *Counter-Terrorism (Temporary Exclusion Orders) Act 2019* (Cth) (TEO Act, CSA 15)

As discussed in Chap. 1, these Acts have been selected from a broader range of Acts amending or adding to Australia's counter-terrorism regime for three key reasons: (a) these Acts represent the most substantive legislative changes to Australia's counter-terrorism regime (b) these Acts each introduce (or substantially amend) new powers, offences or mechanisms that have the potential to have a significant impact on individual rights and (c) each Act has been subject to scrutiny by at least one inquiry-based committee, as well the scrutiny-based committees. In the next section of this Chapter, I will briefly outline the context in which each of these major legislative reforms was introduced.

3.4.1 The First Tranche: The Howard Government's Response to 'September 11' (2001–2003)

Prior to 11 September 2001 there were no specific terrorism offences in federal legislation (Reilly 2007; Williams 2011). However, Australia had an extensive of range of laws at the state and territory level that addressed many of the criminal acts associated with terrorist activity (Hancock Bills Digest 2002a at p. 3). For example, politically motivated violence was already an offence (Crimes Act (Cth) s 30A) and a range of other relevant criminal offences existed at the state and federal level (Hancock, Terrorism and the Law 2002b). Law enforcement and intelligence agencies also already had powers to collect intelligence (e.g. Telecommunications (Interception) Act 1979 (Cth); Australian Security and Intelligence Organisation Act 1979 (Cth); National Crime Authority Act 1984 (Cth)) and Australia had implemented a number of international instruments concerning different types of terrorist activity.[9] Despite this, as Australia witnessed the horror of the 9/11 terrorist attacks on the United States, it became apparent that this legal landscape may not be sufficient to deal with the emerging threat of international terrorism (Williams 2011 at p. 1131).

Following 9/11, the United Nations (UN) Security Council unanimously adopted Resolution 1373 and called for 'improved international cooperation to suppress and respond to acts of terrorism'. Article 2(e) of the Resolution required States to ensure that 'terrorist acts are established as serious criminal offences in domestic laws and regulations and that the punishment duly reflects the seriousness of such terrorist acts'. At the same time, a UN High Commissioner on Human Rights also emphasised that States should exercise caution when enacting new laws to avoid breaching their international human rights, refugee and humanitarian law obligations (see e.g. United Nations Commission on Human Rights 2008). The Howard Government moved quickly to respond to these new international standards (Larkin and Uhr 2009 at p. 241), but it took some months before new legislative measures could be introduced, due to the proroguing of Parliament in early October 2001 (Barber and Johnson 2014).

In December 2001 the re-elected Howard Government announced a series of measures to strengthen Australia's counter-terrorism capabilities, which were introduced into Parliament during 2002.[10] The most substantive of these became the

---

[9]For example, the *Crimes (Hostages) Act 1989* (Cth) implemented the *International Convention Against the Taking of Hostages*, and the *Crimes (Internationally Protected Person) Act 1976* (Cth) implemented the *Convention on the Prevention and Punishment of Crimes against Internationally Protected Persons*.

[10]These laws included: *Security Legislation Amendment (Terrorism) Act 2002* (Cth); *Border Security Legislation Amendment Act 2002* (Cth); *Criminal Code Amendment (Suppression of Terrorist Bombings) Act 2002* (Cth); *Suppression of the Financing of Terrorism Act 2002* (Cth); *Australian Security Intelligence Organisation Legislation Amendment (Terrorism) Act 2003* (Cth); *Crimes Amendment Act 2002* (Cth); *Criminal Code Amendment (Offences Against Australians) Act 2002* (Cth); *Telecommunications Interception Legislation Amendment Act 2002* (Cth); and

Security Legislation Amendment (Terrorism) Bill 2002 (Cth) (SLAT Bills, CSA 1) and the Australian Security Intelligence Organisation Legislation Amendment (Terrorism) Bill 2002 (Cth) (ASIO Bill 2002, CSA 2). These laws introduced the term 'terrorist act' into the Criminal Code Act 1995 (Cth) and created a range of related criminal offences, as well as new law enforcement and intelligence-gathering powers for government agencies, including ASIO. The Bills also set out a process for proscribing an organisation as a 'terrorist organisation' and created a range of 'terrorist organisation' offences (Larkin and Uhr 2009 at p. 241; Hocking 2004b).

A number of observers described this package of legislation as being rushed through Parliament, undermining the usual parliamentary scrutiny process (see e.g. Hocking Terror Laws 2004aat p. 171; Williams 2011; Head 2002; McCulloch 2002). All of the Bills introduced on 12 March 2002 (Security Legislation Amendment (Terrorism) Bill (No 2) 2002 (Cth), Border Security Legislation Amendment Bill 2002 (Cth) and the Telecommunications Interception Legislation Amendment Bill 2002 (Cth).) were passed by the House of Representatives in a single day, prompting Simon Crean, then Leader of the Opposition, to complain during Parliamentary debates on the Bills that while the government spent six months designing the legislation, they only provided the Parliament with 16 h to consider its contents (13 March 2002 at p. 1143). In the Senate, where the Howard Government did not have a majority, the package of Bills were successfully referred to the LCA Legislation Committee for inquiry and report (LCA References Committee SLAT Bills Inquiry 2002). As discussed in Part II, despite its short time frame, this inquiry attracted over 431 submissions and resulted in a number of rights-enhancing amendments to the Bills.

Importantly, this inquiry also saw the ASIO Bill 2002 – which proposed to introduce a new questioning and detention regime for ASIO separated from the package of Bills. The ASIO Bill 2002 was then referred for separate inquiry by both the PJC on ASIO, ASIS and DSD and the LCA References Committee. The PJC on ASIO, ASIS and DSD did not hold back in expressing its strong concerns with the ASIO Bill 2002, describing it as highly controversial and likely to erode the very rights and freedoms that underpinned Australia's democracy (Hocking 2004 Protecting Democracy at p. 322). As discussed below in Chap. 5, these and other strong concerns with the Bill led to a multi-committee scrutiny process that culminated in the Bill being re-introduced in amended form as the Australian Security Intelligence Organisation Legislation Amendment (Terrorism) Bill 2003 (Cth) (ASIO Bill 2003, CSA 3), which finally passed both Houses in mid-2003.

While this package of legislation was making its way through Parliament, on 12 October 2002 a terrorist bombing incident occurred in a nightclub on the Indonesian

---

Criminal Code Amendment (Terrorism) Act 2003 (Cth). In addition to this package of Bills, a range of other legislative measures were introduced in the first half of 2002 that contributed to the Howard Government's counter-terrorism policy framework and that were subject to scrutiny by parliamentary committees. These include the Proceeds of Crime Bill 2002 (Cth), the Proceeds of Crime (Consequential Amendments and Transitional Provisions) Bill 2002 (Cth), and the Criminal Code Amendment (Espionage and Related Offences) Bill 2002 (Cth).

island of Bali, killing 202 people and injuring 209. Among the dead were 88 Australians, leading some to describe this incident as 'Australia's September 11' (see e.g. McDonald 2003; Brenchley 2002). This incident triggered the rapid enactment of the Criminal Code Amendment (Offences Against Australians) Bill 2002 (Cth), which made it an offence to harm or kill Australians overseas. The Criminal Code Amendment (Terrorism) Bill 2003 (Cth) was also introduced to ensure a sound constitutional basis for the new terrorism provisions in the Criminal Code Act 1995 (Cth).

The protection of national security information had also emerged as a priority issue for the Howard Government following the successful prosecutions of Australian intelligence officers in Australia and the US for attempting to sell classified national security information. On 2 April 2003, the Attorney-General referred the issue of the protection of classified security information to the ALRC for inquiry and report, which, as discussed below, would later become relevant to the review and scrutiny of another case study Bill (CSA 5). The year 2003 also saw the introduction of new laws to further broaden ASIO's intelligence-gathering and questioning powers (*ASIO Legislation Amendment Act 2003* (Cth)).

3.4.2 The Second Tranche: Pre-charge Detention and Protection of Security Information (2004–2005)

The second tranche of counter-terrorism legislation saw the Howard Government rapidly expand the powers of law enforcement and intelligence agencies to detain and question people when investigating terrorist-related activity, and the beginnings of a notable 'push back' from sections of the public, who called for greater oversight of these agencies.

The second tranche occurred in the aftermath of the Madrid train bombings in March 2003, which killed 191 people and injured almost 2000 (Reinares 2009). Legislation was introduced to address a range of procedural matters connected to terrorism offences, including the Anti-Terrorism Bill 2004 (Cth) (CSA 4), which amended the *Crimes Act 1914* (Cth) to make special provisions in relation to bail and non-parole periods, investigative periods (which later became known as the Part IC 'dead time' provisions) and periods of arrest for terrorism offences. The Bill also introduced a strict liability component to the offence of training with a terrorist organisation and a new offence of associating with a terrorist organisation. These offences are now contained in the Criminal Code Act 1995 (Cth). The Anti-Terrorism Bill 2004 also amended the *Proceeds of Crime Act 2002* (Cth) to provide for the recovery of literary proceeds derived from offences committed outside Australia and subsequently transferred to Australia.

While these laws made their way through Parliament, there was a renewed push to ensure that the rapidly expanding powers of ASIO and other intelligence agencies were subject to robust parliamentary oversight. For example, in 2003 the PJC into

ASIO, ASIS and DSD recommended an independent inquiry into Australia's intelligence agencies, which resulted in the establishment of the Flood Inquiry in 2004. The Flood Inquiry in turn recommended that the committee's mandate be extended to cover all intelligence agencies and that the committee be renamed the PJCIS (Recommendation 1). This pattern of extension of executive power, followed by recommendations for increased oversight of executive agencies, has characterised Australia's counter-terrorism law-making experience, and is discussed further in Part II and III.

During 2004, the Howard Government introduced a range of other counter-terrorism laws designed to expand the powers of ASIO and the AFP, including increased telecommunications interception (eg, Telecommunications (Interception) Amendment (Stored Communications) Bill 2004 (Cth)) and surveillance powers (National Security Information (Criminal Proceedings) Bill 2004 (Cth). The National Security Information (Criminal Proceedings) Bill 2004 (Cth) (CSA 5) was also introduced to prevent or limit disclosure of national security information in criminal proceedings, without waiting for the detailed recommendations of the ALRC, which was at that time preparing a report on the handling of national security information.

Despite the haste at which legislation was introduced in this second tranche of counter-terrorism law making, these Bills were subject to detailed parliamentary committee inquiries where recommendations were made to narrow the scope of the proposed new powers, introduce new safeguards to limit the laws' impact on individual rights, and improve parliamentary oversight. The changes recommended by the parliamentary committees received strong support from a range of Senators, some of whom demanded further reforms to these laws or completely opposed their passage.

With a full legislative list before the Senate, the Howard Government called a federal election for 9 October 2004 and returned to office with a clear Senate majority for the first time since 1980. The new government moved quickly to reintroduce and pass a number of the counter-terrorism Bills that had previously stalled before the Senate. As discussed further in Part II, many of these Bills were reintroduced in amended form, taking up a significant number of the recommendations made by parliamentary committees prior to the election.

3.4.3 The Third Tranche: Control Orders and Preventative Detention Orders (2005)

The third tranche of counter-terrorism law making further expanded the powers of law enforcement agencies, this time to control or restrict the movement, communications and associations of people suspected of involvement in or knowledge of terrorist-related activity. It signalled a substantive departure from established criminal law principles, and ultimately attracted the attention of the High Court. This third tranche also generated strong public interest, including in the form of high levels of participation in parliamentary committee inquiries into these laws.

This third tranche of counter-terrorism law making occurred in the wake of a number of terrorist attacks that took the lives of Australians (Benson 2013; Michaelsen 2005). These incidents gave the Howard Government the political 'green light' to introduce new regimes to control the movements, associations and communications of those thought to be involved in or have information about terrorist-related activity (control order and preventative detention order regimes), as well as amending existing sedition laws with a view to capturing a much wider range of terrorist-related forms of expression. As discussed further in Chap. 5, these reforms were introduced as part of the Anti-Terrorism Bill (No 2) 2005 (Cth).

Enacting these new laws depended upon the referral of powers by the states and territories to the Commonwealth, and involved multiple levels of negotiation, starting with COAG (COAG 2005). The Howard Government sought to pursue these negotiations without publicly revealing the content of the proposed law. However, on 14 October 2005 the ACT Chief Minister, Jon Stanhope, released a version of the Bill on his website. Stanhope later explained in an interview with the author that he pursued this course of action to provide an opportunity for rigorous public scrutiny of the laws: '[T]hey were proposing some quite draconian legislation without taking the people of Australia into their confidence. That's all I was seeking to do. And I did … want some of the brains around the place to get to look at it.' (Canberra, 27 September 2016). Stanhope also considered it his role, as Chief Minister of a jurisdiction with a recently enacted Human Rights Act, to seek advice about the rights compatibility of the proposed law.

This led to the public release of the Anti-Terrorism Bill (No 2) 2005 (Cth) (Control Orders Bill, CSA 6), which was subject to intense parliamentary debate and scrutiny, led by two specific groups of parliamentarians: the Attorney-General's Backbenchers Committee (and the LCA Legislation Committee (Carne 2007 at p. 43; Grattan 2005). As Part II documents, the work of those backbenchers had important rights-enhancing impacts on the proposed laws (see also Carne 2007 at pp. 41–48). These changes, which could be described as an example of the 'hidden impact' considered in Chap. 7, occurred despite the short time frame given to the LCA Legislation Committee to conduct its inquiry.

As explored in Part III, the scrutiny of this Bill exemplifies both the strengths and weaknesses of Australia's parliamentary model of rights protection. On the one hand, significant rights-enhancing changes were made to the Control Orders Bill that are directly attributable to the work of parliamentary committees and their key participants, despite the short time frames and the government-controlled Senate. On the other hand, the enacted law still contained a range of rights-abrogating features, some of which have since been declared contrary to international human rights standards and repealed in other comparable jurisdictions such as the UK (see e.g. Tyulkina and Williams 2017). These strengths and weaknesses of the rights-protecting role of parliamentary committees are considered further in Part III.

3.4.4 *Time for Review: Parliamentary and Judicial Review of Counter-Terrorism Laws (2005–2008)*

By 2006, some of the Howard Government's counter-terrorism laws had been utilised by intelligence and law enforcement agencies, occasionally giving rise to criminal charges and complaints of misuse or overuse (Williams et al. 2014; Williams 2006; Zifcak 2015; Foot 2007). In addition, early attempts at securing convictions for terrorist offences were complicated by constitutional challenges and appeals, as well as a concerns that juries may struggle with the complex elements of the new offences (Williams et al. 2014).

For example, in one of the first uses of the offences contained in the SLAT Bills, Zaky Mallah was charged with two counts of preparing for a terrorist act on the basis of evidence that he had planned a suicide mission to kill Australian government officials (R v Mallah [2005] NSWSC 317; [2005] NSWSC 358). Mallah was acquitted by a jury for the terrorist related charges, but pleaded guilty to a separate charge of threatening a Commonwealth officer and was jailed for 2.5 years.

In 2004 Joseph Thomas was convicted of financing terrorism offences, after being found guilty of intentionally receiving funds from al-Qaeda and was sentenced to five years imprisonment. Crucial to his conviction was the admission of self-inculpatory statements made by him in the course of a police interview (R v Thomas [2006] VSCA 165 at [96]). However, Thomas' conviction was later overturned on appeal on the grounds that his confession was not freely given to authorities (R v Thomas [2006] VSCA 165). In response, the Government sought to restrict Thomas' liberty by issuing a control order against him, constituting the first time such an order had been made. This led to a constitutional challenge initiated by Thomas (Thomas v Mowbray (2007) 233 CLR 307), wherein the High Court was asked to determine whether the control order regime was consistent with the constitutionally entrenched doctrine of separation of powers (Lynch 2008a, b). The majority of the High Court upheld the validity of the control order regime, despite strong concerns from rights advocates about its potential to allow police to deprive someone of their liberty prior to being charged with a criminal offence (for discussion see Williams 2011; Saul 2008; Lindell 2008; Pintos-Lopez and Williams 2008; for critiques of the High Court decision see Lynch and Reilly 2007; Fairall and Lacey 2007).

The prosecution and conviction of Faheem Khalid Lodhi also provided one of the earliest opportunities for procedure-related terrorism laws to be implemented in practice, including the use of closed court proceedings and substantial in camera argument. Lodhi was charged with four separate terrorist related offences, including offences under s101.6 of the Criminal Code for making enquiries about the availability of chemicals and other information relevant to preparing explosives (*R v Lodhi* [2006] NSWSC 691). Lohdi was convicted of three of the four offences charged, and sentenced to 20 years imprisonment. This sentence was upheld on appeal (Lodhi v R [2007] NSWCCA 360), despite the court finding that Lohdi's conduct was at the early stages of planning. This successful prosecution provided in important early insight into how the courts would approach the relatively 'novel' aspects of the preparatory terrorist offences and the new procedural rules introduced during the Howard period (Broadbent 2007). It also gave rise to a separate challenge (*R v Lodhi* [2006] NSWSC 571; Lodhi v The Queen [2007] 179 A Crim R 470, 487 [67]) to the provisions of the *National Security Information (Criminal and Civil Proceedings) Act 2004* (Cth) on the ground that these laws permitted a person accused of committing terrorist offences to be sentenced through a process incompatible with the exercise of federal judicial power (Williams 2001). The Act was found to be not inconsistent with the exercise of judicial power, on the basis that it was concerned with pre-trial disclosure of evidence rather than setting out a process for excluding evidence during the trial itself (Lodhi v The Queen [2007] 179 A Crim R 470, 487 [67]).

The prosecution of Izhar ul-Haque in 2006, charged with training with a terrorist organisation while overseas, also led to a constitutional challenge – this time relating to whether the Commonwealth had the power to legislate terrorist-related offences with extra-territorial reach. The constitutional validity of the terrorist organisation offences was ultimately upheld in the case of Ul-Haque v The Queen [2006] NSWCCA 241, where the laws were found to be validly enacted under the Commonwealth's 'external affairs' power. This case also led to an independent inquiry that prompted a broader review into the activities and oversight of intelligence agencies, and their relationship with law enforcement, in light of their new legislative powers (Cornall and Black 2011).

In other comparable jurisdictions, such as the UK, efforts were being made to strengthen oversight of the use of counter-terrorism laws (*Prevention of Terrorism Act 2005* (UK); see also Elliott 2006; Lynch 2008a, b) and international human rights bodies began to question whether Australian counter-terrorist laws were compliant with our international human rights obligations (UN Human Rights Committee 2009).

These developments, combined with the expiry of sunset clauses included in a number of the counter-terrorism Acts described above (McGarrity et al. 2012), gave rise to a period of sustained independent review of Australia's counter-terrorism regime, from both within and outside of Parliament. These reviews included the:

- 2006 ALRC Report No 104 *Fighting Words: A Review of Sedition Laws in Australia*;
- 2006 PJCIS's Review of Security and Counter Terrorism Legislation;
- 2006 report of the Security Legislation Review Committee (the Sheller Committee) into the operation, effectiveness and implications of the package of anti-terrorism legislation introduced during 2002 and 2003[11];
- 2007 PJCIS inquiry into the proscription of 'terrorist organisations' under the Criminal Code; and
- the 2008 inquiry by the Hon John Clarke QC into the case of Dr Mohamed Haneef (the Haneef Inquiry).

[11] The package of laws reviewed were: *Security Legislation Amendment (Terrorism) Act 2002* (Cth); *Suppression of the Financing of Terrorism Act 2002* (Cth); *Criminal Code Amendment (Suppression of Terrorist Bombings) Act 2002* (Cth); *Border Security Legislation Amendment Act 2002* (Cth); *Telecommunications Interception Legislation Amendment Act 2002* (Cth) and the *Criminal Code Amendment (Terrorism) Act 2003* (Cth).

Taken together, these inquiries represent an important assessment of the key components of Australia's counter-terrorism laws enacted up until 2008. They attracted significant numbers of submissions and generated mainstream media coverage. As discussed in Part II, the past work of parliamentary committees featured prominently in these reviews, and contributed to important legislative change in the form of the *National Security Legislation Amendment Act 2010* (Cth) (CSA 7) and the *Independent National Security Legislation Monitor Act 2010* (Cth) (INSLM Bill, CSA 8). As discussed below, these two case study Acts contain a range of features that directly reflect some of the recommendations made during these reviews.

The detention and visa cancellation of Dr. Mohamed Haneef, an Indian doctor working in Australia, also gave rise to questions about the use of the extensive new counter-terrorism powers provided to the AFP and intelligence agencies (Pickering and McCulloch 2010). The Haneef case involved the use of the so called 'dead time' provisions of Part IC of the *Crimes Act*, introduced by the *Anti-Terrorism Act 2004* (Cth), which allowed Dr. Haneef to be detained by police for a prolonged period without charge. Dr. Haneef was eventually charged with the offence of 'providing support to a terrorist organisation' and granted bail, but the Minister for Immigration then decided to cancel his visa on character grounds (Clarke 2008 at p. 2–3). An inquiry conducted by Michael John Clarke made a number of findings that were critical of the handling of the case by key government agencies and recommended that the federal government:

- amend the 'dead time' provisions in Part IC of the *Crimes Act*;
- appoint an independent reviewer of terrorism laws; and
- amend the Criminal Code offence of providing support to a terrorist organisation (Clarke 2008 Summary of Recommendations; Head 2009).

As discussed further in Part II, these recommendations, combined with previous recommendations made by parliamentary committees, led to important changes in Australia's counter-terrorism legislative framework and cemented the already popular view that rigorous independent oversight was necessary if executive agencies were to be invested with extraordinary and intrusive investigative powers.

3.4.5 The Fourth Tranche: Updating Australia's Counter-Terrorism Framework (2008–2010)

The 2007 election resulted in a change of government for the first time in 11 years (Barber and Johnson 2014).[12] While national security remained a high-ranking issue among voters, the ALP's campaign included a focus on 'getting the balance right' between security and liberty when it came to counter-terrorism laws (Rudd

[12] The election was held on 24 November 2007. Under the leadership of Kevin Rudd, the ALP was returned to office with 83 seats. The Coalition lost control of the Senate, but still held 37 seats – five more than the government. The balance of power in the Senate was shared between Nick Xenophon, Steve Fielding and the five Greens.

Parliamentary Debates 2008). This coincided with a renewed push by rights advocates for a federal charter or bill of rights for Australia, spurred on by the National Consultation process (McClelland 2008).

In this climate, work was underway to respond to the findings of previous inquiries into Australia's counter-terrorism laws. On 12 August 2009, the then Attorney-General, the Hon Robert McClelland, released a lengthy discussion paper outlining proposed reform options to Australia's counter-terrorism laws, some of which sought to narrow the scope of key provisions and improve safeguards and oversight mechanisms (McClelland 2009; LCA Legislation Committee 2010 at para [1.2]). The PJCIS was asked to conduct an inquiry into the reforms set out in the discussion paper and produced a report that drew heavily from the findings and submissions made to the previous inquiries set out above (LCA Legislation Committee 2010).

In response to the PJCIS report, the government introduced the National Security Legislation Amendment Bill 2010 (Cth) (CSA 8) which contained some, but not all, of the reforms proposed by the discussion paper.[13] Around this time, and also in response to earlier reviews of counter-terrorism laws, the government introduced legislation to establish the position of the Independent National Security Legislation Monitor (*INSLM Act 2010* (Cth), CSA 7) to review and report on the operation, effectiveness and implications of Australia's counter-terrorism and national security legislation on an ongoing basis. The Monitor is also responsible for considering if counter-terrorism and national security laws remain necessary and are proportionate to any threat of terrorism or to national security. This Act was passed in advance of the 2010 federal election, but the position of INSLM was not filled until April 2011. This paved the way for further independent reviews of Australia's counter-terrorism laws to take place, with a specific focus on rights compatibility (Walker 2011). COAG also revisited Australia's counter-terrorism framework in 2012, reflecting on the changes implemented in 2005 by the states and territories relating to the control order and preventative detention order regimes, along with a range of other matters (COAG 2013).

This period of gradual and selective implementation of the findings of past reviews of Australia's counter-terrorism laws demonstrates both the significance and limits of the rights protection role of the parliamentary committee system. On the one hand, as explored in Part II, the impact of the committee system on the content of counter-terrorism laws during this period was direct and generally rights-enhancing, particularly when it came to improving safeguards and enhancing independent oversight of the use of executive powers. However, it is also clear that the ALP government's response left many rights-abrogating features of the legislative framework in place, and further entrenched some of these features (such as the control order regime) into Australia's legal landscape. As Part II documents, while new rights-review bodies may have been established, the politics of 'tough on terror' continued to be persuasive, particularly as the ALP entered its second term in

[13] For example, the Bill pursued the amendments proposed in the discussion paper that related to the treason offences in the Criminal Code; the urging violence offences (previously known as the sedition offences) in the Criminal Code; the 'dead-time provisions' in the *Crimes Act*; the bail provisions in the *Crimes Act*; the introduction into the *Crimes Act* of a new emergency warrantless entry and search power; and *National Security Information (Criminal Proceedings) Act 2004* (Cth).

government and confronted its second leadership change in three years (Barber and Johnson 2014).[14]

During this period a number of successful terrorist-related prosecutions also took place, resulting in numerous prosecutions for preparatory offences and membership of terrorist organisation offences arising out of intelligence gathering and the disruption of plans to undertake terrorist activity in Australia (Renwick 2018 Appendix 1).

3.4.6 *The Fifth Tranche: Dealing with 'Home-Grown' Terrorism (2013–2018)*

The election of the Abbott Coalition Government in 2013 brought with it a new tranche of counter-terrorism law making, squarely focused on confronting the national security challenges presented by Australian citizens who were engaged in terrorist activity overseas (Barker et al. 2014). According to incoming Attorney-General Brandis, Australia had become one of the largest per-capita sources of foreign fighters in the Syrian conflict from countries outside the region (Bergin 2014). This led to significant concerns that foreign fighters returning to Australia posed a real threat to national security (Barker et al. 2014), underscored by terrorist attacks undertaken by so-called 'home-grown' terrorists in the UK and France (Klausen 2015; Zuijdewijn et al. 2014). There was also a push at the international level for States to act to prevent travel and support for foreign terrorist fighters (UN Security Council Resolution 2178 2014). This period also saw a decisive shift away from the previous government's policy commitment to 'human rights', with the incoming Attorney-General instead articulating his vision for the portfolio in the language of 'traditional rights and freedoms' (Chordia and Lynch 2013; Brandis 2013). As will be discussed further in Part III, this had a noticeable impact on the way key participants framed and articulated their concerns about individual rights during this period.

During this period, the Abbott Government introduced a range of new counter-terrorism laws that significantly expanded the pre-existing regime. These included the following case study Acts which authorised:

- the extension of the control order regime and the collection, use and sharing of intelligence information (the *Counter-Terrorism Act 2014 (No 1)*, CSA 10);
- the collection, retention and sharing of telecommunications data (the Data Retention Act, CSA 9);
- the declaration of certain overseas 'zones' as declared areas and the criminalisation of those who travel to those areas (the Foreign Fighters Act, CSA 11); and
- the revocation of citizenship of Australians who travel overseas to engage in or support terrorist activity (the Citizenship Act, CSA 12).

[14] Kevin Rudd became Prime Minister for the second time when he replaced Julia Gillard on 27 June 2013 but was unable to save the ALP from defeat in the 2013 federal election on 7 September 2013, which saw the Coalition Government elected with a comfortable majority in the House.

This legislative agenda continued as Malcolm Turnbull replaced Tony Abbott as the leader of the Coalition Government, and included the following case study Acts which authorised:

- the continued detention of terrorist offenders in prison, after their sentences have been served, where the offender poses an unacceptable risk to the community (the High Risk Offenders Act, CSA 13); and
- new law enforcement powers to compel telecommunication provides to provide technical assistance to decrypt encrypted technologies and access communications and data at points where they are not encrypted (Encryption Act, CSA 14).

As discussed in detail in Part II, each of these laws generated substantial public and parliamentary debate. After more than 10 years, the Australian community had, on the one hand, come to expect counter-terrorism law making as part of the ordinary legislative agenda of incoming Australian Governments and, on the other, become increasingly explicit in its demands for meaningful rights scrutiny of such laws. While the broad policies underpinning the laws received bipartisan support, questions about the proposed laws' infringements on the right to privacy, freedom of movement and the right to citizenship were raised by many commentators and some members of the opposition and cross bench. In addition, questions were raised about the efficacy of these laws as preventative measures, particularly in the context of continued concern about the experience of isolation and discrimination within Australia's Islamic community.

As discussed in detail in Chap. 5, case study Acts 9–14 were all scrutinised by the PJCIS, as well as the SSCSB and the PJCHR, during their passage through Parliament. As discussed further in Chap. 5, this period coincided with a decisive shift towards the PJCIS (as opposed to the LCA Committees) as the parliamentary scrutiny body with the membership, mandate and powers to exert political influence regarding the content of counter-terrorism legislation. These PJCIS inquiries also drew upon the work of the INSLM, who became a source of influential commentary on the legitimacy and effectiveness of proposed counter-terrorism laws, despite unsuccessful efforts by the Abbott Government to repeal the position (Barker et al. 2014).

As Part II also demonstrates, this multi-committee scrutiny of the case study Acts proved to have a significant rights-enhancing impact, despite the rights-abrogating features of many of the enacted provisions. The PJCIS, in particular, appeared to provide a highly influential forum for the major political parties to clarify and narrow the scope of key terms, improve safeguards, and enhance oversight and reporting requirements with respect to the proposed new powers and offences in these Acts. For example, during this period, the PJCIS enjoyed a 100% 'strike rate' in terms of having its recommendations for legislative change reflected in successful government amendments with respect to case study Acts 9–13 (PJCIS Annual Report 2015at p. 3). These changes improved the rights compliance of these Bills in important ways, for example by:

- requiring that telecommunications data be defined in primary legislation, and any data retained by authorities be de-identified or destroyed after two years;
- ensuring that detailed public records be kept of the use of retained telecommunications data;
- protecting the data of journalists from being accessed;
- increasing the oversight powers and review functions of the PJCIS, including to examine the counter-terrorism activities of the Australian Federal Police;
- narrowing the scope of the proposed 'declared area' offences in the Criminal Code and ensuring that such declarations are subject to disallowance by Parliament;
- preserving the safeguards relating to specifying and reviewing the conditions imposed as part of a control order or preventive detention order;
- narrowing the circumstances in which a dual national can have their citizenship 'renounced' by doing something terrorist-related overseas, including by narrowing the range of conduct that can trigger the provisions.

It is important to note that these laws were debated and scrutinised against the backdrop of a number of reports of deeply disturbing acts of terrorism and violence (Fraser 2014). In addition, on 12 September 2014 Prime Minister Abbott announced that Australia's national security threat level had been raised from 'medium' to 'high' (Craw 2014).

Another significant event that occurred during this period would later become known as the 'Sydney Siege'. The handling of the Sydney Siege by police and other authorities was subject to a joint Commonwealth/NSW Government Review (2015). The review was hesitant to recommend sweeping changes to Australia's counter-terrorism regime, and instead aimed to preserve the 'current balance' in the regulatory and legislative counter-terrorism framework (Australian Government and New South Wales Government 2015).

3.4.7 The Sixth Tranche: Post-Conviction Controls and Response to Cyber-Terrorism (2016–2019)

National security expert Jacinta Carroll described 2017 as a 'game changer' in terms of terrorism, with Islamic State's defeat in Iraq and Syria giving rise to an extreme Islamist 'resurgence' and leading to a number of high-casualty attacks including in the United Kingdom, Germany, Sweden, Indonesia and the Philippines (Carroll 2018 at p. 13). Part of Australia's response to this resurgence in terrorist activity was to 'look inwards' to identify local Muslim communities that may be the targets of terrorist propaganda, as well as 'toughening up' border restrictions for returning 'foreign fighters' and increasing the surveillance powers of Australian intelligence agencies (Carroll 2018 at p. 13). Carroll (2018) explains that consolidating and strengthening technical and communication linkage and intelligence sharing with international and regional counter-terrorism bodies has also been a key aspect of Australia's response (at p. 15). Carroll (2018) also documents Australia's success at thwarting threats of terrorism arising at home, noting for example that 'Operation Kastelholm' (undertaken at the end of 2016) disrupted plots to undertake a mass casualty, multiple venue attack in the Melbourne CBD at Christmas time (at pp. 15–16). This Operation later led to prosecutions against those involved.

The years 2016–2019 were also tumultuous in political terms for Australia, with Prime Minister Tony Abbott replaced in a leadership ballot held on 14 September 2015 by Malcolm Turnbull, who was subsequently replaced by Scott Morrison in the lead up to the 2019 Federal Election. During this period, the Coalition Government remained steadfast in its commitment to a 'tough on terror' legislative agenda that including the following three features: (1) keeping convicted terrorists in Australia locked up (leading to the High Risk Offenders Bill in 2016, CSA 14), (2) disrupting online communication between and within terrorist cells by compelling telecommunication providers to assist in the decrypting of telecommunications and data (leading to the introduction of the Encryption Bill in 2018), and (3) preventing Australians who travel overseas to engage in terrorist activity from returning to Australia (leading to the introduction of the Counter-Terrorism (Temporary Exclusion Orders) Bill 2019 (the TEO Bill, CSA 15)).

As discussed further in Chap. 5, these new laws added significantly to the range of coercive, intrusive powers available to law enforcement officers and intelligence agencies investigating counter-terrorism activity. All three Bills also subvert important principles of criminal law, particularly the High Risk Offenders Bill, which establishes a regime of post-conviction detention, and the TEO Bill 2019 (CSA 15), which allows Australian authorities to prevent Australians from returning home on the basis of the Minister's 'reasonable suspicion' of engagement in terrorist activity, potentially rendering them stateless or permanently separated from their families or dependents. The content, rights impact and scrutiny experience of these laws are considered further in Part II of this book.

The period between 2016–2019 also saw the PJCIS engage a range of substantial reviews of pre-existing counter-terrorism laws, including reviews of ASIO's questioning and detention powers (2018), the new 'declared area' offences introduced by the Foreign Fighters Act (2018), and police stop and search powers, the control order and preventative detention order regimes (2018). As discussed further in Chap. 5, these reviews led to recommendations for amendments to the counter-terrorism regime, the great majority of which were rights-enhancing in nature, despite leaving key aspects of the counter-terrorism regime enacted in the earlier tranches in place. The sheer scale and influence of the PJCIS's work during this period highlight the significant impact the Committee is having on the shape of counter-terrorism laws since 2013 (Moulds 2020).

3.5 Institutional Engagement on Rights Issues and the Impact of Parliamentary Committees

The above discussion highlights three essential considerations for the next parts of my research. First, the institutional context and political experiences summarised above explain why parliamentary committees exist and their role in Australia's parliamentary model of rights protection. Secondly, as discussed further in Part III, the key functions and features of the Australian Parliament set the parameters for identifying realistic options for improving the rights-enhancing impact of the committee system. Finally, the rights-intrusive content and proliferation of Australia's counter-terrorism laws demonstrates why we should care about the quality of scrutiny parliamentary committees provide, particularly in the Australian context where there is no Charter or Bill of Rights at the federal level.

As Stephenson explains, if improving the quality of rights scrutiny is understood as an inherently positive goal, the process of identifying reform options must be sensitive to the constitutional principles and values of the particular jurisdiction being considered (Stephenson 2016). This is because these principles and values govern how the institutions of government interact with each other on rights issues. As Stephenson (2016) warns, once established, the practices and structures that govern dialogue between different institutions of government are extremely difficult to shift, and thus rights advocates should make sure that they fully understand the pre-existing institutional dynamic within the jurisdiction they are studying before developing options for reform. As noted in Chap. 2, my research seeks to confront this challenge through integrating the observations made in this chapter throughout the remaining two parts of this book.

By undertaking this approach, the evidence presented in Part II reveals the 'multi-stage' rights review that occurs at the federal level and exposes the direct and indirect institutional interactions that form part of this process (Stephenson 2016 at pp. 6–8). For example, by looking for 'hidden impact', Part II highlights the role the bureaucracy plays in anticipating rights scrutiny by parliamentary committees, and the indirect interaction that occurs between the Parliament and the executive when engaged in this form of rights review. Similarly, by examining the impact parliamentary committees have on the content of proposed laws, Part II exposes the direct institutional engagement that occurs between the Parliament and the executive when the government fails to 'get the balance right' when seeking to enact rights-intrusive counter-terrorism laws.

The results of this analysis identify the characteristics that give particular committees strengths within the Australian system of rights protection. The results also demonstrate that when multiple committees work together their rights-enhancing impact is stronger. These findings in turn inform the reform options set out in Part III. In this way, my research gives practical effect to the analytical approach outlined by Stephenson (2016 at pp. 210–219) and offers jurisdiction-sensitive suggestions for how to enhance the quality of Australia's multi-stage system of rights review.

References

Cases

Lodhi v The Queen (2007) 179 A Crim R 470, 487 [67].
Lodhi v R [2007] NSWCCA 360.
R v Lodhi [2006] NSWSC 571.
R v Lodhi [2006] NSWSC 691.
R v Mallah [2005] NSWSC 317; [2005] NSWSC 358
R v Thomas. (2006). *VSCA*, 165. [4].
Thomas v Mowbray (2007) 233 CLR 307.
Ul-Haque v The Queen. (2006). *NSWCCA*, 241.

Bills

House or Representatives. (2019). *Counter-terrorism (temporary exclusion orders) Bill 2019 (Cth)*. Canberra: Parliament of Australia. https://www.aph.gov.au/Parliamentary_Business/Bills_Legislation/Bills_Search_Results/Result?bId=r6311
House or Representatives. (2019). *Identity-matching services Bill 2019 (Cth)*. Canberra: Parliament of Australia. https://www.aph.gov.au/Parliamentary_Business/Bills_LEGislation/Bills_Search_Results/Result?bId=r6387
House or Representatives. (2019). Australian Passports Amendment (Identity-matching Services) Bill 2019 (Cth). Canberra: Parliament of Australia. https://www.aph.gov.au/Parliamentary_Business/Bills_Legislation/Bills_Search_Results/Result?bId=r6386
House or Representatives. (2019). Counter-terrorism (temporary exclusion orders) Bill 2019 (Cth). Canberra: Parliament of Australia. https://www.aph.gov.au/Parliamentary_Business/Bills_Legislation/Bills_Search_Results/Result?bId=r6311
House of Representatives. (2018). *Telecommunications and Other Legislation Amendment (Assistance and Access) Bill* 2018. Canberra: Parliament of Australia. https://www.aph.gov.au/Parliamentary_Business/Bills_Legislation/Bills_Search_Results/Result?bId=r6195
House of Representatives. (2015). *Telecommunications (Interception and Access) Amendment (Data Retention) Bill* 2015 (Cth). Canberra: Parliament of Australia. https://www.aph.gov.au/Parliamentary_Business/Bills_LEGislation/Bills_Search_Results/Result?bId=r5375
House of Representatives. (2015). *Australian Citizenship Amendment (Allegiance to Australia) Bill* 2015 (Cth). Canberra: Parliament of Australia. https://www.aph.gov.au/Parliamentary_Business/Bills_Legislation/Bills_Search_Results/Result?bId=r5507
House of Representatives. (2014). *Counter-Terrorism Legislation Amendment Bill (No 1) 2014* (Cth). Canberra: Parliament of Australia. https://www.aph.gov.au/Parliamentary_Business/Bills_Legislation/Bills_Search_Results/Result?bId=s982
https://www.aph.gov.au/Parliamentary_Business/Bills_Legislation/Bills_Search_Results/Result?bId=r1808
House of Representatives. (2010). *Human Rights (Parliamentary Scrutiny) Bill* 2011 (Cth). Canberra: Parliament of Australia. https://www.aph.gov.au/Parliamentary_Business/Bills_Legislation/Bills_Search_Results/Result?bId=r4420
House of Representatives. (2010). *National Security Legislation Amendment Bill* 2010 (Cth). Canberra: Parliament of Australia. https://www.aph.gov.au/Parliamentary_Business/Bills_Legislation/Bills_Search_Results/Result?bId=r4435
House of Representatives. (2004). *Anti-terrorism Bill 2004 (Cth)*. Canberra: Parliament of Australia. https://www.aph.gov.au/Parliamentary_Business/Bills_Legislation/Bills_Search_Results/Result?bId=r2032

House of Representatives. (2004). Anti-Terrorism Bill (No 2) 2005 (Cth). Canberra: Parliament of Australia. https://www.aph.gov.au/Parliamentary_Business/Bills_Legislation/Bills_Search_Results/Result?bId=r2469
House of Representatives. (2004). *Surveillance Devices Bill 2004 (Cth)*. Canberra: Parliament of Australia. https://www.aph.gov.au/Parliamentary_Business/Bills_Legislation/Bills_Search_Results/Result?bId=r2010
House of Representatives. (2003). *Australian Security Intelligence Organisation Legislation Amendment (Terrorism) Bill* 2003 (Cth). Canberra: Parliament of Australia. https://www.aph.gov.au/Parliamentary_Business/Bills_Legislation/Bills_Search_Results/Result?bId=r1763
House of Representatives. (2003). *Criminal Code Amendment (Hamas and Lashkar-e-Tayyiba) Bill* 2003 (Cth). Canberra: Parliament of Australia. https://www.aph.gov.au/Parliamentary_Business/Bills_Legislation/Bills_Search_Results/Result?bId=r1925
House of Representatives. (2003). *Criminal Code Amendment (Hizballah) Bill* 2003 (Cth). Canberra: Parliament of Australia. https://www.aph.gov.au/Parliamentary_Business/Bills_Legislation/Bills_Search_Results/Result?bId=r1826
House of Representatives. (2003). *Criminal Code Amendment (Terrorist Organisations) Bill* 2003 (Cth). Canberra: Parliament of Australia.
House of Representatives. (2002). *Criminal Code Amendment (Espionage and Related Offences) Bill* 2002 (Cth). Canberra: Parliament of Australia. https://www.aph.gov.au/Parliamentary_Business/Bills_Legislation/Bills_Search_Results/Result?bId=r1475
House of Representatives (2002). Proceeds of crime Bill 2002 (Cth). Canberra: Parliament of Australia. https://www.aph.gov.au/Parliamentary_Business/Bills_Legislation/Bills_Search_Results/Result?bId=r1467
House of Representatives. (2002). *Proceeds of Crime (Consequential Amendments and Transitional Provisions) Bill* 2002 (Cth). Canberra: Parliament of Australia. https://www.aph.gov.au/Parliamentary_Business/Bills_Legislation/Bills_Search_Results/Result?bId=r1515
House of Representatives. (2002). *Security Legislation Amendment (Terrorism) Bill* 2002 (Cth). Canberra: Parliament of Australia. https://www.aph.gov.au/Parliamentary_Business/Bills_Legislation/Bills_Search_Results/Result?bId=r1516
House of Representatives. (2002). *Australian Security Intelligence Organisation Legislation Amendment (Terrorism) Bill* 2002 (Cth). Canberra: Parliament of Australia. https://www.aph.gov.au/Parliamentary_Business/Bills_Legislation/Bills_Search_Results/Result?bId=r1539
Senate. Counter-Terrorism Legislation Amendment (Foreign Fighters) Bill 2014 (Cth). Canberra: Parliament of Australia. https://www.aph.gov.au/Parliamentary_Business/Bills_LEGislation/Bills_Search_Results/Result?bId=s976
Senate. (2010). *Independent National Security Legislation Monitor Bill* 2010 (Cth). Canberra: Parliament of Australia. https://www.aph.gov.au/Parliamentary_Business/Bills_Legislation/Bills_Search_Results/Result?bId=s712
Senate. (2008). *Independent Reviewer of Terrorism Laws Bill* 2008 (No 2) (Cth). Canberra: Parliament of Australia. https://www.aph.gov.au/Parliamentary_Business/Bills_Legislation/Bills_Search_Results/Result?bId=s634
Senate. (2006). *Criminal Code Amendment (High Risk Terrorist Offenders) Bill* 2016 (Cth). Canberra: Parliament of Australia. https://www.aph.gov.au/Parliamentary_Business/Bills_Legislation/Bills_Search_Results/Result?bId=s1039
Senate. (2004). *Telecommunications (Interception) Amendment (Stored Communications) Bill* 2004 (Cth). Canberra: Parliament of Australia. https://www.aph.gov.au/Parliamentary_Business/Bills_Legislation/Bills_Search_Results/Result?bId=s447
Senate. (2004). *National Security Information (Criminal Proceedings) Bill* 2004 (Cth). Canberra: Parliament of Australia. https://www.aph.gov.au/Parliamentary_Business/Bills_Legislation/Bills_Search_Results/Result?bId=s437

Legislation

Anti-terrorism Act 2004 (Cth).
Anti-Terrorism Act (No 2) 2005 (Cth).
Australian Citizenship Amendment (Allegiance to Australia) Act 2015 (Cth).
Australian Human Rights Commission Act 1986 (Cth).
Australian Security and Intelligence Organisation Act 1979 (Cth).
Australian Security Intelligence Organisation Legislation Amendment (Terrorism) Act 2002 (Cth).
Australian Security Intelligence Organisation Legislation Amendment (Terrorism) Act 2003 (Cth).
Counter-Terrorism Legislation Amendment Act (No 1) 2014 (Cth).
Counter-Terrorism Legislation Amendment (Foreign Fighters) Act 2014 (Cth).
Counter-Terrorism (Temporary Exclusion Orders) Bill 2019 (Cth).
Crimes Act 1914 (Cth).
Criminal Code Act 1995.
Human Rights (Parliamentary Scrutiny) Act 2011 (Cth).
Independent National Security Legislation Monitor Act 2010 (Cth).
Inspector-General of Intelligence and Security Act 1986 (Cth).
Intelligence Services Act 2001 (Cth).
International Convention Against the Taking of Hostages, and the Crimes (Internationally Protected Person) Act 1976 (Cth).
Migration Act 1958 (Cth).
National Crime Authority Act 1984 (Cth).
National Security Information (Criminal Proceedings) Act 2004 (Cth).
National Security Legislation Amendment Act 2010 (Cth).
Ombudsman Act 1976 (Cth).
Parliamentary Joint Committee on Law Enforcement Act 2010 (Cth).
Prevention of Terrorism Act 2005 (UK).
Proceeds of Crime Act 2001 (Cth).
Security Legislation Amendment (Terrorism) Act 2002 (Cth).
Telecommunications (Interception and Access) Amendment Act 2008 (Cth).
Telecommunications (Interception and Access) Amendment (Data Retention) Act 2015 (Cth).
Telecommunications (Interception) Act 1979 (Cth).

International Law Materials

United Nations Security Council Resolution 1373 SC Res 1373, UN SCOR, 4385th mtg, UN Doc S/RES/1373 (28 September 2001).

UN Commission on Human Rights, *Message by 17 independent experts of the Commission on Human Rights on the occasion of Human Rights Day*, S/RES/1805(2008), UN Doc E/CN.4/2002/137 (20 March 2008).

UN Human Rights Committee, *Consideration of Reports Submitted by States Parties Under Article 40 of the Covenant Concluding observations of the Human Rights Committee: Australia*, 95th sess, UN doc CCPR/C/AUS/CO/5 (7 May 2009) [11].

United Nations Security Council Resolution SC Res 2178, UN SCOR, 7272nd mtg, UN Doc S/RES/2178 (24 September 2014). http://www.un.org/en/sc/ctc/docs/2015/SCR%20 2178_2014_EN.pdf.

Parliamentary Materials

Standing Orders

Senate, Parliament of Australia, *Standing Order*, Chapter 5, Orders 17 to 39. (17 November 2017). https://www.aph.gov.au/Parliamentary_Business/Chamber_documents/Senate_chamber_documents/standingorders/b00/b05
Senate, Parliament of Australia, *Standing Order 25* (2000). https://www.aph.gov.au/Parliamentary_Business/Chamber_documents/Senate_chamber_documents/standingorders/b00/b05
Senate, Parliament of Australia, *Standing Order* 24A (*13* February 1997). https://www.aph.gov.au/Parliamentary_Business/Chamber_documents/Senate_chamber_documents/standingorders/b00/b05

Parliamentary Debates

Commonwealth, *Parliamentary Debates*, House of Representatives, 4 December 2008, 12549 (Kevin Rudd, Prime Minister). https://parlinfo.aph.gov.au/parlInfo/search/display/display.w3p;query=Id:%22chamber/hansardr/2008-12-04/0000%22
Commonwealth, *Parliamentary Debates*, Senate, 24 July 2019, 772 (Kristina Keneally). https://www.aph.gov.au/Parliamentary_Business/Hansard/Hansard_Display?bid=chamber/hansards/f1e272cd-753f-4b97-bfb4-516fc5f0f19d/&sid=0000
Commonwealth, *Parliamentary Debates*, House of Representatives, 30 September 2010, 271 (Robert McClelland, Attorney-General). https://parlinfo.aph.gov.au/parlInfo/search/display/display.w3p;query=Id:%22chamber/hansardr/2010-09-30/0000%22
Commonwealth, *Parliamentary Debates*, House of Representatives, 13 March 2002, 1143 (Simon Crean, Leader of the Opposition). https://parlinfo.aph.gov.au/parlInfo/search/display/display.w3p;query=Id:%22chamber/hansardr/2002-03-13/0000%22.

Parliamentary Committee Reports

Parliament of Australia, *Report on the United States*, Senate, Parliamentary Paper No 36 (1956). Canberra: Parliament of Australia.
Parliamentary Joint Committee on Human Rights, Parliament of Australia, *Annual Report 2013–14* (2016) Canberra: Parliament of Australia. https://www.aph.gov.au/Parliamentary_Business/Committees/Joint/Human_Rights/Scrutiny_reports/Annual_Reports/Annual_report_2013_14
Parliamentary Joint Committee on Human Rights, Parliament of Australia, *Annual Report 2015–16* (2017) Canberra: Parliament of Australia. https://www.aph.gov.au/Parliamentary_Business/Committees/Joint/Human_Rights/Scrutiny_reports/Annual_Reports/Annual_Report_2015-16
Parliamentary Joint Committee on Human Rights, Parliament of Australia, *Chair's Tabling Statement* (2016). Canberra: Parliament of Australia. Parliamentary Joint Committee on Human Rights, Parliament of Australia, *Chair's Tabling Statement* (2016). https://www.aph.gov.au/Parliamentary_Business/Committees/Joint/Human_Rights/Statements
Parliamentary Joint Committee on Human Rights, Parliament of Australia, *Guidance Note 1: Drafting Statements of Compatibility* (December 2014) Canberra: Parliament of Australia.

http://www.aph.gov.au/Parliamentary_Business/Committees/Joint/Human_Rights/Guidance_Notes_and_Resources
Parliamentary Joint Committee on Human Rights, Parliament of Australia, *Guidance Note 2: Offence Provisions, Civil Penalties and Human Rights* (December 2014) Canberra: Parliament of Australia.http://www.aph.gov.au/Parliamentary_Business/Committees/Joint/Human_Rights/Guidance_Notes_and_Resources
Parliamentary Joint Committee on Human Rights, Parliament of Australia, *Guide to Human Rights* (June 2015) Canberra: Parliament of Australia. https://www.aph.gov.au/Parliamentary_Business/Committees/Joint/Human_Rights/Guidance_Notes_and_Resources
Parliamentary Joint Committee on Intelligence and Security (2018). *Review of the 'declared area' provisions*. Canberra: Parliament of Australia. https://www.aph.gov.au/Parliamentary_Business/Committees/Joint/Intelligence_and_Security/DeclaredArea
Parliamentary Joint Committee on Intelligence and Security. (2018) *ASIO's questioning and detention powers*. Canberra: Parliament of Australia. https://www.aph.gov.au/Parliamentary_Business/Committees/Joint/Intelligence_and_Security/ASIO/Report
Parliamentary Joint Committee on Intelligence and Security. (2018). *Review of the police stop, search and seizure powers, the control order regime and the preventative detention order regime*. Canberra: Parliament of Australia. https://www.aph.gov.au/Parliamentary_Business/Committees/Joint/Intelligence_and_Security/AFPpowersreview/Report
Parliamentary Joint Committee on Intelligence and Security, (2015). *Annual report of committee activities 2014–2015*. Canberra: Parliament of Australia. https://www.aph.gov.au/Parliamentary_Business/Committees/Joint/Intelligence_and_Security/Annual_Report_2014-15/Report
Parliamentary Joint Committee on Intelligence and Security. (2013). *Inquiry into the potential reforms of Australia's National Security Legislation*. Canberra: Parliament of Australia. http://www.aphref.aph.gov.au/house/committee/pjcis/NSL2012/report.htm
Parliamentary Joint Committee on Intelligence and Security. (2007). *Inquiry into the Terrorist Organisation Listing Provisions of the Criminal Code Act 1995*. Canberra: Parliament of Australia. https://www.aph.gov.au/Parliamentary_Business/Committees/House_of_Representatives_Committees?url=pjcis/proscription/index.htm
Parliamentary Joint Committee on Intelligence and Security. (2006). *Review of Security and Counter Terrorism Legislation*. Canberra: Parliament of Australia. https://www.aph.gov.au/Parliamentary_Business/Committees/House_of_Representatives_Committees?url=pjcis/securityleg/report.htm
Senate Standing Committee on Legal and Constitutional Affairs Legislation Committee. (2010). *Inquiry into the National Security Legislation Amendment Bill 2010 and Parliamentary Joint committee on Law Enforcement Bill 2010*. Canberra: Parliament of Australia. https://www.aph.gov.au/Parliamentary_Business/Committees/Senate/Legal_and_Constitutional_Affairs/Completed_inquiries/2008-10/National_Security_Legislation/index
Senate Standing Committee on Legal and Constitutional Affairs Legislation Committee. (2002). *Inquiry into the Security Legislation Amendment (Terrorism) Bill 2002 [No 2] and Related Bills*. Canberra: Parliament of Australia. https://www.aph.gov.au/Parliamentary_Business/Committees/Senate/Legal_and_Constitutional_Affairs/Completed_inquiries/2002-04/terrorism/index
Senate Standing Committee on Legal and Constitutional Affairs References Committee. (2002). *Inquiry into Australian Security Intelligence Organisation Legislation Amendment (Terrorism) Bill 2002 and Related Matters*. Canberra: Parliament of Australia. http://www.aph.gov.au/~/media/wopapub/senate/committee/legcon_ctte/completed_inquiries/2004_07/witness_protection/report/report_pdf.ashx
Senate Standing Committee on Procedure. (2008). *First report 2008*. Canberra: Parliament of Australia. https://www.aph.gov.au/Parliamentary_Business/Committees/Senate/Procedure/2008/report1/index
Senate Standing Committee on Regulations and Ordinances. (1930). *Report*. Canberra: Parliament of Australia.

Senate Standing Committee for Scrutiny of Bills, Parliament of Australia, Inquiry into the Future Direction and Role of the Scrutiny of Bills Committee (2012). https://www.aph.gov.au/Parliamentary_Business/Committees/Senate/Scrutiny_of_Bills/Completed_inquiries/futuredirection2011/index

Senate Standing Committee on Standing Committees, Parliament of Australia, *Report* (1930).

Senate Legislative and General Purpose Standing Committees, Parliament of Australia, *The First 20 Years 1970–1990* (1990) <http://www.aph.gov.au/Parliamentary_Business/Committees/Senate/Significant_Reports/first20years/index>

Senate Standing Committee for Scrutiny of Bills, Submission to ALRC, *Traditional Rights and Freedoms – Encroachments by Commonwealth Laws* (2014).

Senate Standing Committee for Scrutiny of Bills. (2006). Inquiry into *Entry, Search and Seizure Provisions in Commonwealth Legislation*. Canberra: Parliament of Australia. https://www.aph.gov.au/Parliamentary_Business/Committees/Senate/Scrutiny_of_Bills/Completed_inquiries/entrysearch/report/index

Senate Standing Committee for Scrutiny of Bills. (2017). *Scrutiny News* Canberra: Parliament of Australia http://www.aph.gov.au/Parliamentary_Business/Committees/Senate/Scrutiny_of_Bills/Scrutiny_News

Books/Articles/ Reports/Speeches

Appleby, G., Reilly, A., & Grenfell, L. (Eds.). (2014) *Australian Public Law* (2nd ed.). Oxford: Oxford University Press.

Appleby, G. (2017). Horizontal accountability: The Rights protective promise and fragility of the executive integrity institutions. *Australian Journal of Human Right, 23*, 168–187. https://doi.org/10.1080/1323238X.2017.1363372.

Australian Law Reform Commission. (2006). *Fighting Words: A Review of Sedition Laws in Australia* (ALRC Report No 104). Retrieved from https://www.alrc.gov.au/publication/fighting-words-a-review-of-sedition-laws-in-australia-alrc-report-104/. Accessed 7 Jan 2020.

Australian Law Reform Commission. (2016). *Traditional Rights and Freedoms – Encroachments by Commonwealth Laws* (Report No 129). Retrieved from https://www.alrc.gov.au/publication/traditional-rights-and-freedoms-encroachments-by-commonwealth-laws-alrc-report-129/. Accessed 7 Jan 2020.

Australian Government (2010). National Consultation on Human Rights. Commonwealth of Australia, *Australia's Human Rights Framework* (2010). https://www.ag.gov.au/Consultations/Documents/Publicsubmissionsonthedraftbaselinestudy/AustraliasHumanRightsFramework.pdf

Australian Government and New South Wales Government. (2015). Joint Commonwealth and NSW Review: Martin Place Seige. Sydney. Retrieved from https://www.nsw.gov.au/news-and-events/news/martin-place-siege-joint-commonwealth-new-south-wales-review/. Accessed 12 Jan 2020.

Barker, C., Biddington, M. & Klapdor, M. *Bills Digest Counter-Terrorism Legislation Amendment (Foreign Fighters) Bill* 2014, No 34 of 2014–15, 24 September 2014. Retrieved from https://www.aph.gov.au/Parliamentary_Business/Bills_Legislation/bd/bd1415a/15bd034. Accessed 12 Jan 2020.

Barber, S., & Johnson, S. (2014). Federal election results 1901–2014. Parliamentary research papers 2014–15, Parliamentary Library, Parliament of Australia. Retrieved from http://www.aph.gov.au/About_Parliament/Parliamentary_Departments/Parliamentary_Library/pubs/rp/rp1415/FedElect. Accessed 7 Jan 2020.

Bennett, S. (2004). The Australian Senate (Research paper no 6). Parliamentary Library, Parliament of Australia. Retrieved from https://www.aph.gov.au/About_Parliament/Parliamentary_Departments/Parliamentary_Library/pubs. Accessed 8 Jan 2020.

Benson, S. (2013, October 9) 'Tony Abbott Tells of 2005 Bali Bomb Terror', *news.com.au* (online). http://www.news.com.au/national/tony-abbott-tells-of-2005-bali-bomb-terror/story-fncynjr2-1226735443437

Bergin, A. (2014, May 6). Why Australians shouldn't fight in Syria. *Sydney Morning Herald* (online). http://www.smh.com.au/comment/why-australians-shouldnt-fight-in-syria-20140506-zr5fi.html

Brenchley, F. (2002). I won't forget this week ... for as long as I live. *The Bulletin (Sydney), 29.*

Brandis, G. (2013). *The freedom wars*. Sydney: Speech given at the Sydney Institute. 7 May 2013. http://nofibs.com.au/freedom-wars-the-george-brandis-speech/

Broadbent, N. (2007). *Lodhi v R* [2007] NSWCCA 360. *Australian International Law Journal, 14*, 227–236. http://www.austlii.edu.au/au/journals/AUIntLawJl/recent.html

Burton, L., & Williams, G. (2013). Australia's exclusive parliamentary model of rights protection. *Statute Law Review, 34*, 58–94. https://doi.org/10.1093/slr/hms048.

Byrnes, A. (2020). Economic and social Rights in the Australian parliamentary Human Rights scrutiny process. In J. Debeljak & L. Grenfell (Eds.), *Law- making and Human Rights* (pp. 135–171). Sydney: Thompson Reuters.

Campbell, T., & Morris, S. (2015). Human rights for democracies: A provisional assessment of the Australian Human Rights (Parliamentary Scrutiny) Act 2011. *University of Queensland Law Journal, 34*(1), 7–27.

Carne, G. (2007). Prevent, detain, control and order? Legislative Process and executive outcomes in enacting the Anti-Terrorism Act (No 2) 2005 (Cth)' (2007) 10(1), *Flinders Journal of Law Reform, 10*(1), 17–79. https://eprints.utas.edu.au/3708/

Carroll, J. (2018). Counter-terrorism in Australia. *United Service, 69*(1), 13–17.

Chappell, L., Chesterman, J., & Hill, L. (2012). *The politics of human rights in Australia* (pp. 67–69). Cambridge: Cambridge University Press. https://doi.org/10.1017/CBO9780511841545.

Chesterman, S. (2008). An international rule of law? *The American Journal of Comparative Law, 56*(2), 331–362.

Childs, B. (1992). *The truth about parliamentary committees* (Parl paper no 18). Parliament of Australia. Retrieved from https://www.aph.gov.au/~/~/~/link.aspx?_id=DD64348A4FEC4F94A3332033C6003F64. Accessed 10 Jan 2020.

Chordia, S. & Lynch, A. (2013). The Brandis agenda. *Inside Story* (online), 4 December 2013 http://insidestory.org.au/the-brandis-agenda

Clark, A. I. (1997). *Studies in Australian Constitutional Law.* Sydney: Legal Books, Reprint, 1st Ed. 1901.

Clarke, M.J. (2008) *Report of the Inquiry into the Case of Dr Mohamed Haneef.* Retrieved from https://trove.nla.gov.au/work/35146207. Accessed 7 Jan 2020.

Cooney, B. C. (1991). Speech at T*en Years of Scrutiny – A seminar to mark the tenth anniversary of the Senate Standing Committee for the Scrutiny of Bills,* 25 November 1991, Parliament of Australia, Canberra. Retrieved from https://www.aph.gov.au/Parliamentary_Business/Committees/Senate/Scrutiny_of_Bills/~/media/Committees/Senate/committee/scrutiny/completed_inquiries/work39/report.ashx. Accessed 8 Jan 2020.

Cornall, R., & Black, R. (2011). *2011 Independent review of the Intelligence Community Report*, Canberra: 16 November 2011. https://www.pmc.gov.au/resource-centre/national-security/2011-independent-review-intelligence-community. Accessed 7 Jan 2020.

Council of Australian Governments Counter-Terrorism Review Committee. (2013). *Review of Counter-Terrorism Legislation.* Retrieved from https://www.ag.gov.au/Consultations/Pages/COAGReviewofCounter-TerrorismLegislation.aspx. Accessed 7 Jan 2020.

Council of Australian Governments, *Communiqué – Council of Australian Governments* (27 September 2005), Special Meeting on Terrorism. Retrieved from https://www.coag.gov.au/meeting-outcomes. Accessed 11 Jan 2020.

Craw, V. (2014). *Tony Abbott raises Australia's terror threat to high. news.com.au* (online), 12 September 2014. http://www.news.com.au/national/nsw-act/tony-abbott-raises-australias-terror-threat-to-high/news-story/ac94b904859c79c407eeca9cf3170aa4

Dalla-Pozza, D. (2006). The Conscience of Democracy? The Role of Australian Parliamentary Committees in Enacting Counter-Terrorism Laws. Paper presented at the Australasian Law and Society Conference. Retrieved from http://unsworks.unsw.edu.au/fapi/datastream/unsworks:8439/SOURCE02. Accessed 6 Jan 2020.

Dalla-Pozza, D. (2020). A dual scrutiny mechanism for Australia's counter- terrorism law landscape: The INSLM and the PJCIS. In J. Debeljak & L. Grenfell (Eds.), *Law- making and Human Rights* (pp. 673–700). Sydney: Thompson Reuters.

Debeljak, J., & Grenfell, L. (2020). Contextualising law- making and Human Rights. In J. Debeljak & L. Grenfell (Eds.), *Diverse Australian Landscapes of Law- Making and Human Rights: Contextualising Law- Making and Human Rights* (pp. 2–28). Sydney: Thompson Reuters.

Dicey, A. V. (1959). *Introduction to the Study of the Law of the Constitution* (10th ed.). London: Macmillan.

Dixon, R. (2012). A new (inter)national Human Rights experiment for Australia. *Public Law Review, 23*, 75–80.

Elliott, M. (2006). United Kingdom: Detention without trial and the war on terror. *International Journal of Constitutional Law, 4*, 553–566. https://doi.org/10.1093/icon/mol013.

Evans, C., & Evans, S. (2006). *Australian parliaments and the protection of Human Rights*. Paper presented in the Department of the Senate Occasional Lecture Series, Canberra, 8 December 2006.

Fairall, P., & Lacey, W. (2007). Preventative detention and control orders under Federal law: The case for a Bill of Rights. Melbourne University Law Review 31, 1072–1098. http://www.austlii.edu.au/au/journals/MelbULawRw/2007/40.html

Feldman, D. (2015). Democracy, law and Human Rights: Politics as challenge and opportunity. In M. Hunt, H. J. Hooper, & P. Yowell (Eds.), *Parliaments and Human Rights: Redressing the democratic deficit* (pp. 95–117). Oxford: Hart Publishing.

Fletcher, A. (2018). *Australia's Human Rights scrutiny regime*. Melbourne: Melbourne University Press.

Fletcher, A. (2020). Human rights scrutiny in the federal parliament: smokescreen or democratic solution? In J. Debeljak & L. Grenfell (Eds.), *Law making and human rights: executive and parliamentary scrutiny across australian jurisdictions* (pp. 31–66). Sydney: Thompson Reuters.

Flood, P. (2004). *Report of the inquiry into Australian intelligence agencies*. Canberra: Commonwealth of Australia. Retrieved from https://fas.org/irp/world/australia/flood.pdf. Accessed 7 Jan 2020.

Foot, R. (2007). The United Nations, counter terrorism and Human Rights: Institutional adaptation and embedded ideas. *Human Rights Quarterly, 29*(2), 489–514. https://doi.org/10.1353/hrq.2007.0018.

French, R. (1996). The parliament, the executive, the courts and the people. *Deakin Law Review, 3*, 1–22.

Fraser, K. (2014). The Photo that Will Shock the World: Jihadist Khaled Sharrouf's Son, 7, Holds Severed Head. *The Daily Telegraph* (Sydney, online), 4 August 2014. https://www.dailytelegraph.com.au/news/nsw/the-photo-that-will-shock-the-world-jihadist-khaled-sharroufs-son-7-holds-severed-head/news-story/ea5201d8e7f6fac960022548f51e3b4f

Galligan, B. (1990). *Senate Committees – Can they halt the decline of Parliament* (Parl paper no 12). Canberra: Parliament of Australia. Retrieved from https://www.aph.gov.au/About_Parliament/Senate/Powers_practice_n_procedures/pops. Accessed 8 Jan 2020.

Goldsworthy, J. (1999). *The sovereignty of parliament: History and philosophy*. Oxford: Clarendon Press.

Goldsworthy, J. (2001). Legislative sovereignty and the rule of law. In T. Campbell, K. Ewing, & A. Tomkins (Eds.), *Sceptical essays on Human Rights* (pp. 69–81). Oxford: Oxford University Press.

Goldsworthy, J. (2010). *Parliamentary sovereignty: Contemporary debates*. Cambridge: Cambridge University Press.

Grattan, M. (2005 December 2). A hard slog for backbench rebels as Howard gets his way on key legislation, *The Age*. Melbourne.,

Griffith, J. A. G.,. & Ryle, M., with Wheeler-Booth, M. A. J. (1989). Parliament: Functions, practice and procedures. London: Sweet and Maxwell.
Grenfell, L. (2015). An Australian spectrum of political Rights scrutiny: Continuing to lead by example? *Public Law Review, 26*(1), 19–32.
Hart, H. L. A. (1994). *The concept of law* (2nd ed.). Oxford: Oxford University Press.
Halligan, J. (2007). Accountability in Australia: Control, paradox, and complexity. *Public Administration Quarterly, 31*, 453–479.
Halligan, J., Miller, R., & Power, J. (2007). *Parliament in the twenty-first century: Institutional reform and emerging roles*. Melbourne: Melbourne University Press.
Hancock, N. (2002a). *Bills Digest: Security Legislation Amendment (Terrorism) Bill 2002 [No 2]*, no 126 of 2001–02, 30 April 2002. Retrieved from https://www.aph.gov.au/Parliamentary_Business/Bills_Legislation/bd/bd0102/02bd126. Accessed 11 Jan 2020.
Hancock, N. (2002b). *Terrorism and the Law in Australia: Legislation, commentary and constraints* (Research paper no 12). Department of the Parliamentary Library, Parliament of Australia, 2002. Retrieved from https://www.aph.gov.au/About_Parliament/Parliamentary_Departments/Parliamentary_Library/pubs/rp/rp0102/02rp12. Accessed 11 Jan 2020.
Head, M. (2002). Counter-terrorism" Laws: A threat to political freedom, civil liberties and constitutional Rights. *Melbourne University Law Review, 26*(3), 666; http://www.austlii.edu.au/au/journals/MelbULawRw/2002/34.html
Head, M. (2009). What the Haneef inquiry revealed (and did not). *Alternative Law Journal, 34*(4), 243–247. http://handle.uws.edu.au:8081/1959.7/501401
Hirst, J. (2010, August 25. A chance to end the mindless allegiance of party discipline. *The Sydney Morning Herald* (online) https://www.smh.com.au/politics/federal/a-chance-to-end-the-mindless-allegiance-of-party-discipline-20100824-13q9b.html. Accessed 8 Jan 2020.
Hocking, J. (2004a). *Terror laws: ASIO, counter-terrorism and the threat to democracy*. Sydney: University of New South Wales Press.
Hocking, J. (2004b). Protecting democracy by preserving justice: Even for the Feared and the Hated' (2004) 27 *University of New South Wales Law Journal 27,* 319–342. https://www.austlii.edu.au/cgi-bin/viewtoc/au/journals/UNSWLJ/2004/
Human Rights Consultation Committee. (2009). *National Human Rights Consultation Report.* Retrieved from https://trove.nla.gov.au/work/35853626?selectedversion=NBD44855144. Accessed 7 Jan 2020.
Kinley, D., & Ernst, C. (2012). Exile on main street: Australia's Legislative Agenda for Human Rights. *European Human Rights Law Review, 1*, 58–70.
Klausen, J. (2015). Tweeting the Jihad: Social media networks of Western foreign fighters in Syria and Iraq. *Studies in Conflict and Terrorism, 38*(1), 1–22. https://doi.org/10.1080/1057610X.2014.974948.
Jenkins, H. (2012). *Human Rights are in our hands*. Speech delivered at Australian Human Rights commission, Human Rights at your fingertips, online and in practice, Sydney, 29 October 2012. Retrieved from http://www.aph.gov.au/Parliamentary_Business/Committees/Joint/Human_Rights/~/media/Committees/Senate/committee/humanrights_ctte/statements/pdf/291012.ashx. Accessed 10 Jan 2002.
Larkin, P., & Uhr, J. (2009). Bipartisanship and bicameralism in Australia's "War on Terror": Forcing limits on the extension of executive power. *Journal of Legislative Studies, 15*, 239–256. https://doi.org/10.1080/13572330902933391.
Lindell, G. (2008). The scope of the defence and other powers in the light of *Thomas v Mowbray. Constitutional Law and Policy Review, 10*, 42–53.
Levy, R., & Orr, G. (2016). *The law of deliberative democracy*. London: Routledge.
Lynch, A. (2008a). Thomas v Mowbray: Australia's 'War on Terror' reaches the high court. *Melbourne University Law Review, 32*(3), 1182. http://www5.austlii.edu.au/au/journals/MelbULawRw/2008/37.html
Lynch, L. (2008b). Control orders in Australia: A further case study in the migration of British counter-terrorism law. *Oxford University Commonwealth Law Journal, 8*(2), 159–185.
Lynch, A., & Reilly, A. (2007). The constitutional validity of terrorism orders of control and preventative detention. *Flinders Journal of Law Reform, 10*, 105-143; Available at SSRN: https://www.ssrn.com/abstract=977324 or https://doi.org/10.2139/ssrn.977324

Mason, A. (1996). A new perspective on separation of powers. *Canberra Bulletin of Public 86, Administration* 1.
Marinac, A. (2003). *The usual suspects? Civil Society and Senate Committees*. Paper submitted for the senate baker prize. Retrieved from https://www.aph.gov.au/About_Parliament/Senate/Powers_practice_n_procedures/pops/~/link.aspx?_id=1AF5557C98A84D45A0ACCB0E6C36945D&_z=z. Accessed 10 Jan 2020.
Marsh, I. (2006). *Can Senate Committees contribute to social learning* (Parl paper no 45). Parliament of Australia. Retrieved from https://www.aph.gov.au/About_Parliament/Senate/Research_and_Education/pops/~/link.aspx?_id=AC113D4628DF418F8B4C4AE5782C235A. Accessed 10 Jan 2020.
McClelland, R. (2008). *Australia and International Human Rights: Coming in from the Cold*. Speech delivered at the Human Rights and Equal Opportunity Commission Law Seminar, Sydney, 23 May 2008. Retrieved from https://www.humanrights.gov.au/news/speeches/law-seminar-2008-australia-and-international-human-right-coming-cold-hon-robert. Accessed 7 Jan 2020.
McClelland, R. (2009). *Attorney-General*. National Security Legislation Discussion Paper. Media release, 12 August 2009.
McCulloch, J. (2002). War at Home: National Security Arrangements Post 11 September 2001. *Alternative Law Journal*, *27*(2), 87 http://www.austlii.edu.au/au/journals/AltLawJl/2002/30.html
McDonald, C. (2003). The Bali Bombing. *Summer Bar News: Journal of the New South Wales Bar Association, 3*.
McGarrity, N., Gulati, R., & Williams, G. (2012). Sunset clauses in Australian Anti-Terror Laws. *Adelaide Law Review, 33,* 307–334. https://papers.ssrn.com/sol3/papers.cfm?abstract_id=2213234
Menzies, R. G. (1967). *Central Power in the Australian Commonwealth*. London: Cassell.
Michaelsen, C. (2005). Antiterrorism legislation in Australia: A proportionate response to the terrorist threat? *Studies in Conflict & Terrorism, 28*(4), 321–339. https://doi.org/10.1080/10576100590950138.
Millar, A. (1991). *The world of senate committees* (Parl paper no 12). Parliament of Australia. Retrieved from https://www.aph.gov.au/About_Parliament/Senate/Powers_practice_n_procedures/pops. Accessed 8 Jan 2020.
Minchin, N., & Moore, C. (2010). *Committees Under a Government-Controlled Senate: Lessons From 2005–08* (Parl paper no 54). Parliament of Australia. Retrieved from https://www.aph.gov.au/About_Parliament/Senate/Powers_practice_n_procedures/pops. Accessed 10 Jan 2020.
Moulds, S. (2016). Committees of influence: Parliamentary committees with the capacity to change Australia's counter-terrorism Laws. *Australasian Parliamentary Review, 31*(2), 46–68. https://www.aspg.org.au/wp-content/uploads/2017/07/Paper-Moulds-Sarah.pdf. Accessed 11 Jan 2020.
Moulds, S. (2020). Forum of choice? The legislative impact of the parliamentary joint committee of intelligence and security. *Public Law Review, 29*(4), 287–321.
Mulgan, R. (1996). The Australian senate as a 'House of Review'. *Australian Journal of Political Science, 31*(2), 191–204. https://doi.org/10.1080/10361149651184.
Odgers, J. (2012). *Australian Senate Practice* (13th ed.). Canberra: Commonwealth of Australia.
Paxman, K. (1998). *Referral of Bills to Senate Committees: An Evaluation* (Parl Paper No 31) (1998) 76. Parliament of Australia. Retrieved from https://www.aph.gov.au/-/media/05_About_Parliament/52_Sen/524_Research_and_education/Other_Publications/PSP09_grant.pdf?la=en&hash=3E49498576ED0CCE822777919E1C1EE27AA17407. Accessed 6 Jan 2020.
Pearce, D. (1991). *Ten years of scrutiny*. Seminar to mark the tenth anniversary of the Senate Standing Committee for the Scrutiny of Bills, Canberra, 25 November 1991. Retrieved from http://www.aph.gov.au/Parliamentary_Business/Committees/Senate/Scrutiny_of_Bills/Completed_inquiries. Accessed 7 Jan 2020.
Pickering, S., & McCulloch, K. J. (2010). The Haneef case and counter-terrorism policing in Australia. *Policing and Society, 20*(1), 21–38. https://doi.org/10.1080/10439460903377311.

Pintos-Lopez, H., & Williams G.,(2008). Enemies foreign and domestic: *Thomas v Mowbray* and the new scope of the defence power. *University of Tasmanian Law Review, 27,* 83–110. http://www.austlii.edu.au/au/journals/UTasLawRw/2008/4.pdf

Quick, J., & Garran, R. (2014). *The annotated constitution of the Australian commonwealth.* Sydney: Lexis Nexus, Revised ed.

Rajanayagam, S. (2020). Urgent law- making and the Human Rights (parliamentary scrutiny) act. In J. Debeljak & L. Grenfell (Eds.), *Law- Making and Human Rights* (pp. 647–672). Sydney: Thompson Reuters.

Reid, G. S., & Forrest, M. (1989). *Australia's commonwealth parliament 1901–1988: Ten perspectives.* Melbourne: Melbourne University Press.

Reilly, A. (2007). The processes and consequences of counter-terrorism law reform in Australia: 2001–2005. *Flinders Journal of Law Reform, 10*(1), 81–90. http://www.austlii.edu.au/au/journals/FlinLawJl/2010/3.pdf

Reinares, F. (2009). After the Madrid Bombings: Internal security reforms and prevention of global terrorism in Spain. *Studies in Conflict and Terrorism, 32*(5), 367–388. https://doi.org/10.1080/10576100902836767.

Renwick, J. (2018). Independent National Security Legislation Monitor (Annual report 2017–2018, report no 6, December 2018, 14). Retrieved from http://www.dpmc.gov.au/publications/INSLM/index.cfm. Accessed 7 Jan 2020.

Reynolds, D., & Williams, G. (2020). Evaluating the impact of Australia's federal human rights scrutiny regime. In J. Debeljak & L. Grenfell (Eds.), *Law-making and human rights* (pp. 67–96). Sydney: Thompson Reuters.

Rice, S. (2020). Allowing for dissent: Opening up Human Rights dialogue in the Australian parliament. In J. Debeljak & L. Grenfell (Eds.), *Law- Making and Human Rights* (pp. 99–134). Sydney: Thompson Reuters.

Royal Commission on Intelligence and Security. (1977). *Final Report.* Canberra: Commonwealth of Australia.

Sawer, M., Abjorensen, N., & Larkin, P. (2009). *Australia: The state of democracy.* Sydney: Federation Press.

Saul, B. (2008). Terrorism as crime or war: Militarising crime and disrupting the constitutional settlement?. *Public Law Review 19,* 20; Sydney Centre for International Law Working Paper No. 2; Sydney Centre for International law Working Paper No. 2; Sydney Law School Research Paper No. 08/129. Available at SSRN: https://ssrn.com/abstract=1292588

Security Legislation Review Committee. (2006). *Report of the Security Legislation Review Committee.* Retrieved from https://www.ag.gov.au/NationalSecurity/Counterterrorismlaw/Documents/Report%20of%20the%20Security%20Legislation%20Review%20Committee.pdf. Accessed 7 Jan 2020.

Shell, D. (2001). The history of bicameralism. *Journal of Legislative Studies, 7*(1), 13–18.

Siaroff, A. (2003). Varieties of parliamentarianism in the advanced industrial democracies. *International Political Science Review, 24*(4), 445–464.

Stanhope, J. (2005, Octoer 14). Chief Minister Makes Public Draft Terror Legislation. Media Release, (online). http://www.cmd.act.gov.au/open_government/inform/act_government_media_releases.

Stellios, J., & Palfrey, M. (2012). A new Federal Scheme for the protection of Human Rights. *Australian Institute of Administrative Law Forum, 69,* 13–19.

Stephens, U. (2013). *Opening remarks.* Speech given at the Australian Government and Non-Government Organisations Forum on Human Rights, Old Parliament House, Canberra, 19 June 2013. Retrieved from http://www.aph.gov.au/Parliamentary_Business/Committees/Joint/Human_Rights/~/media/Committees/Senate/committee/humanrights_ctte/statements/pdf/stephens_ngo_forum_190613.ashx. Accessed 11 Jan 2020.

Stephenson, S. (2016). *From dialogue to disagreement in comparative rights constitutionalism.* Sydney: Federation Press.

Stone, A. (2001). The Australian free speech experiment and scepticism about the UK Human Rights Act. In T. E. K. Campbell & A. Tomkins (Eds.), *Sceptical essays on Human Rights* (pp. 391–430)). Oxford: Oxford University Press.

Stone, B. (2005). *Australian Bicameralism: Potential and Performance in State Upper Houses* (Parl paper no 40). Parliament of Australia. Retrieved from https://www.aph.gov.au/About_Parliament/Senate/Powers_practice_n_procedures/pops. Accessed 8 Jan 2020.

Thompson, E. (1998). *The senate and representative democracy* (Senate brief no 10, parliamentary library). Parliament of Australia. Retrieved from https://www.aph.gov.au/About_Parliament/Senate/Powers_practice_n_procedures/~/~/link.aspx?_id=DCF2CDCE8D454BBA9768A9B61474D94F&_z=z. Accessed 10 Jan 202.

Tyulkina, S., & Williams, G. (2017). Combating terrorism in Australia through preventative detention orders. In T. Tullich, R. Anaian-Welsh, S. Bronitt, & S. Murray (Eds.), *Regulating preventative justice: Principle, policy and paradox* (pp. 136–152). Oxford: Routledge. https://doi.org/10.4324/9781315620978.

Uhr, J. (1991). *Speech at Ten Years of Scrutiny'*. Seminar to mark the tenth anniversary of the Senate Standing Committee for the Scrutiny of Bills, Canberra, 25 November 1991. Parliament of Australia. Retrieved at https://www.aph.gov.au/Parliamentary_Business/Committees/Senate/Scrutiny_of_Bills/~/media/Committees/Senate/committee/scrutiny/completed_inquiries/work39/report.ashx. Accessed 10 Jan 2020.

Uhr, J. (1998). The constitutional convention and deliberative democracy. *University of New South Wales Law Journal, 21*(3), 875–881.

Uhr, J. (2006). The role of Australian legislatures in protecting Rights. In T. Campbell, J. Goldsworthy, & A. Stone (Eds.), *Protecting Rights without a Bill of Rights* (pp. 41–62). London: Ashgate.

Walker, B. (2011). Independent National Security Legislation Monitor (Annual report). Retrieved from http://www.dpmc.gov.au/publications/INSLM/index.cfm. Accessed 7 Jan 2020.

Williams, G. (2006). Executive oversight of intelligence agencies in Australia. In Z. K. Goldman & S. J. Rascoff (Eds.), *Global intelligence oversight: Governing security in the twenty-first century*. Oxford: Oxford University Press.

Williams, G. (2011). A decade of Australian Anti-Terror Laws. *Melbourne University Law Review, 35*(3), 1136.

Williams, G., Lynch, A., & McGarrity, N. (2010). *Counter-terrorism and beyond: The culture of law and justice after 9/11*. Oxford: Routledge.

Williams, G., & Lynch, A. (2006). *What Price security? Taking stock of Australia's anti-terror Laws*. Sydney: UNSW Press.

Williams, G., Lynch, A., & McGarrity, N. (2015). *Inside Australia's anti-terrorism Laws and Trials*. Sydney: New South Publishing.

Williams, G., Davis, F., & McGarrity, N. (Eds.). (2014). *Surveillance, counter-terrorism and comparative constitutionalism*. London: Routledge.

Williams, G., & Reynolds, D. (2016). The operation and impact of Australia's parliamentary scrutiny regime for human rights. *Monash University Law Review, 41*(2), 469–508.

Zifcak, S. (2015). Counter-terrorism and Human Rights. In J. Menadue & M. Keating (Eds.), *Fairness, opportunity and security*. Adelaide: ATF Press.

Zuijdewijn, V., Roy, J., & Bakker, E. (2014). *Returning Western foreign fighters: The case of Afghanistan, Bosnia and Somalia* (Background note). International Centre for Counter-Terrorism, The Hague. Retrieved from https://www.icct.nl/download/file/ICCT-De-Roy-van-Zuijdewijn-Bakker-Returning-Western-Foreign-Fighters-June-2014.pdf. Accessed 12 Jan 2020.

Websites

Parliament of Australia. (2016).

History of the Intelligence and Security Committee. http://www.aph.gov.au/Parliamentary_Business/Committees/Joint/Intelligence_and_Security/History_of_the_Intelligence_and_Security_Committee

Part II
Applying the Assessment Framework

Chapter 4
Participation and Legitimacy

Abstract This chapter identifies the key participants in the four committees studied and investigates the 'legitimacy' or 'political authority' of each of these committees as seen by its key participants. Understanding the views and perspectives of key participants in the system helps provide a more holistic picture of the nature of the impact each committee has had on the case study Acts. It also helps to set the parameters of realistic options for improving the rights-enhancing impact of each committee, discussed in Part III. Chapter 5 explores the concept of 'legitimacy' in the context of parliamentary law-making and reflects on the rates and diversity of participation in the parliamentary committee system. The Chapter concludes by identifying an important tension between the 'deliberative' and 'authoritative' attributes of different committees within the Australian Parliament – a theme that is explored further in Part III of the book.

4.1 Why Look for Key Participants and Evidence of Legitimacy?

Part II of my research applies the assessment framework set out in Chap. 2 and describes the overall impact of the four parliamentary committees studied on the case study Acts. This chapter identifies the *key participants* in the parliamentary committee system and looks for evidence of whether particular committees are seen as more *legitimate* by some or all of these participants. This provides important context for the type of influence particular committees can have on decision makers in the legislative process. It can also explain why some committees have had a stronger, or different, impact on the case study Acts than others, which is important when it comes to evaluating the capacity of the committee system to contribute to rights protection. This is because the parliamentary model of rights protection relies on the Parliament and the executive voluntarily developing a culture of rights scrutiny, rather than being required to do so by threat of judicial sanction. To contribute meaningfully to this system, parliamentary committees must therefore have sufficient legitimacy in the eyes of a wide range of participants in the process, including

S. Moulds, *Committees of Influence*, https://doi.org/10.1007/978-981-15-4350-0_4

parliamentarians, government members, public servants and the broader community. As discussed below, my research suggests that parliamentary committees that can generate and sustain high levels of legitimacy among those responsible for developing and drafting proposed laws are well placed to maximise their rights-enhancing impact.

This chapter argues that certain characteristics of individual committees provide them with a higher level of legitimacy or enable them to attract a more diverse range of participants, and this has implications for their capacity to influence the content of a Bill. For example, the SSCSB has well-established relationships with a narrow range of executive-dominated participants, which allows the committee to have strong behind-the-scenes impact on the content of the case study Acts. Whereas for the LCA Committees, attracting many diverse participants to their inquiries is one of the most effective ways for the committees to generate the type of public attention that sometimes translates into rights-enhancing legislative change.

As discussed further below, understanding these different characteristics of particular committees allows practical options for reform to be identified that can improve the way individual committees work together to contribute to rights protection.

4.1.1 Who Are the Key Participants?

In many ways, the entire Australian community is a participant in the parliamentary committee process which forms part of Australia's democratically elected Parliament. However, for the purpose of this evaluation, *key participants* in the parliamentary committee system are those individuals or organisations who either directly engage with the committees, or who rely upon their work when making decisions about proposed laws.

Table 4.1 provides a snapshot of the key participants identified in each of the committees being evaluated in this book, in the context of the case study Acts. The following four tables (Tables 4.2, 4.3, 4.4, and 4.5) provide an overview of the number and diversity of submissions and witnesses to the inquiry-based committees (the LCA Committees and the PJCIS). The relevance of these tables to my research is discussed below.

4.1.2 Rates and Diversity of Participation

4.1.2.1 Strong Performer: The LCA Committees

The above tables tell an important story about the different forms of participation each committee attracts. Rates and diversity of participants in formal parliamentary scrutiny can be an important indicator of the capacity of the committee system to

Table 4.1 Key participants in the four committees studied

Key participants	Ministers	Public servants or government agencies	Parliamentary committee staff	Submission makers or inquiry witnesses	Independent oversight or review bodies	Committee members (2001–2015)	Other parliamentarians
SSCSB	Yes, through regular, formal correspondence	Generally limited to those drafting bills or instructing parliamentary counsel	Committee secretary, legal advisor, secretariat staff	Generally no submission makers or inquiry witnesses for bills scrutiny work	Rare for substantive references to be made	34 members since 2001 including from minor parties	No capacity for participating members
LCA Committees	Yes, though most often via relevant departments; formal correspondence relatively rare	Generally limited to those within the attorney-General's portfolio	Committee secretary, secretariat staff	Large numbers of submissions (up to 400) and a wide range of submission makers	Regular references to and engagement with independent oversight bodies	31 members since 2001 including minor parties and independents	Other senators are regularly involved as participating or substitute members
PJCIS	Yes, though most often via relevant departments; formal correspondence relatively rare	Focused on those agencies within statutory ambit, e.g. ASIO, AFP, ASIS, as well as AGD, PM&C and DIBP	Security cleared committee secretary and secretariat staff plus specialist secondees from the relevant government organisations	Moderate numbers of submissions (up to 230), many repeat submission makers with legal expertise	Regular reference s to and engagement with national security related oversight bodies	Membership includes both houses, 38 members (between 2005 and 2015)	Membership with approval of Prime Minister only. No capacity for participating members
PJCHR	Yes, through regular, formal correspondence	Generally limited to those drafting bills (and statements of compatibility) or instructing parliamentary counsel	Committee secretary, legal advisor, secretariat staff	Generally no submission makers or inquiry witnesses for bills scrutiny work	Regular references to national and international human rights bodies, and independent oversight bodies	Membership includes both houses, 23 members (since establishment in 2012)	No capacity for participating members

Table 4.2 Submission and witness participation rates for case study acts considered by PJCIS

Bill	Submissions	Witnesses (organisations counted as 1)
Counter-Terrorism (Temporary Exclusion Orders) Act 2019 (Cth)	8	4
Telecommunications and Other Legislation Amendment (Assistance and Access) Act 2018	105	31
Criminal Code Amendment (High Risk Terrorist Offenders) Bill 2016	18	7
Australian Citizenship Amendment (Allegiance to Australia) Bill 2015	43	19
Counter-Terrorism Legislation Amendment (Foreign Fighters) Bill 2014	46	18
Counter-Terrorism Legislation Amendment Bill (No. 1) 2014	17	8
Telecommunications (Interception and Access) Amendment (Data Retention) Bill 2015	204	29
Inquiry into potential National Security Legislation reforms 2012	236	38
Counter-Terrorism (Temporary Exclusion Orders) Bill 2019 (Cth)	8	4

Table 4.3 Submission and witness participation rates for case study acts and related inquiries considered by LCA Committees

Bill	Submissions	Witnesses (organisations counted as 1)
Comprehensive revision of the Telecommunications (Interception and Access) Act 1979 (conducted during 2013–2015)	45	27
National Security Legislation Amendment Bill 2010	23	10
Anti-Terrorism Bill (No. 2) 2005	294	21
National Security Information (Criminal Proceedings) Bill 2004	24	5
Anti-terrorism Bill 2004	28	6
Australian Security Intelligence Organisation Legislation Amendment (Terrorism) Bill 2002 [References Committee]	435	22
Security Legislation (Anti-Terrorism) Bills 2002	431	34

contribute to rights protection, particularly when it comes to the inquiry-based committees such as the LCA Committees and the PJCIS (Paxman at p. 76). This is because a diverse range of participants in committee inquiries provides the chance for participants with different views to 'find common ground' (Marinac 2003) or, as Dalla-Pozza (2016) has explained, for parliamentarians to make good on their promise to 'strike the right balance' between safeguarding security and preserving individual liberty when enacting counter-terrorism laws (at p. 273). In her earlier

Table 4.4 Frequent submission makers to PJCIS as percentage of total number

Bill	AGD	ASIO	AFP	Oversight agency	Other government department or agency	AHRC	Law council	Other legal body	Legal academic individual	Legal academic group	% of Total submissions received
Counter-Terrorism (Temporary Exclusion Orders) Act 2019 (Cth)				IGIS	Home Affairs	✓	✓	✓	2	✓	86%
Telecommunications and Other Legislation Amendment (Assistance and Access) Act 2018 (Cth)	✓	✓	✓	Multiple (IGIS, AIC, ombudsman, state agencies)	Home Affairs	✓	✓	✓	✓		12%
Criminal Code Amendment (High Risk Terrorist Offenders) Act 2016 (Cth)	✓		✓	✓		✓	✓	✓	2		87%
Australian Citizenship Amendment (Allegiance to Australia) Bill 2015	✓	✓	✓	✓	Immigration	✓	✓		5	✓	73%
Counter-Terrorism Legislation Amendment (Foreign Fighters) Bill 2014	✓	✓	✓	3 (IGIS, ombudsman, privacy commissioner)	4 (Customs, Foreign Affairs and Trade, Immigration, Australian Crime Commission (ACC))	✓	✓	2	2	✓	94%
Counter-Terrorism Legislation Amendment Bill (No. 1) 2014	✓	✓	✓	✓	Australian Signals Directorate (ASD)	✓		✓		✓	100%
National Security Legislation Amendment Bill (No. 1) 2014	✓	✓		2 (IGIS, privacy commissioner)	ASIS		✓	✓		✓	70%

(continued)

Table 4.4 (continued)

Bill	AGD	ASIO	AFP	Oversight agency	Other government department or agency	AHRC	Law council	Other legal body	Legal academic individual	Legal academic group	% of Total submissions received
Telecommunications (Interception and Access) Amendment (Data Retention) Bill 2015	✓	✓	✓	3 (ombudsman, privacy commissioner)	3 (ACC, Australian Commission for Law Enforcement Integrity (ACLEI) Australian Securities and Investment Commission (ASIC))	✓	✓		✓		41%
Inquiry into potential National Security Legislation reforms 2012	✓	✓	✓	✓	6 (ASIS, DSD, ACC, ACLEI, ASIC, Australian Taxation Office)	✓		3		2	42%

Table 4.5 Frequent submission makers to LCA Committees as percentage of total number of submissions received

Bill	AGD	ASIO	AFP	Oversight agency	Other government department or agency	AHRC	LCA	Other legal body	Legal academic individual	Legal academic group	% Of total submissions received
Comprehensive revision of the Telecommunications (Interception and Access) Act 1979	✓	✓	✓	3 (IGIS, Ombudsman AIC)	3 (ACC, ATO, ACLEI)		✓	✓	✓		48%
National Security Legislation Amendment Bill 2010	✓		✓		✓ (ACC)	✓	✓	✓	✓	2	90%
Anti-Terrorism Bill (No. 2) 2005	✓	✓	✓	2	✓ (AUSTRAC)	✓	✓	✓	2	✓	57%
National Security Information (Criminal Proceedings) Bill 2004	✓						✓	✓			60%
Anti-terrorism Bill 2004	✓		✓					✓	✓	✓	83%
Australian Security Intelligence Organisation Legislation Amendment (Terrorism) Bill 2002	✓	✓	✓				✓	6	2		54%
Security Legislation (Anti-Terrorism) Bills 2002	✓	✓	✓		3 (AUSTRAC, Customs, Immigration)		✓	4	4	✓	47%

2007 study of participation in counter-terrorism related inquiries, Dalla-Pozza found that, while there are many examples of inquiries that attract a diverse range of submission makers, overall, committees had 'mixed success' in functioning as a 'conduit for diverse interests to be heard' (Dalla-Pozza 2007). As Tables 4.4 and 4.5 show, similar results emerge in the context of the case study Acts chosen for my research.

The LCA Committees have the highest overall participation rate, engaging a broad range of Senators, public servants and submission makers. For example, in their respective inquiries into the SLAT Bills in 2002, the LCA Committees each attracted over 400 submissions and heard from well over 20 witnesses. A number of the LCA Committees' features explain why this might be the case. First, as noted in Chap. 3, the LCA Committees are 'inquiry-based' committees, with specific powers to call for public submissions and hold public hearings into Bills or policy issues referred to them by the Senate. Secondly, the Standing Orders governing the LCA Committees enable a large number of Senators to be directly involved as participating or substitute members. For example, in the period between 1 January 2015 and 30 June 2015, 49 Senators participated in the work of the LCA Legislation Committee (Senate 2015, pp. 123–4). This high participation rate among Senators from diverse political and portfolio backgrounds in turn helps to attract a diverse range of regular submission makers, including those who may be opposed to the government's policy objectives in the area of counter-terrorism. For example, in an interview with the author the CEO of Civil Liberties Australia Bill Rowlings said:

> The Senate Legal and Con References committee is a committee where the opposition and the Greens can get things up … normally the opposition or one of the Greens chairs that committee, so that's where you'll get the more interesting analysis of what should be done, …. So that's a very useful committee (Canberra, 24 May 2016).

This relatively diverse rate of participation allows the LCA Committees to contribute to Australia's parliamentary model of rights protection by providing a meaningful public forum for the exchange of views on rights issues arising from proposed laws or policies (Uhr 1998a, p. 879; b, pp. 220, 227; 2001, p. 712; Dalla-Pozza 2007). This diversity of participation also suggests that the LCA Committees provide an effective forum for holding the executive government to account, which, as noted in Chap. 3, is a key function of the Australian Parliament. For these reasons, the reforms I recommend in Part III are designed to enhance these qualities of the LCA Committees, for example by formalising processes for selecting witnesses to guard against unconscious bias (Table 9.1). However, as explored further below, other changes may also be required to ensure that these relatively high rates of participation translate into strong legislative and public impact for the LCA Committees, particularly as they are forced to compete with other inquiry-based committees with cross-cutting mandates, such as the PJCIS.

4.1.2.2 A Narrower Range of Participants for the Technical Scrutiny Committees

As Table 4.1 above shows, the SSCSB and the PJCHR attract a narrower range of key participants, both in terms of direct participation by parliamentarians and external engagement. In many ways, this is completely to be expected. As outlined in Chap. 3, the SSCSB considers itself to be in the business of 'technical scrutiny', which rarely calls for the type of broad public or parliamentary engagement of the LCA Committees. Moreover, as the committee itself has indicated, the unrelenting workload faced by the SSCSB makes it practically impossible for it to encourage active community participation in its Bills scrutiny work (SSCSB 2014).

As Chap. 3 explains, the SSCSB also has highly formalised ways of communicating with proponents of Bills that revolve around the exchange of correspondence, and it generally exercises deference and restraint when formulating its final advice on the compatibility of a Bill with its scrutiny criteria. As a result, the committee's closest working relationships are with a relatively narrow range of public servants who are directly involved in drafting Bills, or providing assistance to Ministers who are required to respond to the committee's requests for further information. As discussed in Chap. 3, the PJCHR also seeks to emulate this 'technical scrutiny' role, at least when it comes to its Bills scrutiny function, and as a result has a similarly limited range of participants. The PJCHR also has specific statutory functions that include inquiring into 'any matter relating to human rights which is referred to it by the Attorney-General': *Human Rights (Parliamentary Scrutiny) Act 2011* (Cth) s 7(c), however this function has been used only sparingly (see Williams and Reynolds 2016).

As set out in Table 4.1, the relatively limited range of participants in the Bills scrutiny functions of the PJCHR and the SSCSB has implications for the capacity of these committees to have a strong rights-enhancing impact on the content of Australia's counter-terrorism laws. For example, as explored further in Chap. 7, this characteristic makes these committees much more reliant on the 'hidden impact' they are able to exert on those responsible for developing counter-terrorism laws before they are introduced into Parliament.

4.1.2.3 The PJCIS Experience

The PJCIS sits somewhere in the middle of the spectrum when it comes to diversity of participation, both in terms of its membership, and the types of submissions it receives to its public inquiries. Unlike the LCA Committees, the membership of the PJCIS is tightly prescribed and leaves no room for participating or substitute members (*Intelligence Services Act 2001* (Cth) s 28(2) and Sch 1). The PJCIS also regularly attracts parliamentarians with experience in the military, law enforcement or related fields, and to date has included only members of the major political parties (although minor parties and independents are not explicitly excluded). This lack of diversity among the membership of the PJCIS led some interviewees to express concern about the potential for this to influence the 'culture' of the committee and its approach to public hearings. For example, in a 2016 interview with the author, Rowlings from Civil Liberties Australia was of the view that:

> The Parliamentary Joint Committee on Intelligence and Security is nothing other than a straight extension of the security forces and the police. … Of the 6–8 regulars it is headed by spooks, or ex-spooks or ex-military or ex-police type people. …
>
> It's a total insiders club. They adopt whatever's put up by the police and security services as gospel and that is taken to be virtually what will apply unless you can overturn it … with dramatic proof that it won't work. … The starting point of that committee is that the police and security services will get 100% of what they want unless somebody from outside the organisation can absolutely demonstrate that it shouldn't be that way. And that is wrong. Fundamentally wrong. … We would suggest that the people who should be on the committee like that are the ones that have voiced concerns. They should not be the ex-spooks, the ex-police, the ex-military people, because we know what their attitudes are, we know that they bring to bear a particular attitude which is totally dismissive of the community point of view (Canberra, 24 May 2016).

In an interview with the author in 2016, Lydia Shelly from the Muslim Legal Network was also 'concerned about the membership of the PJCIS not being very diverse either in terms of political allegiance or life experiences' and noted that this gave rise to negative experiences for witnesses, particularly for groups and individuals who fall outside of the common list of repeat submission makers to public inquiries into counter-terrorism law. For example, Ms Shelly explained that, for non-legally trained community members, even finding out about a parliamentary inquiry into a law that might affect their rights was challenging:

> It is very difficult for everyday Muslims to participate in parliamentary committee inquiries. Often these inquiries are not well known. Key community groups don't find out about them at all, or if they do it is too late for them to coordinate and draft a submission. It seems that the process is set up to capture only a very small group of representatives.
>
> Being legally trained was very important, and pretty much essential to understanding the laws and participating in the inquiry at such short notice. Other Muslim community groups who were interested in participating struggled due to the time frames, and the lack of capacity to get across the detail of the legislation in such a short time and then confront such a hostile committee hearing (via telephone, 2 June 2016).

The Muslim Legal Network's experiences may have been shaped by the subject matter of the committee inquiry and the public nature of the committee hearing, as well as the lack of diversity in the membership of the PJCIS. However, others have also commented on the barriers individuals and groups face when seeking to access committee hearings and to be invited to appear as witnesses (see e.g. Paxman 1998). For Paxman (1998), these barriers arise, at least in part, from the dominance of sophisticated, usually legally qualified, organisations or government departments who are frequently invited by the committees themselves to make submissions or appear as witnesses, as discussed below. Paxman describes these organisations and departments as the 'usual suspects'.

4.1.2.4 The Usual Suspects

Tables 4.4 and 4.5 below suggest that in the case of the LCA Committees' and the PJCIS's inquiries into counter-terrorism law, the 'usual suspects' are government departments and agencies, legal bodies (such as the Law Council of Australia), statutory bodies (such as the AHRC and the INSLM) and academics (including groups such as the Gilbert & Tobin Centre for Public Law).

While generalisations are hard to make across a range of different inquiries into different Bills, Tables 4.4 and 4.5 suggest that, on average, the 'usual suspects' submission makers made up well over half of the witnesses to the PJCIS and LCA Committees' inquiries into the case study Acts (see e.g. LCA Legislation Committee 2002a, 2002b, LCA References Committee 2002) . The dominance of these categories of submission makers is particularly pronounced with respect to the PJCIS, which held six inquiries where 70% or more of the witnesses were from the 'usual suspects' category.

It is noted that the inquiries into the early counter-terrorism reforms, in particular the LCA Committees inquiries into the SLAT Bills, attracted high participation and diversity in terms of witnesses, perhaps because these Bills sought to introduce considerable new, intrusive powers for law enforcement and intelligence agencies. This can be contrasted with some of the inquiries conducted by the PJCIS, which concerned Bills that built upon or refined existing powers rather than introducing new powers. However, this does not fully explain the comparative lack of diversity seen in inquiries conducted by the PJCIS relating to the introduction of new powers in the case of the Foreign Fighters Bill and the Citizenship Bill, which both introduced significant new powers for executive agencies but failed to attract a diverse range of witnesses (PJCIS Foreign Fighters Report 2014; PJCIS Citizenship Bill Report 2015).

This reliance on 'the usual suspects' by the PJCIS may be a result of the relatively informal processes adopted by committees and their secretariats when it comes to calling for submissions and selecting witnesses. As Paxman (1998) explains, the majority of individuals or groups that engage with parliamentary committee inquiries into proposed legislation are those that are already aware of the bill's existence, or who have been contacted directly by other key participants such as parliamentarians or committee secretariat staff (at p. 81).

It is also common for the inquiry committees to develop their own 'lists' of submission makers, with whom they regularly liaise and whom they actively encourage to make submissions or appear as witnesses, as was confirmed by a number of interviews conducted for this book.

In an interview with the author in 2016, a former parliamentary committee secretariat staff member explained that, in their experience, when selecting inquiry witnesses the secretariat would:

> look at the submissions and say, 'Well, these are the people you have to interview or go to a public hearing on, and here are a selection of people you might want to contact.' Then you consider the individual submissions, and unless there's one that's really compelling, well they're just really individuals with views that you might use as references for your report (Canberra, 28 September 2016).

For some, this reliance on a relatively narrow pool of high-quality and sophisticated submission makers is sensible and appropriate, particularly for committees such as the LCA Committees and the PJCIS, which are often required to deal with complex legal issues in their Bills scrutiny function. It means, for example, that those with the capacity and expertise to contribute are actively engaged in the scrutiny system. As the former Chair of the LCA Legislation Committee Patricia Crossin observed in 2010:

> A lot of legislation we deal with in this country would not be shaped into quality legislation were it not for the Law Reform Commission, the Law Council and some of the legal experts who are outside of the Parliament. We rely on their expertise heavily (Crossin 2010, p. 139).

However, consistent reliance upon the 'usual suspects' can give rise to the perception that, when it comes to public inquiries involving these submission makers, 'the same old paths are being trodden … with predictable outcomes'. As discussed below, this in turn dilutes the inquiry-based committees' perceived legitimacy as a deliberative forum, particularly if the voices of those most likely to be negatively affected by the proposed law are excluded from the inquiry, or drowned out by a chorus of 'usual suspects'.

For these reasons, I recommend changes to the practices of the inquiry-based committees to encourage more active engagement with potential submission makers and witnesses from a broader range of organisations and interest groups (Tables 9.1 and 9.2). Of course, improved engagement with a broader cross-section of the community may not automatically result in more (or more diverse) submissions: there may be some sectors of the community that are unwilling to engage or unaware of the benefits of engagement with parliamentary committees for their particular advocacy strategy or interests. For this reason, I also recommend changes to help demonstrate the value of committee participation for the advocacy objectives of a broader range of groups and individuals, for example by documenting the influence committee recommendations can have on the content of legislation (Tables 9.1 and 9.2). These recommendations align with the general agreement among past and present committee members interviewed that a more diverse range of views adds to the quality of the inquiry process.

As will be discussed further in Part III, the above analysis reveals an important tension in the role and impact of different types of parliamentary committees when it comes to scrutinising rights-engaging legislation. On the one hand, the ability to attract and reflect upon a diverse range of perspectives when inquiring into a Bill has positive deliberative implications for the capacity of the committee system to contribute to Australia's parliamentary model of rights protection. On the other hand, as Chap. 5 documents, other committee attributes, such as specialist skills and trusted relationships with the executive, can also lead to a consistently strong legislative impact, which can also have important rights-enhancing results. This tension between committees as deliberative and authoritative forums – and in particular, how these different forums are viewed and used by key participants in the committee system – is discussed in the next part of this chapter.

4.2 Evidence of Legitimacy

The previous section of this chapter identified the key participants in the formal parliamentary scrutiny system and looked at the relevance of different rates and diversity of participation in the inquiries conducted by the committees evaluated in this book. The next section asks whether and why those key participants consider the parliamentary committee system, or particular components of the system, to play a *legitimate* role in the features and functions of the Australian Parliament set out in Chap. 3. As noted in Chap. 2, legitimacy (or political authority) is critical if the committee system is going to contribute to Australia's parliamentary model of rights protection and, as discussed below, the relationship each committee has with parliamentarians, the public and those involved in developing and drafting counter-terrorism laws often determines its overall impact on a Bill.

4.2.1 The Challenge of Gathering Views on Legitimacy

As discussed in Chap. 2, finding evidence of whether or not a committee is seen as more or less legitimate demands consideration of both objective sources of evidence (such as reference to the work of committees in public service guidelines or annual reports of regular submission makers) and the subjective views of the key participants themselves. For example, whether a committee is seen as more legitimate than others may depend upon whether the participant is an 'insider' (such as a member of the government or a public servant) or an 'outside observer' (such as a commentator) or perhaps an ordinary member of the public, with no particular knowledge or interest in the committee system. As a result, my research draws upon interviews conducted with past and present members of parliamentary committees and their staff, regular submission makers and a number of public servants, government officials and statutory bodies who are responsible for developing, drafting and reviewing counter-terrorism laws (Moulds 2018, Appendix A). My research deliberately focuses on this range of participants, rather than the public at large, as they are most likely to reveal the contextual information needed to supplement the other documentary material presented in this part, such as insights into whether past committee scrutiny has been taken into account when developing, drafting or debating a proposed new law.

This approach is designed to infuse my research with the real-life experiences of those directly involved in the committee system; however, it also makes it impossible to completely avoid the risks inherent in undertaking interviews with a selective and relatively small sample of key participants (Moulds 2018, Appendix A). I am aware, for example, that some of my findings could be affected by factors such as the interviewee's seniority and experience, their geographical location, and their political allegiance. In addition, my analysis includes case studies relating to counter-terrorism, which may generate particularly strong responses in those asked to comment on the legitimacy of certain committees. However, it is important to note that indications of legitimacy derived from these interviews are not relied upon in this book to provide *proof* of a committee's impact on a particular counter-terrorism law (which is instead tested by looking for evidence of legislative, public and hidden impact). Rather this material is used to provide a fuller picture of the *context* in which the particular committees operate, and to begin to understand what types of changes to the system would be accepted as realistic by those directly involved in its work. When used in this way, the subjective nature of the interview material adds colour to the documentary evidence used to determine impact without undermining the integrity of my research.

4.2.2 A Spectrum of Legitimacy among Committees

My research suggests that, when it comes to assessing legitimacy, a spectrum of committee experiences emerges. At one end are the SSCSB and the PJCIS, which are attributed high levels of legitimacy by almost all categories of participants, and particularly by those directly involved in the law-making process, such as proponents of Bills, public servants, parliamentary counsel and parliamentarians. At the other end is the PJCHR, a much newer committee clearly struggling to gain legitimacy in the eyes of a wide range of participants. A special place is held by the LCA Committees, whose legitimacy is sometimes questioned by the government of the day, but whose relatively broad and diverse range of participants consistently attribute at least moderate levels of legitimacy across a wide range of functions. This spectrum is summarised in Table 4.6, and discussed further below.

4.2.3 Tensions Between the Deliberative and Authoritative Attributes of Committees

Looking for evidence of legitimacy within the committee system also illustrates the important tension between the *deliberative* and *authoritative* attributes of parliamentary committees. The deliberative attributes of the system (discussed in further detail in Chap. 6) are those that facilitate meaningful forums for the public and a diverse range of parliamentarians to engage in and contribute to the law-making process (Levy and Orr 2016, pp. 4, 22–23). These attributes are most commonly observed with respect to the inquiry-based committees, who regularly hold public hearings and have politically diverse and relatively dynamic committee membership. The authoritative attributes of the committee system are those features of individual committees, including membership, processes and relationships with the executive, that command respect among key decision makers in the system. This authority can manifest in terms of legislative impact (such as amendments being

Table 4.6 Evidence of legitimacy by committee

	Proponents of a bill	Public servants	Parliamentary committee staff	Submission makers	Independent bodies	Media	Parliamentarians
SSCSB	Strong: evidenced by generally timely responses to requests and broad acceptance of scrutiny criteria	Strong: evidenced by scrutiny criteria entrenched as part of 'best practice' for public servants	Strong: evidenced belong service provided by secretariat staff	Moderate: not seen as a forum for directly advancing rights concerns, but regular reference to SSCSB in other inquiries	Moderate: rare to explicitly refer to SSCSB in reports	Moderate: rare to explicitly refer to SSCSB in media reports but generally no criticism	Moderate: strong positive feedback in interviews, but rare to explicitly refer to SSCSB directly· in Hansard
LCA Committees	Mixed views: can be seen as legitimate, but may also be seen as politicised	Modeste: regular participants in hearings but lack of consistent scrutiny criteria can make it difficult to anticipate key issues	Moderate to strong despite heavy and varied workload	Moderate to strong: high volumes of submissions consistently received and a relatively diverse range of submission makers	Moderate to strong: regular reference to and praise for the work of the LCA Committees	Moderate some explicit public discussion; however not all positive	Moderate: regular references to the committee in Hansard, mainly praise but some criticism
PJCIS	Strong: Particularly among major patties. Minor parties and independents more sceptical	Strong: Particularly·by those working most closely on counter-terrorism and nationa1 security related legislation	Strong: staff subject to security clearance and include e clinical experts from law enforcement and intelligence agencies	Moderate: high-quality submissions consistently received but less diversity	Strong: regular references by key oversight and review bodies	Moderate: Some explicit public discussion, mostly positive.	Strong: regular positive references in Hansard, with some criticism from minor parties and independents
PJCHR	Mixed views: can be seen as legitimate, but may also be seen as largely irrelevant	Moderate: scrutiny criteria yet to become entrenched; however, effort applied to preparing SoCs and responding to PJCHR's requests	Moderate: high quality secretariat staff, but not all share same vision for role of PJCHR	Weak to moderate: not seen as forum for advancing concerns re counter-terrorism laws, but some reference to the work of the PJCHR in submissions to other committees	Weak to moderate: some explicit references to the work of the PJCHR in reports	Weak rare to find examples of media discussion of the work of the PJCHR	Weak rare to find references to the PJCHR in Hansard, with some minor party exceptions

made to implement committee recommendations) or behind-the-scenes influence (such as public servants developing legislation in line with the standards set by scrutiny committees). As discussed further below, both of these attributes – deliberative and authoritative – can generate legitimacy for a particular committee, and sometimes pull against each other to reduce or dilute the respect or political authority a committee demands. Of central interest to this book is how these tensions play out when committees work together as a system, and what changes could be made to minimise the tension between these attributes, and improve the rights-enhancing impact of the committee system on federal laws. This discussion, which takes place in Part III, is informed by the views of key participants on the legitimacy attributed to particular committees set out in Table 4.6 and considered further below.

4.2.3.1 SSCSB

Of all the committees studied, the SSCSB appears to generate the most legitimacy (or command the most political authority) among the key participants interviewed, due to its well accepted 'technical scrutiny' character, and the fact that its scrutiny criteria resonates strongly with those involved in the development of legislation. This is also evident from the extent to which the SSCSB's scrutiny criteria are closely reflected in formal guidance materials prepared by government departments (explored further in Chap. 7). Interviews with parliamentarians suggest that other parliamentary committees also attribute strong value and legitimacy to the SSCSB and its reports. For example, in an interview with the author in 2016 Patricia Crossin said that when she was Chair of the LCA Legislation Committee she would:

> always cross-reference the work of the SSCSB, as a first step when getting across the issues. We would draw upon the work of the SSCSB and the other committees whenever we could. The secretariat staff would always be right across the SSCSB report (via telephone 10 August 20126).

These comments were supported by secretariat staff of other committees, such as Secretary of the LCA Committees Committee Sophie Dunstone, who explained that there are now formal processes in place to help ensure parliamentary committee secretariat staff are aware of the findings and reports of the SSCSB (Canberra 23 May 2016).

Submission makers also spoke of the value of the SSCSB reports, particularly in the context of their submissions to other parliamentary committees. For example, in an interview with the author in 2016 a legal submission maker said: 'I refer to them quite a lot. If they've raised concerns or made recommendations about something then we tend to note them in our submissions because that often bolsters the arguments we're making.' (Canberra 24 May 2016).

The SSCSB's Alert Digest system is held in particular regard by many key participants, and works as an "early warning" system, alerting other key participants to the need to look more carefully at the proposed law to determine its rights implications or other impacts (SSCSB 2012, at [4.26]).

The high regard with which the SSCSB is held by its key participants, and in particular, the infusion of the SSCSB's scrutiny criteria within the parliamentary and public service culture, gives it particular strengths when it comes to contributing to Australia's parliamentary model of rights protection, but also limits its capacity to influence the content of federal laws. In this way, the views on the SSCSB in Table 4.6 neatly illustrate the tension described above. For many participants interviewed (including officers at the Office of Parliamentary Counsel interviewed in Canberra on 24 May 2016), the SSCSB is highly respected because it sits outside of the political process, and provides an opportunity for parliamentarians to undertake a non-partisan analysis of a Bill. These same qualities make the SSCSB less diverse in membership and less deliberative in process. In other words, it is because the SSCSB distances itself from the political qualities of the Australian Parliament that it commands the most authority for many participants interviewed, but, as Chap. 5 documents, this same attribute also works to limit its capacity to have a direct legislative impact on the case study Acts.

4.2.3.2 PJCIS

This tension between the deliberative and authoritative roles of committees is also illustrated by the range of views expressed by key participants with respect to the PJCIS in Table 4.6. Many key participants attributed strong legitimacy (or political authority) to the PJCIS because of its strong legislative impact, major-party membership and bipartisan approach to developing recommendations (Department of Prime Minister and Cabinet 2017, pp. 118–19, 121–3). However, as discussed below, these same attributes also led others to question the committee's capacity to provide a meaningful deliberative forum for rights protection.

This tension is illustrated by the views of 'insiders' interviewed, such as Cameron Gifford from the Attorney General's Department who describe the PJCIS as being held in 'high regard' among the executive, in part due to the seniority of its membership and also due to the fact that it is 'a bipartisan committee that makes recommendations that then the government largely supports' (Canberra 23 May 2016). Former PJCIS member former Senator Robert Ray described PJCIS members as 'genuinely prepared to put the national interest first and work through the issues' (via telephone 23 November 2016). Mr Ray said that this 'was different to other committees, where I, like many others, acted in a very partisan way' and he described the PJCIS as 'looking for solutions' and developing compromises 'so as to ensure that the recommendation it wanted to make was able to get through' (Canberra 23 May 2016). The PJCIS's regular use of closed hearings to gather security-sensitive information from agencies (*Intelligence Services Act 2001* (Cth) sch 1, pt. 3), and the committee's practice of utilising secondees from departments or agencies to provide technical assistance to the PJCIS secretariat staff (PJCIS Annual Report 2014–2015), were also cited as examples of measures to foster positive working relationships with key agencies. For example, in an interview with the author in 2016, an Attorney-General's Department (AGD) official described the secondee arrangement with the PJCIS as follows:

> the Committee, through the secretariat, seeks [secondee] assistance and quite logically so, because in a very short space of time it's able to get across a very technical area of law. So the [Attorney-General's Department] might provide a staff member to assist [the committee] to get across the complexities of a Bill, and answer some simple inquiries so that the committee doesn't have to ask everything on notice (Canberra 20 May 2016).

The requirement for PJCIS secretariat staff to have security clearance, and their high level of experience and expertise, was also cited as enhancing the committee's legitimacy, particularly among the public service and the law enforcement and intelligence community. As AGD officer Cameron Gifford said:

> The people at the secretariat who support the PJCIS have been there for a number of years. … [They] also need a security clearance, so that means that [the secretariat staff] have been through that process and been in that position for some time. That's not necessarily the same for the human rights committee, and I understand that there's been a little bit more turnover in terms of the secretariat support for it (Canberra, 23 May 2016).

These 'insider' views can be contrasted with the more critical perspectives offered by other, 'outsider' participants, who express scepticism of the PJCIS's close and trusted working relationship with government and question its legitimacy as a rights-protecting forum. As a former senior member of an oversight body said in an interview with the author in 2016:

> I have some concerns that the PJCIS could be captured by the agencies, and I am really concerned by the use of secondees to the secretariat. I have seen examples of the same person who has worked on the legislation for the agencies then on the secretariat for the committee. This presents a big risk for the impartiality of the committee. I have also seen committee members who are so uncritical of the submissions of agencies. This pro-agency bias is concerning (via telephone 8 November 2016).

The capacity to hold private hearings, which is available to all parliamentary committees but is used frequently by the PJCIS, also gave rise to some questions about the PJCIS's legitimacy for some interviewees. For example, a former senior member of an oversight body said:

> A lot of … information gathering is done in closed sessions, and some of it has to be done in this way, but it really does detract from the purpose of parliamentary scrutiny, which is about public accountability. It doesn't allow others to question the evidence of the agencies. There is no one in those hearings able to contest the agencies' claims, except the IGIS. This is a big contrast to other parliamentary committees, where evidence of departments and agencies is robustly tested by a range of other experts and submission makers. So the role of the IGIS is really important to give the PJCIS a different view (via telephone 8 November 2016).

These different views illustrate the tension between the effectiveness of the PJCIS when it comes to legislative impact (which, as Chap. 5 discusses, appears to be generally rights-enhancing), and its capacity to generate respect among non-government submission makers as a meaningful deliberative forum for rights protection. In other words, the discussion above suggests that for some key participants the PJCIS is a high-impact, authoritative committee, while for others the committee risks being held captive by the executive and its agencies. While this tension is unlikely to be completely resolved, my research suggests that it can be minimised to improve the rights-protecting potential of the committee system. As discussed further in Part III, I argue for changes to the system of committees to preserve the attributes of the PJCIS that give rise to its strong legislative impact, whilst at the same time encouraging other committees to help fulfil the deliberative role sought by 'outsider' participants in the system.

4.2.3.3 LCA Committees

As discussed further in Part III, the LCA Committees provide the counterpoint to the SSCSB when it comes to the tension between the deliberative and authoritative roles of parliamentary committees. The information in Table 4.6 suggests that the LCA Committees are valued as deliberative forums, but do not always attract high levels of legitimacy, particularly among key participants who actively seek to influence the executive government. This is because the diverse membership of the LCA Committees (which include members from major and minor political parties as well as substitute and participating members), coupled with the broad range of issues they inquire into, can be seen by some as diluting their influence in terms of legislative impact. As the interview material reveals, there appears to be some hesitation among key participants when it comes to the capacity of the LCA Committees to influence legislation, alongside general praise for the committees' deliberative function. For example, Rowlings from Civil Liberties Australia told the author that 'the Senate Legal and Con Committee is the most important committee from our perspective' (Canberra, 24 May 2016). This is also reflected in the LCA Committees' strong performance when it comes to rates and diversity of participating in their public inquiries into counter-terrorism Bills, and by the discussion in Chap. 6 relating to public impact, which explains that the LCA Committees are often referenced and praised by post-enactment review bodies (see e.g. ALRC 2006; Security Legislation Review Committee 2006; Clarke 2008) and in parliamentary debates (see Table 6.3). However, not all interviewees consider the LCA Committees to be preferable forums over other committees to make submissions on counter-terrorism laws. For example, in an interview with the author in 2016 a legal submission maker said:

> In my experience when we've put up submissions to the Senate Legal and Constitutional Affairs committee, it's not a particularly effective committee in so far as a lot of recommendations made to it by a range of organisations they tend not to be accepted. Whereas the Parliamentary Committee on Intelligence and Security it has a reputation of trying to achieve bipartisan results. I think that forces members to really negotiate and sit down and discuss the issues of relevance and so that seems to be a committee that's more open to submissions being made from other organisations and possibly accepting some of those recommendations (Canberra 24 May 2016).

This comment demonstrates the important relationship between legitimacy (or political authority) and legislative impact, which can be particularly relevant for sophisticated submission makers looking to 'forum shop' to ensure that their submissions have the best chance of being reflected in committee recommendations that result in legislative change. As discussed further below, since the election of the 44th Parliament in 2013, the PJCIS inquiries into proposed counter-terrorism Bills have completely displaced inquiries into the same Bills by the LCA Committees, and the PJCIS has enjoyed a 100 per cent strike rate when it comes to translating its recommendations for legislative change into enacted amendments.

Other submission makers cited the LCA Committees' heavy and broad-ranging workload as a barrier to having a consistently strong impact on counter-terrorism laws. For example, some public servants interviewed explained that it was much harder to elucidate a clear set of principles, or to anticipate what concerns the LCA Committees may raise, due to the committees' broad mandate and politically diverse and changeable membership.

Despite these mixed views, members and former members described the LCA Committees as particularly valuable spaces for backbench parliamentarians to have an influence on government policy. For example, in an interview with the author Patricia Crossin said that the committee allows you to have:

> access to good quality submissions – particularly from the 25 or so 'usual suspects' in the legal area ... and you can help show up significant flaws in the legislation that the Minister's office or the department has overlooked, or due to sloppy drafting of [Explanatory Memoranda] etc. – these types of issues almost always resulted in legislative amendments to remedy the issue (via telephone 10 August 2016).

Ms Crossin also spoke of the opportunity to help shape policy or the content of legislation through her role as LCA Committee Chair, observing that, even in the context of counter-terrorism Bills that had strong bipartisan support, the committee was able to draw Ministerial attention to rights concerns and push for legislative change.

Taken together, these views illustrate the other side of the tension between deliberative and authoritative roles described with respect to the SSCSB. In other words, the LCA Committees are valued and respected among key participants due to their ability to attract a large number and diverse range of submission makers, and due to their politically diverse membership. However, for those looking to influence government legislation, these same features can present risks and dilute the political authority of the LCA Committees. As discussed in Part III, this has implications for the LCA Committees' future capacity to contribute to the parliamentary model of rights protection. I argue that the challenge for those seeking to improve the parliamentary model of rights protection at the federal level is to encourage the LCA Committees to continue to provide a meaningful deliberative forum for public inquiry into proposed counter-terrorism laws without duplicating the work of other, high-impact inquiry-based committees such as the PJCIS.

4.2.3.4 PJCHR

As Table 4.6 suggests, the PJCHR has struggled to attract strong levels of legitimacy from the majority of key participants (although as noted below, some commentators have expressed a different view). Chief among the reasons for this is the relative youth of the committee, the contested nature of the PJCHR's role and purpose, and a number of structural and procedural issues that lead to its reports not being seen as timely or useful.

(i) The Contested Role and Purpose of the PJCHR

Many people interviewed expressed concern about the confusion that surrounds the ‘proper’ role and purpose of the PJCHR, and considered this a threat to the committee’s legitimacy. The tension between the PJCHR as a ‘technical scrutiny committee’ and its broader inquiry functions is apparent among key participants and scholars (see e.g. Fletcher 2018, pp. 165–175). As an interviewee explained:

> [T]he Act says that the job of the committee is to assess legislation for its compatibility, against human rights standards, and to report to both Houses of Parliament. And that’s the end of the matter really if you want to take the Act as providing that answer to that question, so that is an educative role. It’s not a role to … prevent the passage of legislation that is incompatible with our human rights obligations. But … if you look at the circumstances in which it was introduced, there’s often a little bit of confusion. … [S]o when you look at what was said in the second reading speech, for example, then the purpose of the committee, … is to ensure that human rights considerations are taken into account, not just at this end point, but all the way through the process. And then there are elements of the design of the approach that support that (Canberra, 23 May 2016).

Other key participants were not prepared to accept that ‘technical scrutiny’ was the only legitimate purpose of the PJCHR, and envisaged a more proactive, deliberative role for the committee, where non-government organisations were actively invited to provide evidence to the committee on the rights compatibility of a Bill, in addition to information being provided by government. For example, in an interview in 2016 former PJCHR Legal Advisor Dr Aruna Sathanpally explained:

> If you think that human rights involve political and policy issues then you need evidence, not just technical advice on the law, to help reach conclusions. If the only evidence is from the department, this does not put the committee in the best position to reach conclusions in certain cases. [The PJCHR] could do the job much better if supported by civil society (via telephone 23 June 2016).

The first legal advisor to the PJCHR, Professor Andrew Byrnes, also envisaged proactive engagement by the committee with submission makers and advocacy groups. However, Byrnes also considered the PJCHR to offer particularly strong opportunities to bring human rights considerations to the attention of law and policy makers at the pre-introduction phase, and to ‘have a washback effect or to bring about cultural and bureaucratic change’ (Byrnes 2014; cf. Byrnes 2020). Campbell and Morris made similar observations in their 2015 review of the PJCHR, where they saw the committee as having a primary role in providing opportunities for both the parliament and the executive government to improve their awareness of the human rights issues and impacts arising from the development and enactment of proposed new laws (at p. 8).

For others, it was not just the contested role and purpose of the PJCHR, but also the contested nature of its human rights mandate, that posed a threat to the committee's legitimacy. As an interviewee explained:

> Human rights is … a subject matter that is very polarising. It has the appearance of being ethics laden, morality laden, so that's a difficult thing to pursue totally as a technical matter. … Often there's going to be room for legitimate differences in view, but it can be hard to keep those away from essential policy preferences. So you know, people choose an outcome based on their policy preference in that space, and then give differences in views. So I think it's the nature of human rights itself that [is] so polarising and so, the idea of the committee report saying this legislation is incompatible with the right to 'X' is something that is very difficult for committee members to come to terms with (Canberra, 23 May 2016).

As a number of former PJCHR members have reflected, not all members of the committee or the broader Parliament have a background in international law and some have a deep scepticism of human rights (Williams 2016). For some of these rights sceptics, the PJCHR can be seen as a potentially confrontational committee, pushing a particular international human rights law agenda that has at times been rejected by the government of the day. As former Chair of the PJCHR Senator Dean Smith said in an interview in 2016:

> I made a very, very conscious decision that I would uphold the scrutiny function of the committee even at the risk of pitting myself against the government. The government was quite willing to publicly surrender its human rights obligations to pursue laws and policies in the public interest and that is absolutely within their rights to do so. What is needed [from the committee's point of view] is a strong and rigorous defence of that choice with reference to the human rights standards and the particular policy. The merits of the policy should be debated in the [inquiry-based] committees. That is the place for compromises to be made (via telephone 22 September 2016).

The tension between the PJCHR's desire to achieve a consistent application of a prescribed international human rights scrutiny mandate (informed by international human rights law and sometimes comparative jurisprudence) and the need to develop a more responsive, contestable notion of human rights in the Australian context has been explored by Rice (2020) and Reynolds and Williams (2020) and is discussed further below. The extent to which the PJCHR has been able to successfully navigate this tension also generates a range of responses from key participants. As discussed below, for those who see the PJCHR as attempting to undertake the type of forensic legal analysis sometimes seen within United Nations human rights bodies, often the results are disappointing. Where the PJCHR attempts this approach, the proponent Ministers often obfuscate their duty to engage with the Committee and the Committee's report is seen as less accessible to other potential key participants in the system, including submission makers and media commentators For others who take a broader view of the PJCHR's role, the disappointment is connected to the Committee's failure to integrate the human rights concepts that form part of its scrutiny mandate into Australia's law making culture, or to make any meaningful impact on the content of the laws themselves. In other words, when the PJCHR's language is too broad or deferential to legislative choice, its rights protection impact can be perceived as diluted or weak. The combination of these responses has led to a general cynicism about the extent to which the PJCHR is able to 'make a real difference' when it comes to rights protection in Australia (see e.g. Fletcher 2018, 2020). As discussed further in Part III, it also provides important insights into the existing rights scrutiny culture at the federal level in Australia, and the role the PJCHR plays in the broader parliamentary committee system.

Some submission makers interviewed in 2016 praised the intention behind the establishment of the PJCHR, but were cynical of the extent to which it could have any impact on the shape or content of laws such as counter-terrorism laws. For example, Rowlings from Civil Liberties Australia said:

> The Parliamentary Committee on Human Rights has done as good a job as it can do. Basically, it's like in the old days of cricket they used to have a long stop behind the wicket keeper. That's what that committee is. It's a long stop. It's not in the main game, it's too late to be helping the action, etc. (Canberra, 24 May 2016).

For others, it is the way the PJCHR has approached its human rights analysis that poses a risk to its legitimacy. For example, former INSLM Bret Walker SC praised the work of the PJCHR, but suggested that a more proactive approach could be adopted to identifying and outlining the rights-protecting impact a proposed new counter-terrorism law may have, as well as its negative or rights-infringing consequences. For example, in an interview with the author in 2016 Bret Walker SC explained:

> I think the Human Rights Committee could perhaps more routinely ... start with the rights of what I might call the people who just want to be left alone, and get on with their lives in freedom and peace ... And if you do that, I think a lot of other things fall into place more naturally (Sydney, 30 May 2016).

As scholars such as Williams and Reynolds (2016), Reynolds and Williams (2020) and Fletcher (2018, pp. 165–174) have documented, the processes and practices of the PJCHR have changed over time, leading to differences in the 'look and feel' of the Committee's reports and responding to pressures to consolidate resources, and adding to the overall sense of uncertainly about the place the PJCHR holds within the broader scrutiny system. Fletcher describes the period between 2012 and 13 as the 'golden-era' of the PJCHR, where consensus-only scrutiny reports were issued, and the secretariat had access to a wider range of resources that enabled the PJCHR to contemplate utilising its inquiry functions (Fletcher 2018, pp. 169–174). However, for others, the impact of the PJCHR will only truly be felt once it has been in operation for a longer period of time. For example, former Chair of the PJCHR Senator Smith said:

> The PJCHR needs time to entrench its principles particularly with respect to the House members. This requires more work for the House members to gain an understanding of the scrutiny mechanisms generally and then to understand the particularly human rights standards. It will take time to entrench that scrutiny function.[1]

[1] Interview with Dean Smith, Liberal Senator for Western Australia, former Chair of the Parliamentary Joint Committee on Human Rights (telephone, 22 September 2016).

This view was shared by an interviewee who explained:

> [The] Regulations and Ordinances Committee and Scrutiny of Bills Committee are part of the furniture …. As new members come in quite often they get put on scrutiny committees early in the piece. A big part of our role is to essentially encourage them to approach it as a technical inquiry, as a parliamentarian, rather than as a party member. Both of the scrutiny committees had existential issues when they were first established, and that was really to be expected. It took time to get that status as being part of the furniture. Now, the Human Rights Committee is a new committee and it doesn't have that status yet (Canberra, 23 May 2016).

Another interviewee, Senator Don Farrell said:

> My instinctive feel would be simply a question of time [before PJCHR scrutiny criteria are more entrenched in parliamentary culture]. The Scrutiny of Bills Committee has much more entrenched processes whereas the Human Rights Committee is new and in time they'll develop their own procedures' (Adelaide, 15 November 2016).

(ii) Structural and Procedural Risks to PJCHR's Legitimacy

Structural and procedural features, such as staffing, the handling of dissent (Rice 2020) and timing of tabling of reports (Rajanayagam 2020), have also been identified as risks to the PJCHR's political authority and capacity to influence government legislation. For example, while the first years of the PJCHR's operation were characterised by consensus-style reporting (Byrnes 2014), in later years dissenting reports were included in the rights analysis of the PJCHR. The deteriorating consensus style of reporting undertaken by the PJCHR has been cited by Williams and Burton (2015, p. 257) and Fletcher (2018, p. 175) as contributing to the PJCHR's lack of overall impact on the content and debate of proposed new laws (at p. 257). Reflecting on the emerging dissent within the PJCHR, former Australian Greens Senator Penny Wright told the author that:

> I think it was a really laudable aim to have a consensus report because, in a sense, this isn't about whether members of the committee think what is being proposed is a good idea or a bad idea. The question of what is required for compliance with human rights law is actually pretty settled in most cases. So it was often very clear. It wasn't a maybe; it was a yes or a no. But, in my later time on the committee, we were rarely able to get the committee to acknowledge that.
>
> I feel that, in some ways, the dissent within the committee came about because some latter members of the committee had not worked hard enough to educate themselves about the nature of human rights law.
>
> So, the concern I have is that, where the report routinely contains majority and minority views, it undermines the effectiveness of the report and people can then pick and choose what side they are on, depending on their policy objectives. The outcome is more politicised than principled. It becomes almost irrelevant what the actual human rights law is. That is my main concern. (Adelaide 11 August 2016)

However, others considered dissent to be part of the PJCHR's natural development, having regard to the accepted practice of dissenting reports being regularly issued by other committees in the system, such as the LCA Committees. For example, in an interview with the author in 2016 former PJCHR Legal Professor Simon Rice expressed the view that a dissenting view is of no concern provided it is well reasoned, with reference to the human rights standards that form part of the PJCHR's mandate. However, in his time on the committee Professor Rice said he:

> didn't see a single dissent in the reports which was reasoned. The dissents are nakedly unsubstantiated. They simply, after a long, long explanation about how one part of the committee gets to a conclusion, the other part of the committee says, 'and we say this'. (Sydney 24 May 2016).

(iii) Clarifying the Role and Rights Contribution of the PJCHR

Taken together, these comments highlight the need to clarify whether the legislative review role[2] of PJCHR should be one of 'technical scrutiny' or a more deliberative inquiry function (PJCHR 2017). My research suggests that this is important not just for structural and procedural matters, such as the timing and format of the PJCHR's reports, but also for the PJCHR's overall legitimacy and political authority.

As explored further in Part III, if these roles remain blurred or confused, the PJCHR runs the risk of being rendered ineffectual and uninfluential. Unlike the other committees discussed above, when it comes to Bills scrutiny, the PJCHR will be neither deliberative nor authoritative, and thus struggle to attract legitimacy among key participants. If, on the other hand, the role of the PJCHR is clear and its strengths and weaknesses complemented by other committees in the system, it has strong potential to contribute in a meaningful way to Australia's parliamentary model of rights protection. As discussed further below, I argue that the PJCHR's role should be clarified in favour of its technical scrutiny function, at least with respect to its legislative review function. As explored in detail in Part III, such a 'technical scrutiny' would building upon the existing features of the committee that are most well respected by key participants in the system, and would encourage the PJCHR to more closely emulate the work practices of the SSCSB when it comes to the timeliness and format of its Bills scrutiny reports. While this approach may be disappointing to some rights advocates, particularly those who had hoped the Australian PJCHR would one day more closely resemble its UK counterpart, my research strongly warns against making more radical structural change to a

[2] My focus on is the PJCHR's Bills scrutiny role however I acknowledge that, like the SSCSB, the PJCHR also has the power to hold public inquiries. As noted in Chap. 3, this inquiry-based function has been used relatively infrequently but in 2017 the PJCHR held a public inquiry into pt. IIA of the *Racial Discrimination Act 1975* (Cth) that attracted large numbers of submissions and included multiple public hearings. As discussed further in Part III, I argue that investing in the PJCHR's technical scrutiny role is the best way to maximise its rights-protecting capacity when working together with other committees in the system.

committee that is already at risk of being sidelined or ignored. Instead, my recommendations reflect a more cautious, consolidating approach that recognises that some of the most significant rights-enhancing impacts of the committee system occur 'behind the scenes' and depend upon members of the executive being able to accurately predict and proactively respond to the future parliamentary scrutiny of the laws they initiate.

As discussed further in Part III, this is not to suggest that the PJCHR should be stripped of its powers to conduct public inquiries into Bills or other human rights issues. Further research may still be required to evaluate the potential impact of such inquiries on rights protection, particularly in the context of economic, social and cultural rights, where some commentators and participants have suggested the PJCHR is making a noticeable legislative or public impact (Byrnes 2020; Goldblatt 2017).[3] Nor am I arguing against what Rice (2020) has described as the need to shift to a more 'contestable' notion of human rights standards that encourages active participation from a broader range of voices when it comes to determining the precise contours of the PJCHR's scrutiny mandate. Rather, my findings suggest that clarifying that the *primary* role of the PJCHR is a *scrutiny role* (rather than an inquiry role or investigation of the policy merits of a proposed Bill) may improve its legitimacy among the full range of key participants, and thus improve its potential impact on the content and consideration of federal laws.

4.3 Summary of Findings on Legitimacy

This chapter has begun to illustrate the important tension between the deliberative and authoritative roles of parliamentary committees that runs through each of the committees studied in my research. It demonstrates that high rates of participation from a diverse range of parliamentarians and submission makers can generate respect among key participants, but may also come at the risk of political authority. It also demonstrates that the relationship between a particular committee and the executive can both generate legitimacy (through legislative influence) and give rise to scepticism (through concerns about lack of independence and transparency), depending on the perspective of key participants in the system. This chapter also demonstrates that committees with more tightly controlled membership, entrenched scrutiny criteria and less public engagement can be highly influential for those

[3] For example, Goldblatt has considered the role and impact of the PJCHR in the context of the Committee's inquiry into the *Social Security Legislation Amendment (Fair Incentives to Work) Bill 2012*. Goldblatt observed that the PJCHR provided an "opportunity [for community groups] to frame their concerns with proposed law reforms in human rights terms" and that the PJCHR's exchanges with the Minister on the human rights concerns raised by submission makers "arguably demonstrate[s], at the very least, a growing human rights literacy in parliament in relation to social security" (Goldblatt 2017, p. 183). However, Goldblatt also acknowledged the limits of this impact, noting that "essentially, the workings of the PJCHR seem to take the lack of enforceable rights no further" (Goldblatt 2017, p. 194).

working behind the scenes on the development of legislation. This tension is explored further in Chap. 5, which considers the legislative impact each of the four committees had on the case study Acts. It also sets the scene for the discussion in Part III, where I argue that this tension can be minimised when parliamentary committees work together as a system, and the individual strengths and weaknesses of a particular committee can be complemented by other committees in the system.

References

Bills

House of Representatives. (2015). *Australian Citizenship Amendment (Allegiance to Australia) Bill 2015* (Cth). Canberra: Parliament of Australia.

House of Representatives. Counter-Terrorism Legislation Amendment (Foreign Fighters) Bill 2014 (Cth). Canberra: Parliament of Australia.

Legislation

Intelligence Services Act 2001 (Cth).

Parliamentary Committee Reports

Parliamentary Joint Committee on Human Rights. (2015). *Annual report 2014–15*. Canberra: Parliament of Australia. https://www.aph.gov.au/Parliamentary_Business/Committees/Joint/Human_Rights/Scrutiny_reports/Annual_Reports/Annual_Report_2014-15

Parliamentary Joint Committee on Human Rights. (2017). *Freedom of speech in Australia: Inquiry into Part IIA of the* Racial Discrimination Act 1975 *(Cth) and related procedures under the Australian Human Rights Commission Act 1986 (Cth)*. Canberra: Parliament of Australia. https://www.aph.gov.au/Parliamentary_Business/Committees/Joint/Human_Rights_inquiries/FreedomspeechAustralia/Report

Parliamentary Joint Committee on Intelligence and Security. (2014). *Advisory report on the Counter-Terrorism Legislation Amendment (Foreign Fighters) Bill 2014*. Canberra: Parliament of Australia. http://www.aph.gov.au/~/media/02%20Parliamentary%20Business/24%20Committees/244%20Joint%20Committees/PJCIS/Foreign%20Fighters%20Bill/CommitteeReport_17Oct2014.pdf

Parliamentary Joint Committee on Intelligence and Security. (2015). *Advisory report on the provisions of the Australian Citizenship Amendment (Allegiance to Australia) Bill 2015*. Canberra: Parliament of Australia. http://www.aph.gov.au/~/media/02%20Parliamentary%20Business/24%20Committees/244%20Joint%20Committees/PJCIS/Citizenship/FullReport.pdf?la=en

Senate. (2015). *Work of the Senate*. Canberra: Parliament of Australia. https://www.aph.gov.au/Parliamentary_Business/Chamber_documents/Senate_chamber_documents/Journals_of_the_Senate/2015. Accessed 13 Jan 2020.

Senate Standing Committee for Scrutiny of Bills. (2012). *Inquiry into the future direction and role of the scrutiny of bills committee*. Canberra: Parliament of Australia. https://www.aph.

gov.au/Parliamentary_Business/Committees/Senate/Scrutiny_of_Bills/Completed_inquiries/futuredirection2011/index

Senate Standing Committee for Scrutiny of Bills, Submission to ALRC, *Traditional rights and freedoms – Encroachments by commonwealth laws* (2014).

Senate Standing Committee on Legal and Constitutional Affairs Legislation Committee. (2002a). *Australian Security Intelligence Organisation Legislation Amendment (Terrorism) Bill 2002 and related matters*. Canberra: Parliament of Australia. https://www.aph.gov.au/parliamentary_business/committees/senate/legal_and_constitutional_affairs/completed_inquiries/2002-04/asio_2/report/contents

Senate Standing Committee on Legal and Constitutional Affairs Legislation Committee. (2002b). *Inquiry into the Security Legislation Amendment (Terrorism) Bill 2002 [No. 2] and related bills*. Canberra: Parliament of Australia. https://www.aph.gov.au/Parliamentary_Business/Committees/Senate/Legal_and_Constitutional_Affairs/Completed_inquiries/2002-04/terrorism/index

Senate Standing Committee on Legal and Constitutional Affairs References Committee. (2002). *Inquiry into Australian Security Intelligence Organisation Legislation Amendment (Terrorism) Bill 2002 and related matters*. Canberra: Parliament of Australia. http://www.aph.gov.au/~/media/wopapub/senate/committee/legcon_ctte/completed_inquiries/2004_07/witness_protection/report/report_pdf.ashx

Books/Articles/Reports/Speeches

Australian Law Reform Commission. (2006). *Fighting words: A review of sedition laws in Australia*. ALRC Report No. 104. Retrieved from https://www.alrc.gov.au/publication/fighting-words-a-review-of-sedition-laws-in-australia-alrc-report-104/. Accessed 7 Jan 2020.

Byrnes, A. (2014). *Human rights under the microscope: Reflections on parliamentary scrutiny*. Speech delivered at Law Society of South Australia Continuing Professional Development Program, Adelaide, 11 December 2014. http://www.ahrcentre.org/sites/ahrcentre.org/files/mdocs/Byrnes%20%2D%2D%20%20PJCHR%20-%20handout%20for%20Adelaide%20talk%20December%202014%20revised.pdf

Byrnes, A. (2020). Economic and social rights in the Australian parliamentary human rights scrutiny process. In J. Debeljak & L. Grenfell (Eds.), *Law-making and human rights* (pp. 135–171). Sydney: Thompson Reuters.

Campbell, T., & Morris, S. (2015). Human rights for democracies: A provisional assessment of the Australian Human Rights (Parliamentary Scrutiny) Act 2011. *University of Queensland Law Journal, 34*(1), 7–27.

Clarke, M. J. (2008). *Report of the inquiry into the case of Dr Mohamed Haneef*. Canberra: Government of Australia. Retrieved from https://trove.nla.gov.au/work/35146207. Accessed 7 Jan 2020.

Crossin, P. (2010). *The future of Senate committees: Challenges and opportunities*. Speech delivered at the Senate Committees and Government Accountability Forum, Canberra, December 2010. http://www.aph.gov.au/binaries/senate/pubs/pops/pop54/c11.pdf.

Dalla-Pozza, D. (2007). The conscience of democracy? The role of Australian parliamentary committees in enacting counter-terrorism laws (Working Paper, Australasian study of parliament group conference, 2007). http://www.aspg.org.au/conferences/adelaide2007/Dalla-pozzo.pdf

Dalla-Pozza, D. (2016). Refining the Australian counter-terrorism legislative framework: How deliberative has parliament been? *Public Law Review, 27*(4), 271.

Department of Prime Minister and Cabinet. (2017). *Independent intelligence review*. Canberra: Government of Australia. Retrieved from https://pmc.gov.au/national-security/2017-independent-intelligence-review. Accessed 7 Jan 2020.

Fletcher, A. (2018). *Australia's human rights scrutiny regime*. Melbourne: Melbourne University Press.

Fletcher, A. (2020). Human rights scrutiny in the federal parliament: smokescreen or democratic solution? In J. Debeljak & L. Grenfell (Eds.), *Law making and human rights: executive and parliamentary scrutiny across australian jurisdictions* (pp. 31–66). Sydney: Thompson Reuters.

Goldblatt, G. (2017). Social (in)security and inequality in Australia: The limited role of human rights in the policy debate. In A. Durbach & B. Edgeworth (Eds.), *Law and poverty in Australia: 40 years after the Poverty Commission* (pp. 183–198). Sydney: Federation Press.

Levy, R., & Orr, G. (2016). *The law of deliberative democracy*. London: Routledge.

Moulds, S. P. (2018). *The rights protecting role of parliamentary committees: The case of Australia's counter-terrorism laws* (Doctoral thesis). University of Adelaide, Adelaide, SA, Australia. https://digital.library.adelaide.edu.au/dspace/handle/2440/115212

Paxman, K. (1998). *Referral of bills to Senate committees: An evaluation*. Parl Paper No. 31 (1998) 76. Parliament of Australia. Retrieved from https://www.aph.gov.au/-/media/05_About_Parliament/52_Sen/524_Research_and_education/Other_Publications/PSP09_grant.pdf?la=en&hash=3E49498576ED0CCE822777919E1C1EE27AA17407. Accessed 6 Jan 2020.

Rajanayagam, S. (2020). Urgent law-making and the Human Rights (Parliamentary Scrutiny) Act. In J. Debeljak & L. Grenfell (Eds.), *Law-making and human rights* (pp. 647–672). Sydney: Thompson Reuters.

Reynolds, D., & Williams, G. (2020). Evaluating the impact of Australia's federal human rights scrutiny regime. In J. Debeljak & L. Grenfell (Eds.), *Law-making and human rights* (pp. 67–96). Sydney: Thompson Reuters.

Rice, S. (2020). Allowing for dissent: Opening up human rights dialogue in the Australian parliament. In J. Debeljak & L. Grenfell (Eds.), *Law-making and human rights* (pp. 99–134). Sydney: Thompson Reuters.

Security Legislation Review Committee. (2006). *Report of the Security Legislation Review Committee*. Canberra: Australian Government. Retrieved from https://www.ag.gov.au/NationalSecurity/Counterterrorismlaw/Documents/Report%20of%20the%20Security%20Legislation%20Review%20Committee.pdf. Accessed 7 Jan 2020.

Uhr, J. (1998a). The constitutional convention and deliberative democracy. *University of New South Wales Law Journal, 21,* 875–881. https://search.informit.com.au/documentSummary;dn=110083001406611;res=IELHSS

Uhr, J. (1998b). *Deliberative democracy in Australia: The changing place of parliament*. Cambridge: Cambridge University Press.

Uhr, J. (2001). Parliament and public deliberation: Evaluating the performance of parliament. *University of New South Wales Law Journal, 24,* 708–723. http://www.unswlawjournal.unsw.edu.au/wp-content/uploads/2017/09/24-3-17.pdf

Williams, G. (2016). *Scrutiny of primary legislation principles and challenges: Where are we now and where are we headed?* Speech delivered at the Australia-New Zealand Scrutiny of Legislation Conference, Parliament House, Perth, 12 July 2016. http://www.parliament.wa.gov.au/WebCMS/WebCMS.nsf/resources/file-anzslc-provisional-conference-program/$file/ANZSLC%20Provisional%20Conference%20Program%20V5.pdf

Williams, G., & Burton, L. (2015). Australia's Parliamentary Scrutiny Act: An exclusive parliamentary model of rights protection. In M. Hunt, H. J. Hooper, & P. Yowell (Eds.), *Parliaments and human rights: Redressing the democratic deficit* (pp. 258–279). Oxford: Hart Publishing.

Williams, G., & Reynolds, D. (2016). The operation and impact of Australia's parliamentary scrutiny regime for human rights. *Monash University Law Review, 41*(2), 469–508.

Chapter 5
Legislative Impact

Abstract Chapter 5 sets out evidence of the legislative impact the parliamentary committees had on the case study Acts. As discussed in Chap. 2, evidence of legislative impact – such as whether a successful legislative amendment has been made in response to a specific committee recommendation – can provide an objective source of evidence that points to a committee's overall influence. The nature of the legislative amendment can also provide a strong source of evidence about the committee's contribution to Australia's parliamentary model of rights protection, particularly if it is rights-enhancing (for example by limiting the scope of the rights impact of provision, or subjecting the powers within the provision to safeguards or oversight) or rights-remedying (such as removing the provision completely or removing any rights-abrogating features).

5.1 Why Look for Legislative Impact?

Evidence of the legislative impact of the four parliamentary committees on the case study Acts is a powerful indicator of their overall influence. In addition, as noted in Chap. 4, there is a reciprocal relationship between a committee's legislative impact and its legitimacy, particularly when the Bill in question relates to a key policy platform for the government. Often the political authority attributed to a committee is based on its capacity to influence legislative outcomes; however, if the relationship between the committee and the executive is seen as too close, the committee may lose respect from key participants, particularly non-government submission makers and non-government parliamentarians. Other committees, such as the SSCSB, achieve legislative impact through less direct means, generating strong levels of legitimacy among those most active at the pre-introduction stage, but less visible during parliamentary debates.

As noted in Chap. 1, I have been generally surprised by the extent to which the committees studied were able to generate legislative change to the case study Acts (documented in Chap. 5 below and Moulds 2018). This is because my findings challenge the orthodox view that governments generally resist making changes to

S. Moulds, *Committees of Influence*, https://doi.org/10.1007/978-981-15-4350-0_5

legislation that they have already publicly committed to and introduced into Parliament. As Hiebert (2011) has observed in the UK context, once a government minister has introduced a proposed law, the government is unlikely to entertain any substantial amendments or welcome deliberation or scrutiny of its contents. Hiebert (2011) argues that it is also unlikely to change its mind about pursuing a particular legislative agenda on the basis of an unfavourable report by a parliamentary committee (at p. 63). As Hiebert explains, once the executive government has made a public commitment to a course of action in the form of introducing a Bill, it will be reluctant to accept amendments proposed in Parliament. To do so could risk reagitating discussions already concluded in the party room, reopening internal divisions or signalling government weakness (Hiebert 2015 at p. 52; Hiebert 2011 at pp. 60–1). Such weaknesses in the parliamentary model of rights protection have been well canvassed by Hiebert (2015 at p. 41) and other scholars (Kelly 2011 at p. 272; Feldman 2015 at p. 108; Monk 2001 at p. 7). These perceived weaknesses are emphasised by the fact that members of parliamentary committees are political actors, with political incentives to support or oppose the legislative proposals they are tasked with reviewing, and often with limited independent resources to exert influence over policy-making carried out by the executive. This suggests that parliamentary committees, and in particular government-dominated committees, will be seriously limited when it comes to offering meaningful rights protection, especially when scrutinising laws that affect electorally unpopular groups, such as criminals or terrorists.

This next Chapter of the Book seeks to unpack this assumption and test whether the parliamentary model of rights-protection, and in particular the parliamentary committee system, has had any positive impact on the development and content counter-terrorism laws in Australia.

However, my research also heeds the warnings of those scholars referred to in Chap. 2 when it comes to relying on evidence of legislative impact as an indicator of a committee's overall influence or role in the parliamentary system. I acknowledge, for example, the need for caution when identifying the causal relationship between the work of the committee and the legislative change, and when understanding the significance of the legislative change made. A myriad of factors, including personal or political ambitions, could influence the decision of an individual parliamentarian to introduce or support a legislative amendment. This may be particularly pronounced in the context of an issue such as counter-terrorism, which provokes strong views and attracts media coverage, providing a platform for political ambitions of all types to play out (cf Evans and Evans 2006a, b, c; Benton and Russell 2013; Russell and Benton 2009; Willams and Reynolds 2016) Then there are factors associated with the make-up of the Senate, and the need for the government to secure support for the passage of its legislative agenda from independents, minor parties or the opposition (Lindell 2005). I do not ignore these issues, but seek to factor them in by adopting the following approach:

- explicitly acknowledging the institutional and political context in which a particular case study Bill was introduced, scrutinised, amended and passed;
- looking for clear documentary evidence that the legislative change can be directly attributed to the work of a parliamentary committee, for example by reference to

a committee's recommendation in the supplementary Explanatory Memorandum accompanying the proposed legislative amendments;
- distinguishing between substantive and inconsequential or minor legislative amendments; and
- testing these findings against the views of a range of key participants in the committee system and the other forms of impact a parliamentary committee can have on the law-making process, described in my research as 'public' and 'hidden' forms of impact.

This allows legislative impact to remain a powerful indicator of the overall influence of the committees studied on the content of the case study Acts, without ignoring the equally powerful evidence set out in Chaps. 4, 6 and 7.

To begin the analysis of legislative impact, Table 5.1 set outs the 'strike rate' of the inquiry-based committees (LCA Committees and PJCIS) in terms of translating

Table 5.1 Overview of Legislative Impact

Bill	Amendments directly attributable to committee recommendations	Committee strike rate
Counter-Terrorism (Temporary Exclusion Orders) Bill 2019	11 recommendations, 6 reflected in legislative amendments, 5 partially accepted resulted in further legislative amendments – One of these (rec 7) many advocates consider has not been sufficiently implemented	PJCIS 80%
Telecommunication and Other Legislation Amendment (Assistance and Access) Bill 2018 *NB Enacted Bill referred immediately to PJCIS for further inquiry*	17 PJCIS recommendations, 16 fully or partially accepted, 15 reflected in legislative amendments (1 non-legislative).	PJCIS 94%
Criminal Code Amendment (High Risk Terrorist Offenders) Bill 2016	23 PJCIS recommendations, all reflected in legislative amendments	PJCIS 100%
Australian Citizenship Amendment (Allegiance to Australia) Bill 2015	27 PJCIS recommendations, 25 reflected in legislative amendments (2 changes to the Explanatory Memorandum (EM))	PJCIS 100%
Counter-Terrorism Legislation Amendment (Foreign Fighters) Bill 2014	37 PJCIS recommendations reflected in legislative amendments	PJCIS 100%
Counter-Terrorism Legislation Amendment Bill (No 1) 2014	16 PJCIS recommendations reflected in legislative amendments	PJCIS 100%
Telecommunications (Interception and Access) Amendment (Data Retention) Bill 2015	39 PJCIS recommendations reflected in legislative amendments.	PJCIS 100%
National Security Legislation Amendment Bill 2010	4 LCA Committee recommendations, 3 non-legislative (2 not adopted), 1 legislative (and not adopted).	LCA Committees 0%

(continued)

Table 5.1 (continued)

Bill	Amendments directly attributable to committee recommendations	Committee strike rate
Independent National Security Legislation Monitor Bill 2010	12 Senate Finance and Public Administration Committee (SFPAC) recommendations, 8 reflected in legislative amendments (3 non-legislative).	SFPAC 100%
Anti-Terrorism Bill (No 2) 2005	51 LCA Committee recommendations, 24 were fully implemented by amendments, 13 partially implemented and 5 non-legislative. 8 rejected	LCA Committees 85%
National Security Information (Criminal Proceedings) Bill 2004 *NB Initial Bill lapsed, new Bill introduced*	13 LCA Committee recommendations made. 3 accepted and reflected in substantive changes to the re-introduced Bill, 1 partially implemented and 9 not adopted.	LCA Committees 30%
Anti-terrorism Bill 2004	8 LCA Committee recommendations, 5 reflected in amendments, 1 further amendment supported by Senate but not passed by House.	LCA Committees 65%
ASIO Legislation Amendment (Terrorism) Bill 2003	11 amendments made reflecting the previous LCA Committee and PJC on ASIO, DSD and ASIS recommendations with respect to the 2002 Bill.	LCA Committees and PJ ASIO 100%
Australian Security Intelligence Organisation Legislation Amendment (Terrorism) Bill 2002	15 PJC on ASIO, DSD and ASIS recommendations, 12 reflected in amendments, 2 partially reflected and 1 not adopted. 27 LCA Committee recommendations, 13 reflected in amendments, 8 rejected, 5 rejected but alternative model proposed, 1 non-legislative	PJC ASIO 75% LCA Committees 65%
Security Legislation Amendment (Terrorism) Bill 2002 (No 2) and Other Bills	7 LCA Committee recommendations, 4 reflected in amendments, 3 rejected.	LCA Committees 60%

their recommendations into successful legislative amendments. These committees are the focus of this table as their recommendations are frequently articulated in terms of specific amendments to a Bill, which allows a crude but important calculation of how many recommendations are translated into legislative amendments. The 'technical' scrutiny committees (SSCSB and the PJCHR) are not included in Table 5.1 as their recommendations rarely refer explicitly to legislative amendments, and are instead more commonly couched in terms of matters for the Senate or the Parliament to consider. However, the work of the SSCSB and the PJCHR is included in the following analysis of the overall scrutiny experience for each case study Bill. This allows findings to be made about the legislative impact of each committee on a case study Bill, and demonstrates the overall legislative impact of multi-committee scrutiny.

5.2 Evidence of Legislative Impact

Table 5.1 above provides a broad-brush snapshot of the success rates of the inquiry-based committees in turning their recommendations into legislative outcomes and conveys the strikingly high success rate of the PJCIS, particularly since 2014. It also demonstrates a consistently high success rate (60 per cent or over in almost all cases) experienced by the LCA Committees. Although further research is required to confirm whether this experience is typical of all Bills subject to committee review, these results suggest that both the PJCIS and the LCA Committees are having a relatively strong legislative influence on the case study Acts. This tentative conclusion is considered further below.

To assist in the presentation of material in this chapter, in the next section I analyse three 'phases' of committee scrutiny of the case study Acts. These three phases help navigate the five tranches of counter-terrorism law making discussed in Chap. 3:

- Phase 1 was a period where parliamentary committees' scrutiny of proposed counter-terrorism Bills took place at a fast and furious pace, in a climate where it was still politically viable (at least from the perspective of some members of the opposition and minor parties) to challenge the necessity of certain proposed counter-terrorism measures. During this phase, both the LCA Committees and the PJC on ASIO, DSD and ASIS (which later became the PJCIS) had a modest to moderately strong legislative impact. This phase corresponds to the first three 'tranches' of counter-terrorism law making set out in Chap. 3, all of which occurred under the Howard Government between 2001 and 2007.
- Phase 2 was a period of relatively robust post-enactment review of the case study Acts (both by parliamentary committees and independent bodies) following the election of the Rudd Government, and continued through the Gillard Government. During this phase, the legislative impact of committee scrutiny on proposed new counter-terrorism measures depended heavily on the relationship between the committees' recommendations and the findings of other independent review bodies with respect to pre-existing counter-terrorism laws. This phase corresponds with the 'Time for Review' period and 'tranche 4' of counter-terrorism law making discussed in Chap. 3 and spans the period 2007–2013.
- Phase 3 saw the emergence of the PJCIS as a committee with strong legislative impact, which coincided with the establishment of the PJCHR, and the effective 'sidelining' of the LCA Committees as a forum for reviewing counter-terrorism legislation. Phase 3 coincides with tranche 5 of counter-terrorism law making described in Chap. 3 and covers the period from the election of the Abbott Government, the change of Government leadership to Malcolm Turnbull and then Scott Morrison, until the end of 2018.

In the background of each of these phases is the scrutiny work being undertaken by SSCSB and (since 2012) the PJCHR. As will be discussed below, both of these committees had a discernible legislative impact, but it was less direct than either the PJCIS or the LCA Committees at the height of their respective influence.

The following analysis of these three phases allows for a set of preliminary findings to be made about the overall legislative impact of the parliamentary committee system on the case study Acts. These preliminary findings can then be considered alongside the other components of the assessment framework applied in my research, the public and hidden impacts.

5.3 Three 'Phases' of Parliamentary Scrutiny of the Case Study Bills

5.3.1 Phase 1: Fast and Furious Scrutiny

Phase 1 covers the period from 2001 until 2007, when the Howard Government was in power. Six of the case study Acts were introduced and passed during this period:

- SLAT Acts (CSA 1);
- ASIO Bill 2002 (CSA 2);
- ASIO Act 2003 (CSA 3);
- *Anti-Terrorism Act 2004* (Cth) (CSA 4);
- *National Security Information (Criminal Proceedings) Act 2004* (Cth) (CSA 5); and
- Control Orders Act (CSA 6).

I describe this phase as 'fast and furious scrutiny' due to: (a) the speed at which these new provisions were introduced and scrutinised by parliamentary committees, and (b) the political climate that existed at the time, wherein it was still politically viable for non-government parliamentarians and some government backbenchers to directly question the need for the introduction of new counter-terrorism laws, having regard to existing criminal laws, and law enforcement and intelligence powers.

In this context, the LCA Committees, with their broad membership and strong capacity to conduct wide-ranging and popular public inquiries, were influential when it came to turning recommendations into legislative change. This can be seen with respect to the SLAT Acts, the *Anti-Terrorism Act 2004* (Cth) and the Control Orders Act, but also the ASIO Bill 2002 and ASIO Act 2003 which received an unprecedented level of parliamentary scrutiny and underwent significant change from introduction to enactment. The more specialist PJC on ASIO, DSD and ASIS also featured prominently in the scrutiny of the ASIO Bill 2002. The SSCSB's constant role in reviewing the laws introduced in this phase is less visible; however, as the examples below demonstrate, the issues raised by the SSCSB regularly featured strongly in the reports and recommendations of other parliamentary committees and were sometimes reflected in successful amendments to the Bill.

5.3.1.1 The SLAT Acts (CSA 1)

As noted in Chap. 3, the SLAT Bills[1] marked the beginning of the Howard Government's legislative response to the 11 September 2001 terrorist attacks in the United States (Hancock 2002a, b pp. 25–7). After quickly passing through the House, the SLAT Bills were referred to the LCA Legislation Committee for inquiry and report.[2] Despite having only five weeks to conduct its inquiry, the LCA Legislation Committee received 431 submissions and held public hearings in Sydney, Melbourne and Canberra. A majority report was issued, supported by members from both major political parties, with additional comments and points of dissent provided by the Australian Democrats (LCA Legislation Committee SLAT Bills Report 2002). The report contained seven majority recommendations for amendments to the Bill, including that:

- a defence to the offence of treason be provided relating to the provision of humanitarian aid;
- the definition of 'terrorist act' be narrowed;
- absolute liability be removed as an element of the proposed terrorist act offences, and be replaced with requirement of recklessness;
- the proposed proscription of terrorist organisations regime be amended to ensure that it does 'does not vest a broad and effectively unreviewable discretion in a member of the executive' and provides for 'adequate judicial review of the grounds for declarations of proscription';
- the Attorney-General review the current law on access to stored communications of delayed messages services with a view to introducing a warrant regime;
- the proposed financing of terrorism offences be amended to include an element of intent; and
- changes be made to the proposed asset-freezing provisions (Recommendations 1–7).

Four of these recommendations were rights-enhancing in nature and were reflected in successful amendments to the Bills that were directly attributed to the work of the LCA Legislation Committee in the Supplementary Explanatory Memorandum to the SLAT Bill. As a result, the SLAT Bill was amended to:

- tighten the proposed definition of 'terrorist act' to be inserted in the Criminal Code;
- remove absolute liability and the reverse onus in respect of fault from the terrorism offences;

[1] The SLAT Bills package included the Suppression of the Financing of Terrorism Bill 2002 (Cth), the Criminal Code Amendment (Suppression of Terrorist Bombings) Bill 2002 (Cth), the Border Security Legislation Amendment Bill 2002 (Cth), the Telecommunications Interception Legislation Amendment Bill 2002 (Cth), and the Security Legislation Amendment (Terrorism) Bill 2002 (Cth).

[2] The SLAT Bills were first introduced into Parliament on 13 March 2002, and on 20 March 2002, after passing through the House of Representatives, were referred to the LCA Legislation Committee for inquiry and report by 3 May 2002.

- create a defence to the offence of treason relating to the provision of humanitarian aid; and
- make changes to the proscription regime, including requiring proscription to occur via regulation thereby enabling parliamentary review (Items 4–5, 8, 11–19).

Amendments were also made to the Bills to require the SLAT Acts to be reviewed by the PJC on ASIO, ASIS and DSD (later to become PJCIS) in three years (Supplementary Explanatory Memorandum to SLAT Bills 2020 Items 1 and 20). The SLAT Bills were also scrutinised by the SSCSB, and some legislative amendments, such as those that removed the absolute liability features of the proposed new offences and improved oversight of the terrorist organisation proscription regime, reflected key concerns raised by that committee (SSCSB Alert Digest No 3 of 2002 at pp. 49–52; SSCSB Report No 4 of 2020).

These important legislative changes to the SLAT Bills package are particularly noteworthy having regard to both the short time frames for conducing such a large and complex scrutiny task and the political context for the reforms, coming soon after the 11 September 2001 attacks and after the Howard Government successfully won the 2001 election with a 'tough on terror' mandate.

5.3.1.2 ASIO Bill 2002 and ASIO Act 2003 (CSA 2 and 3)

The ASIO Bill 2002 was the second major counter-terrorism reform package introduced by the Howard Government. This Bill is a particularly interesting case study as it was considered by four separate parliamentary committees and underwent significant legislative change from introduction to enactment.

As noted in Chap. 3, the ASIO Bill 2002 proposed to introduce a new questioning and detention warrant regime (Q&D regime) wherein ASIO officers would be empowered to apply for a warrant to detain, search and/or question persons before a prescribed authority (PJC on ASIO, ASIS and DSD Report on ASIO Bill 2002 at pp. 3–5). The proposed Q&D regime included the power to detain a person (without charge or being suspected of committing an offence) for up to 48 hours, with successive warrants available. The detention could be incommunicado and the person subject to the warrant would have no rights to decline to give information or produce a document. Like the SLAT Bills, the ASIO Bill 2002 was referred to the LCA Legislation Committee; however, it was also referred to the PJC on ASIO, ASIS and DSD for report, with the same tight five-week time frame.[3]

The PJC on ASIO, ASIS and DSD received over 150 written submissions in response to its inquiry and held public hearings in Canberra, Sydney and Melbourne (Report on ASIO Bill 2002 at p. 1). The majority of the submissions called for the Bill to be abandoned or recommended key provisions be removed, and much of the

[3]As it transpired, an extension of time was eventually granted to both committees, with the PJC ASIO reporting on the ASIO Bill on 5 June 2002 and the LCA Legislation Committee tabling its report on 18 June 2002.

PJC on ASIO, ASIS and DSD's oral hearings were devoted to exploring alternative policy options and additional safeguards for witnesses. A consensus report was issued (2002) that included strongly worded concerns about aspects of the Bill and 15 recommendations for amendments, including that the Bill be amended to:

- ensure that persons detained under a Q&D warrant have access to legal representation, and be protected against self-incrimination;
- require all warrants to be issued by a Federal Magistrate and, in those cases where detention will exceed 96 hours, by a Federal Court Judge;
- prescribe a maximum period of detention of seven days, at the expiry of which a person will need to be charged or released;
- provide that a person must have the right to judicial review after 24 hours of detention and every time a subsequent warrant is sought;
- remove the power to detain a person under 18 under a questioning and detention warrant; and
- include a three-year sunset clause for the questioning and detention regime (Recommendations 6, 1, 3, 15, 10, 12).

Of the 15 recommendations made by the PJC on ASIO, ASIS and DSD, 14 were accepted in part or in full, and government amendments were moved in the House to implement the legislative changes recommended by the committee. These amendments were attributed to the work of the Parliamentary Joint Committee on ASIO, ASIS and DSD in the Supplementary Explanatory Memorandum to the ASIO Bill 2002 (Items 23-4). However, as discussed below, although these amendments successfully passed through the House, the ASIO Bill 2002 was blocked by members of the opposition and the minor parties in the Senate, who pushed hard for further changes to be made to the Bill, including amendments to preclude the application of the regime to children and the inclusion of a sunset clause.

The legislative changes attributed to the PJC on ASIO, ASIS and DSD were substantive and rights-enhancing in character, even if they failed to remedy the most pressing of the human rights concerns with the Bill. As former committee member Robert Ray observed in an interview with the author:

> The ASIO 2002 Bills were the perfect example of the [PJC on ASIO, ASIS and DSD] issuing a consensus report recommending changes to a whole raft of provisions that were absolutely over the top and draconian ….
>
> At this time, rights issues were very much in the minds of the committee.
>
> The more intrusive powers, the more protections are required. In the first form of the legislation, there certainly wasn't anywhere enough of these (via telephone 23 November 2016).

The LCA Legislation Committee's concurrent inquiry into the ASIO Bill 2002 was far less comprehensive and reflected an early deference by the LCA Legislation Committee to the more specialist PJC on ASIO, ASIS and DSD, which has intensified in more recent parliamentary inquiries into counter-terrorism law (LCA Legislation Committee Report on the ASIO Bill 2020 at p. 1). The LCA Legislation Committee did not hold any public hearings or make any specific recommendations in its report on the Bill. Instead, it focused on the constitutional concerns raised with respect to the ASIO Bill 2002 by submission makers to both the PJC on ASIO, ASIS and DSD inquiry and the earlier LCA Committee inquiry into the SLAT Bills.[4] Having considered further advice from the AGD on these issues (at pp. 2–3), the majority of the LCA Legislation Committee concluded that, if adopted, the recommendations of the PJC ASIO would largely address all of the constitutional concerns raised by submission makers with respect to the Bill (at pp. 4–5). A dissenting report was provided by Australian Democrats (at pp. 9–11) and by Labor Senator Barney Cooney and Australian Greens Senator Bob Brown (at pp. 11–12).

The SSCSB also scrutinised the ASIO Bill 2002, first through its Alert Digest (No 4 of 2002) and later in its report on the Bill (Report No 12 of 2002). In the Alert Digest, the SSCSB raised a number of concerns and questioned the necessity of the proposed new warrant regime, and whether it was appropriate that police powers should be extended to organisations concerned with the collection of intelligence (Alert Digest No 4 of 2002). Ensuring due process rights for those subject to the proposed new warrants was a central issue for the SSCSB, which observed that:

> The protection of the community from terrorism is obviously a vital concern. However a community that fails to accord its citizens due process, and to protect their rights, even in extreme circumstances, runs the risk of becoming a community different in nature from that which currently exists (Alert Digest No 4 of 2002; Report No 12 of 2002).

On 24 September 2002, the Attorney-General provided a written response to the questions raised by the SSCSB in its Alert Digest (Report No 12 of 2002 at p. 415), referring repeatedly to the government amendments moved in response to the PJC on ASIO, ASIS and DSD which, he asserted, alleviated the SSCSB's concerns (at p. 418). In its final report on the ASIO Bill 2002, the SSCSB concluded that 'the provisions, even after amendment, may continue to be seen to trespass unduly on personal rights and liberties' and found that the 'Senate must therefore decide whether such breaches are acceptable when weighed against the policy objectives of the bill' (Report No 12 of 2002 at p. 418).

As noted above, while nearly all of the recommendations made by the PJC on ASIO, ASIS and DSD were reflected in government amendments to the ASIO Bill 2002 that passed the House, the amended Bill was not agreed to in the Senate. Instead, the Senate referred the ASIO Bill 2002 and related matters to the LCA References Committee for inquiry. This time, led by a non-government majority, the LCA References Committee conducted an extensive public inquiry into the ASIO Bill 2002 that attracted over 400 written submissions and involved public hearings in Canberra, Melbourne and Sydney (LCA References Committee ASIO Bill 2002 Report at p. xix).

Almost all of the submissions received by the LCA References Committee objected to parts or all of the Bill (at pp. 11–22). Like the SSCSB, the LCA

---

[4] The two key constitutional issues of interest to the LCA Committee were (1) 'the constitutionality of the Executive authorising the detention of a person who is not a suspect'; and (2) 'whether the issuing by magistrates of warrants for questioning of an individual is an exercise of executive power that is incompatible with their role'. LCA Legislation Committee Report on the ASIO Bill 2020 at p. 2.

References Committee queried whether it was appropriate to invest an intelligence agency with coercive questioning and detention powers (at p. 22). However the majority of the LCA References Committee supported the passage of the Q&D regime, albeit with some significant changes. This was a significant conclusion for the majority of the committee to reach, particularly in light of the fact that the non-government members of the LCA References Committee enjoyed a majority and in the context of senior Labor Opposition figures strongly calling for an alternative, AFP-based questioning approach.

The committee made 27 recommendations for amendments to the ASIO Bill 2002, some of which included additional comments or provisos expressed by government members. Among the key recommendations were that:

- changes be made to the way questioning and detention warrants are issued;
- clear limits be set on the maximum time period for questioning;
- a person subject to a warrant be given confidential access to lawyer of choice, an interpreter, and the IGIS during questioning;
- procedures and protocols for detention under the proposed warrants be enshrined in regulation;
- the proposed new regime be subject to a three-year sunset clause; and
- the Bill not apply to children (Recommendations 1–3, 4–6, 9, 11–14, 20, 22–23, 26–27).

The majority of the committee concluded that these recommendations provided 'a basis for improving and progressing the legislation, while keeping its provisions within acceptable bounds and respecting the rights and freedoms that are fundamental to the Australian community' (LCA References Committee ASIO Bill 2002 Report at p. xxi). A different view was adopted by the Australian Democrats (pp. 153–4) and Australian Greens (p. 161–2) who concluded that, even with the changes proposed by the majority, the Bill was a 'disproportionate, badly targeted and possibly unconstitutional response' to the threat of terrorism in Australia (at p. 161).

Following the tabling of the LCA References Committee report, the government introduced a range of amendments, implementing a number but not all of the LCA Committee's recommendations and acknowledging the work of the Committee in the Supplementary Explanatory Memorandum to the ASIO Bill 2002. Recommendations 1–3 relating to the issuing authority for warrants were accepted, as were those relating to access to interpreters and the IGIS for those subject to a warrant (recommendations 17–18, 20). The government amendments also sought to address concerns about lack of access to legal representation for those subject to a warrant, but did not fully implement the committee's recommendations on this issue.[5] Nor did the government amendments restrict the proposed warrant regime to adults or introduce a three-year sunset clause. If this is where the legislative story

[5]The government introduced an amendment to create a new proposed s 34AA. This responded in part to Recommendation 6 in the committee's report on the Bill relating to access to legal representation by persons who are the subject of a warrant.

ended, one would have to conclude that the LCA References Committee had only a modest legislative impact on the shape of the ASIO Bill 2002. However, the legislative story continued for some time, with the Bill debated deep into the night by both the House and the Senate during the final couple of sitting days in December 2002. Chief among the issues debated during this period were whether a sunset clause should be included in the Bill and whether the regime should be restricted to adults, as recommended by both the LCA References Committee and the PJC on ASIO, ASIS and DSD. The need to ensure full, confidential access to legal representation and protect the common law privileges of self-incrimination and use immunity also featured strongly, particularly in the amendments moved by Opposition members. The Bill was not passed.

When Parliament resumed the next year, the ASIO Bill 2002 was re-introduced as the ASIO Bill 2003, which incorporated many of the features recommended by the committees discussed above.[6] For example, it included limits on the maximum time period for questioning under a warrant (Items 34C and 34D), a process for a person subject to a warrant to access a lawyer of their choice (albeit a lawyer with a security clearance) (Item 34A), and a restriction to ensure that the questioning and detention regime only applies to people who are 14 years and older, and special regime for those between 14 and 18 (Item 34NA). A three-year sunset clause for the proposed new regime was also included in the enacted Bill.

The ASIO Bill 2002 and ASIO Act 2003 experience highlights how different components of the parliamentary committee system can work together to maximise the overall legislative impact of their scrutiny. Given the political dynamic of this period, and particularly the composition of the Senate, the legislative impact of parliamentary scrutiny on the shape of the enacted ASIO Act 2003 should not be overstated. Indeed, it may have been this political dynamic that provided the opportunity for the committees studied to exert particularly strong legislative influence on the content of the Bills. In any case, given the explicit acknowledgement of the work of the various parliamentary committees in multiple Supplementary Explanatory Memoranda and Hansard speeches accompanying both government and opposition amendments, it is possible to conclude that parliamentary scrutiny of the ASIO Bills had an important rights-enhancing, but not rights-remedying, legislative impact.

5.3.1.3 Anti-Terrorism Act 2004 (CSA 4)

The Anti-Terrorism Bill 2004 was introduced in May 2004, during the height of the public debate around the cases of David Hicks (Brew et al. 2007; Dratel 2008; Bastin and Tamberlin 2008), Mahmoud Habib (Brew et al. 2007; Banham 2016) and the treatment of detainees by the US at Guantanamo Bay (Brew et al. 2007) and six

[6] Interestingly, by this time, there was much broader agreement among major parties in the Parliament about the need for ASIO, rather than the AFP, to be able to exercise the proposed questioning and detention powers. The debate on the reintroduced Bill centred much more closely on the adequacy of the proposed safeguards in the Bill. For further discussion see Chap. 6.

months prior to the 2004 federal election, after which the Howard Government had a majority in the Senate. The Bill was also introduced in the shadow of the Madrid bombings, the Abu Ghraib scandal, the ul-Haque case and some of the first terrorism charges being laid in Australia (see e.g., *R v Ul-Haque* [2007] NSWSC 1251; Ray 2007; Horsburgh and Manas 2008; Sorial 2008).

As explained in the Explanatory Memorandum, one of the key purposes of the Anti-Terrorism Bill 2004 was to extend existing *Crimes Act 1915* (Cth) powers to enable AFP officers to detain people without charge for the purpose of investigating possible terrorist related activity (known as the Part IC changes). The Bill also extended the existing proceeds of crime regime to ensure that it applied to proceeds derived from literary works.

The Bill was referred to the LCA Legislation Committee for inquiry and report (2004), as well as being considered by the SSCSB (Alert Digest No 6 of 2004). After holding a 12-day inquiry, involving only a relatively small number of submissions and one public hearing, the LCA Legislation Committee issued a report containing eight recommendations focused on:

- improving judicial oversight of the use of the proposed new Part IC powers (recommendation 1);
- ensuring clear criteria for proscription of organisations for foreign incursion laws (recommendations 2–4);
- tightening proposed proceeds of crime laws relating to literary proceeds and ensuring no retrospective operation (recommendations 6–7); and
- opposing recognition of military commissions in proceeds of crime laws (recommendation 8).

The government accepted the first two of these sets of recommendations and introduced amendments to that effect (Supplementary Explanatory Memorandum Amendments (4)–(8)). The government amendments also addressed the issue of retrospectivity (Amendment (1)) but otherwise rejected the remaining LCA Committee's recommendations.

The SSCSB report on the Bill focused exclusively on the Part IC changes that would permit law enforcement authorities to detain a person without charge, and without judicial oversight (Alert Digest No 6 of 2004 at p. 5). While not directly attributed to the SSCSB, some of the successful government amendments improved the judicial oversight of the use of the Part IC provisions in line with the issues considered by the SSCSB.

On this basis, is it possible to conclude that the formal parliamentary scrutiny of the Anti-Terrorism Bill 2004 had a rights-enhancing legislative impact on the Bill, in so far as it led to the introduction of additional safeguards and more precise, proscriptive criteria on the use of executive power. However, the central pillars of the reforms remained intact, including a new detention without charge regime, and more expansive proceeds of crime provisions.[7]

5.3.1.4 National Security Information (Criminal Proceedings) Bill 2004 (Cth)

As noted in Chap. 3, 2004 also saw the introduction of a regime designed to protect classified national security information from being disclosed in federal criminal court proceedings, loosely based on a similar regime implemented in the UK (House of Commons 2005). The regime proposed in the National Security Information (Criminal Proceedings) Bill 2004 sought to preclude the public, and the defendant, from accessing information that was relevant and sometimes critical to the prosecution case, where revealing that information could be considered prejudicial to national security (clauses 22–29; Varghese 2004 at p. 4). It also proposed to introduce a system of security clearances for defence lawyers engaged in terrorism-related trials (clause 34).

Once passed by the House, the Bill was referred to the LCA Legislation Committee for inquiry and report (2004). During the inquiry, which attracted almost exclusively legal bodies and only modest numbers of submissions, the Attorney-General's Department and the Director of Public Prosecutions argued strongly in favour of changes, providing examples of the gaps in the pre-existing law in this area. Although a legal mechanism already existed to preclude the publication of information prejudicial to national security in court proceedings, known as 'public interest immunity', the government argued that this was a 'blunt' instrument to deal with national security information relevant to terrorist offending. This became an obstacle in the case of *R v Lappas and Dowling* [2001] ACTSC 115, which the Attorney-General cited as a precipitant for the National Security Information (Criminal Proceedings) Bill 2004 (Cth) (Varghese 2004at p. 4). Other submission makers queried the need for changes in light of other laws that they argued already provided for protection of sensitive information (Law Council of Australia Submission No 8 2004 at paras [3.5]–[3.8]).

The LCA Legislation Committee's report focused heavily on legal process rights, reflecting the predominantly legal character its key submission makers (see e.g. Chap. 3.) Legal organisations were particularly concerned about the proposed system of security clearances for lawyers, and the implications for the independence of the legal profession, particularly if security clearances were denied or delayed by the Attorney-General. The LCA Legislation Committee made 13 recommendations including that:

---

[7] Two additional amendments were made to the Bill following the issue of the LCA Legislation Committee report that detract from established criminal law principles and common law rights. These amendments remove the presumption against bail for people charged with terrorism offences and provide for minimum non-parole periods for persons convicted of, and sentenced to imprisonment for, terrorism offences. Supplementary Explanatory Memorandum, Anti-Terrorism Bill 2004 (Cth) Item 1B and Item 1C.

- the court[8] retains its discretion to determine whether proceedings are open or closed (recommendation 1);
- the court be required to provide a written statement outlining the reasons for holding proceedings in-camera (recommendation 2);
- defendants and their legal representatives can only be excluded from hearings in limited specified circumstances (recommendation 6);
- the court be required, when making an order to exclude a witness from the proceedings, to be satisfied that the exclusion of the witness would not impair the ability of the defendant to make his or her defence (recommendation 8); and
- the court be required, when making an order for non-disclosure, to be satisfied that the redacted documentation to be adduced as evidence would provide the defendant with substantially the same ability to make his or her defence as would disclosure of the source document (recommendation 7).

The SSCSB also considered the Bill in a very short report focused on the weight to be attributed by the court exercising federal jurisdiction to the rights of the accused when considering whether to exclude national security information from the defendant (Alert Digest No 11 of 2004 at pp. 29–30). The SSCSB also noted the lack of a requirement for the Attorney-General to provide reasons when issuing an evidential certificate under the Bill (at p. 31).

Parliament was prorogued before the government issued its formal response to the LCA Legislation Committee's report. However, shortly after the Howard Government was re-elected, a new Bill was introduced that included a number of features recommended by the LCA Committee, including: a narrower definition of 'national security'; a requirement to provide reasons for holding a hearing in camera; power for the court to make decisions about how national security information could be used prior to trial; and the preservation of the court's discretion to make decisions about the admissibility of evidence (see Supplementary Explanatory Memorandum General Outline and notes on clauses 1–3, 21–3, 29, 31–32; Varghese 2004 at p. 4). The new Bill also allowed the court to stay proceedings if the defendant could not be assured a fair trial, provided that a security-cleared lawyer could not be excluded from closed hearings, and ensured that defendants have the opportunity to make submissions before evidence or witnesses are excluded (clause 29). The new Bill also provided that 'substantial adverse effect' on the conduct of the defence must be a factor considered by the court in deciding to exclude evidence or witnesses or withdraw a statement or facts (clause 31(7).

These rights-enhancing features of the new Bill attributable to the work of the LCA Committee are particularly noteworthy coming after the Howard Government had been re-elected with an increased majority and with the prospect of a Senate majority in coming months.

---

[8] In the National Security Information (Criminal Proceedings) Bill 2004 (Cth) and related committee inquiry reports, 'court' refers to 'court exercising federal jurisdiction, where the offence or any of the offences concerned are against a law of the Commonwealth': see *National Security Information (Criminal Proceedings) Act 2004* (Cth) s 8.

5.3.1.5 The Control Orders Act (CSA 6)

As noted in Chap. 3, the Control Orders Bill contained some of the most significant additions to the counter-terrorism framework in Australia, introducing new powers to restrict the rights and liberties of people thought to be involved in terrorist activity that fell well outside of the established principles of criminal law. Among other reforms, it introduced preventative detention orders, control orders and updated sedition offences into the federal criminal law (Harris-Rimmer 2005; Carne 2007; Fairall and Lacey 2007; Tyulkina and Williams 2017). The Bill was also exceptional in terms of the speed at which it moved through Parliament; enacted just 41 days after introduction, despite attracting strong public attention and receiving second reading speeches by over 50 parliamentarians.

When the Control Orders Bill was introduced into the House, it was referred immediately to the LCA Legislation Committee for inquiry and report. After only 25 days, and having received nearly 300 submissions and hearing from 21 witnesses, the LCA Legislation Committee issued its report (2005). The report contained 51 recommendations for change, 17 concerning the proposed preventative detention order regime and designed to address the key concerns of submission makers. Recommendations made by the LCA Committee to address these matters translated into over 30 successful amendments to the preventative detention order regime in the Bill that were directly attributed to the work of the committee in the Supplementary Explanatory Memorandum (Schedule 4 Items 25–64) and in the second reading speech of Senator George Brandis, then representing the Attorney-General in the Senate (5 December 2005, at p. 18). The amendments included changes to how the preventative detention order regime would apply to children, including making express provision for children subject to a control order to have contact with their parents or other support persons (Supplementary Explanatory Memorandum Item 47). Changes were also recommended with respect to the proposed control order regime, including amendments designed to improve access to natural justice and procedural fairness (LCA Legislation Committee Report 2005 Chap. 4 and Recommendations 19–26). These recommendations also translated into successful government amendments (particularly to clause 104) that were attributed to the work of the LCA Committee and improved the procedural fairness of the control order regime, for example by requiring that the person subject to the interim order be provided with notice of an application for confirmation, and relevant information supporting that application (Supplementary Explanatory Memorandum Item 13).

The LCA Committee also recommended that the proposed new sedition offences in Schedule 7 of the Bill be left out of the Bill and instead referred to the ALRC for detailed consideration by the ALRC (Recommendations 27 and 28). As an alternative, the majority recommended that the proposed sedition offences be amended in significant respects (Recommendation 9). While the sedition offences ultimately remained in the Bill, they were amended to clarify the burden of proof and expand the proposed 'good faith defence' in the manner set out by the LCA Committee (Anti-Terrorism Bill (No 2) 2005 Items 68–72). The government also adopted the LCA Committee's recommendation to refer the sedition offences to the ALRC for inquiry (see ALRC 2006).

Overall, in response to the LCA Committee's report, the government introduced 74 amendments to the Bill, the great majority of which could be described as 'rights-enhancing'. However, many of the LCA Committee recommendations were not implemented, or not implemented in full by the government (see e.g. recommendations 25, 27 and 29), although some of these recommendations were reflected in unsuccessful opposition amendments, such as setting out a process for independent review of the preventative detention order regime or introducing a five-year sunset clause.

The SSCSB also reported on the Control Orders Bill (Alert Digest No 13 of 2005 at p. 13), focusing on the provisions of the Bill that sought to exclude judicial review (at p. 13), the retrospective operation of certain key provisions, and the abrogation of common law privileges (at pp. 14–16). In its usual style, the SSCSB left these matters to the Senate as a whole to consider. While none of the government amendments to the Bill were directly attributed to the work of the SSCSB, the issues raised by the SSCSB featured prominently in the report of the LCA Committee (2005 at pp. 13–14, 24–7, 48 and 143), which in turn led to a number of successful government amendments and had the effect of at least partially alleviating some of the concerns raised by the SSCSB (see Supplementary Explanatory Memorandum Anti-Terrorism Bill (No 2) 2005 (Cth)). Interestingly, the PJCIS (as it was by now known) did not receive a reference to inquire into the Control Orders Bill, signalling that, at least at this time, the LCA Committee remained the 'forum of choice' for large-scale public inquiries into proposed new counter-terrorism laws.

Taken together, the Bills in this first phase demonstrate that, even where there is bipartisan support for strong legislative responses to new threats to Australia's national security, parliamentary committees can have a rights-enhancing impact on the content of the laws passed. As discussed further in Chap. 6, this can occur even when the Bills are rushed through Parliament and is greatly enhanced when more than one committee is involved in scrutinising or reviewing a proposed law. While the case study Acts enacted during this phase continue to raise serious rights concerns and have been cited by some scholars as evidence of the weaknesses of the parliamentary model of rights protection (Carne 2015; Williams 2011; Lynch 2006; Tyulkina and Williams 2017; and Reynolds and Williams 2017), the rights implications of these laws would have been significantly worse had parliamentary committees not been able to effect significant legislative change. As the next phase reveals, the rights-enhancing impact of parliamentary committees can also have a longer-term effect, helping to shape the development of new provisions and providing the basis for further independent review of Australia's counter-terrorism framework.

5.3.2 *Phase 2: Consolidating Reform of Counter-Terrorism Laws*

The second 'phase' of parliamentary scrutiny of counter-terrorism law was a period covering 2008–2012, commencing with the defeat of the Howard Government and the election of the Rudd Government. As noted in Chap. 3, this period saw review and reform of pre-existing counter-terrorism laws and the introduction of new oversight mechanisms to help 'strike the right balance' between national security and individual rights and freedoms. For scholars in the UK, this period might also be described as a period of 'post-legislative scrutiny' of Australia's counter-terrorism laws (Moulds 2019a, b).

This phase also saw the establishment of the PJCHR in response to the findings of the National Consultation. This period also coincided with a number of specific cases that drew public attention to the scope of the new powers given to intelligence and law enforcement agencies, and the risks associated with the use of those powers, including the case of Dr. Mohamed Haneef (Clarke 2008).

Two Bills illustrate this phase of the legislative impact: the National Security Legislation Amendment Bill 2010 and the INSLM Bill 2010. Together these Bills constitute the most significant legislative activity in the area of counter-terrorism by the Rudd and Gillard Governments, and reflect many years of independent review of Australia's counter-terrorism framework introduced since 2001. These Bills are also different in character to the phase 1 Bills discussed above, as they were introduced in an effort to consolidate the existing counter-terrorism framework, rather than in response to an emerging threat to national security. As the below discussion reveals, although neither of these Bills were referred to the PJCIS following their introduction, the past work of the PJCIS featured strongly in their development. In this way, this phase marks the beginning of the rise of the PJCIS as a committee with significant influence on the shape of Australia's counter-terrorism laws.

5.3.2.1 The INSLM Act (CSA 7)

As noted in Chap. 3, the INSLM Bill had its origins in past reviews of counter-terrorism legislation, including reviews conducted by the PJCIS in 2006 (Review of Security and Counter Terrorism Legislation) and 2007 (Review of Terrorist Listing Provisions), the Sheller Committee (2006) and the Haneef Inquiry (Clarke 2008 at pp. 255–6). It also represented the culmination of previous efforts by Liberal backbenchers Humphries and Troeth to introduce similar legislation in 2008 (Independent Reviewer of Terrorism Laws Bill 2008 [No 2]). The purpose of the INSLM Bill was to establish the statutory position of the National Security Legislation Monitor to review Australia's counter-terrorism and national security legislation with a view to determining whether it was 'effective in deterring and preventing terrorism' and other threats to Australia's security and consistent with Australia's human rights obligations and contains appropriate safeguards for protecting individual rights (clause 3).

Although previous incarnations of the Bill had been considered by the LCA Legislation Committee (2008), the 2010 INSLM Bill was reviewed by the Senate Finance and Public Administration Committee (SFPAC) in 2009.[9] The SFPAC conducted a relatively small public inquiry and drew heavily from past scrutiny reports including the LCA Committee's inquiry into the Independent Reviewer of Terrorism Laws Bill 2008 (No 2) (Cth) and other inquiries into counter-terrorism laws that recommended the establishment of an INSLM. The SFPCA issued a consensus report that contained 12 recommendations for amendment but otherwise supported the Bill. These recommendations included: a name change (adding 'independent' to the Monitor's title), power for the INSLM to conduct its own inquiries, power for the PJCIS to refer matters to the INSLM for inquiry and report, and providing the INSLM with an explicit mandate to assess whether the counter-terrorism laws were consistent with Australia's international human rights obligations (SFPAC 2009 Recommendations 2, 5 and 6). The government implemented all of these recommendations as amendments to the Bill. In addition, the key features of the INSLM Bill were drawn from provisions already considered by the LCA Committee in its 2008 inquiry into the previous incarnations of the Bill. Thus, it is possible to conclude that, in this case, the parliamentary committee system had a substantial legislative impact on the enacted law. As ALP Senator Ludwig, then Special Minister of State, observed during the second reading debate on the INSLM Bill:

> In many respects, the bill we are considering today reflects the considerable work of both the joint and the Senate committees in drawing attention to and developing proposals to fix a gap in the security legislation identified by both committees, as well as independent reviews of counterterrorism legislation since 2001. I recognise the work of my Senate and House colleagues from all parties on this important issue. To a great extent the bill is the fruit of a properly functioning parliament working at its best (3 February 2010 at 209).

As will be discussed further below, the work of the INSLM has had a significant and predominantly rights-enhancing impact on the shape of subsequent changes to Australia's counter-terrorism laws, despite the Abbott Government's attempts to abolish the office, delays in appointing or re-appointing an INSLM, and delays in government responses to successive INSLM reports. As discussed by Dalla-Pozza in her 2020 examination of the way the INSLM and the PJCIS have worked together to scrutinise Australia's counter-terrorism laws, the INSLM holds a special place in the review and accountability framework. At its best, the INSLM has the potential to undertake the type of independent, rights-focused, post-legislative scrutiny that facilitates practical legislative and policy changes. The establishment of the INSLM has also provided submission makers, experts and government agencies with an

---

[9] Senate, Parliament of Australia, *Standing Order* 25 (15 July 2014) provides for the appointment of a legislative and general purpose standing committee on Finance and Public Administration. The SFPAC maintains oversight over two portfolios: Prime Minister and Cabinet and Finance (including Indigenous Affairs). The SFPAC has membership structure and inquiry powers similar to that of the LCA Committees. Its Legislation Committee has a government Chair and government majority, while its Reference Committee has a non-government Chair and non-government majority.

alternative forum within which to reflect on the practical implementation of Australia's counter-terrorism laws, which was seen as highly valuable by many participants interviewed for this book. For example, in an interview with the author, Law Council of Australia Criminal Law Committee member Mr. Phillip Boulten SC said:

> The Monitor's work is really important. … The Monitor acts over and above politics. Both of [the appointed Monitors] have been very diligent and effective in the way in which they conduct their inquiries. They engaged with the Law Council and other contributing bodies in a very thorough and open-minded way. Their reports go past immediate use value. In many respects, they're the real conscience of both the PJCIS and the Parliament on these issues (Sydney 31 May 2016).

However, as Dalla-Pozza (2020) documents, the position of INSLM remains vulnerable to executive neglect, particularly given the INSLM's limited powers to initiate its own inquiries outside of the annual report process. This has led successive INSLM's to recommend that there be an express power for the INLSM to report on a matter or matters within its statutory mandate on a more urgent, responsive basis and that the INSLM Act be amended to require formal government response to INSLM reports within 12 months of delivery of the reports (INSLM Annual Report 2017–2018 pp. 10). If implemented, these recommendations would help to 'close the loop' when it comes to post-legislative scrutiny of Australia's counter-terrorism laws – particularly if the work of the INSLM continues to be closely integrated to the scrutiny functions undertaken by the PJCIS.

5.3.2.2 National Security Legislation Amendment Act 2010 (Cth) (CSA 8)

The National Security Legislation Amendment Bill 2010 (Cth) is another example of a Bill introduced in response to a series of independent reviews of Australia's counter-terrorism provisions introduced since 2002. As noted in Chap. 3, the National Security Legislation Amendment Bill 2010 (Cth) was preceded by a discussion paper circulated by the Attorney-General's Department in August 2009 (McClelland 2009). Some, but not all, of the proposals contained in the discussion paper were included in the Bill. The changes proposed in the Bill included amendments to the treason and sedition offences, changes to the 'dead time' provisions in Part IC of the *Crimes Act 1914* (Cth) (Item 16), changes to the operation of the *National Security Information (Criminal and Civil Proceedings) Act 2004* (Cth) (Schedule 8) and expanded oversight powers for the IGIS (Schedule 9). The discussion paper and the Bill formed part of an attempt by the Rudd Government to ensure that Australia's counter-terrorism laws strike the right 'balance' between the Government's need to protect Australians from threats to national security, and the need to ensure accountability for intrusive action and protection for key civil liberties and the rule of law (Attorney General's Department 2009 at p. 2). The discussion paper approach also provided the opportunity for prosecutorial agencies and legal experts to provide the government and the parliament more broadly with evidence about the ways in which the courts had applied and interpreted a number of new terrorist-act related offences implemented in the Phase 1 stage. For example, submission makers warned the PJCIS about the need to ensure key elements of the urging violence against groups offences contained in Division 80 of the Criminal Code aligned with established criminal law principles and were capable of being clearly explained to juries. As noted below, these matters were considered in detail by the LCA Committee in its 2010 report (pp. 20–29).

Following its introduction, the National Security Legislation Amendment Bill 2010 (Cth) was referred to the LCA Legislation Committee for inquiry and report (2010). The committee received 23 submissions, largely from legal organisations, law reform bodies, government departments and law enforcement agencies and held a public hearing in Melbourne. A number of submission makers expressed concern that the issues they raised in submissions in response to the discussion paper were not addressed in the Bill.[10] These included concerns about the proposed new 'urging violence' offences (LCA Committee Report 2010 at paras [3.22]–[3.62], the pre-charge detention provisions in Part IC of the *Crimes Act 1915* (Cth) (at paras [3.76]–[3.128]), and the system of security-cleared lawyers under the *National Security Information (Civil and Criminal Proceedings) Act 2004* (Cth) (at paras [3.129]–[3.136]). Some submission makers (such as the Castan Centre for Human Rights and the Law Council of Australia) also expressed concern that the Bill did not make substantive changes to the existing control orders and preventative detention order regimes, and proposed only relatively minor changes to the proscription regime and terrorist organisation offences.

The majority of the LCA Legislation Committee recommended four amendments, including that the government reissue the Explanatory Memorandum to clarify the reasons for introducing the proposed new 'urging violence' offences and remove the element of 'good faith' from the proposed defence to the new offences (LCA Committee Report 2010 Recommendations 1 and 2). It also recommended that the ALRC conduct a public inquiry into the pre-charge detention regime in Part IC of the *Crimes Act 1915* (Cth) (Recommendation 3) and amend the regime to limit the amount of time that a person can be held in detention to a maximum of three days (Recommendation 4). The Liberal Senators of the LCA Legislation Committee did not agree with this last recommendation, preferring evidence given by law enforcement officers that a maximum of seven days pre-charge detention was more appropriate. A dissenting report was provided by the Australian Greens, who argued that the legislation should not proceed until reviewed by the newly created position of INSLM.

The SSCSB also considered the Bill (Alert Digest No 5 of 2010 at p. 267), focusing its attention on the commencement of the new treason-related offences (at pp. 268–70). The SSCSB expressed concern about the proposed reversal of proof to

---

[10] See, eg, Castan Centre for Human Rights Law, Monash University, Submission No 9; Gilbert & Tobin Centre of Public Law, Submission No 10; National Association of Community Legal Centres, Submission No 13; Civil Liberties Australia, Submission No 14; Law Council of Australia, Submission No 22 to LCA Legislation Committee Inquiry 2010.

apply to these new offences where the conduct is undertaken for the purposes of humanitarian assistance (at pp. 270–1).

The original Bill lapsed with the proroguing of Parliament on 28 September 2010 without any amendments being introduced. An identical Bill was then reintroduced, with only minor changes to the Explanatory Memorandum, and without any substantive changes to address the LCA Legislation Committee's recommendations. At first blush, this would suggest that formal parliamentary scrutiny of the Bill had no discernible legislative impact at all. However, this would obscure the strong influence of the previous recommendations made by the PJCIS in its 2007 and 2006 inquiries, which featured strongly in both the discussion paper and in the Explanatory Memorandum accompanying the Bill. In fact, many of the key features of the Bill reflected the government's attempt to implement the outstanding recommendations of the PJCIS and were attributed as such in both the Explanatory Memorandum and in the second reading speeches on the Bill. For example the following rights-enhancing features of the Bill were attributed to previous recommendations made by the PJCIS:

- changes to clarify the content and narrow the scope of the treason offences;
- changes to the time frames relating to the proscription of terrorist organisations, to provide improved opportunities for organisations subject to proscription orders to challenge their proscription;
- changes to ensure parliamentary oversight over the proscription process by continuing to require the PJCIS to review regulations that prescribe terrorist organisations; and
- changes to the listing process for the proscription of terrorist organisations relating to UN instruments, to narrow the scope of 'automatic' listing provisions (Items 1, 3–4).

Taken together, the two Bills in this phase of scrutiny provide examples of the legislative impact of the *system* of parliamentary committees, demonstrating that, even when a particular committee struggles to have its recommendations translated into legislative change, the cumulative effect of past committee inquiries and reports can be significant and rights-enhancing. This phase also points to the cumulative rights-enhancing effect of multiple stages of rights review, whether from parliamentary committees or other independent review bodies, which increasingly features the PJCIS as a key player. In this case, the use of the discussion paper consultation technique was particularly useful in generating evidence-based submissions from a wide range of key participants and experts, even if some of these participants later expressed disappointment at the extent to which their concerns were reflected in the enacted legislation.

Taken together, this phase of parliamentary scrutiny can also be characterised as a form of 'post-legislative scrutiny' – a term made popular by the Law Commission of England and Wales in 2006, and more recently through international development activities led by the Westminster Foundation for Democracy (WFD) (De Vrieze and Hasson 2017). The concept of 'post-legislative scrutiny' generally denotes the process of reviewing *enacted* (rather than proposed) laws to determine whether the provisions have been implemented or enforced and to evaluate the impact or effectiveness of the laws (Law Commission of England and Wales 2006). In the UK context the scope of post-legislative scrutiny, and the scrutiny criteria to be applied, are determined through formal parliamentary committee processes supported by systematic reporting by government departments (Caygill 2019; Calpinska 2006). As described above, in the Australian context, the approach to post-legislative scrutiny is more ad hoc and likely to involve a range of parliamentary and non-parliamentary actors and mechanisms including the use of sunset clauses, the inclusion of legislative provisions that prescribe post-enactment scrutiny functions to the PJCIS and other statutory bodies such as the INSLM (Moulds 2019a, b), and the establishment of non-parliamentary committees of inquiry to review the application of the laws in particular contexts. The overall impact of this ad hoc form of post-legislative scrutiny – and the central and influential role played by the PJCIS in this process – is considered below in Part III and discussed by Dalla-Pozza (2020).

5.3.3 Phase 3: The Rise of the PJCIS and the Introduction of the PJCHR

Phase 3 of parliamentary scrutiny of counter-terrorism law commenced at the election of the Abbott Government in 2013 and continued up until the end of 2015, taking in 'tranche 5' of the counter-terrorism law-making experience described in Chap. 3 and incorporating the following case study Acts:

- Data Retention Act (CSA 9);
- *Counter-Terrorism Legislation Amendment Act (No 1) 2014* (Cth) (CSA 10);
- Foreign Fighters Act (CSA 11);
- Citizenship Act (CSA 12);
- High Risk Offenders Act (CSA 13); and
- Encryption Act (CSA 14)
- TEO Bill (CSA 15)

In this phase it is possible to see two distinct trends occurring. The first is the complete sidelining of the LCA Committees as a forum for inquiring into proposed changes to counter-terrorism laws. The second is the 100 per cent 'strike rate' of the PJCIS in translating its recommendations for legislative change into successful amendments (see e.g. PJCIS Annual Report 2014–2015 at p. 3; see also Dalla-Pozza 2020), at least between the years. This dramatic rise in legislative impact attributable to the PJCIS occurred against the backdrop of the newly operational INSLM and the now functioning PJCHR, and generates important insights for the discussion in Part III of my research. Towards the end of this period of parliamentary scrutiny it is also possible to identify signs of fragility when it comes to the legislative impact of the PJCIS, with the experience of the TEO Bill (CSA 15) a particularly interesting example. As discussed below, this fragility was closely followed by another example of powerful legislative impact, in the form of the PCJIS's complete rejection of the Identity-Matching Services Bill 2019 (Cth) and the Australian Passports Amendment (Identity-matching Services) Bill 2019 (Cth) – referred to collectively as the 'Identity Matching Laws'– highlighting the particularly fascinating and dynamic contribution the PJCIS makes to the broader federal parliamentary committee system and to Australia's parliamentary model of rights protection.

5.3.3.1 The Data Retention Act (CSA 10)

The Data Retention Bill provides a useful case study to examine the longer-term legislative impact of the PJCIS, and the role of the LCA Committees in providing a forum for extensive public debate on bold new legislative reforms. The Bill, which was introduced by the Abbott Government, had its origins in a proposal first floated by the Gillard Government in a discussion paper developed by the then Attorney-General the Hon Nicola Roxon MP in May 2012.[11] The Roxon discussion paper was referred to the PJCIS for inquiry and report, in what became known as the Inquiry into the Potential Reforms of Australian's National Security Legislation (PJCIS 2013 at pp. xii–xix). The inquiry lasted for just over a year and attracted 236 written submissions. Five public hearings were held in Sydney, Melbourne and Canberra. The PJCIS tabled its report in June 2013 making 43 recommendations, three directly related to data retention (Recommendations 42 and 43). One of these recommendations suggested that, if such a regime was to be pursued, draft legislation should be developed and released for public consultation, and should include a range of specific features (Recommendation 42). In particular, the PJCIS wanted to ensure that any future mandatory data retention regime applies only to meta-data and not content, that maximum limits of no more than two years apply to the retention of data, and that the regime should include a robust, mandatory reporting and oversight schemes, including mandatory breach notification and review of access to data by the Ombudsman and the IGIS. In addition, the PJCIS recommended that if a mandatory data retention regime was pursued, the PJCIS should have a clear oversight role and review the regime within three years (recommendation 43). These became critical considerations in the PJCIS's subsequent inquiry into the Data Retention Bill.

Some months after the PJCIS had issued its report, and following the election of the Abbott Government in 2013, the newly constituted Senate asked the non-government majority LCA References Committee to undertake a 'comprehensive revision of the *Telecommunications (Interception and Access) Act 1979* (Cth)' (LCA References Committee 2015). The LCA References Committee was asked to have particular regard to recent recommendations made by the ALRC (2008 Recommendation 71), and the recommendations of the PJCIS inquiry described

---

[11] The package of reforms included 'telecommunications interception reform, telecommunications sector security reform and Australian intelligence community reform', and drew upon findings and recommendations made in previous inquiries and reports, including ALRC, *For Your Information: Australian Privacy Law and Practice*, Report No 108 (May 2008), particularly Recommendation 71.2.

above. The LCA References Committee received 46 submissions and held six public hearings. The inquiry was lengthy, with a final report not issued until 23 March 2015. During that time, the LCA References Committee received substantial comment on the issue of mandatory data retention and by the later stages of the committee's inquiry the government had announced that it would be introducing the Data Retention Bill (which occurred on 30 October 2014).

The LCA References Committee Chair, Australian Greens Senator Scott Ludlam, and the other committee members could not reach agreement on the key issues raised during the inquiry. As a result, the final report includes a lengthy Chair's report, containing six recommendations, including that the Data Retention Bill be withdrawn (LCA References Committee 2015 Chairs Minority Report). The Chair's report also recommended that, if the Data Retention Bill was not withdrawn, a number of changes be made, including that telecommunications 'data' be defined in the Bill and that data only be accessed via a warrant. The government Senators opposed the Chair's report and instead recommended that the *Telecommunications (Interception and Access) Act 1979* (Cth) be amended to provide a single attribute-based warrant scheme to apply to telecommunications content and that the Data Retention Bill be passed by the Senate (LCA References Committee 2015 Comments from Opposition Senators).

Meanwhile, on 21 November 2014, the Data Retention Bill was referred to the PJCIS for inquiry and report (2015). The then Attorney-General George Brandis also provided the PJCIS with a draft 'data-set' listing the specific types of telecommunications information that telecommunication service providers would need to retain (PJCIS 2015 at paras [1.14]–[1.15]. The Explanatory Memorandum accompanying the Bill included numerous references to the 2013 PJCIS inquiry and described some provisions of the Bill as implementing the relevant PJCIS recommendations (Items 6–7).

In response to its Data Retention Bill inquiry, the PJCIS received 204 submissions and held three public hearings over December and January 2015.[12] The PJCIS's consensus report was tabled on 27 February 2015 (almost a month before the tabling of the LCA References Committee's report). It looked carefully at the matters set out in the PJCIS's 2013 report and noted the failure of the government to provide the PJCIS with draft legislation to consider prior to introducing the Bill into Parliament. Detailed consideration, and significant media attention, was also given to what would fall within the 'data set' to be retained under the regime (PJCIS 2015; Brew 2012). The PJCIS's 2015 report also referred extensively to the work of other parliamentary committees and independent reviews, including the LCA References Committee, the SSCSB and the PJCHR.[13] Consideration was also given

[12] The PJCIS also held one private hearing and received three private briefings from relevant agencies in Canberra, and visited the Australian Federal Police headquarters for further operational briefings.

[13] For example, direct reference was made to the inquiry conducted by the LCA Committee at pages 36, 47, 60 and 141; direct reference was made to the PJCHR at 38, 87, 98, 232, 234–5 and 247; direct reference was made to the SSCSB at 74, 163, 191 and 209.

to the relevant human rights standards, particular the right to privacy protected by Article 17 of the ICCPR, (see e.g. PJCIS 2015 at pp. 36, 42, 52 and 55) and to the way these issues were dealt with by the government in the SoC accompanying the Bill. Particularly strong concerns were raised by media groups about the impact of the regime on journalists and their sources, and on their ability to report on matters relevant to national security or government activity that may be in the public interest. The PJCIS made 39 recommendations for amendments to the Bill, including that:

- the relevant data set be defined in primary legislation;
- the Bill make it clear that service providers are not required to collect and retain customer passwords, PINs, web-browsing histories or other destination information;
- data retained be de-identified or destroyed after two years;
- the Bill include detailed reporting and oversight regimes, including detailed reporting requirements to the PJCIS; and
- that a separate parliamentary inquiry be instigated into the impact of the proposed provisions on journalists and their sources.[14]

On 3 March 2015 the government announced that it would accept all of the PJCIS's recommendations (Brandis and Turnbull 2015) and moved quickly to introduce amendments. All of the government amendments to the Bill were passed and revised and supplementary Explanatory Memoranda issued attributing the amendments directly to the work of the PJCIS. The government also agreed to commence a separate PJCIS inquiry into the impact of the regime on journalists (PJCIS 2015 Journalist's Source). Following pressure from the ALP Opposition and media groups, the government introduced amendments to establish a 'journalist information warrant', designed to protect the confidentiality of journalists' sources (Supplementary Explanatory Memorandum Data Retention Bill). As discussed further in Chap. 6, frequent reference was made to the PJCIS's recommendations during the second reading debates on the Bill and further unsuccessful amendments were introduced in the Senate by the minor parties and independents, building on the issues raised by submission makers to both the LCA References Committee and the PJCIS.[15]

The Data Retention Bill was also considered by the PJCHR (Fifteenth Report of 44th Parliament 2014 at p. 10) in a report tabled well in advance of either the PJCIS or LCA References Committee reports. The PJCHR's report focused on the potential for the Bill to unjustifiably interfere with the right to privacy protected by

[14] The PJCIS also recommended that the government provide a response to the outstanding recommendations from the PJCIS's 2013 report by 1 July 2015 and made recommendations to limit the range of agencies able to access retained data and to strengthen safeguards relating to the sharing and use of data between agencies.

[15] For example, Australian Greens Senator Scott Ludlam introduced unsuccessful amendments to extend the 'journalist information warrant' scheme to all access to data retained under the Bill, which was also included in amendments circulated by Senator Leyonhjelm.

Article 17 of the ICCPR (at p. 18). In a relatively unusual step, the PJCHR issued a consensus recommendation that the Bill be amended to:

> provide that access to retained data be granted only on the basis of a warrant approved by a court or independent administrative tribunal, taking into account the necessity of access for the purpose of preventing or detecting serious crime and defined objective grounds as set out [earlier in the report] (at p. 18).

The PJCHR also recommended that the Bill be amended to define the types of data that are to be retained, and to limit the range of agencies with access to retained data (at pp. 14, 16–17). The PJCHR also sought further information from the Attorney-General as to the proportionality and necessity of imposing a two-year mandatory retention period, having regard to the privacy and other rights impacts of the proposed regime (at p. 15) and recommended that consideration be given to amending the proposed scheme to ensure that individuals were notified when their data have been accessed (at p. 21). While the PJCHR did not receive a positive response to its recommendations for amendment from the government, many of its concerns were noted in the reports of both the LCA References Committee and the PJCIS, and many of its recommendations were reflected in the PJCIS's recommendations.[16]

The Data Retention Bill was also scrutinised by the SSCSB (Alert Digest No 16 of 2014 at p. 2; Report No 1 of 2015 at p. 113). In its Alert Digest, the SSCSB expressed concerns about the extent to which the Bill interfered with the right to privacy, and the way the Bill left many key matters, including the meaning of 'data', to delegated legislation.[17] In its final report on the Bill, issued after the government had agreed to implement the PJCIS recommendations, the SSCSB reiterated its strong concerns about the use of delegated legislation and instruments to prescribe the type of data to be retained under the scheme and to list the types of agencies that would have access to such data (Report No 1 of 2015 at pp. 118).

Taken together, the Data Retention Bill experience provides another example of the cumulative legislative impact of multi-committee review. In this case, the PJCIS had a strong, direct legislative impact, with all of its recommendations implemented though successful government amendments. In addition, the PJCIS's 2013 report provided the framework for much of the public and parliamentary debate on the Data Retention Bill when introduced. The work of the LCA References Committee, the PJCHR and the SSCSB is also evident in the submissions to the PJCIS and in the PJCIS's report on the Bill. Further, many of the recommendations made by the PJCHR and issues raised by the SSCSB were reflected in legislative amendments

---

[16] However, it should be noted that the recommendation that data only be accessed with a warrant did not form part of the PJCIS's recommendations and was only reflected in government amendments to the Bill in so far as it applied to journalists.

[17] The SSCSB also requested advice from the government about other mechanisms to increase parliamentary oversight in relation to regulations prescribing the data set, those prescribing additional services to which the data set will apply and ministerial declarations of further authorities and bodies as a 'criminal law enforcement agency'. (SSCSB, Alert Digest No 16 of 2014 at pp. 2, 6).

introduced in response to the PJCIS report (PJCIS 2015 Journalist's Sources Recommendations 2, 3, 10 and 13). These committee reports may have also influenced opposition and minor party parliamentarians to pressure the government to introduce the 'journalist information warrant' regime.

As discussed in Chap. 6, the Data Retention Bill related to a subject matter that was intrinsically interesting to media organisations and journalists, which no doubt influenced the significant public attention the Bill received. However, the very large number of submissions to the committee inquiries, and the diversity of the organisations and individuals providing evidence, suggests that parliamentary committees provided a practical forum for parliamentarians and sophisticated submission makers to develop concrete ways of ameliorating some of the rights-abrogating features of the proposed legislation. In these types of scenarios, where public support for rights-enhancing change is strong, government backbenchers, opposition members and minor parties may be particularly strident in their push for reform, even with respect to Bills that had originally received bipartisan support. As discussed further in Chap. 6, this can be a sign of the important role parliamentary committees play in fostering deliberative democracy at the federal level.

5.3.3.2 The Foreign Fighters Act 2014 (CSA 11)

As noted in Chap. 3, the Abbott Government introduced the Foreign Fighters Bill in response to the 'serious and ongoing terrorist threat' posed to Australia by the return of 'foreign fighters' (those Australians who have participated in foreign conflicts or undertaken training with extremist groups overseas) (Explanatory Memorandum Foreign Fighters Bill 2014 at para [1]). The Bill amended 22 separate Acts.[18] Its key provisions included: the establishment of a new offence of entering a 'declared area' in which a terrorist organisation is engaging in hostile activity (Item 110); a new offence of 'advocating terrorism'(Item 61); amendments to the terrorist organisation training offences (Items 68–71); the introduction of a delayed notification search warrant regime (Item 51); and a ten-year extension of the control order and preventative detention order regimes, and the questioning and detention regime (Items 72–180).

Despite moving rapidly through Parliament,[19] four separate parliamentary committees scrutinised the Foreign Fighters Bill, but not the LCA Committees. This

[18] The Commonwealth Acts include: *Crimes (Foreign Incursions and Recruitment) Act 1978* (Cth); *Criminal Code Act 1995* (Cth); *Crimes Act 1914* (Cth); *Australian Security Intelligence Organisation 1979* (Cth); *Intelligence Services Act 2001* (Cth); *Telecommunications (Interception and Access) Act 1979* (Cth); *Australian Passports Act 2005* (Cth); *Customs Act 1901* (Cth); *Anti-Money Laundering and Counter-Terrorism Financing Act 2006* (Cth); *Migration Act 1958* (Cth); *Foreign Evidence Act 1994* (Cth); *A New Tax System (Family Assistance) Act 1999* (Cth); *Paid Parental Leave Act 2010* (Cth); *Social Security Act 1991* (Cth); *Social Security (Administration) Act 1999* (Cth).

[19] The Bill was introduced on 24 September 2014 and passed on 30 October 2014.

decision adopted by the government members of the LCA Committees (and opposed by the non-government members) was made on the basis that the PJCIS was already inquiring into the Bill (LCA Legislation Committee Foreign Fighters Bill Report 2014).

The PJCIS's three-week inquiry into the Bill attracted over 50 submissions, involved three days of hearings, and resulted in an extensive consensus report (2014). In its report, the PJCIS referred extensively to past independent reviews and parliamentary committee reports, including the 2012 and 2013 INSLM annual reports (see e.g. pp. 63, 77 and 79) and the 2012 COAG review of the control order and preventative detention order regimes and stop and search powers (at pp. 52 and 63). The PJCIS accepted the evidence provided from government agencies on the need for the new offences and powers proposed in the Bill. However, it also acknowledged the rights-intrusive nature of the proposed new measures, and warned of the need to ensure that the proposed provisions were accompanied by strong safeguards and oversight mechanisms (see e.g. para [2.39]. This is reflected in the PJCIS's 36 recommendations, which included:

- improving the safeguards in the preventative detention order regime to include the requirement for the Ombudsman to be notified of certain events;
- introducing a new sunset clause (24 months after the next election) for the questioning and detention regime, the control order and preventative detention order regime and the stop, search and seizure powers relating to terrorism offences;
- increasing the PJCIS's oversight powers to include the counter-terrorism activities of the AFP;
- limiting the definition of 'hostile activity' in the proposed new offences to conduct which would be considered to be a 'serious offence' if undertaken within Australia;
- ensuring that declarations of declared areas for the purposes of the new offences can only be made by the Minister for Foreign Affairs and only if a 'terrorist organisation is engaging in a hostile activity' in that area. These declarations must be in the form of disallowable instruments and subject to disallowance by Parliament;
- requiring the PJCIS to conduct a review of each 'declared area' declaration made, within the disallowance period for each declaration; and
- subjecting the proposed new declared area offences to a sunset clause two years after the next election (Recommendations 12–14, 16, 18–20).

The government agreed to implement all of these recommendations (Brandis 2014a, b) and introduced amendments to this effect, directly referencing the work of the PJCIS in second reading speeches and in supplementary Explanatory Memoranda. The government amendments were passed, as well as amendments proposed by the opposition in the Senate, which inserted a 'legitimate purpose' exception into the new declared areas offence regime.[20] The opposition also moved successful amendments to clarify that the 'advocating terrorism' offence does not apply to 'a person who engages in good faith in public discussion of any genuine academic, artistic, scientific, political or religious matter'.[21]

The SSCSB also considered the Bill, initially in a special Alert Digest tabled out of session (SSCSB Alert Digest Relating to the Foreign Fighters Bill 2014) and later in two separate, longer reports, both issued in 2014. These latter reports were tabled just as the Bill was reaching the second reading stage in the Senate, and just prior to passage of the amended Bill in the House. In its Alert Digest and subsequent reports, the SSCSB referred to the relevant findings and recommendations of the INSLM and requested further information on why the government sought to depart in some respects from the INSLM's recommendations. A key consideration for the SSCSB was whether persons subject to the proposed new executive powers in the Bill (such as passport or visa cancellation powers) had access to judicial review and the rules of natural justice. In his response to the SSCSB's Alert Digest, the Attorney-General undertook to include further information in the revised Explanatory Memorandum (SSCSB Further Report Relating to the Foreign Fighters Bill 2014 at pp. 3–7). The Attorney-General also noted the government's acceptance of the full range of PJCIS recommendations, which he asserted addressed many of the SSCSB's concerns (at pp. 5–13). Some issues, particularly those relating to access to judicial review following passport or visa cancellation decisions and those features of the Bill that diluted pre-existing safeguards for the control orders or preventative detention orders regime, continued to raise concerns for the SSCSB, which ultimately left these issues to the Senate as a whole to consider.

The PJCHR also considered the Bill (Fourteenth Report of 44th Parliament 2014 at p. 3) but tabled its report *after* the conclusion of the second reading debate on the Bill in the Senate, and just two days before the amended Bill passed through the House. The PJCHR expressed strong frustration at the time frame it was given to scrutinise this complex legislation and provide rights analysis on the pre-existing control order regime, which had been introduced prior to the establishment of the PJCHR and therefore had not previously been subject to detailed consideration by the committee (see e.g. para [1.20]. The PJCHR made a series of requests for further information about the rights compatibility of the control orders regime, and to substantiate claims in the SoC that the proposed new measures were a necessary and proportionate response to the threat posed by foreign fighters to Australian national security.[22] The PJCHR also made a number of consensus findings of incompatibility

[20] Under this amendment, the declared area offence provision does not apply if the person enters or remains in the area for a legitimate purpose such as providing aid of a humanitarian nature, performing an official duty, working in a professional capacity as a journalist or making a bona fide visit to a family member.

[21] Unsuccessful amendments were also moved by the Australian Greens and independent Senator David Leyonhjelm, addressing some of the concerns raised by the PJCHR.

[22] These included requests for further advice from the Attorney-General on: whether the operation of the counter-terrorism laws will, in practice, be compatible with the rights to equality and non-discrimination and whether the proposed introduction of the power to suspend passports for up to 14 days is compatible with the right to freedom of movement.

with a number of human rights and recommended legislative amendments. For example, it found that:

- the control order regime and the preventative detention order regime is likely to be incompatible with Article 9 and 14 of the ICCPR (at pp. 15–25);
- the proposed delayed notification search warrant regime should be amended to require an applicant to demonstrate that it is not possible to obtain the evidence in another way (at pp. 29–34);
- the declared area offence provision is likely to be incompatible with the right to a fair trial and the presumption of innocence, unnecessarily restricts freedom of movement, and is likely to be incompatible with the right to equality and non-discrimination (at pp. 34–7); and
- the advocating terrorism offence provision, as currently drafted, is likely to be incompatible with the right to freedom of opinion and expression (at pp. 50–2).

Unlike the SSCSB, the PJCHR did not receive a response to its requests for further information or advice from the Attorney-General. As a result, the Bill was passed with amendments on 30 October 2014 that did not directly address the full range of rights concerns later raised by the PJCHR.

When taken together, the parliamentary scrutiny of this Bill had an important rights-enhancing legislative impact, despite the very tight time frame for undertaking inquiries and the complexity and range of new measures proposed. However, as discussed further in Chap. 6, the Foreign Fighters Bill is also an example of how the work of the PJCHR can be frustrated by the very short times between the introduction of a Bill and the second reading debate. Despite making findings of rights incompatibility and specific recommendations for amendment, the PJCHR's efforts to influence the content of the Bill were stifled as a result of its report being tabled after the conclusion of the second reading debate on the Bill in the Senate. This meant that Senators did not have access to the views of PJCHR prior to voting on the Bill, and members of the House received the PJCHR report just days before the amended Bill was passed. In addition, submissions makers to the PJCIS inquiry did not have access to the PJCHR's analysis of the Bill, and were therefore unable to integrate the PJCHR's concerns into their advocacy.

5.3.3.3 Counter-Terrorism Legislation Amendment Act (No 1) 2014 (Cth) (CSA 10)

Just a month after introducing the Foreign Fighters Bill, and before that Bill had passed, the government introduced the Counter-Terrorism Legislation Amendment Bill (No 1) 2014. This Bill expanded the grounds upon which a control order can be requested and issued, reduced the information required to be provided to the Attorney-General when seeking an interim control order, and extended the time before material must be provided to the Attorney-General where a request for an urgent interim control order has been made (Items 6–29). The Bill also requires the Attorney-General to advise the PJCIS before amending a regulation that lists a terrorist organisation and to allow the committee to review any proposed change during the disallowance period.

The Bill was referred to the PJCIS (but not the LCA Committees) for a short inquiry that attracted 17 written submissions and involved one public hearing. Many submissions drew attention to the INSLM's 2012 recommendation that control orders were 'not effective, not appropriate and not necessary' and that the regime should be repealed (Walker 2012 at pp. 4 and 44). Some submissions also noted that the Bill's proposal to expand the control order regime was being pursued despite the majority of the COAG Review Committee having recommended strengthening safeguards in the *existing* control order regime (PJCIS Report 2014 at p. 11). In its report on the Counter-Terrorism Legislation Amendment Bill, the PJCIS referred to the work of the INSLM and the committee's own consideration of the control order regime as part of its inquiry into the Foreign Fighters Bill (see e.g. p. 22). The report also noted that some of the safeguards proposed by COAG were not reflected in the Bill, such as the introduction of a system of 'Special Advocates' who would be able to access classified information and act on behalf of individuals. Some committee members supported the introduction of such a regime to accompany the changes proposed by the Bill (Recommendation 1 and p. 24). The PJCIS also noted that the extended delay in appointing the INSLM left a gap in accountability and oversight of the control order regime (at p. 23) and recommended that the position be filled as a matter of urgency. Other recommendations included that:

- the meaning of a number of key terms be clarified;
- when seeking the Attorney-General's consent to request an interim control order, the AFP must provide the Attorney-General with a statement of facts relating to why the order should be made, and any known facts as to why it should *not* be made;
- requests to obtain the Attorney-General's consent to apply for an interim order should be dealt with within eight hours; and
- the pre-existing safeguards relating to specifying and reviewing the conditions imposed as part of a control order should be re-instated (Recommendations 3–5).

The government agreed to accept, or 'accept in principle', all of the PJCIS's recommendations (Brandis 2014a, b) and introduced a number of successful government amendments to the Bill, and a supplementary Explanatory Memorandum attributing the legislative changes to the work of the PJCIS.[23]

On the same day, the PJCHR tabled its report on the Bill (Sixteenth Report of the 44th Parliament) containing strong criticisms of the SoC (at para [1.39]), and noting that a far more detailed assessment of the control order regime's compliance with human rights should have been provided. The PJCHR also expressed the view that the proposed changes should not go ahead until an INSLM was appointed (at para

[23] Thirty successful government amendments were made to reflect the 15 recommendations made by the PJCIS. Nine unsuccessful amendments were moved by Senator Wright that also aimed to improve the Bill's compliance with human rights. The Bill passed both Houses on 2 December 2014 and received Royal Assent on 12 December 2014.

[1.32]) and sought further information on these and other matters from the Attorney-General. However, no response was provided until 11 February 2015, well after the passage of the Bill.

The SSCSB also considered the Counter-Terrorism Legislation Amendment Bill (No 1) 2014 (Alert Digest 15 of 2014), referring to its detailed comments on the control order regime contained in its extensive reports on the Foreign Fighters Bill (at pp. 29–31). Like the PJCHR, the SSCSB also expressed concern that the provisions proposed in this Bill would expand the scope of the regime while also removing key safeguards (at pp. 33–35). The SSCSB requested further information on why the Bill departed from past findings made by the PJCIS, and failed to address the concerns raised by the INSLM (at pp. 29–35). However, these requests for information were not answered prior to the passage of the Bill (see SSCSB Report No 1 of 2015).

The scrutiny experience of this Bill demonstrates a convergence of rights concerns being expressed by three different committees, but reveals that only one committee (the PJCIS) was able to translate these concerns into legislative change. The technical scrutiny committees were sidelined in this case by the lack of timely responses from the proponent Minister to their requests for information, which meant that their concluded views on the Bill were not available to parliamentarians at the vital second reading stage. Nor were they available to submission makers to the PJCIS. These issues will be discussed further in Part III, where a range of strategies are suggested to address the reporting practices of the SSCSB and the PJCHR and to encourage more collaboration between the technical scrutiny and inquiry-based committees.

5.3.3.4 The Citizenship Act (CSA 12)

The Citizenship Bill was introduced in June 2015 in the context of escalating global and local concerns about the threat posed by 'foreign fighters' and 'home-grown terrorists' (Harrison-Smith 2015; Pillai 2014). It included a range of new measures designed to remove the Australian citizenship of anyone who travels overseas to participate in or support terrorist activity (Schedule 1). Among many other provisions, the Citizenship Bill introduced three new ways in which an Australian dual national can cease to be an Australian citizen: (1) engaging in specified terrorist-related conduct, (2) fighting for, or being in the service of, a declared terrorist organisation, or (3) being convicted of a prescribed terrorism offence.

The Bill was referred to the PJCIS for inquiry and report (2015). The Attorney-General also asked the PJCIS to consider whether proposed conviction-based cessation of citizenship provisions should apply retrospectively to convictions prior to the commencement of the Act. An attempt by the Australian Greens to have the Citizenship Bill referred to the LCA Legislation Committee was defeated (Senate Debates 25 June 2015 at 4600). The Bill was also considered by the SSCSB (Alert

Digest No 7 of 2015) and the PJCHR (Twenty-Fifth Report of the 44th Parliament 2015).[24]

The PJCIS received 43 submissions and seven supplementary submissions to its inquiry, and held three public hearings in addition to receiving private briefings. This culminated in an extensive report containing 26 recommendations for amendment, subject to which the PJCIS recommended that the Bill be passed. All of these recommendations were accepted and reflected in successful government amendments (see Supplementary Explanatory Memorandum to the Citizenship Bill). In a number of instances, these changes could be described as rights-enhancing. For example, the amendments:

- make it clear that before a dual national can have their citizenship 'renounced' by doing something terrorist-related overseas, they must at least have *intended* to engage in the particular prescribed conduct (rather than been reckless or negligent) (amended cl 33AA(3));
- narrow the range of conduct that can trigger the renunciation provisions, from the previously low-level 'damage to Commonwealth property' to a tighter list of conduct with a closer connection to an actual terrorist act (amended cl 33AA(2));
- require the Minister for Immigration to notify the person who has 'renounced' their citizenship that he or she is no longer an Australian, and set out the person's rights of review (amended cl 33AA(11)); and
- make it clear that the laws cannot be applied to children under 14 (amended cl 33AA(1)).

The PJCHR, which was by now chaired by the Hon Phillip Ruddock MP, also considered the Citizenship Bill in a lengthy and detailed report (Twenty-Fifth Report of the 44th Parliament 2015). In its report, the PJCHR criticised many aspects of the SoC, in particular its failure to provide reasoning or evidence that the measures were reasonable to address a 'pressing or substantial concern' (at p. 11). The PJCHR also questioned the proportionality of having the citizenship revocation provisions trigged by offences that included damaging Commonwealth property and other relatively minor offences (at p. 11), and expressed concerns with respect to:

- the lack of clarity around how decisions will be made by the Minister or officials to revoke a person's citizenship (at p. 13); and
- whether depriving a person of citizenship, and therefore potentially exposing them to deportation, is compatible with Australia's non-refoulement obligations (at pp. 23–24).

[24] The PJCIS issued its report on the Citizenship Bill on 4 September 2015. The PJCHR issued its report with respect to the Citizenship Bill almost a month before the PJCIS on 11 August 2015. The SSCSB issued its report on 12 August 2015. This relatively relaxed legislative time frame may be explained by the change of Australia's Prime Minister from Tony Abbott to Malcolm Turnbull on 15 September 2015, which may have delayed the debates on the Citizenship Bill for longer than usual.

The PJCHR requested further information from the Attorney-General and Minister for Immigration on these and other matters, but did not wait for a response before tabling its report on 11 August 2015. This proved prudent, as further advice from the Minister for Immigration was not received until 11 January 2016 (PJCHR Thirty-Sixth Report of 44th Parliament 2016 Ch 2).

The SSCSB also considered the Citizenship Bill in its Alert Digest tabled prior to the resumption of the second reading debate on the Bill (Alert Digest No 7 of 2015 at p. 3), and raised a number of strongly worded concerns (see e.g. p. 10). For example, it said that: 'serious issues of fairness arise given that a person may lose their citizenship on the basis of criminal conduct *without any of the protections associated with a criminal trial*' (emphasis in original, p. 6). The SSCSB also found the 'automatic' nature of the cessation of citizenship provisions to be highly problematic (at p. 7), and sought further explanations about why these provisions were considered necessary from the Minister of Immigration. Like the PJCHR, the SSCSB did not receive a response to its requests for further information until several months after the enactment of the Citizenship Bill (SSCSB Report No 4 of 2016); however, the SSCSB's concerns were noted by the PJCIS in its report and by a number of submission makers to the PJCIS inquiry.[25]

Parliamentary scrutiny of the Citizenship Bill is another strong example of the cumulative and rights-enhancing legislative impact of multi-committee scrutiny of a Bill. In this case, the legislative impact of the PJCIS was clearly more direct, but was underpinned by the analysis provided by the SSCSB and its robust exchange of correspondence with the executive. Similarly, while the PJCHR may not have had a direct legislative impact, it was successful in alerting Parliament to the issues to consider when passing laws of this nature due to its decision to table its report prior to the commencement of the second reading debate, despite not receiving a response from the Minister. As discussed further in Part III, early reporting by the PJCHR on rights-engaging Bills (even in the absence of a response from the proponent Minister) is one of the key recommendations of my research.

5.3.3.5 The High Risk Offenders Act (CSA 13)

Timeliness of PJCHR reporting again came into focus in the context of the High Risk Offenders Bill, which provides an interesting example of how significant rights-enhancing legislative amendments can be achieved in a relatively short time period, this time as a result of a combination of a strongly worded SSCSB report, specific recommendations for amendment from the PJCHR and an influential PJCIS inquiry.

[25] For example, PJCIS Recommendations 2, 6, 8, 9 were designed to narrow the scope of the offences to which the conviction-based provisions of the Bill would apply, responding to concerns raised by the SSCSB. A range of other PJCIS recommendations reflect concerns raised by the SSCSB, for example those relating to concerns about adequate judicial review: see PJCIS Report on the Citizenship Bill 2015 Recommendation 14.

The High Risk Offenders Bill was introduced into the Senate following COAG discussions at about how Australian jurisdictions should work together to counter the risk poses by convicted terrorist offenders, who may still hold nefarious intent, being released from prison on the expiry of their custodial sentences (PJCIS Report High Risk Offenders Bill 2016 at p. 4). The Bill proposed a continuing detention order (CDO) regime that allows for the continued detention of convicted 'terrorist offenders' who are assessed by a judge in civil proceedings to present an 'unacceptable risk' to the community following the completion of their custodial sentence (Explanatory Memorandum High Risk Offenders Bill 2016 at para [3]). These orders can only be obtained if the Court is satisfied that no other alternative, less restrictive means exist for preventing the 'unacceptable risk' posed by the person's release (High Risk Offenders Bill proposed s105A.7(1)). Under the Bill, once a person is detained for these purposes, they should be treated 'in a way that is appropriate to their status as a person who is not serving a sentence of imprisonment' (proposed s105A.4(1)) – a feature designed to align with what the Government described as the Bill's *preventative* rather than *punitive* character (Explanatory Memorandum at paras [9]–[13]). However, this characterisation was contested by the PJCHR, the SSCSB and the PJCIS and each committee raised strong concerns about the punitive impact of the Bill in their scrutiny reports. Those involved in the PJCIS inquiry into the Bill (such as the Law Council of Australia) also raised concerns about whether the new continuing detention order regime was needed in the first place, submitting that the existing control order and preventative detention order regime could already be applied to any convicted terrorist who, upon release, continued to pose a threat to the Australian community. Similar issues and concerns were the subject of the PJCHR's consideration of the Bill, which was the first of the three committees scrutinising the Bill to issue its preliminary report on 11 October 2016 (Seventh Report of 2016 at p. 14).

A key focus of the PJCHR's report was the character of the detention being authorised as well as the conditions of detention for those subject to continuing detention orders. While the PJCHR accepted that the Bill was introduced for the purpose of protecting the community from the risk of terrorist attacks, it did not accept that it was purely preventative in character and asked for further information about the type of safeguards included in the Bill, and the extent to which these worked to ensure the detention imposed was limited to that strictly necessary to achieve the purported preventative aim (at para [1.62]). The PJCHR also asked for more information about the extent to which the CDO regime was designed to counter the specific concerns raised by international human rights bodies with respect to similar regimes in other jurisdictions, and raised concerns with respect to the application of the civil standard of proof to proceedings (at paras [1.69]–[1.81]). In an interesting departure from its normal practice, the PJCHR set out a number of specific legislative options for addressing its concerns, referring, for example, to the criminal standard of proof under section 40 of the *Dangerous Sexual Offenders Act 2006* (WA) as preferred option for dealing with standards of proof to that employed in the Bill.

These detailed and direct requests for timely information about the Bill by the PJCHR went unheeded by the Government for many months, well after the Bill had been passed. As a result, the PJCHR was unable to conclude its assessment of the Bill while it was still in Parliament. It did, however, issue a second scrutiny report on the Bill (Eighth Report of 2016) wherein the PJCHR concluded that in the absence of the further information it was unable to find the proposed continuing detention regime compatible with the right to liberty (PJCIS Report 2016 at [1.85]).

Just one day after the PJCHR delivered this relatively forcefully worded report, the SSCSB issued its Alert Digest report on the Bill (Alert Digest No 7 of 2016 p. 54), followed by a final Report, tabled on 30 November 2016 (SSCSB Report No 10 of 2016). Like the PJCHR, the SSCSB was highly critical of the Bill, raising strongly worded concerns that depart from the usual cautious and somewhat deferential style of the SSCSB (Moulds 2017). Frustration was also expressed at the lack of substantive response by the relevant Minister to the issued raised by the SSCSB in its Alert Digest (Moulds 2017). Of particular concern was the claim that the detention authorised by the Bill was of a *preventative* rather than *punitive* character, with the SSCSB explaining that it considered the material contained in the Explanatory Memorandum to be insufficient to substantiate this claim.

The High Risk Offenders Bill was also considered by the PJCIS (2016) which tabled its report on the Bill prior to the close of the second reading speeches on the Bill. By then, both the PJCHR and the SSCSB had issued their first reports on the Bill, but had yet to receive responses to their requests for information from the Attorney General. The PJCIS's report was far more detailed and included material obtained from 23 written submissions and from witnesses at a public inquiry. The PJCIS ultimately supported the passage of the Bill, but made this support conditional on the implementation of 23 recommendations for amendments to be made to the Bill and the Explanatory Memorandum.

The recommendations of the PJCIS align closely with the concerns raised by the PJCHR and SSCSB reports and in its report about the punitive character of the detention authorised by the Bill, and the PJCIS refers to the work of these scrutiny committees in its analysis (see eg. para [1.83]). The PJCIS report also covers many operational and procedural features of the Bill in more detail than either the SSCSB or the PJCHR which in turn become the focus of many of its recommendations. For example, the PJCIS recommended that the Bill be amended to:

- Narrow the scope of offences to which the CDO regime applies by removing treason offences and those offences relating to the publication of recruitment advertisements (Recommendation 2).
- Increasing the level of detail required in applications for CDOs and clarifying and strengthening the court's role in approving interim CDOs (Recommendations 6, 9 and 14).
- Increasing the level of oversight for the CDO regime and including a sunset clause of ten years duration. (Recommendations 18–20).

Like the SSCSB and the PJCHR, the PJCIS also considered the legality and rights compliance of other similar continuing detention orders in other Australian jurisdictions. Consideration was given to the case of *Fardon v Attorney-General (Qld)* (2004) 233 CLR 575 which concerned the legality of the preventative detention regime in place in Queensland for sexual offenders, and in particular, whether it was compatible with the separation of powers doctrine central to Chapter III of the Australian Constitution (see also PJCIS Report 2016 at paras [1.61]). Through the PJCIS's inquiry process the Government confirmed that it had sought advice from the Solicitor General and the Australian Government Solicitor on the constitutional validity of the Bill. The PJCIS recommended that the Government obtain further legal advice from the Solicitor General or equivalent on the final form of the Bill.

All 23 of the PJCIS's recommendations were accepted by the Government and amendments to the High Risk Offenders Bill were moved to this effect on 28 November 2016. A supplementary Explanatory Memorandum was also tabled, attributing the amendments to the work of the PJCIS. The role of the PJCIS in securing these legislative changes was also noted in many of the second reading speeches on the Bill.

Taken together, the multi-committee scrutiny of the High Risk Offenders Bill tells us something important about the differences in the way the three committees approach their scrutiny role, and their relationships with the executive Government. The scrutiny experience of the High Risk Offenders Bill also provides another example of the potentially cumulative benefit of parliamentary committees working together to improve the quality and rights compliance of a proposed law. In this case study example, there is a high degree of public and behind-the-scenes engagement between each of the three committees, who share rights concerns with the content of the proposed CDO regime, and who share frustration at the lack of timely response from the proponent Minister for more information. All three committees also share a common interest in accessing further legal advice about the constitutionality or lawfulness of the proposed CDO regime, with the PJCIS able to facilitate a more direct 'dialogue' with the Government on this and other issues by virtue of its public hearing powers, whilst the PJCHR and SSCSB wait for an answer to their more formal written correspondence. On the other hand, the strongly-worded and timely issue of the initial scrutiny reports by the PJCHR and SSCSB raised the alarm about the concerning features of this Bill early and strongly enough to feature both in submissions to the PJCIS and in the report of the PJCIS itself. In these ways the High Risk Offenders Bill case brings into focus a number of themes emerging from this phase of parliamentary scrutiny of Australian counter-terrorism laws. It illustrates, for example, that multi-committee review significantly improves both the breadth and the quality of the information available to the Parliament about the Bill and leads to significant rights enhancing improvements with the PJCIS appearing particularly well placed to have a strong and direct legislative impact. The High Risk Offenders Bill also shows that the scrutiny committees can continue to play in influential role in the amendment process even if their Final Reports are delayed, provided that parliamentarians and submission makers are able to publish their preliminary thoughts on the Bill. These and other interactions between individual committees within the system are explored in further detail in Chap. 8.

5.3.3.6 The Encryption Act (CSA 14)

Another example of the system of committees working together to achieve rights-enhancing results is the Encryption Bill, which was introduced into Parliament in September 2018. Central to the scrutiny experience of the Encryption Bill is the growing dominance of the PJCIs, both as a pre-enactment scrutiny body, and as a post-enactment review body. As discussed below, parliamentary scrutiny of this Bill brought the members of the PJCIS in direct and public conflict with the proponent Minister and the Prime Minister, and bipartisan support for its enactment was made conditional on an immediate post-enactment referral to the PJCIS for further inquiry. As with the other Bills discussed in this phase, the PJCIS was at the centre of the lawmaking process, dominating the public and parliamentary debate on the content of the Bill, and directly influencing its content.

The purpose of the Encryption Bill is to give law enforcement and intelligence officers access to certain communications and data for the purposes of 'disrupting and investigating criminal activity and threats to national security, including organised crime and terrorism.' (Barker et al. 2018 at p. 7).[26] The Bill was introduced in response to the challenges posed by the 'increasing prevalence of encrypted data and communications' to those agencies seeking to investigate, disrupt and prevent serious organised crime or threats to national security (Barker et al. 2018 at p. 7). This nefarious use of encryption is sometimes known as 'going dark', and the extent of the challenge for law enforcement and intelligence agencies appears to be increasing (Barker et al. 2018 at p. 10).

The measures in the Bill empower law enforcement and intelligence agencies to access industry assistance to decrypt encrypted technologies and to gain access to communications and data at points where they are not encrypted. Central to the Bill are the provisions that *require* industry to provide law enforcement and intelligence agenise with assistance to decrypt encrypted data. Schedule 1 of the Bill sets out circumstances in which providing this assistance is *voluntary* (a technical assistance request) or *mandatory* (a technical assistance notice or technical capability notice). The Bill also contains amendments that broader the powers of law enforcement and intelligence agencies to covertly access data held in a target computer (Schedule 2)[27] and that expand the situations in which law enforcement officers may require a person to provide assistance or face a custodial sentence or significant financial penalty. The Bill also provides ASIO with new coercive powers under the assistance order regime, modelled on the regime available to law enforcement agencies.

The Encryption Bill has been subject to sustained, multi-layered public and parliamentary scrutiny, including through an Exposure Draft department-led

[26] The Bill amends a number of Acts including the *Telecommunications Act 1997*, the *Australian Security Intelligence Organisation Act 1979* and the *Surveillance Devices Act 2004*.

[27] The amendments expand the powers available under computer access warrants and authorisations executed by the ASIO, including by allowing ASIO to intercept a communication for the purpose of executing a computer access warrant and undertake activities to conceal access after the expiry of a warrant.

consultation process and by the PJCIS. This scrutiny has occurred against the backdrop of a clear intention on the part of the Coalition Government to enact the proposed provisions as quickly as possible (Morrison 2018; Dutton 2018). The Bill also forms part of Australia's response to international efforts to combat cybercrime and ensure that appropriate decryption powers are available to Australian intelligence and law enforcement authorities (Morrison 2018; Dutton 2018).

In April 2018, following earlier industry consultations, the Government released an Exposure Draft of the Bill for public comment (Taylor 2018). The Department of Home Affairs received close to 16,000 submissions, including 55 detailed substantive submissions from industry groups, civil society, government bodies and individuals (PJCIS Report Encryption Bill 2018 at p. 41). The focus of the vast majority of these submissions was on the proposed changes to the coercive powers of law enforcement bodies to require industry assistance to decrypt data. While some amendments were made to the Exposure Draft to address some of the issues raised by industry and other bodies, many of the key features remained in the Bill when it was introduced into Parliament in 20 September 2018.

The timing of the introduction of the Encryption Bill, just weeks before the end of the sitting period for 2018, had an impact on the capacity of the parliamentary committee system to scrutinise and report on the Bill. However, as discussed further below, in the case of the Encryption Bill, this tight time frame did not necessarily dilute the legislative impact of the parliamentary scrutiny applied to the Bill, as it ultimately resulted in a post-enactment reference to the PJCIS, as well as over 100 Government amendments made to the Bill prior to enactment in response to the PJCIS inquiry.

The Bill was also subject to scrutiny by the SSCSB and the PJCHR, whose reports set the scene for the rights issues that were later considered by the PJCIS and its submission makers. For example, the SSCSB's scrutiny report (Twelfth Scrutiny Digest of 2018 at pp. 12–49), centred around three themes:

- the breadth and intrusive nature of the powers conferred on the Executive, and the limited parliamentary scrutiny or judicial oversight of the use of those powers (at pp. 26–7),
- the impact of the new measures on the right to procedural fairness where matters may be brought before the courts arising from the exercise of powers amended or introduced in the Bill (at p. 30); and
- the privacy implications for individuals, including the potential impact on the privacy of innocent third parties (at p. 32).

Further information from the proponent Minister was sought on each of these issues and following consideration of the Minister's response, the SSCSB issued a second report on the Encryption Bill whereby it expressed ongoing concerns with respect the themes described above (at p. 33).

As discussed below, these themes featured strongly in the submissions made to the PJCIS's pre-enactment and post enactment inquiry into the Encryption Bill. They were also mirrored in the rights analysis undertaken by the PJCHR in its detailed scrutiny of the Encryption Bill (Report 11 of 2018 at pp. 24–71). Like the

SSCSB, the PJCHR drew attention to the potential impact of the Bill on the right to privacy, and questioned the proportionality or compatibility of measures in relation to this right. The PJCHR also raised concerns with respect to the limitations on an individual's ability to seek legal recourse where they may be affected by actions pursuant to one of the proposed measures, which depart significantly from the right to a fair trial and fair hearing or the right to an effective remedy (at p. 50). The Committee sought further information on this matter from the Minister in its first report on the Bill and received a response which was discussed in the PJCHR's second report on the Bill (at p. 51). In this second report on the Bill, the PJCHR observed that while the need to access encrypted data for law enforcement and national security purposes was a legitimate objective, in its view, the Bill as drafted was 'unlikely to constitute a proportionate limitation on the rights to privacy and freedom of expression and is therefore likely to be incompatible with those rights' (at p. 69). The PJCHR said that it was 'unable to conclude that the measure is compatible with the right to an effective remedy' and noted that the Minister's response 'did not fully address the committee's inquiries in relation to these complex issues.' (at p. 71.) This exchange set the scene for ongoing tensions between the proposed Minister and the parliamentary committee system with respect to this Bill, which were particularly pronounced in the case of the PJCIS inquiry, as discussed further below.

The PJCIS's public inquiry into the Bill took place against the backdrop of sustained pressure from Prime Minister Turnbull and proponent Minister, the Hon Peter Dutton MP, to see the Bill passed quickly. Despite the very short time frame for submissions, the PJCIS received 105 written submissions from a range of individuals and organisations, many of which framed their concerns with reference to or in similar language as that contained in the SSCSB and PJCHR's reports (PJCIS Report 2018, in particular submissions no 29, 76 and 60). Even those submission makers who were strongly in favour of the Bill and the coercive powers it introduced (e.g. submission no 42) recommended that the scope of the Bill be narrowed so that the coercive powers included could only be used for matters that relate to serious criminal activity, such as terrorism and espionage.

Following the receipt of submissions, the PJCIS quickly scheduled public hearings involving representatives from industry, government and community organisations to discuss their concerns with the Bill (PJCIS Report 2018 at p. 3). Further hearings were scheduled to hear from other submission makers, however before those hearings could take place the Prime Minister and Minister for Home Affairs asked the PJCIS to expedite its inquiry to facilitate debate on the Bill in both Houses during the final sitting fortnight of 2018 (Morrison 2018; Dutton 2018). In response to this time pressure, the Chair Andrew Hastie MP and Deputy Chair Anthony Byrne MP of the PJCIS responded by issuing a statement underscoring the need for the Committee to undertake its scrutiny task in a careful and bipartisan way, and noted that

> Since 2014, the Committee has considered 15 substantive national security bills and made over 300 recommendations for amendment, all of which have been accepted by government. These reports have been carefully developed to ensure that new powers are

proportionate and appropriately balanced with human rights and privacy, and that commensurate oversight and accountability is provided (Canberra, 22 November 2018).

Submission makers also raised concerns at the short time frame for the inquiry and questioned the necessity for the urgent passage of all or parts of the Bill (PJCIS Report 2018 at p. 13).

In what could be considered a mild act of defiance, the PJCIS went ahead with the public hearings on 28 November 2018 as scheduled. The PJCIS issued its report on the Encryption Bill shortly after this hearing, on 3 December 2018, and just days before the Bill was to be debated again in the House and the Senate on 6 December 2018, the last sitting day of the year. The PJCIS report was very short, containing only some brief comments on the consultation process and timing, as well as 17 bipartisan recommendations for changes to be made to the Bill. Subject to these changes, the Committee recommended that the Bill be passed as a matter of urgency, noting that 'there is a genuine and immediate need for agencies to have tools to respond to the challenge of encrypted communications' (at para [1.10]).

The 17 changes recommended by the PJCIS centred on the following key themes:

- narrowing the scope of the coercive industry assistance measures for example by requiring a threshold of maximum penalty of 3 years imprisonment or more before they can be used for criminal law enforcement (Recommendation 2);
- improving oversight measures, for example by increasing the power of Ombudsman to inspect and gather information (Recommendation 4) and responding to some of the recommendations made by the IGIS to strengthen oversight of the Bill (Recommendation 5);
- incorporating concepts of reasonableness, proportionality and external oversight into the process of issuing notices for coercive industry assistance measures (Recommendation 11); and
- subjecting the new laws to immediate post-enactment review by the PJCIS (Recommendation 16), and further review by the INSLM within 18 months of commencement (Recommendation 14).

While each of these recommendations can described as rights-enhancing in nature, for many submission makers (see e.g. submissions no 29, 76 and 60) and some committee members they did not go far enough to address the strong concerns with the Bill, particularly concerns with respect to the coercive nature of industry assistance powers. This is reflected in the Additional Comments provided by the Labor members of the PJCIS, which explain that although the Labor members support the 17 changes recommended by the Committee, they 'do not consider that these amendments address all of the problems in this Bill.' Keen to ensure the powers proposed in the Bill, which were described by law enforcement and intelligence agencies as 'urgently needed', were enacted before the Christmas period, the Labor Opposition supported the passage of the amendment Bill. However, it made its support for the Bill conditional on the government's undertaking that the PJCIS will committee will continue its inquiry into the Bill into 2019, and that a separate statutory review will be undertaken by the INSLM within 18 months of the legislation coming into effect. The Labor members of the PJCIS said that:

> These separate processes provide an opportunity to resolve our ongoing concerns about the Bill with the assistance of industry, experts, and civil liberties groups, whilst also upholding our responsibility to keep Australians safe.
>
> This compromise is emblematic of the balancing exercise that the committee has undertaken in all its work over the decades. The government should not walk away from it again. (PJCIS Additional Comments).

In response to the PJCIS's report, the Government moved 167 amendments in the House of Representatives that directly respond to the PJCIS recommendations (Supplementary Explanatory Memorandum Encryption Bill 2018). Further amendments prepared in response to the PJCIS report were moved in the Senate by Labor Senator Penny Wong, some of which were reflected in the successful Government amendments. While there remains some dispute over the extent to which each of the 17 recommendations made by the PJCIS were fully implemented, the direct and substantial legislative impact of the PJCIS is clear. The scope of the powers proposed in the Encryption Bill, and, the oversight mechanisms governing the use of those powers, were significantly modified because of the PJCIS inquiry.

Also clear is the growing dominance of the PJCIS as a *post-enactment* scrutiny body, as evidenced by the fact that the Labor Opposition's support for the Encryption Bill was made conditional upon an immediate referral to the PJCIS for further consideration. As discussed in Chap. 6, this trend solidifies the longer-term impact of the PJCIS on the shape of Australia's counter-terrorism laws and maximises the potential for submission makers to utilise the material contained in the reports of the scrutiny committees, including reports that were tabled close to or after the closing date for PJCIS submissions during the original inquiry. In other words, as discussed further in the next Chapter, *post* enactment review by the PJCIS of counter-terrorism laws enhances the opportunities for different committees within the system to work together and increases the overall legislative impact of the committee system on the shape of the enacted laws.

5.3.3.7 The TEO Bill (CSA 15)

The complex and influential position of the PJCIS within the parliamentary committee system is also evident in the context of the TEO Bill, where the recommendations made by the PJCIS had a significant rights-enhancing legislative impact, despite the fact that not all recommendations were implemented in full by the Government.

The TEO Bill was first introduced on 21 February 2019 and was designed to implement a new scheme for excluding Australian citizens who may have been involved in or supported terrorist activity overseas and are seeking to return to Australia (Tillett 2018). The purpose of the scheme was 'to protect the community from terrorism', allowing the return of Australians who travel overseas to join terrorist organisations to be 'carefully managed' by authorities (Explanatory

Memorandum TEO Bill at p. 16). Under the Bill, the Minister of Home Affairs can make an order preventing an Australian citizen from re-entering the country if one of two conditions are met. The first is where the Minister suspects on 'reasonable grounds' that the making the order would 'substantially assist' in preventing terrorism-related activity or preventing support for terrorist activity or a terrorist organisation upon the person's return to Australia (TEO Bill clause 10(2)(a)). The second is where the person has been assessed by ASIO to be a security risk, 'for reasons related to politically motivated violence' (clause 10(2)(b)). The order can be in force for up to two years from the date of making the order. Under the scheme, the only way a person subject to an exclusion order can come into Australia is to request a return permit, which can be issued by the Minister with conditions attached, including conditions preventing the citizen from entering Australia for up to twelve months (clause 15). Clause 17 of the Bill specifically provides that the Minister is not required to observe any requirements of procedural fairness when exercising these powers.

When first introduced, the TEO Bill was strongly opposed by legal experts and human rights groups who raised concerns that the scheme would invest broad and disproportionate powers in the Executive, be contrary to Australia's international human rights obligations (particularly rights to citizenship and freedom of movement) and conflict with constitutional principles (Irving 2019).[28] Questions were raised as to the need for such a scheme, having regard to the existence of the Control Order regime which effectively allowed the executive to restrict the movements and associations of any individuals considered to give rise to a risk of terrorist activity.

The TEO Bill was quickly referred to the PJCIS for inquiry and report and was also subjected to scrutiny by the SSCSB and the PJCHR. The PJCIS inquiry commenced on 22 February 2019 with submissions due by 8 March 2019. Only eight submissions were received and five witnesses called to provide evidence to the Committee at a hearing in Canberra on 15 March 2019. The PJCIS issued its report on the TEO Bill in April 2019, just prior to the dissolution of Parliament ahead of the Federal Election. As noted below, the TEO Bill was re-introduced into Parliament in amended form on 4 July 2019 by the re-constituted Morrison Government.

During its inquiry into the Bill, the PJCIS considered issues relating to the necessity of and rationale for a TEO scheme; the constitutional validity of the Bill; the absence of judicial authorisation under the proposed TEO scheme; the lack of clarity surrounding the threshold test for the making of a TEO; the exclusion of procedural fairness, and limitations on the ability to seek independent review, and the relationship between the Bill and Australia's international obligations, including in relation to the right to enter one's own country and the rights of children (PCJIS Report 2019 at para [2.1]).

---

[28] Irving distils the key constitutional questions arising from the Bill as follows: "First, does the Executive have the constitutional power to exclude citizens on the grounds that they may commit or support an act of terrorism, and to attach conditions on a TEO, the breach of which attracts imprisonment? Second, does the Commonwealth have the power in the first place to pass a law that prevents an Australian citizen from entering Australia?". (Irving 2019 p. 68.)

During the PJCIS inquiry, many submission makers highlighted the lack of safeguards within the TEO scheme proposed in the Bill and the UK temporary exclusion orders scheme (*Counter-Terrorism and Security Act 2015* (UK); see also Fenwick 2018) which was influential in the design of the Australian legislation. Under the UK legislation, a court's authorisation for the making of a TEO is required, whereas under the Australian scheme, no judicial oversight was provided and there was no requirement that standards of procedural fairness be observed. In its submission to the PJCIS, the Law Council highlighted the fact that under the Bill, the Minister was able to make exclusionary orders preventing an Australian citizen from re-entering the country *without* requiring an assessment by the Australian Security Intelligence Organisation (ASIO) and without adequate judicial oversight (Law Council Submission to PJCIS Report 2019). The Law Council pointed out that under the Bill, the Minister also had the power to attach significant conditions to an exclusion order or entry permit (which can apply to adults and children over 14) the breach of which attracts serious criminal penalties. Concerns were also raised that many of the key terms and tests contained in the Bill were inadequately defined, leading to a lack of precision as to the grounds required to make an exclusion order and inadequate provision for procedural fairness.

The PJCIS acknowledged many of these concerns, and in an unanimous report (2019), recommended that the Bill be amended in significant ways. A theme running through a number of the PJCIS's recommendations was to more closely align the proposed TEO regime with the control order regime, particularly when it comes to safeguards, oversight and reporting requirements. This saw the PJCIS recommend that TEOs and conditions imposed in return permits be made by 'issuing authorities' (being a judge, a retired judge or a senior member of the Administrative Appeals Tribunal) on application by the Minister, rather than by the Minister alone (Recommendations 5 and 7). These recommendations were designed to respond to strong concerns raised during the PJCIS inquiry about the lack of judicial oversight of the issuing of TEOs and the lack of procedural fairness safeguards. This recommendation was also supported by appendices to the PJCIS's report which compared the key features of the proposed TEO regime with those of the existing control order regime, and the TEO regime implemented in the UK. The PJCIS further recommended that in respect of urgent situations, the Minister may issue a temporary exclusion order, or impose a condition in a return permit, without the approval of an issuing authority, provided that the Minister obtain the approval of an issuing authority as soon as reasonably practicable, and if the issuing authority does not approve of the temporary exclusion order, the Minister must immediately revoke the order.

The Government did not accept these recommendations, instead re-introducing the Bill in July 2019 with new provisions setting out a process for TEOs to be referred to a 'reviewing authority' (TEO Bill 2019 s14) (either a former superior court judge or senior member of the Administrative Appeals Tribunal) acting *in a personal capacity* and empowered to consider whether or not the order was *lawful* (but not permitted to review the merits of the order) (s23).

The PCJIS also recommended a range of other rights-enhancing changes to the TEO Bill that were accepted (at least in part) by the Government and reflected in the revised version of the Bill that was re-introduced into Parliament in July 2019. For example, the PJCIS recommended amending the range of factors to which the Minister must have regard when issuing a TEO to include whether the person has a lawful ability to stay in their current location for the duration of the order, whether the person has a lawful ability to enter a third country (for example, due to holding a passport or residency visa for that third country), and the likelihood of the person being detained, mistreated or harmed if the person has no lawful ability to stay in their current location, and no lawful ability to enter a third country, for the duration of the order (PJCIS Report 2019 Recommendation 1).

The PJCIS also recommended amending the matters to which the Minister should have regard when imposing conditions on a return permit to include the impact of the conditions on the person's individual circumstances, including in relation to their dependents (if any), and requiring the Minister to be satisfied that the conditions are 'reasonably necessary, and reasonably appropriate and adapted' on an individual *and* a holistic basis (Recommendation 3). This recommendation was designed to bring the return permit provisions more closely into line with the existing control order regime, and also 'ensure the potential impact of conditions on the children of return permit applicants are taken into account' (at para [2.112]).

Recommendations were also made to amend the Bill to provide more detail as to the range of factors the Minister should have regard to when determining the best interests of the child when making orders with respect to children between 14 and 17, including the child's age, maturity, sex, background, physical and mental health, right to receive an education, and other matters (Recommendation 4).

The Government also implemented the PJCIS's recommendations relating to reporting requirements and parliamentary oversight (Recommendations 14–18), however the implementation of these recommendations occurred within the context of a rejection of the 'issuing authority' recommendation discussed above, which limits the type of information reflected in reports and available to parliamentary and statutory oversight authorities.

The PJCIS also recommended that the Government seek further legal advice as to the constitutionality of the Bill. This recommendation was discussed during the Second Reading debate on the TEO Bill, particularly by the ALP Opposition and the Centre Alliance Senators, but was not adopted by the Government and ultimately, was not pressed by the ALP Opposition who finally expressed support for the Bill in July 2019 despite a number of the PJCIS's recommendations not being reflected in legislative amendments to the Bill (Karp 2019).

Improving safeguards and oversight mechanisms was also central to the recommendations of the scrutiny committees in their reports on the TEO Bill which were issued on 24 July 2019 (SSCSB) and 30 July 2019 (PJCHR). For example, in its report the SSCSB drew attention to the fact that the TEOs issued under the Bill 'severely limits the citizenship rights of Australians to freely enter their country of nationality and could potentially leave an Australian citizen stranded in a conflict zone' and raised concerns about subjecting persons to return permits with strict monitoring conditions 'without any requirement that the person needs to have been convicted of, let alone charged with, any offence' (Scrutiny Digest 3 of 2019 at p. 32). These and other concerns about the impact of TEOs on individual rights led the SSCSB to suggest that 'consideration should be given to providing for some form of merits review of the minister's broad discretionary powers, and to increase parliamentary oversight of the measures, such as requiring a sunset provision' (at para [1.133]). The SSCSB was also concerned about the provisions of the Bill that removed the obligation of the minister to observe the requirements of procedural fairness (at para [1.134]).

Similar concerns were noted by the PJCHR in its report on the Bill, who observed that the absence of merits review of the Minister's decisions to issue TEOs or impose conditions under return permits, coupled with the significant impact of the Bill on individual rights, raised serious questions as to the proportionality of the measures contained in the Bill (PJCHR Scrutiny Report 3 of 2019). The PJCHR's report also included a detailed discussion of the impact of the Bill on children aged between 14 and 17, noting that it was 'not apparent' that the Bill provides for 'systematic or active consideration of the best interests of an affected child in determining whether to make a TEO or impose conditions on a permit.' (at [1.198]–[1.199]).

Taken together, there are two ways of viewing the scrutiny experience of the TEO Bill. On the one hand, it is possible to use this Bill as an example of the flaws inherent within parliamentary rights scrutiny system: neither the SSCSB nor the PJCHR were able to table their reports before the commencement of second reading debate on the Bill, and the PJCIS – despite its previous 100% strike rate in terms of transforming recommendations into legislative amendments – failed to attract Government support for the full range of its unanimous recommendations. On the other hand, and as discussed further in Chap. 8, the scrutiny experience of the TEO Bill can also be used in support of the theory being developed in this book, namely that when multiple parliamentary committees review a Bill, even within tight time frames and the highly politically charged context of a Federal Election, important rights enhancing changes can occur. Although not all of the PJCIS's recommendations were adopted by the Government, the contrast between the TEO Bill as first introduced in February 2019 and that passed in July 2019 is stark. The first iteration contained no review process for issuing TEOs, no specific criteria to be considered by the Minister with respect to the impact on the adult or child subject to the order, and very little by way or reporting and oversight. The enacted legislation contained a (limited) review mechanism, a much more extensive range of factors for the Minister to consider when issuing TEOs or imposing conditions on returning individuals and a multi-layered oversight and reporting regime. These changes – whilst not sufficient to address the full range of rights concerns arising from the Bill – remain significant and suggest that even when the PJCIS does not enjoy the full support of the Government of the day, it can continue to shape enacted legislation in rights-enhancing ways.

5.3.3.8 An Epilogue: The Identity Matching Laws

Although not part of the case study Acts for this research, it is interesting to note that the PJCIS has continued to flex its scrutiny muscle well into 2019, culminating in a flat-out rejection of the Government's proposed identity matching laws in September 2019. The Identity-Matching Services Bill 2019 (Cth) and the Australian Passports Amendment (Identity-matching Services) Bill 2019 (Cth) – referred to collectively as the 'Identity Matching Laws' – aim to set up a national 'hub' (administered by the Department of Home Affairs) that would allow facial images and other identity information to be shared across the country (Petrie 2019 at p. 3). As the *Bills Digest* explains, under the proposed Identity Matching Laws, the Department of Home Affairs is tasked with creating and administering a central 'hub' through which requests for identity matching services can be received and actioned, and identity information (including facial imagery) can be shared between government agencies, and in some cases, private organisations (Petrie 2019 at p. 3). The scheme gives effect to an agreement reached by the Commonwealth and the States and Territories in 2017 to facilitate the 'secure, automated and accountable' exchange of identity information to help combat identity crime and to promote community safety (COAG 2017 Recital A p. 2). Using the COAG Agreement as its authority, the federal Government drafted the Identity Matching Laws to provide the broad framework for the identity matching 'hub' through which participating agencies and organisations can request and transmit information, including facial images on drivers' licences and passports (Explanatory Memorandum Identity Matching Services Bill 2019 Outline). Much of the detail is left to the Regulations and subsequent intergovernmental agreements, meaning that the range of agencies that can potentially access, share and use this sensitive information is broad and can be extended to private bodies (see e.g. Identity Matching Services Bill 2019 (Cth), clauses 7(2) and 7(3)).

While the rationale behind the proposed laws includes faster identity matching in times of disaster or national emergency, the regime has been heavily criticised by rights groups as an attempt at 'mass surveillance' and an egregious breach of individual privacy (see eg. Digital Rights Watch 2017; Moulds 2019a, b). Insufficient safeguards and oversight, and lack of clarity around key terms and tests were cited as particularly problematic features of these proposed laws. (Moulds 2019a, b).

On 24 October 2019 the PJCIS issued a report that largely acknowledged these concerns, calling for significant changes to the proposed laws to ensure stronger protections for privacy and other safeguards against misuse (Recommendation 1). The PJCIS recommended that, if pursued, the identity-matching regime must be 'subject to Parliamentary oversight and reasonable, proportionate and transparent functionality' and should be subject to annual reporting, with key details of the regime set out in primary legislation rather than left to Executive discretion (Recommendation 2). In addition to these recommendations, the PJCIS said that the proposed legislation should *not proceed* in its current form (Recommendation 4). This is a significant, rights protecting recommendation for a Government-chaired, Government majority committee to make, particularly in the context of the membership of the PJCIS (vetted personally by the Prime Minister) and its close relationships with the security agencies. Bucking against the orthodox view of the impotence of parliamentary committees as tools for rights protection, the PJCIS appears to have a significant rights protective significant impact on the shape of these laws. By highlighting a range of rights concerns in its consensus, bipartisan report, the PJCIS has effectively stopped the proposed legislation from proceeding any further through Parliament (although it remains to be seen whether this a permanent or temporary stay).

As explored further in Part III, this suggests that, despite the orthodox view of many rights scholars who have good reason to be sceptical about the effectiveness of Australia's parliamentary model of rights protection, the PJCIS is capable of drawing attention to proposed laws that breach individual rights and taking decisive action to at least improve the compatibility of proposed national security laws with human rights standards.

5.4 Summary of Findings on Legislative Impact

The analysis above suggests that parliamentary committees had a significant rights-enhancing legislative impact on the case study Acts, despite strong bipartisan support for 'tough on terror' policies and even in the context of short reporting time frames and lack of timely responses to requests for information from proponents of a Bill. For example, the evidence set out above suggests that the work of parliamentary committees directly contributed to the following rights-enhancing changes to the case study Acts:

- narrowing the scope of a number of key definitions used in the counter-terrorism legislative framework, including the definition of 'terrorist act' (SLAT Bills inquiries);
- removing absolute liability and reverse onus of proof provisions from the terrorist act related offences introduced by the SLAT Bills and contained in Division 101 of the Criminal Code (SLAT Bills inquiries);
- inserting defences within these terrorist act offences for the provision of humanitarian aid (SLAT Bills inquiries);
- ensuring the power to proscribe terrorist organisations is subject to parliamentary review (SLAT Bills inquiries);
- subjecting each major tranche of counter-terrorism reform to mandatory and regular parliamentary review, for example through the use of sunset clauses (e.g ASIO Bills inquiries) or referral to the PJCIS or INSLM (e.g. Control Order Bill inquires, Data Retention Bill inquiries, Citizenship Bill inquiries);
- subjecting each new law enforcement and intelligence agency power to a raft of detailed reporting requirements and oversight by the Ombudsman and/or the IGIS (e.g. ASIO Bills inquiries);

- ensuring persons detained under an ASIO questioning and detention warrant are adults, have access to legal representation, are protected against self-incrimination and have access to judicial review of detention at regular intervals (ASIO Bills inquiries);
- ensuring that pre-charge detention of people thought to have information relevant to terrorist investigations is subject to judicial oversight and maximum time limits (Anti-Terrorism Bill 2004 inquires);
- re-instating the court's discretion to ensure that a person receives a fair trial when certain national security information is handled in 'closed court', and limiting the potential to exclude relevant information from the defendant in counter-terrorism trials (National Security Information Bills inquiries);
- ensuring people subject to control orders and preventative detention orders can understand and challenge the material relied upon to make the order and limiting the regime to adults only (Control Order Bills inquiries);
- establishing the position of Independent National Security Legislation Monitor and ensuring the Monitor has a specific mandate to consider the human rights implications of Australia's counter-terrorism laws (INSLM Bills inquiries);
- narrowing the scope of terrorist related treason offences (National Security Legislation Amendment Bill inquiries);
- requiring that telecommunications data be defined in primary legislation, and any data retained by authorities be de-identified or destroyed after two years (Data Retention Bill inquiries);
- ensuring that detailed public records be kept of the use of retained telecommunications data (Data Retention Bill inquiries);
- protecting the data of journalists from being accessed (Data Retention Bill inquiries);
- increasing the oversight powers and review functions of the PJCIS, including to examine the counter-terrorism activities of the Australian Federal Police (Foreign Fighters Bill inquiries);
- narrowing the scope of the proposed 'declared area' offences in the Criminal Code and ensuring that such declarations are subject to disallowance by parliament (Foreign Fighters Bill inquiries);
- preserving the safeguards relating to specifying and reviewing the conditions imposed as part of a control order or preventive detention order (Foreign Fighters Bill inquiries); and
- narrowing the circumstances in which a dual national can have their citizenship 'renounced' by doing something terrorist-related overseas, including by narrowing the range of conduct that can trigger the provisions; and making it clear that the laws cannot be applied to children under 14 (Citizenship Bill inquiries).

The strength of this legislative impact varied from committee to committee. For example, the PJCIS was a particularly strong performer, enjoying a high 'strike rate' (particularly since 2013) when it came to translating recommendations into legislative change, but also when it came to the rights-enhancing significance of the amendments it generated. The LCA Committees were particularly active in the first phase of scrutiny described above, generating popular and influential public inquiries that had important, rights-enhancing legislative outcomes, even if the LCA Committee recommendations were not implemented as consistently as those of the PJCIS in the post-2013 period. The fact that the LCA Committees have been effectively sidelined as forums to review counter-terrorism law since 2013 illustrates the dynamic nature of the committee system and is an important sign that a committee's legislative impact can shift significantly over time.

The evidence set out above also makes it clear that it was not just the inquiry-based committees that had a legislative influence on the case study Acts; the technical scrutiny committees also played an important, if less direct, role. The work of the technical scrutiny committees armed the inquiry-based committees and their submission makers with the information and analysis they needed to substantiate and justify the legislative changes they recommended. This is explored further in the next chapter.

Perhaps most significantly, the above analysis demonstrates that it is when multiple committees work together to scrutinise and review a Bill that the most significant legislative impact is felt. This is evident in both the early cases of the Control Order Bill and ASIO Bill 2002, which were considered by the SSCSB, PJC ASIO and the LCA Committees, and in the post-2013 Bills which were considered by the PJCIS, SSCSB and the PJCHR. As discussed further in Part III, this suggests that, by working together, the committees can address the tensions in legitimacy and participation discussed in Chap. 4 – with the technical scrutiny committees providing legitimate and clear analytical frameworks for submission makers to draw upon and the inquiry-based committees providing participatory forums to develop specific recommendations for reform. This has important implications for the types of changes I recommend in Part III. For example, it encourages an approach that enhances the value and utility of the reports and publications issued by the SSCSB and the PJCHR from the perspective of the inquiry-based committees and their submission makers. It also suggests a need to preserve the features of the PJCIS that help account for its consistently strong legislative impact on the case study Acts, including its strong relationships with the executive and its agencies. As will be discussed further in the next chapter, this approach is supported by the findings made with respect to the public and hidden impacts of the parliamentary committees studied.

Despite the significant list of changes above, it is important to underscore again that, in the vast majority of cases, the legislative impact that is occurring as a result of parliamentary committee scrutiny is rights-*enhancing*, even if the amendments made regularly fail to completely remedy the concerning features of the proposed new counter-terrorism measure.

As discussed in Chap. 1, this may give rise to scepticism by some scholars about the overall strength of the committee system as a component of Australia's parliamentary model of rights protection. However, as explored further in Part III, the significance of the amendments attributable to parliamentary committee work should not be underestimated, even if they are far from perfect from a rights advocate's perspective.

In addition, the type of successful rights-enhancing legislative changes attributable to parliamentary scrutiny suggest that a rights-scrutiny culture may be emerging at the federal level that could be valuable for those seeking to improve (or even replace) Australia's current model of rights protection. For example, from the case study Acts above, the most common rights-enhancing amendments that can be directly attributable to committees included: clarifying and narrowing the scope of new investigative powers or offences; introducing stronger safeguards or protections for common law privileges and procedural fairness; requiring ongoing independent or parliamentary oversight or review; limiting the discretion to be applied by members of the executive; and/or limiting the effect of new measures or offences on children. Provisions that sought to give Ministers or law enforcement or intelligence officers powers to interfere with rights of speech, association, privacy, citizenship or procedural fairness also appeared to attract significant attention from the committees, and generated legislative amendments that sought to dilute or limit this interference. These commonly emerging rights and scrutiny principles are explored further in the next chapter and in Part III of the book, where it is noted that further research is needed to determine whether this finding could have broader application beyond the case study adopted in my research.

References

Bills

House or Representatives. (2019). *Identity-matching Services Bill 2019* (Cth). Canberra: Parliament of Australia. https://www.aph.gov.au/Parliamentary_Business/Bills_LEGislation/Bills_Search_Results/Result?bId=r6387

House or Representatives. (2019). *Australian Passports Amendment (Identity-matching Services) Bill 2019* (Cth). Canberra: Parliament of Australia. https://www.aph.gov.au/Parliamentary_Business/Bills_Legislation/Bills_Search_Results/Result?bId=r6386

House or Representatives. (2019). *Counter-Terrorism (Temporary Exclusion Orders) Bill 2019* (Cth). Canberra: Parliament of Australia. https://www.aph.gov.au/Parliamentary_Business/Bills_Legislation/Bills_Search_Results/Result?bId=r6311

House of Representatives. (2018) *Telecommunications and Other Legislation Amendment (Assistance and Access) Bill 2018*. Canberra: Parliament of Australia. https://www.aph.gov.au/Parliamentary_Business/Bills_Legislation/Bills_Search_Results/Result?bId=r6195

House of Representatives. (2015) *Telecommunications (Interception and Access) Amendment (Data Retention) Bill 2015* (Cth). Canberra: Parliament of Australia. https://www.aph.gov.au/Parliamentary_Business/Bills_LEGislation/Bills_Search_Results/Result?bId=r5375

House of Representatives. (2015). *Australian Citizenship Amendment (Allegiance to Australia) Bill 2015* (Cth). Canberra: Parliament of Australia. https://www.aph.gov.au/Parliamentary_Business/Bills_Legislation/Bills_Search_Results/Result?bId=r5507

House of Representatives. (2014). *Counter-Terrorism Legislation Amendment Bill (No 1) 2014* (Cth). Canberra: Parliament of Australia. https://www.aph.gov.au/Parliamentary_Business/Bills_Legislation/Bills_Search_Results/Result?bId=s982. https://www.aph.gov.au/Parliamentary_Business/Bills_Legislation/Bills_Search_Results/Result?bId=r1808

House of Representatives. (2010). *Human Rights (Parliamentary Scrutiny) Bill 2011* (Cth). Canberra: Parliament of Australia. https://www.aph.gov.au/Parliamentary_Business/Bills_Legislation/Bills_Search_Results/Result?bId=r4420

House of Representatives. (2010). *National Security Legislation Amendment Bill 2010* (Cth). Canberra: Parliament of Australia. https://www.aph.gov.au/Parliamentary_Business/Bills_Legislation/Bills_Search_Results/Result?bId=r4435

House of Representatives. (2004). *Anti-terrorism Bill 2004* (Cth). Canberra: Parliament of Australia. https://www.aph.gov.au/Parliamentary_Business/Bills_Legislation/Bills_Search_Results/Result?bId=r2032

House of Representatives. (2004). *Anti-Terrorism Bill (No 2) 2005* (Cth). Canberra: Parliament of Australia. https://www.aph.gov.au/Parliamentary_Business/Bills_Legislation/Bills_Search_Results/Result?bId=r2469

House of Representatives. (2004) *Surveillance Devices Bill 2004* (Cth). Canberra: Parliament of Australia. https://www.aph.gov.au/Parliamentary_Business/Bills_Legislation/Bills_Search_Results/Result?bId=r2010

House of Representatives. (2003). *Australian Security Intelligence Organisation Legislation Amendment (Terrorism) Bill 2003* (Cth). Canberra: Parliament of Australia. https://www.aph.gov.au/Parliamentary_Business/Bills_Legislation/Bills_Search_Results/Result?bId=r1763

House of Representatives. (2003). *Criminal Code Amendment (Hamas and Lashkar-e-Tayyiba) Bill 2003* (Cth). Canberra: Parliament of Australia. https://www.aph.gov.au/Parliamentary_Business/Bills_Legislation/Bills_Search_Results/Result?bId=r1925

House of Representatives. (2003). *Criminal Code Amendment (Hizballah) Bill 2003* (Cth). Canberra: Parliament of Australia. https://www.aph.gov.au/Parliamentary_Business/Bills_Legislation/Bills_Search_Results/Result?bId=r1826

House of Representatives. (2003). *Criminal Code Amendment (Terrorist Organisations) Bill 2003* (Cth). Canberra: Parliament of Australia.

House of Representatives. (2002). *Criminal Code Amendment (Espionage and Related Offences) Bill 2002* (Cth). Canberra: Parliament of Australia. https://www.aph.gov.au/Parliamentary_Business/Bills_Legislation/Bills_Search_Results/Result?bId=r1475

House of Representatives. (2002). *Proceeds of Crime Bill 2002* (Cth). Canberra: Parliament of Australia. https://www.aph.gov.au/Parliamentary_Business/Bills_Legislation/Bills_Search_Results/Result?bId=r1467

House of Representatives. (2002). *Proceeds of Crime (Consequential Amendments and Transitional Provisions) Bill 2002* (Cth). Canberra: Parliament of Australia. https://www.aph.gov.au/Parliamentary_Business/Bills_Legislation/Bills_Search_Results/Result?bId=r1515

House of Representatives. (2002). *Security Legislation Amendment (Terrorism) Bill 2002* (Cth). Canberra: Parliament of Australia. https://www.aph.gov.au/Parliamentary_Business/Bills_Legislation/Bills_Search_Results/Result?bId=r1516

House of Representatives. (2002). *Australian Security Intelligence Organisation Legislation Amendment (Terrorism) Bill 2002* (Cth). Canberra: Parliament of Australia. https://www.aph.gov.au/Parliamentary_Business/Bills_Legislation/Bills_Search_Results/Result?bId=r1539

Senate. *Counter-Terrorism Legislation Amendment (Foreign Fighters) Bill 2014* (Cth). Canberra: Parliament of Australia. https://www.aph.gov.au/Parliamentary_Business/Bills_LEGislation/Bills_Search_Results/Result?bId=s976

Senate. (2010). *Independent National Security Legislation Monitor Bill 2010* (Cth). Canberra: Parliament of Australia. https://www.aph.gov.au/Parliamentary_Business/Bills_Legislation/Bills_Search_Results/Result?bId=s712

Senate. (2008). *Independent Reviewer of Terrorism Laws Bill 2008* (No 2) (Cth). Canberra: Parliament of Australia. https://www.aph.gov.au/Parliamentary_Business/Bills_Legislation/Bills_Search_Results/Result?bId=s634

Senate. (2006). *Criminal Code Amendment (High Risk Terrorist Offenders) Bill 2016* (Cth). Canberra: Parliament of Australia. https://www.aph.gov.au/Parliamentary_Business/Bills_Legislation/Bills_Search_Results/Result?bId=s1039

Senate. (2004). *Telecommunications (Interception) Amendment (Stored Communications) Bill 2004* (Cth). Canberra: Parliament of Australia. https://www.aph.gov.au/Parliamentary_Business/Bills_Legislation/Bills_Search_Results/Result?bId=s447

Senate. (2004). *National Security Information (Criminal Proceedings) Bill 2004* (Cth). Canberra: Parliament of Australia. https://www.aph.gov.au/Parliamentary_Business/Bills_Legislation/Bills_Search_Results/Result?bId=s437

Explanatory Memorandum

House or Representatives. (2019). *Explanatory Memorandum, Identity Matching Services Bill 2019* (Cth). Canberra: Parliament of Australia. https://www.aph.gov.au/Parliamentary_Business/Bills_Legislation/Bills_Search_Results/Result?bId=r6387

House or Representatives. (2019). *Explanatory Memorandum to the Counter-Terrorism (Temporary Exclusion Orders) Bill 2019* (Cth). https://parlinfo.aph.gov.au/parlInfo/search/display/display.w3p;query=Id%3A%22legislation%2Fems%2Fr6311_ems_8d59d6e9-8c8b-4704-8314-69696a5b9ba8%22

House of Representatives. (2018). Supplementary Explanatory Memorandum *Telecommunications and Other Legislation Amendment (Assistance and Access) Bill 2018.* Canberra: Parliament of Australia. https://parlinfo.aph.gov.au/parlInfo/search/display/display.w3p;query=Id%3A%22legislation%2Fems%2Fr6195_ems_b832c54b-6091-41ca-baf4-35bb94a856e8%22

House of Representatives. (2014). *Explanatory Memorandum, Telecommunications (Interception and Access) Amendment (Data Retention) Bill 2014.* Canberra: Parliament of Australia. https://parlinfo.aph.gov.au/parlInfo/search/display/display.w3p;query=Id%3A%22legislation%2Fems%2Fr5375_ems_e6cf11b4-5a4e-41bc-ae27-031e2b90e001%22

House of Representatives. (2015). *Supplementary Explanatory Memorandum, Australian Citizenship Amendment (Allegiance to Australia) Bill 2015* (Cth). Canberra: Parliament of Australia. https://parlinfo.aph.gov.au/parlInfo/search/display/display.w3p;query=Id%3A%22legislation%2Fems%2Fr5507_ems_13fb76d4-b057-4b2b-aacd-ec06e738b5ee%22

House of Representatives. (2015). *Revised Explanatory Memorandum, Telecommunications (Interception and Access) Amendment (Data Retention) Bill 2014* (Cth). Canberra: Parliament of Australia. https://parlinfo.aph.gov.au/parlInfo/search/display/display.w3p;query=Id%3A%22legislation%2Fems%2Fr5375_ems_ac4732e1-5116-4d8f-8de5-0ead3828012c%22

House of Representatives. (2015). *Supplementary Explanatory Memorandum, Telecommunications (Interception and Access) Amendment (Data Retention) Bill 2014* (Cth). Canberra: Parliament of Australia. https://parlinfo.aph.gov.au/parlInfo/search/display/display.w3p;query=Id%3A%22legislation%2Fems%2Fr5375_ems_1fc1188e-ecfb-4772-9b9d-334dc9ff53a2%22

House of Representatives. (2005). *Supplementary Explanatory Memorandum, Anti-Terrorism Bill (No 2) 2005* (Cth). Canberra: Parliament of Australia. https://parlinfo.aph.gov.au/parlInfo/search/display/display.w3p;query=Id%3A%22legislation%2Fems%2Fr2469_ems_9ae6228d-e3c5-46d9-af1e-745712d818d5%22

House of Representatives. (2004). *Explanatory Memorandum, Anti-Terrorism Bill 2004* (Cth). Canberra: Parliament of Australia. https://www.aph.gov.au/Parliamentary_Business/Bills_Legislation/Bills_Search_Results/Result?bId=r2032

House of Representatives. (2004). *Supplementary Explanatory Memorandum, Anti-Terrorism Bill 2004* (Cth). Canberra: Parliament of Australia. https://parlinfo.aph.gov.au/parlInfo/search/display/display.w3p;query=Id%3A%22legislation%2Fems%2Fr2032_ems_e14e356e-896e-4e12-9b54-5fd15b3b7546%22

House of Representatives. (2002). *Supplementary Explanatory Memorandum, Australian Security Intelligence Organisation Amendment (Terrorism) Bill 2002* (Cth). Canberra: Parliament of Australia. https://www.aph.gov.au/Parliamentary_Business/Bills_Legislation/Bills_Search_Results/Result?bId=r1539

House of Representatives. (2002). *Supplementary Explanatory Memorandum, Security Legislation Amendment (Terrorism) Bill 2002 [No 2] and Related Bills* (Cth). Canberra: Parliament of Australia. https://parlinfo.aph.gov.au/parlInfo/search/display/display.w3p;query=Id%3A%22legislation%2Fems%2Fr1517_ems_a24dfca8-f231-4b62-8603-2bfdac23cc89%22

Senate. (2014). *Supplementary Explanatory Memorandum, Counter-Terrorism Legislation Amendment Bill (No 1) 2014* (Cth). Canberra: Parliament of Australia. https://parlinfo.aph.gov.au/parlInfo/search/display/display.w3p;query=Id%3A%22legislation%2Fems%2Fs982_ems_5ada80a9-3dc6-4894-b301-1618320acafd%22

Senate. (2016). *Supplementary Explanatory Memorandum, Criminal Code Amendment (High Risk Terrorist Offenders) Bill 2016*. Canberra: Parliament of Australia. https://parlinfo.aph.gov.au/parlInfo/search/display/display.w3p;query=Id%3A%22legislation%2Fems%2Fs1039_ems_3b9b5af2-90d5-44b2-aefe-06ed5ea3392d%22

Senate. (2016). *Explanatory Memorandum, Criminal Code Amendment (High Risk Terrorist Offenders) Bill 2016*. Canberra: Parliament of Australia. https://parlinfo.aph.gov.au/parlInfo/search/display/display.w3p;query=Id%3A%22legislation%2Fems%2Fs1039_ems_ed2c97b3-8122-4fcd-99e9-c30362b7d85a%22

Senate. (2014). *Explanatory Memorandum, Counter-Terrorism Amendment (Foreign Fighters) Bill 2014* (Cth). Canberra: Parliament of Australia. https://parlinfo.aph.gov.au/parlInfo/search/display/display.w3p;query=Id%3A%22legislation%2Fems%2Fs976_ems_d5aff32a-9c65-43b1-a13e-8ffd4c023831%22

Senate. (2014). *Supplementary Counter-Terrorism Legislation Amendment (Foreign Fighters) Bill 2014* (Cth). Canberra: Parliament of Australia. https://parlinfo.aph.gov.au/parlInfo/search/display/display.w3p;query=Id%3A%22legislation%2Fems%2Fs976_ems_11c68f3b-9a58-4dea-97b2-25de6aa4d825%22

Senate. (2004) Supplementary Explanatory *National Security Information (Criminal Proceedings) Bill 2004* (Cth). Canberra: Parliament of Australia. https://parlinfo.aph.gov.au/parlInfo/search/display/display.w3p;query=Id%3A%22legislation%2Fems%2Fs437_ems_5ae4cdfe-d0bd-4aaf-bf5e-a3b4ac5a03a6%22

Legislation

Anti-terrorism Act 2004 (Cth).
Anti-Terrorism Act (No 2) 2005 (Cth).
Australian Citizenship Amendment (Allegiance to Australia) Act 2015 (Cth).
Australian Passports Act 2005 (Cth).
Australian Security and Intelligence Organisation Act 1979 (Cth).
Australian Security Intelligence Organisation Legislation Amendment (Terrorism) Act 2002 (Cth).
Australian Security Intelligence Organisation Legislation Amendment (Terrorism) Act 2003 (Cth).
Counter-Terrorism Legislation Amendment Act (No 1) 2014 (Cth).
Counter-Terrorism Legislation Amendment (Foreign Fighters) Act 2014 (Cth).
Independent National Security Legislation Monitor Act 2010 (Cth).
Intelligence Services Act 2001 (Cth).
National Security Information (Criminal Proceedings) Act 2004 (Cth).
National Security Legislation Amendment Act 2010 (Cth).
Parliamentary Joint Committee on Law Enforcement Act 2010 (Cth).
Prevention of Terrorism Act 2005 (UK).
Security Legislation Amendment (Terrorism) Act 2002 (Cth).
Telecommunications (Interception and Access) Amendment Act 2008 (Cth).
Telecommunications (Interception and Access) Amendment (Data Retention) Act 2015 (Cth).
Telecommunications (Interception) Act 1979 (Cth).

Parliamentary Debates

Commonwealth, *Parliamentary Debates*, Senate, 25 June 2015, 4600 (Penny Wright). https://parlinfo.aph.gov.au/parlInfo/search/display/display.w3p;query=Id:%22chamber/hansards/99c8aee1-aa1b-48da-8cdc-593fed2e4d62/0000%22

Commonwealth, *Parliamentary Debates*, Senate, 3 February 2010, 209 (Joseph Ludwig, Special Minister for State). https://parlinfo.aph.gov.au/parlInfo/search/display/display.w3p;query=Id:%22chamber/hansards/2010-02-03/0000%22

Commonwealth, *Parliamentary Debates*, Senate, 5 December 2005, 18 (George Brandis). https://parlinfo.aph.gov.au/parlInfo/search/display/display.w3p;query=Id%3A%22chamber%2Fhansards%2F2005-12-05%2F0011%22

Parliamentary Committee Reports

House of Commons Constitutional Affairs Committee. (2005) Parliament of the United Kingdom, *Constitutional Affairs – Seventh Report*. London: Stationary Office. https://publications.parliament.uk/pa/cm200405/cmselect/cmconst/323/32302.htm

Parliamentary Joint Committee on Human Rights. (2019). *Human Rights Scrutiny Report 3 of 2019*, (30 July 2019). Canberra: Parliament of Australia. https://www.aph.gov.au/Parliamentary_Business/Committees/Joint/Human_Rights/Scrutiny_reports/2019/Report_3_of_2019

Parliamentary Joint Committee on Human Rights. (2018). *Report 11 of 2018* (16 October 2018) Canberra: Parliament of Australia. https://www.aph.gov.au/Parliamentary_Business/Committees/Joint/Human_Rights/Scrutiny_reports/2018

Parliamentary Joint Committee on Human Rights. (2016). *Report 8 of 2016* (9 November 2016). Canberra: Parliament of Australia. https://www.aph.gov.au/Parliamentary_Business/Committees/Joint/Human_Rights/Scrutiny_reports/2016

Parliamentary Joint Committee on Human Rights. (2016). *Report 7 of 2016* (11 October 2016). Canberra: Parliament of Australia. https://www.aph.gov.au/Parliamentary_Business/Committees/Joint/Human_Rights/Scrutiny_reports/2016

Parliamentary Joint Committee on Human Rights. (2016). *Thirty-Sixth Report of the 44th Parliament.* Canberra: Parliament of Australia. https://www.aph.gov.au/Parliamentary_Business/Committees/Joint/Human_Rights/Scrutiny_reports/2016/Thirty-sixth_Report_of_the_44th_Parliament

Parliamentary Joint Committee on Human Rights. (2015). *Twenty-Fifth Report of the 44th Parliament.* Canberra: Parliament of Australia. https://www.aph.gov.au/Parliamentary_Business/Committees/Joint/Human_Rights/Scrutiny_reports/2015/Twenty-fifth_Report_of_the_44th_Parliament

Parliamentary Joint Committee on Human Rights. (2015). *Annual Report 2014–15* (2015). Canberra: Parliament of Australia. https://www.aph.gov.au/Parliamentary_Business/Committees/Joint/Human_Rights/Scrutiny_reports/Annual_Reports/Annual_Report_2014-15

Parliamentary Joint Committee on Human Rights. (2014). *Fifteenth Report of 44th Parliament.* Canberra: Parliament of Australia. https://www.aph.gov.au/Parliamentary_Business/Committees/Joint/Human_Rights/Scrutiny_reports/2014/Fifteenth_Report_of_the_44th_Parliament

Parliamentary Joint Committee on Human Rights. (2014). *Sixteenth Report of 44th Parliament* (2014). Canberra: Parliament of Australia. https://www.aph.gov.au/Parliamentary_Business/Committees/Joint/Human_Rights/Scrutiny_reports/2014/Sixteenth_Report_of_the_44th_Parliament

Parliamentary Joint Committee on Human Rights. (2014). *Fourteenth Report of 44th Parliament.* Canberra: Parliament of Australia. https://www.aph.gov.au/Parliamentary_Business/Committees/Joint/Human_Rights/Scrutiny_reports/2014/Fourteenth_Report_of_the_44th_Paliament

Parliamentary Joint Committee on Intelligence and Security. (2019). *Advisory report on the Identity-matching Services Bill 2019 and the Australian Passports Amendment (Identity-matching Services) Bill 2019*. Canberra: Parliament of Australia. https://www.aph.gov.au/Parliamentary_Business/Committees/Joint/Intelligence_and_Security/Identity-Matching2019/Report

Parliamentary Joint Committee of Intelligence and Security. (2019). *Advisory Report on the Counter-Terrorism (Temporary Exclusion Orders) Bill*. Canberra: Parliament of Australia. https://www.aph.gov.au/Parliamentary_Business/Committees/Joint/Intelligence_and_Security/CTTEOBill2019/

Parliamentary Joint Committee on Intelligence and Security. (2018). *Joint statement by Chair and Deputy Chair, media release, 22 November 2018*. Canberra: Parliament of Australia. Retrieved from https://www.aph.gov.au/Parliamentary_Business/Committees/Joint/Intelligence_and_Security/TelcoAmendmentBill2018/Media_Releases. Accessed 15 Jan 2020.

Parliamentary Joint Committee on Intelligence and Security. (2018). *Advisory Report on the Telecommunications and Other Legislation Amendment (Assistance and Access) Bill 2018* (2018). Canberra: Parliament of Australia. https://www.aph.gov.au/Parliamentary_Business/Committees/Joint/Intelligence_and_Security/TelcoAmendmentBill2018/Report_1

Parliamentary Joint Committee on Intelligence and Security. (2016). *Advisory Report on the Criminal Code Amendment (High Risk Terrorist Offenders) Bill 2016*. Canberra: Parliament of Australia. https://www.aph.gov.au/Parliamentary_Business/Committees/Joint/Intelligence_and_Security/HRTOBill/Report-HTML

Parliamentary Joint Committee on Intelligence and Security. (2015). *Advisory Report on the Provisions of the Australian Citizenship Amendment (Allegiance to Australia) Bill 2015*. Canberra: Parliament of Australia. http://www.aph.gov.au/~/media/02%20Parliamentary%20Business/24%20Committees/244%20Joint%20Committees/PJCIS/Citizenship/FullReport.pdf?la=en

Parliamentary Joint Committee on Intelligence and Security. (2015). *Advisory Report on the Telecommunications (Interception and Access) Amendment (Data Retention) Bill 2014* (2015). Parliament of Australia. https://www.aph.gov.au/Parliamentary_Business/Committees/Joint/Intelligence_and_Security/Data_Retention/Report

Parliamentary Joint Committee on Intelligence and Security. (2014). *Advisory Report on the Counter-Terrorism Legislation Amendment (Foreign Fighters) Bill 2014*. Canberra: Parliament of Australia. http://www.aph.gov.au/~/media/02%20Parliamentary%20Business/24%20Committees/244%20Joint%20Committees/PJCIS/Foreign%20Fighters%20Bill/CommitteeReport_17Oct2014.pdf

Parliamentary Joint Committee on Intelligence and Security. (2014). *Advisory Report on the Provisions of the Counter-Terrorism Legislation Amendment Bill (No 1) 2014*. Canberra: Parliament of Australia. https://www.aph.gov.au/Parliamentary_Business/Committees/Joint/Intelligence_and_Security/Amendment_Bill/Report1

Parliamentary Joint Committee on Intelligence and Security. (2015). *Inquiry into the Authorisation of Access to Telecommunications Data to Identify a Journalist's Source*. Canberra: Parliament of Australia. https://www.aph.gov.au/Parliamentary_Business/Committees/Joint/Intelligence_and_Security/access_to_journalists_dat

Parliamentary Joint Committee on Intelligence and Security. (2013). *Inquiry into the Potential Reforms of Australia's National Security Legislation*. Canberra: Parliament of Australia. http://www.aphref.aph.gov.au/house/committee/pjcis/NSL2012/report.htm

Parliamentary Joint Committee on Intelligence and Security. (2006). *Review of Security and Counter Terrorism Legislation*. Canberra: Parliament of Australia. https://www.aph.gov.au/Parliamentary_Business/Committees/House_of_Representatives_Committees?url=pjcis/securityleg/report.htm

Parliamentary Joint Committee on Australian Security Intelligence Organisation, Australian Secret Intelligence Service, and Defence Signals Directorate. (2002). *Advisory Report on the Australian Security Intelligence Organisation Legislation Amendment (Terrorism) Bill 2002*

(2002). Canberra: Parliament of Australia. https://www.aph.gov.au/Parliamentary_Business/Committees/House_of_Representatives_Committees?url=pjcaad/terrorbill2002/terror-index.htm

Senate Standing Committee of Scrutiny of Bill. (2019). *Scrutiny Digest 2 of 2019*. (28 March 2019). Canberra: Parliament of Australia. https://www.aph.gov.au/Parliamentary_Business/Committees/Senate/Scrutiny_of_Bills/Scrutiny_Digest

Senate Standing Committee for the Scrutiny of Bills. (2018). *Twelfth Scrutiny Digest of 2018*, (17 October 2018). Canberra: Parliament of Australia. https://www.aph.gov.au/Parliamentary_Business/Committees/Senate/Scrutiny_of_Bills/Scrutiny_Digest/2018

Senate Standing Committee for the Scrutiny of Bills. (2016). *Tenth Report of 2016*, (30 November 016). Canberra: Parliament of Australia. https://www.aph.gov.au/Parliamentary_Business/Committees/Senate/Scrutiny_of_Bills/Reports/2016/index

Senate Standing Committee for Scrutiny of Bills. (2016). *Report No 4 of 2016*. Canberra: Parliament of Australia. https://www.aph.gov.au/Parliamentary_Business/Committees/Senate/Scrutiny_of_Bills/Reports/2016/index

Senate Standing Committee for Scrutiny of Bills. (2016). *Alert Digest No 7 of 2016* (12 October 2016). Canberra: Parliament of Australia. https://www.aph.gov.au/Parliamentary_Business/Committees/Senate/Scrutiny_of_Bills/Alerts_Digests/2016/index

Senate Standing Committee for the Scrutiny of Bills. (2015). *Alert Digest No 7 of 2015*. (12 August 2015). Canberra: Parliament of Australia. https://www.aph.gov.au/Parliamentary_Business/Committees/Senate/Scrutiny_of_Bills/Alerts_Digests/2015/index

Senate Standing Committee for Scrutiny of Bills. (2015). *Report No 1 of 2015*. Canberra: Parliament of Australia. https://www.aph.gov.au/Parliamentary_Business/Committees/Senate/Scrutiny_of_Bills/Reports/2015/index

Senate Standing Committee on Legal and Constitutional Affairs References Committee. (2015). Parliament of Australia, *Comprehensive Revision of Telecommunications (Interception and Access) Act 1979*. Canberra: Parliament of Australia. https://www.aph.gov.au/Parliamentary_Business/Committees/Senate/Legal_and_Constitutional_Affairs/Comprehensive_revision_of_TIA_Act

Senate Standing Committee for Scrutiny of Bills. (2014). *Alert Digest No 16 of 2014* (26 November 2014). Canberra: Parliament of Australia. https://www.aph.gov.au/Parliamentary_Business/Committees/Senate/Scrutiny_of_Bills/Alerts_Digests/2014/index

Senate Standing Committee for Scrutiny of Bills. (2014). *Alert Digest No 15 of 2014* (19 November 2014). Canberra: Parliament of Australia. https://www.aph.gov.au/Parliamentary_Business/Committees/Senate/Scrutiny_of_Bills/Alerts_Digests/2014/index

Senate Standing Committee for Scrutiny of Bills. (2014). *Alert Digest Relating to the Counter-Terrorism Legislation Amendment (Foreign Fighters) Bill 2014* (2014). Canberra: Parliament of Australia. https://www.aph.gov.au/Parliamentary_Business/Committees/Senate/Scrutiny_of_Bills/Alerts_Digests/2014/index

Senate Standing Committee for Scrutiny of Bills. (2014). *Further Report Relating to the Counter-Terrorism Legislation Amendment (Foreign Fighters) Bill 2014* (2014). Canberra: Parliament of Australia. https://www.aph.gov.au/Parliamentary_Business/Committees/Senate/Scrutiny_of_Bills/Alerts_Digests/2014/index

Senate Standing Committee for Scrutiny of Bills. (2014). *Report Relating to the Counter-Terrorism Legislation Amendment (Foreign Fighters) Bill 2014* (2014). Canberra: Parliament of Australia. https://www.aph.gov.au/Parliamentary_Business/Committees/Senate/Scrutiny_of_Bills/Alerts_Digests/2014/index

Senate Standing Committee on Legal and Constitutional Affairs Legislation Committee. (2014). *Report on Counter-Terrorism Legislation Amendment (Foreign Fighters) Bills 2014*. Canberra: Parliament of Australia. https://www.aph.gov.au/Parliamentary_Business/Committees/Senate/Legal_and_Constitutional_Affairs/Foreign_Fighters

Senate Standing Committee for Scrutiny of Bills. (2010). *Alert Digest No 5 of 2010* (12 May 2010). Canberra: Parliament of Australia. https://www.aph.gov.au/Parliamentary_Business/Committees/Senate/Scrutiny_of_Bills/Alerts_Digests/2010/index

Senate Standing Committee on Legal and Constitutional Affairs Legislation Committee. (2010). *Inquiry into the National Security Legislation Amendment Bill 2010 and Parliamentary Joint Committee on Law Enforcement Bill 2010*. Canberra: Parliament of Australia. https://www.aph.gov.au/Parliamentary_Business/Committees/Senate/Legal_and_Constitutional_Affairs/Completed_inquiries/2008-10/National_Security_Legislation/index

Senate Standing Committee on Finance and Public Administration. (2009). *Inquiry into National Security Legislation Monitor Bill 2009* (2009). Canberra: Parliament of Australia. https://www.aph.gov.au/Parliamentary_Business/Committees/Senate/Finance_and_Public_Administration/Completed_inquiries/2008-10/national_security_leg/report/index

Senate Standing Committee on Legal and Constitutional Affairs Legislation Committee. (2008). Parliament of Australia, *Independent Reviewer of Terrorism Laws Bill 2008 [No 2]*. Canberra: Parliament of Australia. https://www.aph.gov.au/Parliamentary_Business/Committees/Senate/Legal_and_Constitutional_Affairs/Completed_inquiries/2008-10/terrorism/index

Senate Standing c Affairs Legislation Committee. (2005). *Provisions of the Anti-Terrorism Bill (No 2) 2005*. Canberra: Parliament of Australia. https://www.aph.gov.au/Parliamentary_Business/Committees/Senate/Legal_and_Constitutional_Affairs/Completed_inquiries/2004-07/terrorism/report/index

Senate Standing Committee for Scrutiny of Bills. (2005). *Alert Digest No 13 of 2005* (11 November 2005). Canberra: Parliament of Australia. https://www.aph.gov.au/Parliamentary_Business/Committees/Senate/Scrutiny_of_Bills/Alerts_Digests/2005/index

Senate Standing Committee for Scrutiny of Bills. (2004). *Alert Digest No 11 of 2004* (11 October 2004). Canberra: Parliament of Australia. https://www.aph.gov.au/Parliamentary_Business/Committees/Senate/Scrutiny_of_Bills/Alerts_Digests/2006/index

Senate Standing Committee for Scrutiny of Bills. (2004). *Alert Digest No 6 of 2004* (12 May 2004). Canberra: Parliament of Australia. https://www.aph.gov.au/Parliamentary_Business/Committees/Senate/Scrutiny_of_Bills/Alerts_Digests/2006/index

Senate Standing Committee on Legal and Constitutional Affairs Legislation Committee. (2004). *Inquiry into the Anti-Terrorism Bill 2004*. Canberra: Parliament of Australia. https://www.aph.gov.au/Parliamentary_Business/Committees/Senate/Legal_and_Constitutional_Affairs/Completed_inquiries/2002-04/anti_terrorism04/index

Senate Standing Committee on Legal and Constitutional Affairs Legislation Committee. (2004). Parliament of Australia, *Provisions of the National Security Information (Criminal Proceedings) Bill 2004 and the National Security Information (Criminal Proceedings) (Consequential Amendments) Bill 2004*. Canberra: Parliament of Australia. https://www.aph.gov.au/parliamentary_business/committees/senate/legal_and_constitutional_affairs/completed_inquiries/2002-04/national_security/index

Senate Standing Committee on Legal and Constitutional Affairs Legislation Committee. (2002). *Australian Security Intelligence Organisation Legislation Amendment (Terrorism) Bill 2002 and Related Matters* (2002). Canberra: Parliament of Australia. https://www.aph.gov.au/parliamentary_business/committees/senate/legal_and_constitutional_affairs/completed_inquiries/2002-04/asio_2/report/contents

Senate Standing Committee on Legal and Constitutional Affairs References Committee. (2002). *Inquiry into Australian Security Intelligence Organisation Legislation Amendment (Terrorism) Bill 2002 and Related Matters*. Canberra: Parliament of Australia. http://www.aph.gov.au/~/media/wopapub/senate/committee/legcon_ctte/completed_inquiries/2004_07/witness_protection/report/report_pdf.ashx

Senate Standing Committee for Scrutiny of Bills. (2002). *Alert Digest No 3 of 2002* (20 March 2002). Canberra: Parliament of Australia. https://www.aph.gov.au/Parliamentary_Business/Committees/Senate/Scrutiny_of_Bills/Alerts_Digests/2002/index

Senate Standing Committee for Scrutiny of Bills. (2002). *Alert Digest No 4 of 2002* (15 May 2002). Canberra: Parliament of Australia. https://www.aph.gov.au/Parliamentary_Business/Committees/Senate/Scrutiny_of_Bills/Alerts_Digests/2002/index

Senate Standing Committee for Scrutiny of Bills. (2002). *Report No 12 of 2002* (2002). Canberra: Parliament of Australia. https://www.aph.gov.au/Parliamentary_Business/Committees/Senate/Scrutiny_of_Bills/Reports/2002/index

Senate Standing Committee for Scrutiny of Bills. (2002). *Report No 4 of 2002* (2002). Canberra: Parliament of Australia. https://www.aph.gov.au/Parliamentary_Business/Committees/Senate/Scrutiny_of_Bills/Reports/2002/index

Books/Articles/Reports/Speeches

Attorney-General's Department. (2009). *National Security Legislation Discussion Paper* (August 2009). Canberra: Government of Australia.

Australian Law Reform Commission. (2006). *Fighting Words: A Review of Sedition Laws in Australia.* ALRC Report No 104. Retrieved from https://www.alrc.gov.au/publication/fighting-words-a-review-of-sedition-laws-in-australia-alrc-report-104/. Accessed 7 Jan 2020.

Australian Law Reform Commission. (2008). For Your Information: Australian Privacy Law and Practice, Report No 108 (May 2008). Retrieved from https://www.alrc.gov.au/publication/for-your-information-australian-privacy-law-and-practice-alrc-report-108/. Accessed 16 Jan 2020.

Banham, C. (2016). The Power of Human Rights Rituals: Torture and the Australian Context. *Australian Journal of Human Rights, 22*(1), 67–83. https://doi.org/10.1080/1323-238X.2016.11882158.

Barker, C., Portillo-Castro, H., & Biddington, M. (2018). *Bills Digest: Telecommunications and Other Legislation Amendment (Assistance and Access) Bill 2018* No 49 of 2018–19, 3 December 2018. https://www.aph.gov.au/Parliamentary_Business/Bills_Legislation/bd/bd1819a/19bd049

Bastin, L., & Tamberlin, B. (2008). David Hicks in the Australian Court: Past and future legal issues. *Australian Law Journal, 82*(11), 774–785.

Brandis, G. (2014a). Government Response to the Committee's Report on the Foreign Fighters Bill. Attorney-General, Media Release, 22 October 2014, Canberra.

Brandis, G. (2014b). Government Response to Committee Report on the Counter-Terrorism Legislation Amendment Bill (No. 1) 2014'. Attorney-General, Media Release, 25 November 2014, Canberra.

Brandis, G., & Turnbull, M. (2015). Attorney-General and Minister for Communications. Government response to committee report on the Telecommunications (Interception and Access) Amendment (Data Retention) Bill 2014. Media Release, 3 April 2015.

Benton, M., & Russell, M. (2013). Assessing the impact of parliamentary oversight committees: The select committees in the British house of commons. *Parliamentary Affairs, 66*, 772–797.

Brew, N. (2012). *Telecommunications data retention – An overview* Background Note Parliamentary Library. Canberra: Parliament of Australia. Retrieved from https://www.aph.gov.au/About_Parliament/Parliamentary_Departments/Parliamentary_Library/pubs/BN/2012-2013/DataRetention. Accessed 17 Jan 2020.

Brew, N., Jordan, R., & Harris-Rimmer, S. (2007). Australians in Guantanamo Bay: A Chronology of the Detention of Mamdouh Habib and David Hicks. Chronologies Online, Parliamentary Library, Commonwealth, 2007. Retrieved from. https://www.aph.gov.au/About_Parliament/Parliamentary_Departments/Parliamentary_Library/Publications_Archive/online/AustraliansGuantanamoBay. Accessed 14 Jan 2020.

Calpinska, L. (2006). Post-Legislative Scrutiny of Acts of Parliament. *Commonwealth Law Bulletin, 32*(3), 191–204.

Carne, G. (2007). Prevent, Detain, Control and Order? Legislative Process and Executive Outcomes in Enacting the Anti-Terrorism Act (No 2) 2005 (Cth)'. *Flinders Journal of Law Reform, 10*(1), 17–79. https://eprints.utas.edu.au/3708/

Carne, G. (2015). Re-Orientating Human Rights Meanings and Understandings? Reviving and Revisiting Australian Human Rights Exceptionalism through a Liberal Democratic Rights Agenda. *Flinders Law Review Journal, 17,* 1–67. http://www.austlii.edu.au/au/journals/FlinLawJl/2015/1.pdf

Caygill, T. (2019). Legislation Under Review: An Assessment of Post Legislative Scrutiny Recommendations in the UK Parliament. *Journal of Legislative Studies, 25*(2), 295–313.

Clarke, M. J. (2008). Report of the Inquiry into the Case of Dr Mohamed Haneef. Canberra: Government of Australia. Retrieved from https://trove.nla.gov.au/work/35146207. Accessed 7 Jan 2020.

Council of Australian Governments. (2017). *Intergovernmental Agreement on Identity Matching Services*, agreed to on 5 October 2017, Canberra. Retrieved from https://www.coag.gov.au/sites/default/files/agreements/iga-identity-matching-services.pdf. Accessed 15 Jan 2020.

Dalla-Pozza, D. (2020). A dual scrutiny mechanism for Australia's counter-terrorism law landscape: The INSLM and the PJCIS. In J. Debeljak & L. Grenfell (Eds.), *Law-making and human rights* (pp. 673–700). Sydney: Thompson Reuters.

De Vrieze, F., & Hasson, V. (2017). *Post Legislative Scrutiny: Comparative Study of Practices of Post-Legislative Scrutiny in Selected Parliaments and the Rationale for its Place in Democracy Assistance* (2017, Westminster Foundation for Democracy, London).

Digital Rights Watch. (2017). Comprehensive national face database incompatible with a free society, Media Release, 6 October 2017 (online) Digital Rights Watch, (2017). Retrieved from https://digitalrightswatch.org.au/2017/10/06/comprehensive-national-face-database-incompatible-with-a-free-society/. Accessed 15 Jan 2020.

Dratel, J. T. (2008). Navigating the New Military Commissions: The Case of David Hicks. *New York City Law Review, 10*, 385–392. https://doi.org/10.31641/clr100210.

Dutton, P. (2018). (Minister for Home Affairs), Transcript of interview with Laura Jayes and Kieran Gilbert: First Edition, Sky News, media release, 21 November 2018. Retrieved from https://parlinfo.aph.gov.au/parlInfo/search/display/display.w3p;query=Id%3A%22media%2Fpressrel%2F6345652%22. Accessed 15 Jan 2020.

Evans, C., & Evans, S. (2006a). Australian Parliaments and the Protection of Human Rights. Paper presented in the Department of the Senate Occasional Lecture Series, Canberra, 8 December 2006.

Evans, C., & Evans, S. (2006b). Evaluating the Human Rights Performance of Legislatures. *Human Rights Law Review, 6*, 545–569. https://doi.org/10.1093/hrlr/ngl012.

Evans, C., & Evans, S. (2006c). Legislative Scrutiny Committees and Parliamentary Conceptions of Human Rights. *Public Law* 785.

Fairall, P., & Lacey, W. (2007). *Preventative Detention and Control Orders under Federal Law: The Case for a Bill of Rights. Melbourne University Law Review, 31,* 1072–1098. http://www.austlii.edu.au/au/journals/MelbULawRw/2007/40.html

Feldman, D. (2015). Democracy, Law and Human Rights: Politics as challenge and opportunity. In M. Hunt, H. J. Hooper, & P. Yowell (Eds.), *Parliaments and Human Rights: Redressing the Democratic Deficit* (pp. 95–117). Oxford: Hart Publishing.

Fenwick, H. (2018). Reconciling International Human Rights Law with Executive Non-trial-Based Counter-Terror Measures: The Case of UK Temporary Exclusion Orders. In P. Auriel, O. Beaud, & C. Wellman (Eds.), *The Rule of Crisis Terrorism, Emergency Legislation and the Rule of Law* (pp. 157–183). Springer. https://doi.org/10.1007/978-3-319-74473-5.

Hancock, N. (2002a). *Bills Digest: Security Legislation Amendment (Terrorism) Bill 2002 [No 2],* No 126 of 2001–02, 30 April 2002. Retrieved from https://www.aph.gov.au/Parliamentary_Business/Bills_Legislation/bd/bd0102/02bd126. Accessed 11 Jan 2020.

Hancock, N. (2002b). Terrorism and the Law in Australia: Legislation, Commentary and Constraints. Research Paper No 12, Department of the Parliamentary Library, Parliament of Australia, 2002. Retrieved from https://www.aph.gov.au/About_Parliament/Parliamentary_Departments/Parliamentary_Library/pubs/rp/rp0102/02rp12. Accessed 11 Jan 2020.

Harris-Rimmer, S. (2005) *Bills Digest Anti-Terrorism Bill (No 2)*, No 64 of 2005, 18 November 2005. https://www.aph.gov.au/Parliamentary_Business/Bills_Legislation/bd/bd0506/06bd064

Harrison-Smith, M. (2015). *Bills Digest: Australian Citizenship Amendment (Allegiance to Australia) Bill 2015*, No 15 of 2015, September 2015. Department of Parliamentary Services. Canberra: Parliament of Australia. Retrieved from https://parlinfo.aph.gov.au/parlInfo/search/display/display.w3p;query=Id%3A%22legislation%2Fbillsdgs%2F4050570%22. Accessed 7 Jan 2020.

Hiebert, J. L. (2011). Governing like judges? In T. Campbell, K. D. Ewing, & A. Tomkins (Eds.), *The Legal Protection of Human Rights: Sceptical essays* (pp. 40–65). Oxford: Oxford University Press.

Hiebert, J. L. (2015). Legislative rights review: Addressing the gap between ideals and constraints. In M. Hunt, H. J. Hooper, & P. Yowell (Eds.), *Parliaments and Human Rights: Redressing the Democratic Deficit* (pp. 39–56). Oxford: Hart Publishing.

Horsburgh, N., & Manas, F. M. (2008). Strengths and weaknesses of grassroots jihadist networks: The Madrid bombings. *Studies in Conflict and Terrorism, 31*(1), 17–39. https://doi.org/10.1080/10576100701767148.

Irving, H. (2019). Citizenship and constitutional law: Can we come home now?: 'Temporary Exclusion Orders Act' raises serious constitutional concerns. *Law Society of NSW Journal, 59*, 68–70. https://lsj.com.au/articles/can-we-come-home-now-temporary-exclusion-orders-act-raises-serious-constitutional-concerns/

Karp, P. (2019, July 21). Coalition accused of ignoring bipartisan advice over scrutiny of security powers. *The Guardian*, online. https://www.theguardian.com/australia-news/2019/jul/21/coalition-accused-of-ignoring-bipartisan-advice-over-scrutiny-of-security-powers

Kelly, J. (2011). A difficult dialogue: Statements of compatibility and the Victorian Charter of Human Rights and Responsibilities Act. *Australian Journal of Political Science, 46*, 257–279. https://doi.org/10.1080/10361146.2010.517181.

Law Commission of England and Wales. (2006) *Post legislative scrutiny* (October 2006). London: Stationary Offence. Cm 6945.

Law Council of Australia. (2004). Submission No 8 to Senate Standing Committee on Legal and Constitutional Affairs Legislation Committee. *Provisions of the National Security Information (Criminal Proceedings) Bill 2004 and the National Security Information (Criminal Proceedings) (Consequential Amendments) Bill 2004*. Canberra: Parliament of Australia.

Lindell, L. (2005). How (and whether?) to evaluate Parliamentary Committees – From a lawyer's perspective. August *About the House* 55.

Lynch, A. (2006). Legislating with urgency – The Enactment of the Anti-Terrorism Act (No 1) 2005. *Melbourne University Law Review, 30*(3), 747–781.

McClelland, R. (2009). Attorney-General. National Security Legislation Discussion Paper. Media Release, 12 August 2009.

Monk, D. (2001). A framework for evaluating the performance of committees in Westminster Parliaments. *Journal of Legislative Studies, 16*, 1–13. https://doi.org/10.1080/13572330903541904.

Morrison, S. (2018). (Prime Minister), Transcript of press conference with the Minister for Home Affairs, Sydney, media release, 22 November 2018. Retrieved from https://www.pm.gov.au/media/press-conference-minister-home-affairs. Accessed 15 Jan 2020.

Moulds, S. P. (2017). Committees in Dialogue: Parliamentary Scrutiny of the High Risk Terrorist Offenders Bill. AusPubLaw Blog, 30 January 2017. https://auspublaw.org/2017/01/committees-in-dialogue. Accessed 7 Jan 2020.

Moulds, S. P. (2018). *The rights protecting role of parliamentary committees: The case of Australia's counter-terrorism laws* (Doctoral thesis). University of Adelaide, Adelaide, South Australia, Australia. https://digital.library.adelaide.edu.au/dspace/handle/2440/115212

Moulds, S. P. (2019a, October 25). Why the government's proposed facial recognition database is causing such alarm. *The Conversation* online. https://theconversation.com/why-the-governments-proposed-facial-recognition-database-is-causing-such-alarm-125811

Moulds, S. P. (2019b). Parliamentary Rights Scrutiny and Counter-Terrorism Lawmaking in Australia. *Journal of South East Asian Human Rights, 3*(2), 185–230. https://doi.org/10.19184/jseahr.v3i2.13461.

Petrie, C. (2019). Department of Parliamentary Services, *Bills Digest* (Digest No 21 of 2019) Claire Petrie, Law and Bills Digest section, Bills Digest No 21, 2019-20 Identity-matching Services Bill 2019 and Australian Passports Amendment (Identity-matching Services) Bill 2019 (26 August 2019). Canberra: Parliament of Australia. https://parlinfo.aph.gov.au/parlInfo/download/legislation/billsdgs/6875141/upload_binary/6875141.pdf;fileType=application/pdf

Pillai, S. (2014). The rights and responsibilities of Australian citizenship: A legislative analysis. *Melbourne University Law Review, 37*(3), 736–785.

Reynolds, D., & Williams, G. (2017). *A Charter of Rights for Australia* (4th ed.). Sydney: NewSouth Books.

Ross Ray, R. (2007). Policing in the Shadow of Australia's Anti-terror Laws. *Lawyers Weekly, 366*, 20.

Russell, M., & Benton, M. (2009, June 24). *Assessing the policy impact of parliament: Methodological challenges and possible future approaches*. Paper presented at the Public Service Association Legislative Studies Specialist Group Conference, London. Retrieved from https://www.academia.edu/2069151/Assessing_the_policy_impact_of_Parliament_Methodological_challenges_and_possible_future_approaches. Accessed 7 Jan 2020.

Security Legislation Review Committee. (2006). *Report of the Security Legislation Review Committee*. Canberra: Australian Government. Retrieved from https://www.ag.gov.au/NationalSecurity/Counterterrorismlaw/Documents/Report%20of%20the%20Security%20Legislation%20Review%20Committee.pdf. Accessed 7 Jan 2020.

Sorial, S. (2008). The use and abuse of power and why we need a bill of rights: The ASIO (Terrorism) Amendment Act 2003 (Cth) and the Case of R v Ul-Haque. *Monash University Law Review, 34*(2), 400–429.

Taylor, A. (2018). Minister for Law Enforcement and Cyber Security Public consultation commences on new Assistance and Access Bill, media release, 14 August 2018, Canberra.

Tillett, A. (2018). Dual national terrorists to lose citizenship in Morrison plan. *The Australian Financial Review*. Canberra. 23 November 2018, 2. https://www.afr.com/politics/dual-national-terrorists-to-be-stripped-of-australian-citizenship-scott-morrison-20181122-h1880w

Tyulkina, S., & Williams, G. (2017). Combating terrorism in Australia through preventative detention orders. In T. Tullich, R. Anaian-Welsh, S. Bronitt, & S. Murray (Eds.), *Regulating preventative justice: Principle, policy and paradox* (pp. 136–152). Oxford: Routledge. https://doi.org/10.4324/9781315620978.

Varghese, J. (2004). National Security Information (Criminal Proceedings) Bill 2004. *Bills Digest No 59* 2004–2005. 9 August 2004. Retrieved from https://www.aph.gov.au/Parliamentary_Business/Bills_Legislation/bd/bd0405/05bd059. Accessed 16 Jan 2020.

Walker, B. (2012). *Independent national security legislation monitor, declassified annual report* (2012). http://www.dpmc.gov.au/publications/INSLM/index.cfm. Accessed 7 Jan 2020.

Williams, G. (2011). A decade of Australian Anti-Terror Laws. *Melbourne University Law Review, 35*(3), 1136. http://classic.austlii.edu.au/au/journals/MelbULawRw/2011/38.html

Willams, G., & Reynolds, D. (2016). The operation and impact of Australia's Parliamentary Scrutiny Regime for Human Rights. *Monash University Law Review, 41*(2), 469–508.

Chapter 6
Public Impact

Abstract This chapter sets out evidence of the *public impact* of the four parliamentary committees studied on the case study Acts. 'Public impact' means evidence that the parliamentary committee influenced or was considered in public or parliamentary debate on the case study Act or during a post-enactment review of the Act. Evidence of public impact includes reference to the findings or recommendations of a committee in Hansard, media reports or academic commentary, or in reports of post-enactment oversight bodies or review mechanisms. As this chapter explores, the public impact of parliamentary committee work on the way counter-terrorism laws are made, and on their content, can be significant particularly when a longer-term perspective is adopted. This chapter identifies the important deliberative role parliamentary committees play in Australian law making and suggests that a rights-scrutiny culture may be beginning to develop at the federal level that could be a relevant factor to consider when identifying options to improve Australia's parliamentary model of rights protection.

6.1 Why Look for Public Impact?

Public impact is distinct from legislative impact (considered in Chap. 5) because it looks for influence beyond amendments to a clause of a Bill; however, there is necessarily a clear relationship between the two. A committee with a strong, direct legislative impact will invariably feature in the parliamentary debate on a proposed law, for example when proponents of the law refer to the recommendations of the committee when introducing amendments. In addition, members of committees with strong legislative impact may frequently refer to their involvement in the committee when debating the proposed law in Parliament and in public. However, evidence of public impact does not merely reflect strong legislative impact. Looking for evidence of public impact can also identify the long-term influence of parliamentary scrutiny on the content of the law, recognising that sometimes it can take years for the full impact of the work of parliamentary committees to become apparent. As Darren Dick from the Australian Human Rights Commission told the author,

S. Moulds, *Committees of Influence*, https://doi.org/10.1007/978-981-15-4350-0_6

speaking of the PJCHR and its long-term impact on the Northern Territory Intervention legislation:

> I think it's clear that if you judge [the impact of the PJCHR] at that initial point at when that legislation came in, and ask whether committee processes were sufficient at the time, your answer is no, but if you look at it seven years later, you see the way things changed, then it's very clear that [the committee processes] had a very significant impact (Sydney 31 May 2019).

Examining public impact is particularly important for understanding how committees contribute to the parliamentary model of rights protection in Australia. As discussed in Chap. 3, parliamentary committees can help establish a 'culture of rights scrutiny' by providing a forum for members to share their views on a proposed law, including pointing out what they consider to be the rights implications of the proposed law. This can help identify any unintended or unjustified rights implications arising from a proposed law, and generate new, less rights-intrusive, legislative or policy options. Parliamentary committees can also help parliamentarians to weigh competing arguments or different policy options (Uhr 1998 at p. 25; Dalla-Pozza 2016 at p. 272), either through the public process conducted by the inquiry-based committees, or through the consideration of written analysis provided by the technical scrutiny committees. This weighing process becomes particularly relevant when considering the enactment of counter-terrorism laws which, as Dalla-Pozza (2016) explains, are regularly accompanied by the claim that counter-terrorism laws must strike an appropriate 'balance' between safeguarding Australia's national security and preserving individual rights and liberties (at p. 272–4). This bipartisan commitment to 'striking the right balance' when enacting counter-terrorism laws is evident from Dalla-Pozza's earlier study (2008) and my research (Moulds 2018), even if the enacted outcomes leave some commentators sceptical of the efficacy of this process (see e.g. Williams 2011; Lynch 2006; Rajanayagam 2015; Fletcher 2018).

One way to test whether the Parliament has engaged in this weighing process in a meaningful way is to look at the role parliamentary committees play in the development of a particular law. This is because a committee inquiry, or an independent analysis of the key features of a Bill, can demonstrate the capacity of Parliament to gather and disperse information, or bring new voices into the public debate (Shaw 1998; Griffith 2005). It can also provide insights into the nature of the parliamentary debate that occurred on the proposed law, including the time allocated for debate, whether alternative policy options were considered, and whether the impact of the law on individual rights was discussed.

This chapter argues that the public impact parliamentary committees had on the case study Acts was significant and generally rights-enhancing. This was particularly the case when multiple committees worked together to scrutinise proposed provisions and offered less rights-intrusive policy alternatives for governments to consider. This chapter also suggests that there may be an emerging commonality when it comes to the types of rights the parliamentary committees in this study focus on when scrutinising the case study Acts, and those discussed in parliamentary and public debates on the case study Acts. As explored further in Part III, this in turn reveals something useful about the rights-scrutiny culture that may be developing at the federal level.

6.2 Time for Parliamentary Scrutiny and Debate

If the work of parliamentary committees is going to have any impact on the content of a proposed law there must be adequate time for parliamentary scrutiny to take place (Uhr 1993 at 347; Aldons 2003). The counter-terrorism law-making experience outlined in Chap. 3 suggests that this may not always be the case, as some of the case study Bills were 'rushed' through Parliament with little, if any, time for calm, considered parliamentary debate (Rajanayagam 2020; Lynch 2006; Williams and McDonald 2007; Williams et al. 2014; Burton and Williams 2013).

As noted in Chap. 5, where the second reading debate on a Bill concludes prior to the tabling of a committee's report, the opportunity for that committee to have an immediate impact on the enacted law or on the parliamentary debate can be severely limited (eg PJCHR Fourteenth Report of 2014 at p. 3). This is because parliamentarians are required to make a public statement about the merits of a proposed Bill without the benefit of the information generated from the committee's inquiry, or the analysis contained in the committee's scrutiny report. Interviews undertaken by the author with the Office of Parliamentary Counsel in 2016 also suggest that short time periods between committee reporting and the commencement of second reading debates also add pressure to those responsible for drafting the Bill and any government amendments made in response to committee recommendations.

For some committees, the Senate Standing Orders provide some protection against the resumption of the second reading debate prior to the tabling of committee reports. For example, the Senate Standing Orders provide that a second reading debate cannot resume until the tabling of the reports of any relevant Senate committees (Senate Standing Orders 38 and 62). However, while designed to guard against uninformed debate, these orders can sometimes add to the time pressures experienced by Senate committees and their staff. As LCA Committee Secretary Committee Secretary Sophie Dunstone explained in an interview in 2016:

> The Senate doesn't bring on Bills for debate until committee reports are tabled, and so that's partly where some of that time pressure on committee inquiries is borne out. Governments don't want their legislative timetable delayed by committee inquiries and reporting. So often it will be the day that the committee's report is tabled, or the very next day, that the Bill is listed for debate (Canberra 23 May 2016).

The same Standing Orders do not apply to the tabling of joint committee reports, meaning that the second reading debate on a Bill can commence *prior* to the tabling of a joint committee report. As noted in Chap. 5, this has led to occasions where the PJCHR has not had sufficient time to table its report on a case study Bill prior to the resumption of the second reading debate in either the Senate or the House.

For Dalla-Pozza (2016), providing adequate time for meaningful parliamentary scrutiny of proposed laws is integral to 'striking the right balance' between liberty and security when enacting counter-terrorism laws. Like many other scholars (e.g. Lynch 2006; Fletcher 2018), Dalla-Pozza's work (2008; 2016) suggests that a shorter time allocated for scrutiny results in poorer quality scrutiny. While the evidence presented in this chapter certainly confirms that a committee that is unable to table its report prior to the completion of the second reading debate on the Bill will struggle to have a strong impact on the content of the law, my research also presents a more complex picture of the relationship between the *time* allocated for scrutiny and the *strength* of the impact of the scrutiny on the Bill. My research suggests that other factors may be at play that have more influence on the overall impact of parliamentary committees on the case study Acts than time alone. These findings are discussed in further detail below, and are supported by Table 6.1, which summarises how much time was allocated to formal parliamentary scrutiny and parliamentary debate for each case study Act. This table also draws upon information from Chap. 4 to help identify whether tight periods have a correlation with lower levels of public or parliamentary participation.

6.2.1 Period Between Introduction and Enactment

Table 6.1 suggests that the shortest time between introduction and enactment occurred with the Foreign Fighters Bill (39 days), closely followed by the Control Orders Bill (41 days). As Dalla-Pozza (2016) notes, these Bills have experiences in common other than short time frames. In particular, both were introduced in response to an asserted serious and imminent threat to national security.[1] Both Bills also made significant changes to Australia's criminal law framework, with important consequences for individual rights. However, there are also important differences between these Bills and their parliamentary scrutiny experiences. While both Bills proceeded through Parliament quickly, the Control Orders Bill was able to attract considerable public and parliamentary attention. For example, the LCA References Committee's inquiry into the Control Orders Bill attracted 294 submissions and 52 second reading speeches (Dalla-Pozza 2016 at p. 281; Appleby 2015). In addition, both the LCA Committee's report and the SSCSB report on the Control Orders Bill were tabled in advance (although only just) of the resumption of the second reading debate.[2] Thus, at least when compared with the other Bills in my

[1]As discussed in Chap. 3, for the Control Orders Bill, this was the threat posed by the London Bombing experience; in the case of the Foreign Fighters Bill, the threat concerned the return of Australians following participation in terrorist activities overseas.

[2]As noted in Chap. 3, the Bill also required the states and territories to introduce similar laws and thus was proceeded by a COAG process which, through the actions of ACT Chief Minister Jon Stanhope, provided an opportunity for the media and the community to be made aware of the key features of the Bill.

Table 6.1 Time periods for scrutiny and debate of counter-terrorism laws

	Introduction to enactment	Time for scrutiny	Time for submissions	Number of submissions	Public hearings	Second reading speeches	Committee of the whole debate
Security Legislation Amendment (Terrorism) Bill 2002 [No. 2] and Other	94 days	38 days (LCA)	13 days (LCA)	431 (LCA)	4 days (LCA)	27	3 days Senate
Australian Security Intelligence Organisation Legislation Amendment (Terrorism) Bill 2002 No 1	240 days	89 days (PJCASIO) 80 days (LCA)	30 days	150 (PJC ASIO) Nil (LCA)	3 days (PJC ASIO)	36	3 days Senate
Australian Security Intelligence Organisation Legislation Amendment (Terrorism) Bill 2003	90 days	43 days (LCA Refs)	17 days	435 (LCA Ref)	3 days (LCA Ref)	23	4 days Senate
Anti-Terrorism Bill 2004	48 days	5 weeks, (LCA)	12 days (LCA)	28	1 day (LCA)	13	2 days Senate
National Security Information (Criminal Proceedings) Bill 2004 (Cth)	195 days (*lapsed and reintroduced*)	63 days (LCA)	16 days	23	1 day (LCA)	5	2 days Senate 1 day House
Anti-Terrorism Bill (No 2) 2005	41 days	25 days, (LCA)	8 days	294	3 days (LCA)	52	1 day Senate
National Security Legislation Amendment Bill 2010	240 days (*lapsed and reintroduced*)	3 months (LCA)	32 days	23	1 day	19	2 days House 1 day Senate
Independent National Security Legislation Monitor Bill 2010	285 days	42 days (SCFPA)	32 days	15	1 day	21	1 day Senate
Counter-Terrorism Legislation Amendment (Foreign Fighters) Bill 2014	39 days	23 days (PJCIS)	9 days	46	3 days	21,	2 days Senate 1 day House
Counter-Terrorism Legislation Amendment Bill (No 1) 2014	6 weeks	21 days (PJCIS)	11 days	17	1 day	15	2 days in Senate

(continued)

Table 6.1 (continued)

	Introduction to enactment	Time for scrutiny	Time for submissions	Number of submissions	Public hearings	Second reading speeches	Committee of the whole debate
Telecommunication (Interception and Access) Amendment (Data Retention) Bill 2014	5.5 months	96 days (PJCIS)	58 days (PJCIS)	204	3 days	41	3 days Senate 1 day House
Citizenship Amendment (Allegiance to Australia) Bill 2015	5.5 months	72 days (PJCIS)	26 days	43	3 days	68	3 days Senate 1 day House
Criminal Code Amendment (High Risk Terrorist Offenders) Bill 2016	2.5 months	53 days (PJCIS)	28 days	18	1 day	14	1 day House 1 day Senate
Telecommunication and Other Legislation Amendment (Assistance and Access) Bill 2018	2.5 months	73 days (PJCIS)	21 days	105	2 days	20	1 day House 1 day Senate
Counter-Terrorism (Temporary Exclusion Orders) Bill 2019	5 months	42 days (PJCIS)	15 days	8	1 day	21	1 day House 2 days Senate

case study, the short time between introduction and enactment of the Control Order Bill did not appear to act as a serious impediment to robust parliamentary scrutiny of this Bill. As discussed in Chap. 5, important legislative changes were made to the content of the Anti-terrorism Bill (No 2) 2005 that can described as rights-enhancing.

The Foreign Fighters Bill is another example of strong legislative impact by a parliamentary committee, despite short time frames between introduction and enactment. As discussed above, all of the PJCIS's recommendations with respect to the Foreign Fighters Bill were reflected in successful government amendments, and many of these had important rights-enhancing consequences. Unlike the Control Order Bill experience however, the Foreign Fighters Bill's swift passage through parliament effectively sidelined the PJCHR and the SSCSB, who were unable to table their reports on the Bill prior to the resumption of the second reading debate. It is also noted that only 46 submissions were made to the PJCIS inquiry, suggesting a much lower public engagement with the committee process than that experienced with respect to the Control Orders Bill.

The High Risk Offenders Bill provides another interesting example of multi-committee scrutiny taking place quickly with considerable legislative impact. At first blush, the High Risk Offenders Bill case study appears to be an example of the weaknesses of the current scrutiny system. Neither the SSCSB nor the PJCHR were able to issue their final reports on the Bill before the Bill was passed. Both the SSCSB and the PJCHR (and even the PJCIS) expressed genuine frustration at the lack of timely Government responses to requests for further information following initial scrutiny reports. However, on the other hand, both the PJCHR and the SSCSB were able to issue strongly worded, clear and direct initial scrutiny reports on the Bill that proved to be highly useful to other key participants in the parliamentary committee system including the PJCIS. This in turn led to a detailed 125 page report by the PJCIS which investigated in more detail each of the issues flagged by the scrutiny committees in their initial reports, and facilitated a more direct dialogue with the executive through the use of the public hearing function. Further, as noted above, the Government accepted all of the PJCIS's 23 recommendations and moved amendments to this effect on 28 November 2016. It also tabled a supplementary Explanatory Memorandum (2016) that directly attributed the amendments to the recommendations made by the PJCIS. In other words, the High Risk Offenders Bill case study seems to suggest that *timing* of reporting is critical – but *short* time frames might not be fatal, provided key participants have access to the right types of information at the right time. It also demonstrates the sophistication of many frequent submission makers to the PJCIS inquiries, who are actively looking to access and utilise reports of the SSCSB and the PJCHR, even if those reports are only preliminary in nature. It suggests that the 'alert' system provided by the SSCSB and emulated to a lesser extent by the PJCHR may be at least a partial panacea to the concerns raised by other scholars about short time frames for committee scrutiny of proposed laws, particularly if further thought is given to how to improve the accessibly and visibility of these 'alerts' to key participants in the system. These findings are reflected in the recommendations made in Chaps. 8 and 9 of this book.

Other case study examples also help to bolster my claim that while very short time frames *can* have an influence on the nature and quality of parliamentary scrutiny, they do not necessarily *determine* the strength of the public or legislative impact a committee can have.

The longest periods shown in Table 6.1 also illustrate this point. Both the National Security Legislation Amendment Bill 2010 and the INSLM Bill were before Parliament for around 8–9 months. In many ways, these longer periods are not surprising, as these Bills were not introduced in response to a particular terrorist threat, but rather to a series of reviews of Australia's counter-terrorism framework. These Bills could also be described as less rights intrusive, and more rights protective, than many of the other case study Acts. However, what is interesting is the fact that the longer time frames provided for scrutiny of these Bills did not result in more submissions to committees, or in additional parliamentary debate. In fact, these Bills received lower than average numbers of submissions, relatively short periods of parliamentary debate and a relatively small number of legislative changes attributable to parliamentary scrutiny. As noted in Chap. 5 and discussed further below, for these Bills, it was the work of previous parliamentary committee inquiries into counter-terrorism laws that proved influential at the pre-legislative phase, rather than the more direct committee scrutiny of their provisions once the Bills had been introduced.

In this way, the findings of my research could be described as counter-intuitive: I find that time may not be the key determinative factor in terms of the quality of parliamentary scrutiny a Bill receives. My research suggests that factors other than time periods may have an influence on the quality of scrutiny a proposed law receives, and on the rights-enhancing impact a parliamentary committee can have. One of these factors has already been identified as a central theme of my research, that is, the cumulative rights-enhancing effect of multiple committee scrutiny of a particular Bill. Another factor appears to be the extent to which a Bill attracts a range of sophisticated non-government actors to participate in the parliamentary committee process, which in turn increases the volume of public debate on a Bill, and provides important political incentives for parliamentarians to carefully 'weigh' competing public interests and policy options when making decisions about a Bill. These two factors are explored further below and set the foundations for a number of reform recommendations set out in Part III.

Table 6.2 References to parliamentary committee scrutiny

Bill	References to parliamentary committee scrutiny
TOTAL	283 of 356 speeches (78%)
Counter-Terrorism (Temporary Exclusion Orders) Bill 2019	21 of 22 speeches (95%) 21 references to PJCIS
Telecommunications and Other Legislation (Assistance and Access) Bill 2018	20 of 20 speeches (100%) 20 substantive references to PJCIS
Criminal Code Amendment (High Risk Terrorist Offenders) Bill 2016	12 of 14 speeches (85%) 12 substantive references to PJCIS
Counter-Terrorism Legislation Amendment (Foreign Fighters) Bill 2014	19 of 31 speeches (60%) 19 references to PJCIS, 3 references to PJCHR, 2 references to LCA Committees being excluded (Greens)
Counter-Terrorism Legislation Amendment Bill (No 1) 2014	12 of 15 speeches (80%) 12 references to PJCIS, 3 references to PJCHR
National Security Legislation Amendment Bill 2010	15 of 19 speeches (78%) 5 references to LCA Committees, 11 references to past inquiries being addressed by this Bill, all of which included reference to PJCIS
Independent National Security Legislation Monitor Bill 2010	17 of 21 speeches (80%) 7 references to Senate Finance and PA Committee, 10 references to work of past committees
Anti-Terrorism Bill (No 2) 2005	24 of 52 speeches (46%) 24 substantive references to LCA Committees
National Security Information (Criminal Proceedings) Bill 2004 (Cth)	5 of 5 speeches (100%) 5 substantive references to LCA Committees
Anti-terrorism Bill 2004	7 of 13 speeches (53%) 7 substantive references to LCA Committees
Australian Security Intelligence Organisation Legislation Amendment (Terrorism) Bill 2002	25 of 36 speeches (75%) 25 substantive references to PJC ASIO, 11 substantive references to LCA Committees, 3 references to Scrutiny of Bills
Australian Security Intelligence Organisation Legislation Amendment (Terrorism) Bill 2003	14 of 23 speeches (66%) 14 references to past parliamentary inquiries into the 2002 Bill
Security Legislation Amendment (Terrorism) Bill (No 2) 2002 and Other Bills	17 of 27 speeches (62%) 17 references to LCA Committees

6.3 Influence of Parliamentary Committees on the Public Debate on the Case Study Bills

6.3.1 Parliamentary Debates

One way to measure the impact of committees on parliamentary debate is to look for direct references to committee work in Hansard debates on the case study Acts. Care must be taken not to overstate the significance of a reference to a committee in parliamentary debates. It is not possible to identify with any precision what a parliamentarian was *actually* thinking when debating a Bill, or what made him or her vote in a certain way. The political reality may be that the parliamentarian was simply reciting a series of dot points circulated by the proponent Minister or Shadow Minister without any independent reflection on the merits of the Bill. Alternatively, a parliamentarian might refer to the work of a committee that they are a member of simply to bolster their own reputation. However, the words deliberately chosen for parliamentary speeches do provide some indication of the type of issues parliamentarians want the public to understand as important in their deliberation on a particular Bill. For these reasons, evidence derived from Hansard debates on the case study Acts provides a useful basis on which to begin to measure public impact in my research.

Table 6.2 provides an overview of the frequency with which the four parliamentary committees studied were referred to during parliamentary debates on the case study Acts. It shows that around three quarters of second reading speeches made on the case study Acts referred to scrutiny undertaken by at least one of the four parliamentary committees studied.

It is clear from Table 6.2 that committees featured prominently in parliamentary debates on the case study Acts. It is also clear that the PJCIS and the LCA Committees received far more references than the PJCHR or the SSCSB, with the PJCIS featuring particularly strongly in the debates since 2013. While opposition and minor parties referred more frequently to parliamentary committees than government members with respect to some Bills (for example with respect to the Control Orders Bill) it is not uncommon for government members to make substantive references to the work of parliamentary committees in their second reading speeches (for example the debates on the Citizenship Bill).

Of interest is the fact that the debate on the two Bills which attracted the highest number of second reading speeches – the Citizenship Bill and the Control Order Bill – contained fewer direct references to the work of parliamentary committees than those Bills that moved through Parliament with much less debate. As will be explored further below, this may be because these Bills invoked strong rights discussions within the broader community, which may have provided incentives for parliamentarians to refer directly to submission makers to the inquiry committees, rather than relying on the reports of the inquiry-based committees themselves. The same trend is apparent with respect to the debates on the ASIO Bill 2002, the ASIO Bill 2003 and the SLAT Bills, which also contained fewer direct references to parliamentary committees. This can be contrasted with the two Bills that attracted the least number of submissions to committee inquiries and lower numbers of second reading speeches: the National Security Information (Criminal Proceedings) Bill 2004 (Cth) and the National Security Legislation Amendment Bill 2010. For these Bills, there was a common deference to the work of parliamentary committees as evidence that the 'weighing process' described above had occurred. At both ends of this spectrum, the public impact of parliamentary committees (and in particular the inquiry-based committees) was strong. The inquiry-based committees provided the forum for rights concerns about the Bills to be raised, and parliamentarians were keen to emphasise the importance of the committees undertaking this role (either by deferring to the committee's report, or quoting directly from the committee's submission makers) when justifying their position on a particular Bill.

Care must be taken not to overstate the influence of parliamentary committees on parliamentary debates on counter-terrorism, or to equate reference to external review with positive rights outcomes. As Blackbourn has explored in the context of counter-terrorism law-making in the United Kingdom, the trend towards referring these laws to external bodies for review has done little to remedy the rights-abrogating nature of the enacted laws (Blackbourn 2018). As discussed further in Part III, this perspective is also relevant in the Australian content, where some of Australia's most significant counter-terrorism laws (such as the control order regime) have been referred to external bodies for review on multiple occasions and continue to contain features that depart from human rights principles. However, as discussed in Part I, the focus of my research is not to argue that intra-parliamentary or extra-parliamentary scrutiny of enacted laws is a *sufficient* form a rights protection when it comes to counter-terrorism law making, but rather to highlight the *significance* of the legislative, public and hidden impact of the parliamentary committee system on the shape of Australian counterterrorism laws. In this way, my research highlights how, when the system of committees work together, the long and short term impact of parliamentary scrutiny can be significant, and can be rights-enhancing in nature.

The above analysis further suggests that the consistent and substantive discussion of the value and role of parliamentary committees during second reading debates across party lines and successive parliaments, coupled with the very real legislative impact of parliamentary committees, tells us something important about the rights-scrutiny culture within the federal Parliament, that should be kept in mind by rights advocates when considering what changes might need to be made to improve the outcomes of Australia's parliamentary model of rights protection.

6.3.2 *Signs of an Emerging Rights-Scrutiny Culture within the Federal Parliament*

An analysis of the parliamentary debates on the case study Acts reveals useful insights into the way the Parliament discusses rights and suggests that a particular rights-scrutiny culture may be emerging that has an important relationship with the mandates of the technical scrutiny committees considered in this book. This argument is supported by three compelling observations from the second reading debates on the case study Acts. The first is the propensity for second reading speeches on the case study Acts to include discussions of the need to 'balance' competing rights related to the protection of the community from the threat of terrorism, and the individual rights of those affected by the proposed law. For example, of the 334 second reading speeches made on the case study Acts, my analysis suggests that around

70 per cent included some discussion of 'rights' (as inclusively defined in Chap. 1) and the need to consider these rights in light of competing public interests. As noted below, my research is alive to the fact that a reference to 'balancing' does not provide an assurance that the speaker has in fact carefully considered the competing rights and interests, or applied international human rights principles to resolving tensions between rights. However, the fact that the speaker at the very least intends to *give the impression* that they have engaged in this exercise is itself noteworthy, and relevant to identifying whether a relevant rights scrutiny culture may be emerging.

The second compelling observation is the apparent preference (69%) for discussing rights with reference to the broad language featuring in the SSCSB's mandate (such as 'individual rights and liberties' and 'limits on executive power') as opposed to referring directly to international human rights law (such as 'Article 14 of the ICCPR') (30%). Interestingly, there was no dramatic increase in references to international human rights concepts following the establishment of the PJCHR, suggesting that, outside of a handful of human rights 'champions' (discussed further in Chap. 8), the work of the PJCHR was not able to generate a strong response from parliamentarians in the context of debating the case study Acts (consistent with findings made by Williams and Reynolds 2016).

The third compelling observation is the repeated reference to the same types of rights scrutiny principles across the second reading speeches for the 15 case study Acts. These rights and scrutiny principles closely reflect the type of rights analysis found in reports of the committees considered in Chap. 5, and can be described as follows:

- The proposed provisions and Explanatory Memorandum should be clearly drafted so the meaning and policy aim is clear to Parliament.
- The expansion of executive power must come with procedural fairness guarantees: including access to legal representation, preservation of common law privileges and access to judicial review.
- Parliament should have access to information about how government departments and agencies are using their powers.
- If the law is designed to respond to an extraordinary set of circumstances, Parliament should be required to revisit the law to determine whether it is still needed.
- New criminal offences should have clearly defined physical and mental elements, allocate the burden of proof to the prosecution, ensure access to legal representation, and not apply retrospectively.
- Any restriction of free speech should be accompanied by exceptions to promote robust debate on matters of public interest.
- Freedom of association and the right to privacy should not be unduly burdened and any restriction should be subject to independent oversight.
- The proposed law should not infringe freedom of religion, and should respect Australia's ethnic and cultural diversity.
- The rights of children require special protection.

Taken together, these observations suggest that a particular rights-scrutiny culture may be emerging at the federal level that warrants further documentation and investigation. These observations also share themes with the examination of other key aspects of Australia's parliamentary model of rights protection collated by Debeljak and Grenfell (2020). For example, common among the work of Byrnes (2020), Rice (2020), Fletcher (2020) and Reynolds and Williams (2020) is a recognition that there is something unique about the way the Australian parliament engages with human rights standards and the way different institutions of government interact with each other during the rights scrutiny process. This 'uniqueness' appears to be generated by a shared commitment among many key participants to parliamentary sovereignty, the realities of a parliament dominated by a powerful executive and a general mistrust of both the courts and international human rights bodies when it comes to resolving complex rights issues in Australia. As the authors above document, these unique features lead to clear shortcomings when it comes to meaningful rights protection, but as explored in Part III, if embraced through the parliamentary committee process, these same features also give rise to new opportunities and possibilities for the development of a more robust, organically developing rights-scrutiny culture in Australia.

Many observers may be sceptical of the value of what I have described as an emerging rights-scrutiny culture within the Australian Parliament, noting for example that common references to 'balancing' in parliamentary debates are not reliable evidence that meaningful deliberation has taken place or that less rights-intrusive means of achieving the same policy end have been considered (see e.g. Williams 2005; McCulloch 2015). In some instances, they argue, it is just part of the standard political rhetoric used by both major parties to 'soften' or 'hide' the rights-intrusive nature of the laws they are enacting. This view was also supported by some of the interview material. For example, Bill Rowlings from Civil Liberties Australia said that often the lack of a clear analytical framework being applied when parliamentarians speak of 'balance' leaves submission makers and the public more broadly cynical about their commitment to genuinely looking for ways to avoid disproportionate interferences with individuals' rights (Canberra 24 May 2016).

However, my research points to an interesting relationship between the repeated reference to 'balancing' and the nature of the parliamentary committee scrutiny of the Bill (Chordia 2016). The more popular the committee inquiry leading up to the second reading debate, the more confident parliamentarians appear to be in asserting that the 'right balance has been struck'. There is also a strong relationship between (a) those Bills that attract a large number of submission makers to parliamentary inquiries and (b) those Bills that attract the most significant references to rights concepts in parliamentary debates. This suggests that, when the Parliament talks about the work of its committees, it is more likely to discuss 'rights' and is more explicit about the need to strike the right 'balance' when enacting counter-terrorism laws. Further, as established in Chap. 5, where multi-committee scrutiny occurs, there is also a strong chance that it will result in meaningful rights-enhancing legislative change. This suggests that some form of meaningful rights scrutiny took place, at least with respect to the case study Acts, that could be improved and built upon.

Others may consider that I am presenting an overly optimistic view of the rights-scrutiny culture in the federal Parliament, particularly since the election of the Abbott government (can Ham and Chappell 2017 at pp. 166–7; Carne 2015). For example, for Carne (2015), the Brandis-led shift away from international human rights discourse towards the language of individual freedoms points to 'a renewed and deliberate distinctiveness and differentiation' in the away policy makers and law makers approach human rights (at p. 65) that has 'proven grossly ineffectual' in providing meaningful review and critique of Australia's counter-terrorism laws (at p. 67).

Before conducting this research, I shared Carne's concerns that the 'liberal democratic rights agenda' promoted by Attorney-General Brandis would dilute rights scrutiny at the federal level and impact negatively on the human rights literacy of the Parliament. However, as discussed further in Part III, my research challenges Carne's assumptions on a number of fronts. First, my research demonstrates that the counter-terrorism laws debated and enacted during 2013–14 attracted a rights discourse that moved beyond the 'liberal democratic rights agenda', both within the Parliament and within the broader media commentary on the laws. This discourse included, for example, reliance on specific human rights analysis undertaken by the PJCHR by influential submission makers to other parliamentary committees, as well as a focus by the PJCIS and SSCSB on issues such as appropriate parliamentary oversight of the use of executive power and the impact of the law on religious or ethnic minorities. Secondly, my research challenges the conventional wisdom (see e.g. Dalla-Pozza 2016; Appleby 2015; Lynch 2006) that short time periods for parliamentary review lead to poor scrutiny outcomes, but highlighting that a range of other factors are determinative on the quality of parliamentary scrutiny of counter-terrorism laws, chief among these being the capacity of the system of parliament committees to work together to conduct public hearings and provide submission makers and parliamentarians with access to scrutiny committee reports. Finally, my research demonstrates that during 2013–14, the PJCIS had a 100 per cent 'strike rate' in terms of translating its recommendations into legislative amendments, and the vast majority of these amendments were rights-enhancing in nature (even if they did not remedy the full range of rights concerns with the Bills).

Thus, while rights advocates may be correct to hold concerns about the scope of the 'liberal democratic rights agenda' promoted by the Abbott Government, my research suggests that this 'agenda' has not prevented the development of a particular rights-scrutiny culture at the federal level that could, if documented and investigated further, be useful for identifying what type of reforms will be most successful at improving rights protection in Australia. In fact, as discussed further in Part III, my research suggests that investigating and articulating this rights scrutiny culture is a critical first step for anyone interested in improving the current parliamentary model of rights protection, or for anyone developing or evaluating options for reform of this model.

In addition, understanding this emerging rights-scrutiny culture could help to distinguish between what Levy and Orr (2016) describe as the difference between 'conceptual balancing' (which often takes the form of trading off values or interests against others) and 'deliberative accommodation' (which often involves searching for a common ground between different values or interests) (at pp. 67–70). For these authors, deliberative accommodation methodologies are preferable to conceptual balancing approaches as they encourage a broader range of views to be heard, involve mutual learning and persuasion and depend on inclusiveness, rather than 'trade offs' between rights holders (Levy and Orr 2016 at pp. 197). My research suggests that, when working together as a system, parliamentary committees may be beginning to show signs of 'deliberative accommodation' (that is, a capacity to gather information from diverse sources, reflect on that information and adjust their views accordingly) at least in the context of reviewing the case study Acts. As discussed further in Part III, understanding this emerging rights-scrutiny culture could also help contextualise what Stephenson has described as the 'institutional disagreements' that occur on rights issues within the federal jurisdiction, which could in turn help to identify options for improving Australia's parliamentary model of rights protection (Stephenson 2016 at p. 8).

6.4 Media Commentary

The final snapshot of public impact being considered in this chapter is media commentary on the case study Bills. Table 6.3 lists references to the work of committees in media commentary on the case study Acts, found through searches of an Australian media database.[3] While this is by no means a comprehensive catalogue of the public commentary on counter-terrorism law making in Australia,[4] it provides a glimpse into the extent to which parliamentary committee work featured in the broader public debate on the Bills.

Table 6.3 largely confirms the trends described above with respect to the parliamentary debates on the case study Acts. For example, the Control Orders Bill, the Data Retention Bill and the Citizenship Bill all received high levels of media

[3] The database used for this purpose was the Australia/New Zealand Reference Centre accessed through the University of Adelaide Library. This database is supported by EBSCO Host and provides access to Australian and New Zealand newspapers, magazines, and radio and television transcripts. Searches were also undertaken on 'Google' with the 'News' tab 'Australia only' selected. References to individual articles referring to the case study Acts are set out in Moulds 2018 Appendix C.

[4] For example, Table 6.3 does not show the very large volume of media and academic commentary that refers in general terms to Australia's response to terrorism, or that documents or discusses particular local and international terrorist events or threats. Even a cursory examination of this volume of material reveals that articles or reports referring to parliamentary scrutiny of proposed new counter-terrorism measures comprise a small minority. This must be kept in mind when evaluating the public impact of the parliamentary committee system on the public debate on these laws.

Table 6.3 Public commentary on the case study bills and the role of parliamentary scrutiny

	Media articles	Reference to parliamentary scrutiny	Reference to rights issues
Security Legislation Amendment (Terrorism) Bill 2002 (No 2) and Other	18 *NB some cross over with ASIO Bills (below)*	Yes, references to LCA Committees, also criticism of legislative process	Yes, focus on procedural rights, freedom of association, freedom of speech
ASIO Legislation Amendment (Terrorism) Bill 2002 and 2003	39 *NB some cross over with SLAT Bills (above)*	Yes, extensive references to LCA Committees' and PJC ASIO Committee's inquiries, including quotations from submission makers and recommendations.	Yes, extensive discussion of rights and civil liberties including specific references to right to free speech, rights of children, access to legal representation, incommunicado detention
Anti-Terrorism Bill 2004	None found		
National Security Information (Criminal Proceedings) Bill 2004	11	Yes, references to LCA Committees	Yes, strong focus on procedural rights, eg right to access legal representation, open justice
Anti-Terrorism Bill (No 2) 2005	Over 200 *NB including after enactment*	Yes, references to work of LCA Committees	Yes, extensive discussion of rights issues, including reference to international human rights law
National Security Legislation Amendment Bill 2010	10 *NB most focused on Haneef Inquiry*	Yes, references to past reviews including by PJCIS, LCA Committees but more commonly to Haneef Inquiry	Yes, in general terms and with reference to the Haneef case.
Independent National Security Legislation Monitor Bill 2010	10	Yes, references to SCFPA but also PJCIS and Sheller Committee	Yes, with particular reference to 'balancing' rights and national security
Counter-Terrorism Legislation Amendment (Foreign Fighters) Bill 2014	33	Yes, references to PJCIS and 'Senate Committees' examining the Bill. NB also reference to INSLM and IGIS	Yes, particular reference to procedural fairness and fair trial principles, freedom of movement
Counter-Terrorism Legislation Amendment Bill (No 1) 2014	None found		
Telecommunication (Interception and Access) Amendment (Data Retention) Bill 2014	Over 250	Yes, some references to both PJCIS and LCA Committees	Yes, particularly strong and repeated references to right to privacy

(continued)

Table 6.3 (continued)

	Media articles	Reference to parliamentary scrutiny	Reference to rights issues
Citizenship Amendment (Allegiance to Australia) Bill 2015	126	Yes, frequent references to work of PJCIS and INSLM	Yes, including specific references to procedural fairness, legal right to access citizenship, indefinite detention, freedom of speech, right to equality
Criminal Code Amendment (High Risk Terrorist Offenders) Bill 2016	37	Yes, frequent references to work of PJCIS	Yes, including specific references to freedom from post-conviction detention
Telecommunications and Other Legislation (Assistance and Access) Bill 2018	358	Yes, frequent references to the work of the PJCIS	Yes, particularly strong and repeated references to right to privacy
Counter-Terrorism (Temporary Exclusion Orders) Bill	74	Yes, frequent references to the work of the PJCIS	Yes, including specific focus on rights to nationality/statelessness and constitutional issues

attention, and public commentary on these Bills included regular references to rights issues, as well as references to parliamentary scrutiny processes. These Bills also attracted large numbers of submission makers to committee inquiries and, in the case of the Control Orders Bill and the Data Retention Bill, were scrutinised by at least three separate committees. This suggests that there is a causal relationship between the rights-engaging nature of the content of the Bill, the number of submissions a committee inquiry attracts, and the rate of media attention a Bill receives. The interviews I conducted for my research (such as those conducted with Civil Liberties Australia, Muslim Legal Network and the Law Council of Australia) also suggest that often it is the referral of a Bill to a committee for inquiry that provides important trigger points for public advocacy by sophisticated submission makers. This can include direct media engagement by these bodies in order to highlight the rights issues arising from the Bill (see e.g. Wroe 2015; Civil Liberties Australia 2005).

A similar experience can be observed with respect to the SLAT Bills and the ASIO Bills, as well as the Foreign Fighters Bill, which all generated significant media attention. In the case of the SLAT and ASIO Bills, the media commentary included strident criticism of the proposed new measures containing references to human rights principles, rule of law principles and comparative examples (see e.g. Sydney Morning Herald 2002; Nicholson 2002). The speed at which these laws were 'pushed through' Parliament was also frequently noted, although the work of the LCA Committees was praised and submissions to those committees frequently quoted (see e.g. Courier Mail 2002; Kirk 2002). This again suggests that the conduct of public inquiries by parliamentary committees, particularly those involving large numbers of sophisticated non-government submission makers, helps to generate strong media interest in the Bill.

This relatively strong media interest may also help explain the rights-enhancing nature of the legislative amendments made to the Bills noted above that can be attributed to the work of parliamentary committees. This is supported by interviews conducted for this book, which suggest that public statements by reputable submission makers about the rights concerns arising from a proposed Bill can provide useful 'cover' for backbenchers or non-government members to push for their respective parties to give effect to rights-enhancing committee recommendations by way of legislative amendment.

Despite these persuasive examples, it is clear that there is not always a causal relationship between the rights-engaging nature of the Bill, the popularity of the committee inquiry and the level of media attention generated. For example, the Anti-Terrorism Bill 2004 attracted very little media attention when introduced, despite introducing rights-intrusive new powers including the so called 'dead time' provisions in Part IC of the *Crimes Ac 1915* (Cth), which permitted the police to detain a person (potentially incommunicado) who may have relevant information about terrorist activities for extensive periods without charge. These provisions appeared to 'slide under the radar' at the time the Bill was introduced, only to attract much more significant media and academic attention in subsequent years (sparked by the Haneef case and the subsequent inquiry) (see e.g. Hammer 2008). This suggests that rights-engaging provisions may not always attract media and submission maker attention at the time of introduction. Something more may be needed (such as the opportunity to observe the laws in action) before media attention will occur.

Another interesting example is the National Security Information (Criminal Proceedings) Bill 2004. Despite only attracting a relatively modest number of submissions and second reading speeches in Parliament, this Bill managed to attract stronger than expected media attention (see e.g. Banham and O'Malley 2005; Walters 2004). This could be explained by the concerted 'campaign' against the Bill developed and prosecuted by legal organisations and journalists, both of whom had direct interests in drawing attention to the provisions of the Bill that would restrict their professional roles in terrorist-related trials. In the case of the legal organisations, it was the proposal to 'security clear' lawyers that generated particular concern, as well as the 'closed court' provisions that aimed to protect national security information from disclosure in criminal trials. This example underscores the role that sophisticated submission makers play in generating media attention on proposed laws, which is frequently triggered by the referral of the Bill to an inquiry-based committee.

With these findings in mind, it is unsurprising that the inquiry-based committees dominate media references to committees in Table 6.3, as these are the committees that provide the forum for submission makers to publicly articulate their concerns about a proposed law. Inquiry-based committees also provide a forum for parliamentarians to directly question the proponents of a Bill, often adding an element of drama to the public hearing experience that is of interest to the media. The technical scrutiny committees are very rarely referred to in media commentary on the Bills;

however, this does not mean that their analysis is completely absent from the public discourse. Table 6.3 suggests that public commentary on the case study Bills almost invariably included references to rights, and in particular the need to 'balance' competing rights or public interests or to ensure oversight and safeguards to protect rights. In many instances, broad reference was made to international human rights law principles or the principles applied by the SSCSB. This could suggest that the scrutiny criteria being applied by the technical scrutiny committees resonated to some degree within the public commentary on the Bills. However, it may also be explained by the fact that sophisticated submission makers regularly focus on rights issues, and the public commentary simply reflects their concerns. In either case, as Chaps. 4 and 5 suggest, the provision of rights-related analysis of a Bill by the SSCSB and the PJCHR appears to assist submission makers to justify and articulate their concerns about a proposed law, which in turn appears to inform the rights-related discussions that occur within the inquiry-based committees and in the public commentary on the law. These different strengths and weaknesses between the inquiry-based and technical scrutiny committees are considered in detail in Chap. 8, and help inform the recommendations made in Part III of my research.

6.5 Influence of Formal Parliamentary Scrutiny on Post-Enactment Review of the Case Study Bills

The final area of public impact considered in this chapter is the role parliamentary committees play in post-enactment reviews of the case study Acts. Looking for this form of public impact helps to identify whether parliamentary committees are having a longer-term impact on the content of the case study Acts. For example, the LCA Legislation Committee's recommendations with respect to the Control Orders Bill relating to the proposed new sedition offences featured prominently in the ALRC's 2006 report *Fighting Words: A Review of Sedition Laws in Australia* (particularly Recommendations 1-3 and 9), and then later in parliamentary debate on the National Security Legislation Amendment Bill 2010, which implemented a number of the ALRC's recommended reforms (LCA Legislation Committee Control Orders Bill Report 2005).

Another example is the 2006 Sheller Review, which drew upon the work of the LCA Legislation Committee and the PJC on ASIO, ASIS and DSD in their inquiries into the SLAT Bills, the ASIO Bills and the Control Orders Bill (see e.g. p. 6). For example, in line with the recommendations made by these committees, the Sheller Review recommended that the process for proscribing a terrorist organisation be made more transparent by providing persons affected with notification and the right to be heard in opposition (Recommendation 3). It also recommended that the term 'threat of action' be removed from the definition of 'terrorist act' (Recommendation 7), the advocating terrorism offence be narrowed (Recommendation 9), the offence of 'associating with terrorist organisations' be repealed (Recommendation 15), and consideration be given to the establishment of a Special Advocate and/or Public Interest Monitor. The Rudd Government later referred to the recommendations made by the Sheller Committee as the basis for a number of the provisions contained in the *National Security Legislation Amendment Act 2010* (Cth).

The work of parliamentary committees also featured in the 2008 Haneef Report, with Mr. Clarke echoing concerns raised about the relevant provisions of Part IC of the *Crimes Act 1915* (Cth) by the LCA Legislation Committee in its inquiry into the Anti-Terrorism Bill 2004 (Clarke 2008 at pp. 242–3). The Haneef Report also recommended that consideration be given to the appointment of an Independent Reviewer of counter-terrorism laws (Recommendation 4). As discussed above, the government gave legislative effect to some of these recommendations in the *National Security Legislation Amendment Act 2010* (Cth) and the *INSLM Act 2010* (Cth).

The 2012 COAG Review of Counter Terrorism Legislation also referred to past parliamentary committee scrutiny of the control order and preventative detention order regimes (COAG 2013). For example, 33 references were made to the work of the PJCIS, with much less frequent reference being made to the LCA Committees. Other independent post-enactment reviews were also discussed, including the Sheller Review.

The COAG Committee also recommended 47 changes to a range of counter-terrorism provisions subject to the review, many of which reflected the recommendations previously made by parliamentary committees. For example, the COAG Committee recommended changes to clarify and narrow the scope of the definition of 'advocates' in the advocating terrorism offence in s 102.1(1A) of the Criminal Code (Recommendation 13). The LCA Committee (Recommendation 31) made a similar recommendation in its report on the Control Orders Bill. The COAG Committee also recommended the removal of strict liability elements in the terrorist organisation offences (Recommendation 18), similar to recommendations made by the LCA Committee in its report on the SLAT Bills (Recommendations 3 and 4).

Although the government only supported a handful of the COAG Committee recommendations, the recommendation for the introduction of a nationwide system of 'Special Advocates' (Recommendation 13) to participate in control order proceedings later found its way into the PJCIS's report on the Counter-Terrorism Legislation Amendment Bill (No 1) 2014 (Recommendation 19-24).

The period between 2016–2019 also saw the PJCIS engage a range of substantial reviews of pre-existing counter-terrorism laws, including reviews of ASIO's questioning and detention powers, the new 'declared area' offences introduced by the Foreign Fighters Act, and police stop and search powers, the control order and preventative detention order regimes. These reviews provided a further opportunity for submission makers to past PJCIS and INSLM inquiries to re-agitate for reform to some of the most rights-impacted aspects of Australia's counter-terrorism regime. It also provided the PJCIS with a second opportunity to reflect upon the implementation of its past recommendations and press for further change. As noted in Chap. 3, this period also provides a useful example of Australia's ad hoc, multi-faceted model of 'post-legislative scrutiny' (Moulds 2020) or the 'dual scrutiny' experience of counter-terrorism law making in Australia as explored by Dalla-Pozza (2020), that while easy to dismiss at first blush as an executive controlled form of legislative review, in fact holds important insights for other jurisdictions exploring the benefits and shortcomings of systematic or organically emerging forms of post-enactment rights review (Moulds 2020).

A strong example is the PJCIS's 2017–8 inquiry into ASIO's questioning and detention powers. In its 2018 report following this inquiry, the PJCIS explored the ongoing need for and utility of the questioning and detention regimes, reflecting on a range of data collected by other oversight bodies including the IGIS, and on a range of previous recommendations made by the PJCIS and the INSLM. It observed that 'over time this framework has become limited in its utility' and asked ASIO officers to develop several reform proposals which were considered in detailed by the PJCIS and other submission makers. The PJCIS also reflected on the principles that should underpin a future compulsory questioning model, having regard to the findings of INSLM Gyles who found that ASIO's questioning and detention powers to be 'unwieldy and warranted reform' (Gyles 2016; pp. 51–52 and PJCIS 2018 Recommendation 1). While the PJCIS ultimately recommended that ASIO's compulsory questioning powers be retained (Recommendation 1), it recommended repeal of ASIO's detention powers under the regime (Recommendation 2).

In making this significant, rights-enhancing recommendation the PJCIS not only demonstrated the long-term impact parliamentary scrutiny of counter-terrorism laws can have, but also provided a strong factual and policy basis for other parliamentarians of all political persuasions to support reform in this area. For example, before recommending that the detention powers be repealed, the Committee asked ASIO for a hypothetical scenario which would demonstrate why the detention powers were necessary in the 2017 context. The PJCIS carefully worked through each of these scenarios, gathering evidence from other submission makers to ensure that the risk presented by each scenario could be addressed by referring to alternative powers already available to law enforcement or intelligence officers (2018 at pp. 31–33). The PJCIS also pointed to the 'non-use' of the detention powers over the last 14 years (at p. 40), despite this coinciding with period of heightened counter-terrorism activity. It noted that even the Attorney General's Department conceded in its submission to the PJCIS that the non-use of the detention powers was at least partly due to the extensive range of other law enforcement and intelligence gathering powers available to agencies, such as Part IC of the Crimes Act and preventative detention orders (at p. 40). ASIO also told the PJCIS that it was 'not wedded to the current model of detention' (p. 40) and therefore open to exploring legislative alternatives. Using this evidence base as a foundation, the PJCIS then considered the human rights and constitutional concerns with the detention powers before concluding that 'the current provisions are no longer the appropriate response to the threat of terrorism' ant that the current detention framework should be repealed (p. 40). While the Government has yet to respond to the PJCIS's recommendations in this report, this recommendation in particular signals an important milestone in review of counter-terrorism laws in Australia, and if the PJCIS's track record of turning its recommendations into successful reforms is anything to go by, may result in *rights-remedying* change on this occasion.

Regardless of the legislative outcome of the PJCIS's 2018 inquiry into ASIO's questioning and detention powers, the above examples demonstrate that the scrutiny work undertaken by the four parliamentary committees studied had an influence on post-enactment reviews of counter-terrorism laws, which in turn were at least moderately effective at making rights-enhancing changes to the content of the case study Acts. This supports the finding made earlier in this chapter that parliamentary committees appear to play an important supportive role in the broader public debate on how to 'strike the right balance' when it comes to counter-terrorism laws. As noted above, the contribution each committee makes to the public debate on the case study Acts may not always be immediately apparent and depends on their particular strengths and characteristics. As discussed further below, I argue that capitalising on these different strengths of individual committees within the system, and encouraging multi-committee collaboration, is the key to improving the rights-protecting capacity of the parliamentary committee system.

6.6 Summary of Findings on Public Impact

By looking at the influence of parliamentary committees on parliamentary debates, media commentary and post-enactment review it is possible to get a glimpse of the broader impact of the committee system on the case study Acts. The above analysis shows that, when the committee system provided genuine opportunities for public hearings to be conducted into the case study Acts, the public impact was considerable, particularly when sophisticated submission makers who had the capacity to generate media attention participated. This in turn provided strong incentives for parliamentarians to engage with rights issues and discuss committee inquiries when debating the relevant Bill. This is apparent in the LCA Committees' and PJCIS's inquiries into the most controversial case study Acts, such as the ASIO Bills, the Control Order Bill and the Citizenship Bill, but also in the context of less controversial Bills, such as the National Security Information (Criminal Proceedings) Bill 2004.

The above analysis also demonstrates that the public impact of committee work can occur many years after enactment, as evident in the reports and recommendations of the post-enactment review bodies discussed above. This suggests that committee recommendations for legislative amendment that were rejected or 'slipped under the radar' at the time of initial scrutiny can be revived by post-enactment review, providing the committee system with a second chance to influence the shape and operation of these laws.

This chapter also considered whether the time allocated for parliamentary scrutiny of the case study Acts determined the quality of scrutiny undertaken. The results suggest that, while tabling committee reports prior to the conclusion of the second reading debate on a Bill *is* critical if a committee is to have an immediate influence on the content of the Bill, short time frames for scrutiny do not necessarily negate the potential for rights-enhancing legislative and public impacts. In particular, the examples discussed above suggest that large public inquiries can take place in short periods, which can in turn generate robust parliamentary debate and strong media attention and give rise to rights-enhancing legislative change. While this type of 'fast and furious' scrutiny could be particularly problematic for less well-resourced submission makers, it suggests that timing might not be everything when it comes to rights scrutiny of proposed laws.

Finally, this chapter identifies that, when it comes to debating proposed counter-terrorism Bills in the Parliament and the media, there is a positive relationship between the work of the four parliamentary committees studied and the consideration of a particular range of rights and other scrutiny principles. While it may be too early to tell whether this collection of rights and scrutiny principles resonates across other subject areas, I argue that the development of this rights-scrutiny culture is a relevant factor to consider when identifying options to improve Australia's parliamentary model of rights protection.

References

Bills

House of Representatives. (2015). *Telecommunications (Interception and Access) Amendment (Data Retention) Bill* 2015 (Cth). Canberra: Parliament of Australia. https://www.aph.gov.au/Parliamentary_Business/Bills_LEGislation/Bills_Search_Results/Result?bId=r5375

House of Representatives. (2015). *Australian Citizenship Amendment (Allegiance to Australia) Bill* 2015 (Cth). Canberra: Parliament of Australia. https://www.aph.gov.au/Parliamentary_Business/Bills_Legislation/Bills_Search_Results/Result?bId=r5507

House of Representatives. (2014). *Counter-Terrorism Legislation Amendment Bill (No 1) 2014* (Cth). Canberra: Parliament of Australia. https://www.aph.gov.au/Parliamentary_Business/Bills_Legislation/Bills_Search_Results/Result?bId=s982, https://www.aph.gov.au/Parliamentary_Business/Bills_Legislation/Bills_Search_Results/Result?bId=r1808

House of Representatives. (2010). *National Security Legislation Amendment Bill* 2010 (Cth). Canberra: Parliament of Australia. https://www.aph.gov.au/Parliamentary_Business/Bills_Legislation/Bills_Search_Results/Result?bId=r4435

House of Representatives. (2004). Anti-Terrorism Bill (No 2) 2005 (Cth). Canberra: Parliament of Australia. https://www.aph.gov.au/Parliamentary_Business/Bills_Legislation/Bills_Search_Results/Result?bId=r2469

Senate. Counter-Terrorism Legislation Amendment (Foreign Fighters) Bill 2014 (Cth). Canberra: Parliament of Australia. https://www.aph.gov.au/Parliamentary_Business/Bills_LEGislation/Bills_Search_Results/Result?bId=s976

Senate. (2006). *Criminal Code Amendment (High Risk Terrorist Offenders) Bill* 2016 (Cth). Canberra: Parliament of Australia. https://www.aph.gov.au/Parliamentary_Business/Bills_Legislation/Bills_Search_Results/Result?bId=s1039

Explanatory Memorandum

Senate. Supplementary Explanatory Memorandum, Criminal Code Amendment (High Risk Terrorist Offenders) Bill 2016. Canberra: Parliament of Australia. https://parlinfo.aph.gov.au/parlInfo/search/display/display.w3p;query=Id%3A%22legislation%2Fems%2Fs1039_ems_3b9b5af2-90d5-44b2-aefe-06ed5ea3392d%22

Standing Orders

Senate, Parliament of Australia, *Standing Order*, Chapter 5, Order 38 (24 August 1994.); https://www.aph.gov.au/Parliamentary_Business/Chamber_documents/Senate_chamber_documents/standingorders/b00/b05
Senate, Parliament of Australia, *Standing Order*, Chapter 9, Order 62 (14 October 1991). https://www.aph.gov.au/Parliamentary_Business/Chamber_documents/Senate_chamber_documents/standingorders/b00/~/~/~/link.aspx?_id=EBF13C7DAF2B48C6938BF3FEE5E28E07&_z=z

Parliamentary Committee Reports

Parliamentary Joint Committee on Human Rights. (2017). *Second Human Rights Scrutiny Report of 2017* (21 March 2017) Canberra: Parliament of Australia. https://www.aph.gov.au/Parliamentary_Business/Committees/Joint/Human_Rights/Scrutiny_reports/2017/Report_2_of_2017
Parliamentary Joint Committee on Human Rights. (2014). *Fourteenth Report of 44th Parliament* Canberra: Parliament of Australia. https://www.aph.gov.au/Parliamentary_Business/Committees/Joint/Human_Rights/Scrutiny_reports/2014/Fourteenth_Report_of_the_44th_Paliament
Parliamentary Joint Committee on Intelligence and Security. (2018). *Review of ASIO's questioning and detention powers* (2018). Canberra: Parliament of Australia. https://www.aph.gov.au/Parliamentary_Business/Committees/Joint/Intelligence_and_Security/ASIO
Parliamentary Joint Committee on Intelligence and Security. (2016). Advisory Report on the Criminal Code Amendment (High Risk Terrorist Offenders) Bill 2016. Canberra: Parliament of Australia. https://www.aph.gov.au/Parliamentary_Business/Committees/Joint/Intelligence_and_Security/HRTOBill/Report-HTML
Senate Standing Committee on Legal and Constitutional Affairs Legislation Committee. (2005). Provisions of the Anti-Terrorism Bill (No 2) 2005. Canberra: Parliament of Australia. https://www.aph.gov.au/Parliamentary_Business/Committees/Senate/Legal_and_Constitutional_Affairs/Completed_inquiries/2004-07/terrorism/report/index
Senate Standing Committee for Scrutiny of Bills. (2016). Report No 4 of 2016. Canberra: Parliament of Australia. https://www.aph.gov.au/Parliamentary_Business/Committees/Senate/Scrutiny_of_Bills/Reports/2016/index

Books/Articles/Reports/Speeches

Aldons, M. (2003). Problems with parliamentary Committee evaluation: Light at the end of the tunnel? *Australasian Parliamentary Review, 18*(1), 79–86.
Appleby, G. (2015). The 2014 counter-terrorism reforms in review. *Public Law Review, 26*(1), 4–7.
Australian Law Reform Commission. (2006). *Fighting Words: A Review of Sedition Laws in Australia*. ALRC Report No 104. Retrieved from https://www.alrc.gov.au/publication/fighting-words-a-review-of-sedition-laws-in-australia-alrc-report-104/. Accessed 7 Jan 2020.
Banham, C. & O'Malley, N. (2005, September 6). Rights at risk in security crackdown. *The Sydney Morning Herald* (Sydney), 6 September 2005, 2.
Blackbourn, J. (2018). Accountability, counter-terrorism and civil liberties. *Kings Law Journal, 29(2),* 297. https://doi.org/10.1080/09615768.2018.1502070.
Burton, L., & Williams, G. (2013). Australia's exclusive parliamentary model of rights protection. *Statute Law Review, 34*, 58–94. https://doi.org/10.1093/slr/hms048.
Byrnes, A. (2020). Economic and social rights in the Australian parliamentary human rights scrutiny process. In J. Debeljak & L. Grenfell (Eds.), *Law- making and human rights* (pp. 135–171). Sydney: Thompson Reuters.

Carne, G. (2015). Re-orientating human rights meanings and understandings? Reviving and revisiting Australian human rights exceptionalism through a Liberal democratic rights agenda. *Flinders Law Review Journal, 17*, 1–67. http://www.austlii.edu.au/au/journals/FlinLawJl/2015/1.pdf.

Chordia, S. (2016). *The problem of balancing: Structured proportionality and tiered scrutiny*. Harvard Law School Visiting Scholar Colloquium Series, Harvard Law School, Cambridge, 30 November 2016.

Civil Liberties Australia. (2005). Need for Proposed Anti-terror Laws Still Unexplained. Media Release, 28 September 2005; Canberra.

Clarke, M. J. (2008) *Report of the inquiry into the case of Dr Mohamed Haneef*. Canberra: Government of Australia. Retrieved from https://trove.nla.gov.au/work/35146207. Accessed 7 Jan 2020.

Council of Australian Governments Counter-Terrorism Review Committee. (2013). *Review of Counter-Terrorism Legislation*. Retrieved from https://www.ag.gov.au/Consultations/Pages/COAGReviewofCounter-TerrorismLegislation.aspx. Accessed 7 Jan 2020.

Courier Mail (Eds). (2002, May 11). Flaws in Terror Laws Exposed. *The Courier Mail* (Brisbane), 11 May 2002, 22.

Dalla-Pozza, D. (2008). Promoting deliberative debate? The submissions and oral evidence provided to Australian parliamentary committees in the creation of counter-terrorism laws. *Australasian Parliamentary Review, 21*(1), 39–61.

Dalla-Pozza, D. (2016). Refining the Australian counter-terrorism legislative framework: How deliberative has parliament been? *Public Law Review, 27*(4), 271.

Dalla-Pozza, D. (2020). A dual scrutiny mechanism for Australia's counter-terrorism law landscape: The INSLM and the PJCIS. In J. Debeljak & L. Grenfell (Eds.), *Law-making and human rights* (pp. 673–700). Sydney: Thompson Reuters.

Debeljak, J., & Grenfell, L. (2020). Future directions for engaging with human rights in law-making: Is a culture of justification emerging across Australian jurisdictions? In J. Debeljak & L. Grenfell (Eds.), *Law- Making and Human Rights* (pp. 789–818). Sydney: Thompson Reuters.

Fletcher, A. (2018). *Australia's human rights scrutiny regime*. Melbourne: Melbourne University Press.

Fletcher, A. (2020). Human rights scrutiny in the Federal Parliament: Smokescreen or democratic solution? In J. Debeljak & L. Grenfell (Eds.), *Law- making and human rights* (pp. 31–63). Sydney: Thompson Reuters.

Griffith, G (2005). Parliament and accountability: The role of parliamentary oversight committees. Briefing Paper No 12/05. Parliamentary Library Research Service, New South Wales. Retrieved from https://www.parliament.nsw.gov.au/researchpapers/Documents/parliament-and-accountability-the-role-of-parlia/Parliament%20and%20Accountability%20BRIEFING%20Paper%20and%20INDEX.pdf. Accessed 10 Jan 2020.

Gyles, R. (2016). Independent National Security Legislation Monitor, *Report on Certain Questioning and Detention Powers in Relation to* Terrorism. Canberra. Retrieved from https://www.inslm.gov.au/reviews-reports/certain-questioning-and-detention-powers-relation-terorism. Accessed 16 Jan 2020.

Hammer, C. (2008, May 16). Haneef Case Weak, FOI Papers Show. *The Age* (online), 16 May 2008, http://www.theage.com.au/news/national/haneef-case-weak-foi-papers-how/2008/05/15/1210765057432.html

Kirk, L. (2002, December 23). Balance Terror Fight and Liberties. *The Advertiser* (Adelaide), 23 December 2002, 18.

Levy, R., & Orr, G. (2016). *The law of deliberative democracy*. London: Routledge.

Lynch, A. (2006). Legislating with Urgency – the Enactment of the Anti-Terrorism Act (No 1) 2005. *Melbourne University Law Review, 30*(3), 747–781.

McCulloch, J. (2015). Human rights and terror laws. *Precedent, 128*, 26–29.

Moulds, S. P. (2018). *The rights protecting role of parliamentary committees: The case of Australia's counter-terrorism laws* (Doctoral thesis). University of Adelaide, Adelaide, South Australia, Australia. https://digital.library.adelaide.edu.au/dspace/handle/2440/115212

Moulds, S. P. (2020). Parliamentary committees facilitating parliamentary deliberation: A case study of marriage equality reform. In J. Debeljak & L. Grenfell (Eds.), *Law making and human rights* (pp. 745–786). Sydney: Thompson Reuters.

Nicholson, B. (2002). Protect Our Values, Georgio Urges. The Sunday Age (Melbourne), 29 September 2002, 6.

Rajanayagam, S. (2015). Does parliament do enough? Evaluating statements of compatibility under the human rights (Parliamentary Scrutiny) Act. *University of New South Wales Law Journal, 38*(3), 1046–1077.

Rajanayagam, S. (2020). Urgent law-making and the human rights (parliamentary scrutiny) act. In J. Debeljak & L. Grenfell (Eds.), *Law-making and human rights* (pp. 647–672). Sydney: Thompson Reuters.

Reynolds, D., & Williams, G. (2020). Evaluating the impact of Australia's Federal human rights scrutiny regime. In J. Debeljak & L. Grenfell (Eds.), *Law- Making and human rights* (pp. 67–96). Sydney: Thompson Reuters.

Rice, S. (2020). Allowing for dissent: Opening up human rights dialogue in the Australian parliament. In J. Debeljak & L. Grenfell (Eds.), *Law- making and human rights* (pp. 99–134). Sydney: Thompson Reuters.

Security Legislation Review Committee. (2006). *Report of the security legislation review Committee*. Canberra: Australian Government (Sheller Review). Retrieved from https://www.ag.gov.au/NationalSecurity/Counterterrorismlaw/Documents/Report%20of%20the%20Security%20Legislation%20Review%20Committee.pdf. Accessed 7 Jan 2020.

Shaw, M. (1998). Parliamentary committees: A global perspective. *Journal of Legislative Studies, 4*(1), 225–251. https://doi.org/10.1080/13572339808420547.

Stephenson, S. (2016). *From dialogue to disagreement in comparative rights constitutionalism*. Sydney: Federation Press.

Sydney Morning Herald. (Ed) (2002, November 28). Other Threats to Freedom', *The Sydney Morning Herald* (Sydney), 28 November 2002, 12. Sydney: Thompson Reuters.

Uhr, J. (1993). Parliamentary measures: Evaluating Parliament's policy role. In I. Marsh (Ed.), *Governing in the 1990s: An agenda for the decade* (p. 347). Sydney: CEDA/Longman.

Uhr, J. (1998). *Deliberative democracy in Australia: The changing place of parliament*. Cambridge: Cambridge University Press.

van Ham, C. & Chappell, L. (2017). Democracy and human rights: A tripartite conceptual framework. (2017) Australian Journal of Human Rights 23*(2),* 143–167. https://doi.org/10.1080/1323238X.2017.1371927.

Walters, P. (2004, September 12). Press lobby wins reforms to National Security Crime Bill. *The Australian* (National), 12 September 2004, 17.

Williams, G. (2005, September 28). *Losing our balance in fortress Australia* (p. 23). Canberra: Australian Financial Review.

Williams, G.(2011). A decade of Australian Anti-Terror Laws. *Melbourne University Law Review, 35(3)*, 1136. http://classic.austlii.edu.au/au/journals/MelbULawRw/2011/38.html

Williams, G., & McDonald, E. (2007). Combating terrorism: Australia's *Criminal Code* since September 11, 2001. *Griffith Law Review, 16*, 27–54. https://doi.org/10.1080/10383441.2007.10854581.

Willams, G., & Reynolds, D. (2016). The operation and impact of Australia's parliamentary scrutiny regime for human rights. *Monash University Law Review, 41*(2), 469–508.

Williams, G., Davis, F., & McGarrity, N. (Eds.). (2014). *Surveillance, counter-terrorism and comparative constitutionalism*. London: Routledge.

Wroe, D. (2015, June 26). Law council blasts new citizenship terrorism Laws as much too broad. *The Sydney Morning Herald* (online), 26 June 2015. http://www.smh.com.au/federal-politics/political-news/law-council-blasts-new-citizenship-terrorism-laws-as-much-too-broad-20150626-ghyqqx.html

Chapter 7
Hidden Impact

Abstract This chapter sets out evidence of the *hidden* or *behind-the-scenes* impact of the four parliamentary committees on the case study Acts. 'Hidden impact' means the role a parliamentary committee, or the system of committees, plays in the pre-introduction development of a Bill. This type of impact is described as 'hidden' as it often occurs prior to a Bill being introduced into Parliament and concerns the activities of public servants and parliamentary counsel, outside of the public gaze. This chapter focuses particularly on the role of public servants, parliamentary counsel and parliamentary committee staff and gathers evidence and insights from interviews with these key players in the process. This chapter further develops the findings made in Chap. 6 to identify some key features of an emerging rights scrutiny culture within the Australian Parliament, whilst also identifying the barriers key 'behind the scenes' participants face when seeking to improve the rights compliance of Australia's counter-terrorism laws.

7.1 Why Look for Hidden or Behind-the-Scenes Impact of Parliamentary Committees?

As discussed in Chap. 2, looking for hidden impact is a critical part of the methodology employed in this book and integral to providing a holistic insight into the effectiveness of parliamentary models of rights protection. As Hiebert's work on parliamentary rights protection in Canada and the United Kingdom reveals, a culture of rights protection observed and practiced by public servants, parliamentary counsel and others working behind the scenes has a profound impact on the quality and nature of rights outcomes (see e.g. Hiebert 2011, 2012, 2015). For example, when lawmakers and legislative drafters are focused on avoiding rights-based litigation rather than advancing alternative policy options, such as Hiebert explores in the UK and Canadian context, this flows through to the parliamentary debate on proposed legislative provisions, and to the content of the provisions themselves (Hiebert 2015 at p. 39). In other words, the behind the scenes culture has an impact on the nature and scope of rights outcomes achieved. As explored below, the Australian

S. Moulds, *Committees of Influence*, https://doi.org/10.1007/978-981-15-4350-0_7

experience suggests that when policy makers and drafters have incentives to propose alternative, less rights-intrusive policy options for proponent Ministers to consider, drawn from past parliamentary committee engagement with similar issues, the rights-implications can be significant, particularly when considered over time.

Evidence of hidden impact can take the form of publicly available materials published by the government and its departments to guide policy development and ensure consistency in legislative drafting. This provides an insight into the extent to which public servants are required or encouraged to have regard to the work of parliamentary committees when undertaking their work. However, documentary evidence alone is unlikely to provide a clear sense of whether public servants are *actually* having regard to the work of parliamentary committees. This requires a more subjective analysis. In my research this was achieved by interviewing key participants in the law-making process.[1]

Looking for hidden impact is particularly relevant when considering the parliamentary committee system's contribution to rights protection in Australia. This is because, for many commentators, the best opportunity to effect rights-enhancing change within an exclusively parliamentary model of rights protection is at the pre-introduction stage (Hiebert 2012). As noted in Chap. 1, once a Bill has been introduced into Parliament, the proponent Minister has made a public political commitment to its policy objectives that can be very hard to shift even in the face of compelling arguments about the Bill's negative rights consequences (Hiebert 2015 at p. 52; Monk 2010 at p. 7; Feldman 2015 at p. 108; Aldons 2003). Conversely, a proposed Bill can be adjusted to lessen the potential rights impact or to improve rights protection at the pre-introduction stage with far less political risk for the proponent. Pursuant to this approach, the people best able to achieve this rights-enhancing change are those working behind the scenes such as public servants or parliamentary counsel, rather than those involved in the post-introduction public debate on the Bill, who are necessarily curtailed by the political realities of the day. This behind-the-scenes rights-enhancing change is sometimes described as a 'culture of rights compliance' and is seen by some as a key component of successful rights protection (see e.g. Fletcher 2018; Debeljak 2013 at p. 39; Evans and Evans 2006a, b, c).

The hidden impact of the parliamentary committees also has important implications for the tension described in Chap. 4 relating to the legitimacy attributed to different types of parliamentary committees. For example, my research finds that an inquiry-based parliamentary committee that attracts a high rate of participation will be in the minds of those responsible for developing and implementing legislation,

[1]As noted in Chap. 2, as part of this research, I interviewed public servants who were directly responsible for developing or drafting the case study Bills, including those from the AGD, Department of Immigration and Border Protection (DIBP), AFP and OPC. I also conducted interviews with current and past parliamentarians and parliamentary staff. Although not statistically representative, these interviews provide a useful insight into the role parliamentary committees play in the development of proposed laws from the perspective of a broad range of players in the legislative development and drafting process. Further information about the interview selection process is contained in Moulds 2018 Appendix A.

and prudent proponents of Bills will adopt strategies to anticipate or avoid public criticism by such committees. In this way, the inquiry-based committees may have a strong 'hidden impact' on the development of laws. My research also shows that the 'technical scrutiny' committees, and in particular the SSCSB, may also generate a strong hidden impact – not because of their capacity to generate public interest, but rather because the scrutiny criteria the SSCSB applies is entrenched in the practices of public servants and parliamentary counsel. In other words, the SSCSB commands political authority among this category of key participants precisely because it is seen to be removed from the political discourse on the Bill.

Understanding these different forms of 'hidden impact' helps uncover new opportunities to improve the rights-protecting capacity of the committee system, in addition to exposing some of the system's key challenges and weaknesses. In particular, as discussed further in Part III, the findings in this chapter warn against reforms that radically alter the features of the committee system that currently resonate strongly with those responsible for developing and drafting proposed laws. For this reason, I argue that, instead of relying on one particular committee, such as the PJCHR, to generate a culture of rights compliance among law makers at the federal level, it may be more useful to consider how the *system* of parliamentary committees could be adjusted or changed to encourage rights considerations at the pre-introduction stage.

7.2 Documentary Evidence

As noted above, the behind-the-scenes impact of parliamentary committees is evident from explicit references to parliamentary committees or their scrutiny criteria in guidance and other materials prepared for those public servants directly engaged in developing and drafting proposed laws. For example, the Department of the Prime Minister and Cabinet's *Legislation Handbook* (2017) provides a summary of the legislative process, beginning from submitting a legislative proposal for consideration and ending with passage through Parliament, and is an authoritative source of guidance for public servants. The *Legislation Handbook* also contains a number of explicit references to the work of parliamentary committees and the scrutiny criteria they apply. For example, it explicitly refers to parliamentary committees when describing the consultation required when developing legislation (p. 1) and when highlighting specific matters for consideration, such as whether the proposed Bill includes changes to criminal law principles (p. 29) or departures from Australia's international human rights obligations (p. 31). The sections of the *Legislation Handbook* relating to the preparation of Explanatory Memoranda and SoCs also include references to parliamentary committees (pp. 43–44), as do the sections describing a Bill's journey through Parliament (pp. 65–77).

The SSCSB and the PJCHR feature particularly prominently in the *Legislation Handbook*, and the scrutiny criteria applied by the SSCSB, and to a lesser extent the PJCHR, are often pointed to as a useful checklist for public servants when developing proposed legislation (SSCSB 2012 at [2.30]). For example, during the 2012 inquiry into the future direction of the SSCSB, the then Clerk of the Senate observed:

> [T]he committee's most effective work has been in influencing approaches to, and standards in, the drafting of legislation and the provision of supporting documentation (such as, explanatory memoranda). Although some of the committee's work in this area might be characterised as formulaic, there is a risk that, if the committee stepped away from this work, it would not take long for drafting standards to reflect the absence of a watch dog (SSCSB 2012 at [2.31]).

The strong influence of the SSCSB on the development and drafting of legislation is also evident from the Drafting Directions published on the Office of Parliamentary Counsel's (OPC's) website. These Drafting Directions are used regularly by the OPC to assist departmental staff to prepare clear drafting instructions for proposed laws. A handful of these directions are particularly relevant for those providing instructions with respect to counter-terrorism laws, and each of these Drafting Directions explicitly refer to the work of the SSCSB and occasionally the PJCHR, and/or discuss key components of the scrutiny criteria applied by these committees (Office of Parliamentary Counsel 2017). In many cases, these directions are intended to operate as a prompt for the instructing departmental officer either to obtain specific legal advice about the particular provision that engages the scrutiny criteria, or to consider alternative policy options that would avoid engaging the criteria in such a way. For example:

- Drafting Direction 3.1 (2017) includes a requirement to consider whether the proposed Bill may infringe upon or engage the implied freedom of political communication (pp. 6–7). This encourages careful consideration of both constitutional compliance, but also rights principles including freedom of speech.
- Drafting Direction 3.5 (2015) encourages instructors to have regard to the Attorney General's Department's *Guide to Framing Commonwealth Offences, Infringement Notices and Enforcement Powers* (2017) (the Guide to Commonwealth Offences) when proposing legislation that includes criminal offences. This encourages consideration of the range of rights issues previously considered by the SSCSB, such as burden and onus of proof, extended liability offences, coercive powers, and clear drafting of the elements of a criminal offence (Direction 3.5 at p. 5).
- Direction 4.2 (2016) sets out the circumstances in which the OPC will refer a draft Bill to a department other than the instructing department for advice or comment. These include the requirement that a draft Bill be referred to the Office for International Law (OIL) if it proposes to, or may, engage or infringe Australia's international obligations, including the human rights obligations contained in the treaties that comprise the PJCHR mandate.

The above examples, which are replicated in other public servant guidance materials, suggest that the technical scrutiny committees have an important behind-the-scenes impact on the key actors in the development of legislation (see e.g. Guide to Framing Commonwealth Offences 2017). The Drafting Directions also demonstrate the 'gatekeeper' role played by the OPC when it comes to ensuring that instructing departments seek specialist advice if they intend to pursue policy options that infringe upon the scrutiny criteria applied by these committees. As discussed below, this gatekeeper role is further confirmed by interviews conducted with OPC staff and public servants.

7.3 Interview Material

Interviews conducted with those involved in the development of the case study Acts[2] confirm that parliamentary committees can have a rights-enhancing impact on the content of proposed laws and contribute to the 'culture of rights compliance' within the federal public service. However, the interviews also help elucidate the limits of parliamentary committees as a form of pre-introduction rights protection. In particular, the interviews highlight that, at key stages of the policy development process, the rights-enhancing impact of committees may hinge on the value attributed to parliamentary scrutiny by the proponent Minister or his or her Cabinet colleagues.

This section of this chapter summarises what the interviews reveal about the *pre-introduction* impact of parliamentary committees. These interviews also help illustrate the tension between the deliberative and authoritative roles of parliamentary committees discussed above. The interviews suggest, for example, that the inquiry-based, deliberative committees with strong legislative and public impact, such as the PJCIS, are at the forefront of the minds of those involved in the development of the case study Bills. The interviews also confirm that the technical scrutiny committees, and in particular the SSCSB, command authority and respect among those tasked with drafting proposed new laws. As discussed further in Chap. 8, this again highlights the benefit of considering the different strengths and weaknesses of particular committees in the system when developing reform options to improve rights protection at the federal level. This is discussed in further detail below and in Part III.

7.3.1 The 'Technical Scrutiny' Committees

Interviews with senior officers from the OPC confirm the influential role of the SSCSB when it comes to drafting proposed laws and liaising with instructing departments. For example, in an interview with the author, First Parliamentary Counsel Peter Quiggin explained that thc OPC has a database of SSCSB reports that assist parliamentary counsel to keep on top of relevant issues with respect to Bills that they may be drafting (Adelaide, 3 August 2016).

---

[2]A full list of interviews conducted for this research is available at Moulds 2018 Appendix A.

In addition, the fact that many of the SSCSB's common concerns are articulated in the Guide to Commonwealth Offences makes reference to the work of the SSCSB a particularly efficient way for OPC staff to alert instructing departments to potential concerns about proposed counter-terrorism legislation. In interviews with the author in Canberra in 2016 OPC officers also explained that the SSCSB criteria reflect 'best practice' standards when it comes to the development of policy and legislation, and provide a strong indication of how key terms within a proposed Bill may be later interpreted by the courts:

> Well I think at the end of the day, a lot of the principles that are looked at by Senate Scrutiny of Bills Committee are around the principles of legality, … and so that sort of infiltrates all aspects of public life when you are talking about legislating for what citizens can and can't do. …
>
> And those things are at the forefront of our minds when we are drafting for example. So if you want to interfere with fundamental rights, you need to be express and clear about that, and if you are not, you run the risk of the court reading down what you are trying to do. And we do have those discussions with instructors (Meredith Leigh and Naomi Carde, Office of Parliamentary Counsel, Canberra, 24 May 2016).

This 'alert raising' role undertaken by parliamentary counsel, and the collaborative and iterative approach to developing 'best practice' standards that occurs between parliamentary committees, parliamentary counsel and instructing departments gives us a glimpse of what Hiebert has described as the 'culture of rights' within the executive (see e.g. Hiebert 2015), which unlike the UK or Canadian experience, is not informed or enforced by the judiciary, but rather forms part of a shared experience of providing sound, and efficient policy advice to proponent Ministers and the parliament.

The OPC officers also confirmed that the technical scrutiny committees, rather than the inquiry-based committees, have the strongest influence on their work. This confirms the findings in Chap. 4 relating to the particular strengths the SSCSB holds among this category of key participants arising from its deliberate refusal to engage in policy matters when scrutinising a Bill. Like the SSCSB, the OPC also refuses to provide advice on policy matters, and sees its role as providing 'technical' advice.

As observed by Maureen Weeks, Deputy Clerk of the Senate, the SSCSB's 'clear' and 'consistently applied' scrutiny criteria also gives it a distinct advantage over the newer and broader-mandated PJCHR when it comes to ease of integration into drafting and policy development practice (Canberra 23 May 2016). In other words, the ability of the SSCSB to articulate its concerns with a Bill as 'technical' or 'legal' in character, rather than being directed at the political or policy context of the Bill, appear to give it advantages over the PJCHR which is still exploring how to conceptualise, express and apply its wide-ranging rights-scrutiny criteria which necessarily demands a more detailed engagement between the PJCHR and the policy basis of the proposed law. For example, an AGD official explained:

> The principles [applied by the SSCSB] are very specific … it's very clear what choice is the better one to make. And then if you feel in the circumstances there are a series of reasons why you need to make the choice that could contravene or raise concerns with a principle,

> you should have a set of reasons and be able to clearly articulate what they are and how you've weighed it up (Canberra 23 May 2016).

In a similar vein, former PJCHR Legal Advisor Professor Simon Rice observed:

> One of the advantages that the [SSCSB and the SSCRO] have is they're scrutinising against a limited, well defined and well understood range of criteria, that by and large conservative politicians will accept as indicators of good government. So there is nothing political really in what they are doing. ...
>
> So when the [SSCSB] says there's a problem here with the right of review, that's probably the nearest they get to a policy contest. ... [B]y and large, what they are doing is helping the government shape their legislation in a good governance kind of way (Sydney 24 May 2016).

This perspective brings into focus the work of others, including Hiebert, Williams, Reynolds and Burton, who have sought to evaluate and explain the challenges associated with scrutinising laws for compliance with a wide range of human rights criteria (Fletcher 2018; Hiebert 2015; Williams and Reynolds 2016; Williams and Burton 2015 at p. 257). For example, Williams and Burton (2015) have pointed to the length and complexity of the PJCHR's mandate as being a particularly challenge aspect of the committee's role and one that could be having a negative impact on its effectiveness as a rights protecting mechanism (at p. 257). My research echoes this warning, highlighting that at least in the Australian context, there are substantive benefits in presenting rights scrutiny criteria as being 'technical' in character, and therefore existing outside of the party-political discourse on the policy of a Bill (which the SSCSB appears to be able to achieve), as opposed to engaging in an evaluation of possible policy alternatives against a very broad and much less familiar set of internationally protected human rights. As discussed further, in this way, my research both endorses and challenges the findings of Hiebert, Williams and Burton when it comes to the role of the PJCHR in developing a culture of rights among behind-the-scenes law makers. Like Hiebert, Williams and Burton, I agree with the need to think carefully about the rights scrutiny criteria applied by parliamentary committees, but my work also points to the need to ensure that specialist human rights committees within the Australian system are perceived as undertaking 'technical' rather than 'policy-based' scrutiny to ensure its legitimacy – and therefore overall impact—as part of the parliamentary model of rights protection in Australia.

For example, my research suggests that for public servants who are directly engaged in policy and legislation development, the well-entrenched nature of the SSCSB's scrutiny criteria contrasts with the more nebulous mandate of the PJCHR, which has proved challenging for some public servants to integrate into their policy practice (see e.g. Fletcher 2018; Dixon 2012). For example, the interview material highlights the distinct lack of familiarity with international human rights law concepts among public servants responsible for developing legislation prior to the introduction of the PJCHR, particularly among those outside of the AGD. It suggests that even after the introduction of the PJCHR and the requirement to prepare SoCs for every Bill, many public servants have been slow familiarise themselves with these concepts (see Fletcher 2018; Manning 2015). This has resulted in a significant divergence in the levels of engagement with human rights issues across the public service and in the quality of SOCs prepared (PJCHR Annual Report 2012–13 at pp. 10–12). This was also reflected in the interview material; for example, one interviewee said:

> [E]ven fairly recently, anecdotally you hear that departments are getting correspondence from the Human Rights Committee and they just don't understand what it is. They certainly know what they're getting when they get a scrutiny of Bills letter, but even as recently as in the last couple of years, [there have been] stories about departments still struggling to work out what is this all about (Canberra 23 May 2016).

As discussed further in Part III, this divergence in experience in preparing SoCs across the public service, and the general lack of familiarity with engaging in a detailed way with international human rights law among Australian public servants, compounds the sense that the PJCHR is doing something outside of the traditional scrutiny function, and adds to its general lack of legitimacy among behind-the-scenes law makers. This is not to say that SoCs have not had a positive impact on improving the rights-literacy of the public service – as noted below, this impact appears to be steadily increasing - but rather to underscore the benefits of being perceived as a 'technician's scrutiny committee' when it comes to effecting short and long term rights-enhancing change in the Australian parliamentary context.

In fact, my research suggests that unless the proponent Minister takes a personal interest in producing high quality SoCs, the instructing department is unlikely to prioritise their preparation of this material. This point was also expressed by former PJCHR Legal Advisor Professor Simon Rice, who pointed to the important leadership role played by the proponent Minister when it comes to ensuring human rights compliance is taken seriously at the pre-introduction phase. Professor Rice said:

> If the Minister says to the department 'give me a human rights compatible piece of legislation' they will. If a Minister doesn't care or bother, then you need a department to come up with it. And sometimes the Minister won't care and sometimes they'll say 'what's this crap?' So I actually think the message coming down [is very important]. It's the Minister who has to table [the statement]. It's the Minister who has to give the speech. It's the Minister who gets the correspondence from the committee. If they don't care, why should the departments bother? (Sydney 24 May 2016).

This response goes to the heart of what Hiebert (2015) describes in her work as the rights-scrutiny culture within different systems of parliamentary rights protection, where the behind-the-scenes focus is on the political or institutional outcomes (see also Stephenson 2016 at p. 8.). As explored further in Part III, it suggests that when looking to improve the quality of Australia's parliamentary model of rights protection, it is vital to consider the 'hidden impact' of parliamentary committees on the law making process and on the culture of rights compliance within the executive.

This discussion should not dilute the potential of individual mechanisms, such as SoCs, to have a positive rights impact on the law making process in Australia. My research suggests that despite these significant challenges, and broad variations in knowledge and experience across departments, those working directly to improve the quality of SoCs share some optimism about the potential for this mechanism to have a meaningful impact on the development of counter-terrorism laws. For example, some policy officers who were responsible for preparing SoCs for the case study Acts suggest that, at least within their divisions, a range of formal and informal processes are in place to help ensure that high-quality SoCs are produced. This includes: formal and 'on the job' training on the preparation of SoCs; the practice of obtaining advice early from OIL on the content of department-drafted SoCs; genuine engagement with the PJCHR on the quality of SoCs; and an informal 'lessons learnt' process. This appears to be translating into a greater human rights awareness at least among some senior AGD officers, and those responsible for developing counter-terrorism laws, particularly as the PJCHR gains experience and develops a broader range of materials and guidance notes directed at public servants and other behind-the-scenes participants. As former National Security Branch officer Cameron Gifford said:

> My earlier [policy roles] would probably have had less of a sharper focus on human rights and international obligations and that's probably to some extent the result of the creation of the human rights compatibility statements, but also, you can now see that the committees themselves are having those considerations in a sharper focus than they used to have as well (Canberra 23 May 2016).

The PJCHR has also commented on the improving quality of SoCs (see e.g. Annual Report 2013–14 at para [3.30]) and noted that in many cases SoCs were providing sufficient information to assist the PJCHR in its analysis of the rights compatibility of proposed laws (at [3.31]). However, the PJCHR also observed that:

> [A] significant number of bills and legislative instruments during the reporting period failed to provide sufficient information or supporting evidence to justify potential limitations of human rights. … In particular, the committee noted that proponents of legislation often claimed that measures engaging human rights were 'reasonable, necessary and proportionate' without providing any supporting analysis or empirical evidence. …
>
> In a number of cases, the committee noted that additional information provided by the legislation proponent addressed the committee's concerns, but should have been included in the statement of compatibility for the bill or instrument in the first instance (PJCHR Annual Report 2013–14, published in 2016, at para [3.32]–[3.34]).

The material above suggests that the requirement to issue SoCs may be starting to have an impact on the development of legislation, although there remain significant concerns about the veracity of this process when policy is 'Minister driven' and SoCs are 'retro-fitted' to already finalised legislation. The interviews also suggest that, considering the low base of human-rights literacy among the public service prior to the introduction of the PJCHR, there now appear to be some foundations (at least within the AGD) upon which to improve the capacity of the public service to engage with rights in a meaningful way.

The implications of these findings for improving the rights-protecting capacity of the parliamentary committee system are discussed further in Part III, where recommendations are made to build upon the particular strengths of the SSCSB when it comes to influencing the pre-introduction development of legislation. Changes are also proposed to the processes of the PJCHR to capitalise on its modest but improving capacity to guide legislative drafters and policy makers.

7.3.2 *The 'Inquiry-Based' Committees*

The interviews I conducted for this research, combined with the material discussed in Chap. 6, suggest that the inquiry-based committees, such as the PJCIS and LCA Committees, can also have a pre-introduction impact on the development of proposed counter-terrorism laws. This most commonly takes two forms: as an impetus for the legislative proposal itself or as part of the risk assessment process that policy officers undertake in anticipation of future parliamentary scrutiny. Those responsible for developing proposed counter-terrorism laws confirmed that, while often the impetus for these laws is operational or Minister driven, past parliamentary committee recommendations regularly feature as a source of particular provisions. For example, former AGD National Security Branch Cameron Gifford said:

> [F]or instance, if we're taking something forward like we did with the Foreign Fighters Act, that was very much a theme about how to address that particular challenge and we did draw together a range of recommendations that had been around for quite some time to address that issue. So it's not necessarily that you're always developing new laws in relation to a policy gap, but sometimes there's something that's already sitting in the background where you go, actually this is the right response, for this particular challenge, at this particular time (Canberra 23 May 2016).

The AGD officers interviewed also emphasised the important role policy staff play in ensuring the legislative response to an identified operational need is balanced, and has regard to any relevant previous parliamentary reviews or inquiries. For example, Tony Alderman, Manager of Government and Communications explained that often the policy officer works as a 'translator' between the operational staff (such as police or intelligence officers) and the Parliament (telephone interview 6 June 2016). In this role, the policy officer is regularly engaged in seeking detailed information from operational staff about *why* they need a particular power or new offence provision. The policy officer may also be involved in developing safeguards that limit the use of the new power or scope of the new offence, in order to develop a legislative proposal that is more likely to withstand public and parliamentary scrutiny. For example, an AGD official explained that past parliamentary inquiries and recommendations influence:

> the conversations that we in this department might have with agencies about well, what's the operational justification, how far do we need to go, we need to have some accountability here. [We often say] 'Yes we know that in practice you are above board and behave appropriately but the public and senate committees will be looking for more than just your word that you do things properly, some mechanisms for assuring the, for assurance about that'. So it definitely shapes the conversations in developing those provisions (Canberra, 23 May 2016).

Those working on policy development of counter-terrorism laws also said that the anticipation of future inquiry-based parliamentary scrutiny can sharpen their focus on developing a strong evidence base for the policy goals of the law and help identify the safeguards or oversight mechanisms that might be needed to guard against unfair or unjustified intrusion on the rights of particular groups in the community.

For example, Tony Alderman, Manager of Government and Communications, AFP, said:

> In the AFP's view, parliamentary committees and their processes are very useful and very valuable. They provide an opportunity for the AFP to outline a case for necessity, provide an operational context, clarifying the extensive existing oversight mechanisms applying to the AFP, and demonstrate the range of transparency and accountability measures and point to any safeguards (telephone 6 June 2016).

For these policy officers, their approach was less about avoiding questions from a committee inquiry, and more about the need to ensure that, when developing legislation in response to operational need, consideration is given to the types of issues parliamentary committees are likely to focus on in any future scrutiny of the proposed Bill. As Cameron Gifford said:

> It's not so much what's going to come through the PJCIS, we always try and put forward a piece of legislation which is the most balanced legislation as well as meeting the operational need, but also, only engaging rights to the extent that it is absolutely necessary (Canberra 23 May 2016).

The interviews also suggest that there is a practice of reflection on past parliamentary committee inquiries when AGD officers are engaged in the early stages of development of a Bill that proposes changes to existing counter-terrorism laws. As a former AGD official explained:

> It would be remiss of us not to consider previous committee observations. And that's even where the composition of a committee has changed, because it is part of a process through which previous amendments have been considered. Even if that committee has changed, even if the government has changed, it's illustrative of the views and questions we might get. So even if it doesn't affect the policy direction, it certainly affects how we consider the issues and present that advice to government and then how we might engage with our stakeholders (Canberra 30 May 2016).

This suggest that senior public servants leading the government's counter-terrorism policy response take the views of parliamentary committees seriously and reflect in a genuine way on the views of other participants in the committee system, including the views of sophisticated submission makers that raise rights-based concerns with legislative or policy proposals. This again signals an opportunity for those interested in improving Australia's parliamentary model of rights protection to invest on the long-term value of public inquiries into proposed counter-terrorism laws, even in cases where the immediate legislative effect of a committee inquiry fails to deliver comprehensive rights-based reform.

My research suggests that this longer term behind the scenes impact of parliamentary committee inquiries reaches beyond policy leaders within the Attorney General's Department. For example, Tony Alderman, Manager of Government and Communications, AFP, explained that the AFP policy team will 'regularly look to see what parliamentary committees have said in the past' and consider whether the AFP should explain the need for the reform to the public (telephone 6 June 2016). Mr. Alderman explained that '[o]ften the AFP can provide a clear public statement of why the reform is needed, how it would benefit from the passage of the law, what the risks are in terms of not passing the law'.

The interview material also suggests that AGD officers take seriously the process of appearing as a witness at a parliamentary inquiry into a Bill and this usually involves the policy development team as well as support from senior operational officers. For counter-terrorism Bills, Cameron Gifford said that the AGD tend to present a 'portfolio appearance' including AFP, and ASIO depending on the nature of the reforms (Canberra 23 May 2016). Mr. Gifford also said:

> We appear then as a witness, and it can take a few hours, it can take a lot longer. More often than not these days we end up going back once or twice. Particularly with the PJCIS, they're pretty keen for us to … make sure that we've examined all the issues that are raised either by the submissions or in oral evidence, where we can come back and provide some additional information in relation to that. Sometimes that means actually coming back a second time to appear as a witness again (Canberra 23 May 2016).

Mr. Gifford also noted that it is common for the department to provide further supplementary submissions to the inquiry-based committees. These submissions regularly respond in detail to the issues raised by other submission makers or witnesses.

Once a committee has made recommendations for changes with respect to a Bill, the responsible department, as well as any government agencies affected, will be required to reflect on the implications of the proposed change and advise the proponent Minister. Drafting instructions will then be provided to the OPC if the Minister intends to implement changes recommended by parliamentary committees by way of amendment to the Bill. This process can be assisted by prior anticipation of scrutiny by OPC staff and their instructors, particularly in the context of 'controversial Bills' such as those relating to national security, where committee consideration of the detailed provisions of a Bill regularly result in rights-enhancing (rather than rights-limiting) change. As Mr. Gifford explained:

> There's usually not huge surprises and that is mostly because we've hopefully done a very good job in terms of actually looking at the issues being raised before the committee, so we're aware of the likely direction the committee potentially may go. It's still very challenging in terms of the time frames that are attached to these things. So you know, the PJCIS inquiry into [the Foreign Fighters Bill], I think happened over the course of a month, which for such a large reform exercise that was quite challenging. It becomes very challenging in terms of the speed at which you need to think and respond to the issues as they are raised, but also the speed at which you're able to implement them. So again, when you get to the government amendment stage, … parliamentary counsel do the most tremendous job of being able to turn those [recommendations] into provisions very very quickly (Canberra 23 May 2016).

This suggests that the inquiry-based committees provide an important behind-the-scenes opportunity for senior public servants to provide direct advice to proponent Ministers on the risks and benefits of adopting particular legislative provisions in light of past or present committee recommendations. This can provide an 'extra' opportunity for such officers to draw attention to those features of the original Bill that have unjustified impacts on rights, or that fail to 'strike the right balance' between operational need and rights protection.

7.4 Summary of Findings on Hidden Impact

This chapter has presented evidence of the hidden impact parliamentary committees can have on the development of proposed laws. For example, the documentary evidence suggests that the work of the SSCSB, and to a lesser extent the PJCHR, features regularly in the materials relied upon by public servants responsible for developing and drafting counter-terrorism legislation. Some of these documents, in particular the *Legislation Handbook*, Drafting Directions and Guide to Commonwealth Offences, translate the abstract principles underpinning the SSCSB and PJCHR mandates into practical checklists to be applied during particular stages of the legislation development process. In this way, these documents may help create a 'culture of rights compliance' within the public service. Over time, they also give rise to the shared view that the scrutiny criteria applied by the SSCSB (and to a lesser extent the PJCHR) reflect 'best practice' when it comes to developing laws. The interview material also suggests that the requirement to introduce all Bills with SoCs has, at the very least, required policy officers to turn their minds to the human rights implications of the legislation they are developing, even if the quality of engagement with human rights concepts varies significantly across departments and ministerial portfolios. The interview material further suggests that the prospect of a public inquiry can sharpen policy officers' focus on the right implications of proposed new provisions and encourage them to develop safeguards or other rights-protecting mechanisms when seeking to translate operational need into legislative form.

While these findings are compelling, it is important to note that, despite the significant hidden impact of the parliamentary committees studied, I do not argue that committee scrutiny provides a *sufficient* form of rights protection when it comes to counter-terrorism laws. As discussed earlier, I recognise that the content of the enacted case study Acts departs in significant ways from human rights standards (see e.g. Williams 2015; Appleby 2015; Lynch and McGarrity 2008). The interview material also reveals that the rights-enhancing hidden impact of parliamentary committees remains vulnerable to a number of dynamic factors. These include:

- the degree of respect with which the proponent Minister holds the particular parliamentary committee (where this is very low, public servants are unlikely to prioritise the preparation of robust policy advice to anticipate or address the committee's concerns);
- the degree to which the policy officers are able to present alternative policy and legislative options to the Minister for consideration (where a Bill is led exclusively from the Minister's office, the scope for public servants to reflect upon or anticipate parliamentary scrutiny is likely to be very narrow); and
- the expertise and experience of the policy officers and parliamentary counsel involved in the development and drafting of the Bill (where awareness of the scrutiny criteria applied by the SSCSB and the PJCHR is very low, the capacity to reflect upon or anticipate parliamentary scrutiny is also low).

As discussed in Part III, these factors point to significant limitations when it comes to parliamentary committees and the generation of a sufficiently strong rights-scrutiny culture at the federal level. However, despite these important considerations, the material set out in this chapter supports the general theme of my research: that the rights-enhancing nature of the parliamentary committee system is most strongly felt when committees work together to influence the development and content of a proposed law. In particular, the above material demonstrates that the complementary strengths of the committees within the system enhance the overall quality of the scrutiny a Bill receives, both before and after introduction. For example, this chapter shows that the technical scrutiny committees, such as the SSCSB, are well placed to have their clearly prescribed mandates integrated into practical guidance for public servants, but cannot expect to hold the same place in the minds of a public servant who is anticipating having to appear as a witness before a public inquiry. Similarly, while the inquiry-based committees are able to generate future policy options with clarity and specificity, they are less able to articulate a particular set of scrutiny criteria that they will apply consistently over time and that can be used in drafting or policy practice manuals.

For these reasons, the recommendations I propose in Part III are designed to encourage particular committees to build upon their individual strengths, and to improve opportunities for committees to work together when scrutinising rights-engaging legislation. They are designed to minimise the tensions between the deliberative and authoritative roles of parliamentary committees, for example by encouraging the technical scrutiny committees to develop practical, accessible guidance for public servants and by supporting technical-based committees to provide meaningful, deliberative forums for proposed new laws to be reviewed and discussed. In this way, the changes I propose are designed to place the full range of parliamentary committees in the minds of those responsible for developing, drafting and introducing proposed new laws, and to maximise the opportunities for rights-enhancing alternatives to legislative provisions to be developed and enacted. These changes are discussed further in the next part of this book.

References

Parliamentary Committee Reports

Parliamentary Joint Committee on Human Rights. (2016). *Annual Report 2013–14*. Canberra: Parliament of Australia. https://www.aph.gov.au/Parliamentary_Business/Committees/Joint/Human_Rights/Scrutiny_reports/Annual_Reports/Annual_report_2013_14.

Parliamentary Joint Committee on Human Rights. (2013). *Annual Report 2012–13*. Canberra: Parliament of Australia. https://www.aph.gov.au/Parliamentary_Business/Committees/Joint/Human_Rights/Scrutiny_reports/Annual_Reports/Annual_report_2012-13/index.

Senate Standing Committee for Scrutiny of Bills. (2012). *Inquiry into the future direction and role of the scrutiny of bills committee*. Canberra: Parliament of Australia. https://www.aph.

gov.au/Parliamentary_Business/Committees/Senate/Scrutiny_of_Bills/Completed_inquiries/futuredirection2011/index.

Books/Articles/Reports/Speeches

Aldons, M. (2003). Problems with parliamentary committee evaluation: Light at the end of the tunnel? *Australasian Parliamentary Review, 18*(1), 79–86.

Appleby, G. (2015). The 2014 counter-terrorism reforms in review. *Public Law Review, 26*(1), 4–7.

Attorney-General's Department. (2017). *Guide to framing commonwealth offences, infringement notices and enforcement powers* (first produced in 2001, updated 2017). Canberra: Government of Australia. Retrieved from https://www.ag.gov.au/Publications/Pages/GuidetoFramingCommonwealthOffencesInfringementNoticesandEnforcementPowers.aspx. Accessed 15 Jan 2020.

Department of the Prime Minister and Cabinet. (2017). *Legislation handbook*. Canberra: Government of Australia. Retrieved from https://www.dpmc.gov.au/resource-centre/government/legislation-handbook. Accessed 7 Jan 2020.

Debeljak, J. (2013). Does Australia need a bill of rights? In M. Castan & P. Gerber (Eds.), *Contemporary perspectives on human rights in Australia* (pp. 37–70). Sydney: Lawbook Co.

Dixon, R. (2012). A new (inter)national human rights experiment for Australia. *Public Law Review, 23*, 75–80.

Evans, C. & Evans, S. (2006a). *Australian parliaments and the protection of human rights*. Paper presented in the Department of the Senate Occasional Lecture Series, Canberra, 8 December 2006.

Evans, C., & Evans, S. (2006b). Evaluating the human rights performance of legislatures. *Human Rights Law Review, 6*, 545–569. https://doi.org/10.1093/hrlr/ngl012.

Evans, C., & Evans, S. (2006c). Legislative scrutiny committees and parliamentary conceptions of human rights. *Public Law, 785*.

Feldman, D. (2015). Democracy, law and human rights: Politics as challenge and opportunity. In M. Hunt, H. J. Hooper, & P. Yowell (Eds.), *Parliaments and human rights: Redressing the democratic deficit* (pp. 95–117). Oxford: Hart Publishing.

Fletcher, A. (2018). *Australia's human rights scrutiny regime*. Melbourne: Melbourne University Press.

Hiebert, J. L. (2011). Governing like judges? In T. Campbell, K. D. Ewing, & A. Tomkins (Eds.), *The legal protection of human rights: Sceptical essays* (pp. 40–65). Oxford: Oxford University Press.

Hiebert, J. L. (2012). Parliamentary engagement with the charter: Rethinking the idea of legislative rights review. *The Supreme Court Law Review: Osgoode's Annual Constitutional Cases Conference, 58*, 87–107. http://digitalcommons.osgoode.yorku.ca/sclr/vol58/iss1/3.

Hiebert, J. L. (2015). Legislative rights review: Addressing the gap between ideals and constraints. In M. Hunt, H. J. Hooper, & P. Yowell (Eds.), *Parliaments and human rights: Redressing the democratic deficit* (pp. 39–56). Oxford: Hart Publishing.

Lynch, A., & McGarrity, N. (2008). Counter-terrorism laws: How neutral laws create fear and anxiety in Australia's Muslim communities. *Alternative Law Journal, 33*(4), 225–228.

Manning, G. (2015). *The human rights (Parliamentary Scrutiny) act*. Speech delivered at APS Human Rights Network, Canberra, 2 December 2015.

Monk, D. (2010). A framework for evaluating the performance of committees in Westminster parliaments. *Journal of Legislative Studies, 16*, 1–13. https://doi.org/10.1080/13572330903541904.

Moulds, S. P. (2018). *The rights protecting role of parliamentary committees: The case of Australia's counter-terrorism laws* (Doctoral thesis). University of Adelaide, Adelaide, South Australia, Australia. https://digital.library.adelaide.edu.au/dspace/handle/2440/115212

Office of Parliamentary Counsel. (2017). *Drafting directions*. Canberra: Government of Australia. Retrieved from https://www.opc.gov.au/drafting-resources/drafting-directions. Accessed 7 Jan 2020.

Stephenson, S. (2016). *From dialogue to disagreement in comparative rights constitutionalism*. Sydney: Federation Press.

Williams, G. (2015). The legal assault on Australian democracy: The annual Blackburn lecture. *Ethos, 236*, 18–23.

Williams, G., & Burton, L. (2015). Australia's parliamentary scrutiny act: An exclusive parliamentary model of rights protection. In M. Hunt, H. J. Hooper, & P. Yowell (Eds.), *Parliaments and human rights: Redressing the democratic deficit* (pp. 258–279). Oxford: Hart Publishing.

Williams, G., & Reynolds, D. (2016). The operation and impact of Australia's parliamentary scrutiny regime for human rights. *Monash University Law Review, 41*(2), 469–508.

Part III
Improving the Rights-Protecting Capacity of the Parliamentary Committee System

At the heart of my research is a need to recognise, evaluate and improve the role the federal parliamentary committee system plays in Australia's parliamentary model of rights protection in Australia. I have set out to do this by examining how parliamentary committees work together as a *system* at the federal level and looking to see what kind of impact this system can have on the shape of the law, the way the law is debated and developed.

The first part of the book explores the central role parliamentary committees play in the Australian parliamentary model of rights protection and demonstrates how the Parliament itself is reliant upon the committee system to perform its representative, deliberative and law-making functions. Once these roles are understood, it becomes clear that the parliamentary committee system holds unique advantages and opportunities for rights advocates looking to invest in or reform Australia's current model of rights protection, and those interested in improving the equality of parliamentary law making in Australia. Part I is focused on *recognising* the role of the parliamentary committee system.

Part II of the book uses the counter-terrorism case study to document exactly what kind of impact parliamentary committees are making on one area of federal law – turning first to legislative impact, then considering the impact of committees on public and parliamentary debate, and finally reflecting on what is going on behind-the-scenes when law makers reflect upon or anticipate the work of the parliamentary committee system as part of our uniquely Australian culture of rights scrutiny at the federal level. Part II is focused on *evaluating* the role the parliamentary committee system plays in rights protection in Australia.

In this final part of the book I bring the focus squarely on *how to improve* the role the federal parliamentary committee system plays in Australia's parliamentary model of rights protection. This part of the book is intended to provide practical suggestions for change that can be implemented by key participants in the system. Part III offers a fresh new perspective on the scholarship in this field and suggests opportunities for further research and investigation for those seeking to invest in, build upon or reform Australia's existing model of rights protection.

As discussed in Part I, I am conscious that the focus of my research is necessarily limited to one compelling, complex case study, which brings with it a focus on civil and political rights, and engages some parliamentary committees more than others. This highlights the need to use my research as a starting point, rather than a final conclusion, when it comes to evaluating the role the federal parliamentary committee system plays in Australia's parliamentary model of rights protection. In addition, my work has not examined the relationship between the courts and parliamentary committees – a relationship explored by Meagher in his evaluation of the PJCHR (Meagher 2014, p. 1) – again underscoring the need for further investigation and research. Thus, I lay no claim to providing a definitive picture of the role the parliamentary committee system plays in rights protection in Australia. Rather I offer a starting point for others to consider when thinking about what changes or investments may need to be made to improve the capacity of the existing system to deliver rights-enhancing, or even rights-remedying, legislative change.

In this final part of the book, I analyse the material presented in Part II to identify the strengths and weaknesses of each of the committees studied and explore options for minimising or resolving the tension between the deliberative and authoritative roles of parliamentary committees. This analysis supports the central argument in my book, namely that only by considering parliamentary committees *working together as a system* can realistic reform proposals be developed. This part concludes by reflecting on the discussion in Chap. 1 regarding the conventional scepticism about the parliamentary model of rights protection, and offers new perspectives on how to improve this system of rights protection.

Part III comprises three chapters that draw upon the material presented earlier in this book. Chapter 8 focuses on capitalising on the rights-protecting potential of the federal system of parliamentary committees, and discusses the complementary strengths of individual committees and the benefits of building upon these strengths to enhance the quality of interactions with other committees in the system. Chapter 9 explores what changes may need to be made to individual committees to support the system-wide changes recommended in Chap. 8. In the Concluding Chapter, I reflect upon the arguments outlined in Chap. 1 relating to Australia's parliamentary model of rights protection in light of the findings of my research, and offer new perspectives on the role and impact of parliamentary committee system on the future of rights protection in Australia.

In this part of the book, I explain how making changes to the processes or powers of individual committees can improve their capacity to have a rights-enhancing impact on proposed laws. However, I also argue that focusing exclusively on individual committees, without understanding how they work as part of a broader system, may overestimate the rights-protecting role of individual committees and miss important system-wide opportunities for practical and sustainable reform. The evidence collected in Part II shows, for example, that parliamentary committees had the most significant rights-enhancing impact on the case study Acts when multiple committees worked together to scrutinise a law. This suggests that improving opportunities for collaboration between committees would improve the rights-enhancing capacity of the system as a whole. The evidence in Part II also shows that those committees that are able to maintain high levels of legitimacy in the eyes of a range of participants have a stronger rights-enhancing impact on the development of the law. This suggests that there is a need to ensure that any reforms to individual committees work to strengthen (rather than disrupt) their legitimacy across the committee system.

In this way, my findings depart in important respects from those made by other commentators who have focused on improving the rights-enhancing capacity, effectiveness or efficiency of particular committees (see e.g. Fletcher 2018; Williams and Burton 2015; Argument 2011), and from the conventional wisdom that parliamentary scrutiny needs to be 'streamlined' and 'slowed down' (see e.g. Lynch). For example, I argue that it is critical to strengthen the technical scrutiny committees' capacity to produce timely, accessible reports that can be relied upon by submission makers to inquiry-based committees, rather than trying to turn these scrutiny committees into more active inquiry-based forums (cf. Williams and Reynolds 2016; Williams and Burton 2015). I also suggest expanding the capacity for multiple inquiry-based committees to hold public hearings into the same Bill, rather than trying to 'streamline' the number of committee hearings being undertaken (Thompson 2016). Drawing upon the evidence base established in Part II, I look to see how the features of high-impact committees (such as the PJCIS) can be emulated within the context of other committees that may not yet be achieving these results, for example by looking to see how expert advisors or departmental liaison officers may be able to add value to the work of a wider range of committees in the system, whilst at the same time ensuring that the legitimacy of the particular committee is preserved This part of the book also emphasises that the hidden impact of parliamentary committees is a particularly fertile ground for improving rights protection (Russell and Benton 2009). In addition, the changes recommended in this book focus almost exclusively on non-legislative changes that can be pursued by committee Chairs, parliamentary staff and public servants (similar to Uhr 1995, p. 53). These changes are also less dependent on strong leadership from the executive than those previously recommended by other scholars (e.g. Rajanayagam 2015; Hiebert 2015), although support at the Ministerial level is encouraged and anticipated.

For these reasons, some rights advocates could view my recommendations as unambitious. This is a view I shared prior to undertaking the research compiled in Part II. However, as discussed further below, the evidence of the important rights-enhancing impact of the parliamentary committee system on the case study Acts has demonstrated the value in building upon (rather than seeking to replace) the practices, functions and powers of the existing parliamentary committee system. As Chap. 10 explains, this demands a more subtle, pragmatic approach than that often recommended by rights advocates who are sceptical of the parliamentary model of rights protection. The next Chapter of this part sets out the guiding principles that should shape this pragmatic approach, which are supported by some more specific calls for action in Chap. 9.

References

Books/Articles/Speeches

Argument, S. (2011, July 21–22). *Of parliament, pigs and lipstick (Slight Return): A defence of the work of legislative scrutiny committees in human rights protection*. Paper presented at the Australian Institute of Administrative Law Forum, Canberra.

Fletcher, A. (2018). *Australia's human rights scrutiny regime*. Melbourne: Melbourne University Press.

Hiebert, J. L. (2015). Legislative rights review: Addressing the gap between ideals and constraints. In M. Hunt, H. J. Hooper, & P. Yowell (Eds.), *Parliaments and human rights: Redressing the democratic deficit* (pp. 39–56). Oxford: Hart Publishing.

Meagher, D. (2014). The human rights (parliamentary scrutiny) Act 2011 (Cth) and the courts. *Federal Law Review, 42*(1), 1–27.

Rajanayagam, S. (2015). Does parliament do enough? Evaluating statements of compatibility under the human rights (parliamentary scrutiny) act. *University of New South Wales Law Journal, 38*(3), 1046–1077.

Russell, M., & Benton, M. (2009, June 24). *Assessing the policy impact of parliament: Methodological challenges and possible future approaches*. Paper presented at the Public Service Association Legislative Studies Specialist Group Conference, London. Retrieved from https://www.academia.edu/2069151/Assessing_the_policy_impact_of_Parliament_Methodological_challenges_and_possible_future_approaches/. Accessed 7 Jan 2020.

Uhr, J. (1995). *Keeping government honest: Preconditions of parliamentary effectiveness* (Parl Paper No 29). Canberra: Parliament of Australia.

Williams, G., & Burton, L. (2015). Australia's parliamentary scrutiny act: An exclusive parliamentary model of rights protection. In M. Hunt, H. J. Hooper, & P. Yowell (Eds.), *Parliaments and human rights: Redressing the democratic deficit* (pp. 258–279). Oxford: Hart Publishing.

Chapter 8
Capitalising on the Rights-Protecting Potential of the System of Parliamentary Committees

Abstract Chapter 8 marks the beginning of Part III of this book, and reflects on the evidence presented in Part II. Chapter 8 argues that only by considering parliamentary committees working together as a system can we propose realistic substantive improvements in the parliamentary model of rights protection. It demonstrates that making changes to the processes, mandates or powers of individual committees provides only limited scope to improve Parliament's rights-protecting capacity. Instead, it is the way different committees in the system work together that provides the most realistic and practical options for meaningful, short-term reform. Chapter 8 begins by explaining why a diversity of attributes with the parliamentary committee system is key to improving rights impacts, before identifying particular opportunities for investing in the existing parliamentary committee system at the federal level in Australia. These include strategies to address high workloads and ensure timely tabling of reports and improve communication and collaboration between individual committees. Chapter 8 also explores reforms designed to acknowledge and document parliamentary committees' contribution to establishing a common rights-scrutiny culture within the Australian Parliament.

8.1 A Diversity of Attributes Is Key to Improving Rights Impacts

A central finding of my research is that *diversity* of attributes, roles, membership and functions is a key strength of the Australian parliamentary committee system. In fact, my research shows that it is the diverse but complementary nature of different committees within the system that gives rise to longer-term, rights-enhancing legislative change. My research suggests that, like any eco-system, the parliamentary committee system is finely balanced and mutually dependent: a change to one component of the system – particularly a radical change- reverberates across the system with short and long term impact across the three tiers studied in this book. This dynamic between committees offers opportunities and warnings for those seeking to improve the capacity of the committee system to contribute to rights

S. Moulds, *Committees of Influence*, https://doi.org/10.1007/978-981-15-4350-0_8

protection in Australia. It is those opportunities and warnings that I seek to explore in this Chapter.

Parts I and II of this book set out the defining characteristics of the four parliamentary committees studied, and provided insights into how key participants in the law-making process view each of the four committees. This in turn uncovered the particular strengths and weaknesses of the individual committees studied and the different rights-enhancing impact the committees had on the case study Acts. For example, the material in Part II suggests that the LCA Committees provide a meaningful deliberative forum by holding popular and diverse public hearings but are not always able to translate their recommendations into legislative change. In contrast, the SSCSB has a strong behind-the-scenes impact as a result of its scrutiny principles being integrated into public service practice, but is rarely directly cited in parliamentary or public debates. As discussed below, understanding the implications of these strengths and weaknesses of the system of committees is central to identifying opportunities to improve rights protection at the federal level.

As discussed in Chap. 3, the LCA Committees and the PJCIS are 'inquiry-based' committees due to their common practice of calling for submissions and holding public hearings. The PJCHR and the SSCSB can be described as 'technical scrutiny' committees, as both are required to scrutinise all Bills against a set of prescribed criteria, and both rarely hold public hearings as part of this Bills scrutiny function. It is hardly surprising that there is a considerable difference between the type of impact an inquiry-based committee has compared with that of a technical scrutiny committee. As outlined in Chap. 3, these categories of committee have distinct goals, functions, processes and powers, some of which are prescribed by legislation or in the Standing Orders. They are not designed to emulate each other. They contribute different things to the parliamentary committee system. What is interesting for this book is that, despite their organic evolution, each category of committee complements the strengths of the other when it comes to scrutinising the case-study Acts. Indeed, the evidence presented in Part II suggests that the highest overall impact on a Bill occurs when these different categories of committees interact in ways that complement each other's strengths. The following analysis aims to explain why this is the case.

8.2 Inquiry-Based Committees Can Provide a Meaningful Deliberative Forum

A central theme emerging from the analysis in Part II is that the practice of calling for and publishing written submissions, and holding public inquiries into Bills, is an integral and highly influential function undertaken by certain committees within the federal system.

As noted above, the practice of calling for submissions and holding public inquiries allows the PJCIS and the LCA Committees to provide a deliberative forum for scrutinising the content of a Bill or policy proposal. Requiring senior public servants or senior police or intelligence officers to appear before a potentially hostile group of parliamentarians can also be a potent way for the inquiry-based committees to hold the government to account. Unlike the relatively passive experience of exchanging formal correspondence with the scrutiny committees, when participating in a public inquiry into a Bill, public servants must personally attend a committee meeting and justify on the public record the particular policy and legislative choice they have made.

The public inquiry function of the PJCIS and LCA Committees also strengthens these committees' capacity to build legitimacy among a wider range of key participants. In particular, establishing relationships with sophisticated submission makers (described in Chap. 4 as the 'usual suspects') can help attract and retain diverse committee membership and legitimacy within the Parliament and the community. Sophisticated submission makers also attract media attention, which can in turn have an impact on the nature of parliamentary debate on the Bill (see Moulds 2018 Appendix C). In addition, as explained in Chaps. 3 and 5, the recommendations made by the inquiry-based committee are specific and directive, often proposing precise amendments to key provisions of the Bill or its Explanatory Memorandum.

The specificity of the recommendations made by the inquiry-based committees, coupled with the legitimacy and public impact they are able to generate, contribute to their comparatively strong legislative impact. This gives these committees important strengths that should be preserved and enhanced when evaluating options to improve the overall rights-enhancing capacity of the parliamentary committee system. It also suggests that these inquiry committees provide a practical opportunity to build upon this existing impact by investing in the type of 'deliberative accommodation' approaches described by Levy and Orr, to encourage a broader range of views to be heard and evaluated in a meaningful way (2016 at pp. 76–80).

As discussed in Chap. 6, when inquiry-based committees have the resources to facilitate a meaningful public inquiry into a Bill – even if faced with tight time frames – they have potential to generate short- and long-term legislative, public and hidden impacts. As a result, these inquiry-based committees warrant serious attention and investment by anyone looking to improve the rights-protecting capacity of the existing system. In many ways, this finding is in line with the work of Levy and Orr (2016), and Dalla-Pozza (2016), and is reflected in calls by Williams Burton (2015) and Williams and Reynolds (2016) to invest more committees, and in particular the PJCHR, with this type of public inquiry function. However, as explored further below, my research sounds a strong warning against this approach. In fact, my research suggests that the potential rights-protecting impact of the parliamentary committee system is dependent upon some committees in the system having the power and capacity to undertake public inquiries and some committees in the system *not* undertaking this inquiry function. As discussed below, my work points to the need to achieve balance in the eco-system, by carefully building upon the features of individual committees that generate legitimacy among key participants, rather than disrupting the environment by making more radical structural changes to the role and function of individual committees.

8.3 Technical Scrutiny Committees Provide Vital Resources for Those Engaged in the Public Inquiry Process

A second central theme emerging from the analysis in Part II is the critical role the scrutiny-based committees play in the federal committee system, and the particularly strong hidden impact these committees can have on the shape and development of the law. More than this, my research finds that the rights-enhancing impact of the inquiry-based committees is in fact *dependent* on the work of the technical scrutiny committees. As discussed further below, the scrutiny experience of the case study Bills suggests that the scrutiny-based committees are a fundamental part of the ecosystem, and a powerful contributor to the 'culture of rights scrutiny' emerging within the Australian parliament and among behind-the-scenes law makers in Australia.

The technical scrutiny committees enhance the legislative and public impact of the inquiry-based committees in three key ways. First, they provide submission makers with reliable information about the purpose and policy objectives of the Bill, and the key features of the Bill that are likely to raise rights concerns. In the case of the SSCSB, this is likely to be in the form of an Alert Digest (more recently described as an 'Initial Scrutiny Report').[1] The use of Alert Digests means that the SSCSB is able to release information that summarises its preliminary concerns with the Bill quickly and in an accessible form, often prior to the close of submissions to the inquiry-based committees and usually before the commencement of the second reading debate on the Bill. This means that, even when the SSCSB's final report on the Bill is delayed because of difficulties associated with obtaining a response from the proponent Minister, submission makers and parliamentarians are at least armed with the SSCSB's preliminary views *before* they are required to articulate their public position on the merits of the Bill.

The reports of the PJCHR can also assist submission makers to inquiry-based committees, but of course this is dependent on submission makers having access to these reports prior to the deadline for receipt of submissions. As the material in Chap. 6 indicates, the tabling of PJCHR reports can sometimes be significantly delayed, and in this circumstance, submission makers and parliamentarians are without the benefit of the PJCHR's views at the point at which they are required to make public decisions on the merits of the Bill. For example, former Chair of the LCA Legislation Committee Patricia Crossin said that while the LCA Committee would endeavour to look at the reports of the PJCHR as part of its work:

[1]As noted in Chap. 3, in 2017, the SSCSB began publishing its scrutiny comments on recently introduced Bills (including responses received on matters previously considered by the committee) in one report, the *Scrutiny Digest*. However, the *Scrutiny Digest* continues to be divided into initial reports on the Bill (previously called 'Alert Digests', now called 'Initial Scrutiny') and concluded reports on the Bill (previously called 'Reports' now called 'Commentary on Ministerial Responses').

> timing was often a problem, particularly when the government was pushing for committee reports to happen quickly. Because that committee [PJCHR] only met when Parliament was sitting it sometimes didn't have the chance to consider the Bill and issue its report when we needed to use it.' (telephone, 10 August 2016).

For this reason, as discussed in Chap. 9, I recommend strategies to increase the PJCHR's capacity to publish its views on the rights compatibility of a Bill at an earlier stage in the legislative process. As Chaps. 4 and 7 explore, the reporting challenges faced by the PJCHR are complicated by the broad scope of the Committee's mandate, which unlike the SSCSB, extends to a very large number of specific human rights derived from the seven core human rights Conventions to which Australia is a party. However, my research suggests that overcoming these challenges is absolutely critical if the PJCHR is to consolidate its place in the parliamentary committee system, and improve its legislative, public and hidden impact on proposed laws.

A second related way the technical scrutiny committees enhance the impact of the inquiry-based committees is by providing a consistent analytical framework to evaluate competing public interests or individual rights. In other words, the technical scrutiny committees can help the inquiry-based committees (and their submission makers) to unpack the idea of 'striking the right balance' between protecting national security and preserving individual rights. As discussed in Chap. 5, the work of the technical scrutiny committees is also evident – albeit in a less direct way – in the recommendations made by the inquiry-based committees, which regularly align with some of the key concerns or issues raised by the technical scrutiny committees (se e.g. LCA Legislation Committee SLAT Bills Report 2002 at pp. 8–9; PJCIS Citizenship Bill Report 2015 Ch 8).

The third, and perhaps most significant, way the technical scrutiny committees enhance the impact of the inquiry-based committees relates to their strong influence on the pre-introduction stage of legislative development. This is outlined in Chap. 7, where the SSCSB was seen to have a particularly strong behind-the-scenes impact. For example, the interview material suggests that the consideration of the SSCSB's scrutiny criteria at the legislative proposal or Bill drafting stage effectively works to triage some of the rights concerning aspects of the Bill well before it enters the formal parliamentary committee system.

This 'alert raising' role undertaken by parliamentary counsel, and the collaborative and iterative approach to developing 'best practice' standards that occurs between parliamentary committees, parliamentary counsel and instructing departments gives us a glimpse of what Hiebert has described as the 'culture of rights' within the executive (Hiebert 2015), which unlike the UK or Canadian experience, is not informed or enforced by the judiciary, but rather forms part of a shared experience of providing sound and efficient policy advice to proponent Ministers and the parliament.

Care must be taken not to overstate the contribution the technical scrutiny committees make to the inquiry-based committees. Other factors, including committee membership and relationships with government agencies, play a significant role. However, the evidence in Part II suggests that the inquiry-based committees and their submission makers regularly rely upon the work of the technical scrutiny committees to inform the content and structure of their submissions and reports. It also suggests that the work of the inquiry-based committees would be substantially more complex without the behind-the-scenes impact of the SSCSB, and to a lesser extent the PJCHR. The converse is also true. The technical scrutiny committees would clearly struggle to have a substantive impact on the shape of proposed laws without the inquiry-based committees, and the media interest and parliamentary attention that comes from holding a public inquiry into a Bill. This suggests that both categories of committees are needed in the parliamentary committee system, and the different strengths of these committees should be preserved and enhanced if the rights-enhancing capacity of the system is to be improved. This finding, derived from the symbiotic relationship that exists between individual committees, pulls against the changes recommended by other scholars who have focused their attention on individual committees.[2] It also informs the recommendations set out below and discussed further in Chap. 10.

8.4 Investing in the System of Committees

The analysis above highlights the particular strengths and weaknesses of each of the four committees studied and shows that when individual committees work together they can have a significant rights-enhancing impact on the development and content of Australia's counter-terrorism laws (summarised above in Chap. 5). This suggests that the rights-enhancing capacity of the committee system could be improved by increasing meaningful collaboration between committees, while preserving and enhancing the particular strengths of the individual committees in the system. With this in mind, the following discussion introduces a range of key findings and recommendations, designed to identify the types of system-wide changes that could work to promote more timely and higher quality collaboration between different committees in the system. These findings are organised around the following key themes: the benefits of multi-committee scrutiny of rights-engaging Bills (building on findings in Chap. 5), the value in investing in committee resources (building on findings in Chap. 6), opportunities to improve communication between committees and key participants (building on findings in Chap. 7), and improving our understanding of parliamentary committees' contribution to the emerging rights-scrutiny culture within the Australian Parliament (explored in Chap. 6). These key themes and associated recommendations are summarised in Table form in Table 8.1. This is followed by committee-specific discussion in Chap. 9, designed to draw attention to

[2] For example, Williams and Burton (2015) advocate changes to the PJCHR that would see the committee more actively engage with submission makers as part of its Bills scrutiny work, including by calling for submissions and holding public inquiries. Similarly, some submission makers to the Future Directions of the SSCSB inquiry called for the SSCSB to take a more active inquiry role as part of its Bills scrutiny process (SSCSB 2012).

the strengths of each of the committees studied, whilst also increasing their capacity to engage efficiently with other committees in the system.

8.4.1 Improving Communication Between Committees and Key Participants

The scrutiny experience of the case study Bills set out in Part II of this book highlights the benefits of improving communication amongst the key participants in the parliamentary committee system. This reflects the theme emerging from Part II that a strong rights-enhancing legislative impact is dependent upon individual committees working together, which in turn demands effective communication among key participants in the system.

My research suggests that improving communication between individual committees within the system, and between committees and key participants, will enhance both the authoritative and deliberative role of the parliamentary committee system, with flow on implications for improved rights protection. For example, as documented in Chap. 7, regular and clear communication between the technical scrutiny committees and public servants can help entrench the criteria that committees apply when they scrutinise policy development and drafting practices. Chap. 7 suggests that the SSCSB has strengths in this area that could be emulated by other committees in the system. This could involve committee secretariat staff liaising with public servants to develop subject-specific Guidance Notes and Drafting Directions. It could also include committee Chairs providing feedback to public servants on high-quality SoCs and EMs, or publicly praising helpful responses to committee requests for information from departments or Ministers. My research suggests that by improving the flow of communication between those involved in drafting and developing the law, and the committees involved in scrutinising the law, the legitimacy of the committee is strengthened, and thus is impact on the content and development of the law can be improved. As discussed further below, this formal and informal exchange of views on what scrutiny criteria should apply, and how scrutiny material should be presented, also contributes to the emerging rights scrutiny culture within the Australian Parliament, and becomes a highly valuable body of information for rights advocates and other scholars to draw upon when evaluating Australia's parliamentary model of rights protection.

As explored below with respect to the PJCIS and the LCA Committees, the relationship between the inquiry-based committees and the public service is also a determinative factor when it comes to long term public and legislative impact. Those committees with strong working relationships with relevant government agencies and senior policy makers, such as the PJCIS, are able to strengthen their rights-enhancing legislative impact by developing, identifying or testing alternative policy options.

The analysis in Part II suggests that how effective communication between the inquiry-based committees and submission makers can improve the deliberative quality of law making in Australia, in line with the findings of other deliberative democracy scholars, including Dalla-Pozza (2006, 2016) and Halligan (2008). The material set out in Chap. 4 suggests that improving the diversity of submission makers beyond what Marinac (2003) has called the 'usual suspects' (at p. 129) can be particularly important in terms of the subsequent legislative and public impact an inquiry-committee can make. This points to the need for inquiry-committees to embrace proactive strategies to attract a more diverse range of submission makers, including updating and expanding invited submission maker lists to ensure individuals and groups beyond the 'usual suspects' are actively encouraged to participate. It could also mean supporting 'new' submission makers by providing fact sheets or examples of what a high-quality submission might look like, or what to expect before a committee hearing. It could include facilitating regular workshops for submission makers and witnesses or establishing a modest hardship fund to support non-government witnesses travelling from regional or remote locations to attend public hearings in person. This is the type of active search for information and meaningful engagement with different perspectives that Levy and Orr (2016) consider to be at the heart of deliberative decision making.

The material in Chaps. 4 and 7 also underscores the integral role the committee Chair plays in facilitating meaningful deliberative forums for scrutiny to take place, and establishing the 'culture' of the committee, including how decision-making processes will work in practice. The interview material further suggests that targeted support may be needed to ensure that less experienced committee Chairs are well placed to undertake this role, particularly Chairs of inquiry-based committees. For this reason, I recommend that training be provided to inquiry-based committee Chairs and members to develop strategies to promote a committee culture where a diverse range of submission makers are encouraged and supported to participate in the inquiry process.

Improving communication between committee members and submission makers not only contributes to the system's capacity to provide a deliberative forum but can also act as a conduit for improved media coverage of the work of committees. As Chap. 6 explained, the key to generating strong media coverage is to attract and retain sophisticated submission makers who proactively utilise the committee process as a key plank of a broader media strategy. Once these sophisticated submission makers regard the committee as a 'forum of choice', they are likely to orient their public advocacy around the committee, which in turn increases executive attention on the committee's work. This also avoids what Larkin (2009) has described as the 'perpetual problem' of attracting media attention for positive committee work (at p. 6).

Underpinning each of these recommendations is the central need to improve communication between the Government and the committees following the issue of committee reports. The analysis set out in Part II makes it clear that the relationship between the Executive Government and the committee system is a key determinative factor in terms of achieving legislative change. This means that it is imperative that proponent Ministers communicate effectively with parliamentary committees. This is particularly important with respect to the technical-scrutiny committees and their requests for further information from the Minister. For this reason, I argue that the rights-enhancing legislative impact of the committee system could be greatly improved by imposing a requirement for proponent Ministers to respond to the requests for information from the 'technical scrutiny' committees as soon as possible, and at the very least, before the conclusion of the second reading debate on the relevant Bill. I also argue that the rights-enhancing legislative impact of the committee system could be greatly improved by imposing a requirement that Government respond to the findings of inquiry before the conclusion of the second reading debate on the relevant Bill (Windsor and Oakshott 2010). These practical changes (discussed further below) would greatly assist in ensuring that all key participants - including other committees within the system - have access to relevant scrutiny information and inquiry reports *before* parliamentary debate on the Bill or issue has concluded. The success of these changes is likely to also depend on the capacity of the committees themselves to produce timely reports, which forms the basis of the next theme of conclusions discussed below.

8.4.2 Increasing Committee Resources and Adopting Strategies to Address High Workloads and Ensure Timely Tabling of Reports

As documented in Chap. 3, parliamentary committees help the Australian Parliament to deliver a number of its key constitutional functions: they provide all members of parliament with the opportunity to engage in detail with the legislative process, are a primary form of parliamentary oversight of executive action and provide a deliverable forum within which the community can share their views and be part of the law making process (Uhr 1998 at pp. 10–11). Given the scale and significance of the committee system's contribution to parliamentary democracy and law making, it is imperative that committees be allocated adequate resources to perform their varied and complex functions.

Moreover, my research suggests that when individual committees have the capacity and resources to work effectively together, they can have a rights-enhancing impact on the shape of Australian laws. This builds upon the earlier work of Evans and Evans (2006a, b, c), who also advocate for further investment in this feature of Australia's parliamentary model of rights protection as well as past reviews of the federal committee system (House Standing Committee on Procedure 2010 at p. 7 and Recommendation 2). My research suggests that this investment should take the form of both financial and human, but argues that even a modest increase in resources could increase the rights-enhancing capacity of the parliamentary committee system. For example, additional secretariat staff for technical scrutiny committees would facilitate further collaboration between the technical scrutiny committees and the inquiry-based committees and assist in the development of targeted resources for public servants and parliamentary counsel to use when developing new laws. Similarly, funding for additional specialist advisors for the inquiry-based committees, such as human rights experts or constitutional law experts, would assist in the identification of practical policy options to replace rights-abrogating provisions.

My research suggests that this relatively modest increase in resources is urgently needed because, despite its impressive contribution to the law-making function of the Australian Parliament, the committee system has experienced a decline in overall funding for several consecutive years (Bergin and Trood 2015; House of Representatives Annual Report 2013–14; Senate Annual Report 2013–14). Concerns about inadequate funding in the face of rapidly expanding workloads have been voiced in the Clerk's Review sections of successive annual reports of the Department of the Senate (Senate Annual Reports 2014–15 at p. 4 and 2015–16 at pp. 3–6), and by many of the parliamentarians interviewed for this book, who also cited the burden of committee work on the resources of their own offices. The need for further support for committee members, in particular committee Chairs, was also acknowledged in the 2010 House Committee on Procedure Review (e.g at para [2.47]).

While successive governments have been slow to respond to the call for extra funding for the parliamentary committee system, the committees themselves have begun to adopt innovative and effective strategies to ensure parliamentary committee staff are responsive to changes in workloads across system, and to maximise administrative efficiencies and resource allocation. For example, the Office of the Senate has co-located the secretariats of the SSCSB, the PJCHR and the SSCRO to form a single Legislative Scrutiny Unit (Parliament of Australia website 2016), and the PJCIS has utilised part-time specialist advisors and secondee arrangements to enhance the quality and range of resources available to parliamentary committees. Some committees have also begun to invest in efficient communication technologies and innovative new practices for holding public hearings. As set out in Table 8.1, I recommend the continuation of these types of strategies, both at the Senate and House level, in addition to the provision of extra funding to the committee system.

In addition to access to adequate resources, my research demonstrates that it is critical that parliamentary committees engaged in Bills scrutiny are in a position to table their reports (or at least their preliminary reports) prior to the resumption of the second reading debate on the Bill. On this basis, I recommend amending the existing Standing Orders for both Houses (see e.g. Senate Standing Order 25A; House of Representatives Standing Order 222) to make it clear that, as a general rule, the second reading debate on a Bill should not proceed unless all relevant committee reports have been tabled. The material in Chap. 7 suggests this is already the accepted practice when it comes to the tabling of Senate committee reports on Bills that were referred to the committees via the Selection of Bills Committee, but does not always apply when it comes to the tabling of joint committee reports (Legislation Handbook 2014 at pp. 65–77).

In making this recommendation, I recognise that Standing Orders can always be changed or suspended by the majority of the relevant House of Parliament, and this is particularly likely when the legislation being considered is considered urgent or relates to national security. Nevertheless, such an order would provide a strong statement of general practice. It would help establish the expectation among parliamentarians that they should have access to the analysis prepared by parliamentary committees *prior* to reaching their conclusions on the merits of the Bill. For example, in an interview with the author in 2016, former Australian Democrats Senator Andrew Bartlett said that this could be further supported by raising the threshold for changing the Standing Orders to a 'super majority', such as 75% or more, rather than 50% of members (telephone, 4 August 2016).

8.4.3 Encouraging Multi-committee Scrutiny of Rights-Engaging Bills

The central theme emerging from the findings of my research is that committees have a more significant impact on the shape and content of the law when they work together as a system. This is well documented in Part II, and in particular Chap. 5. My research suggests that the greater the number of committees that scrutinised a particular case study Act, the greater the rights-enhancing results, particularly when a combination of inquiry-based and technical scrutiny committees was involved. As Chap. 7 documents, scrutiny by multiple committees also appears to provide more opportunities for those involved in legislative development and drafting to draw upon the scrutiny principles applied by the technical scrutiny committees, and to reflect upon the outcome of past committee inquiries. As a result, this book recommends reforms that would encourage and facilitate scrutiny by multiple committees of the same Bill – particularly for those Bills that engage a large number of rights, or that have significant rights implications.[3]

In this next section of the book, I describe what practical changes may be needed to encourage more committees to work tougher more often. My research suggests that the current approach to multi-committee scrutiny and coloration is relatively organic and ad hoc, leading to differences in scrutiny experiences and rights-protection outcomes. I argue that consolidating and formalising existing collaborative practices would greatly assist in promoting multi-committee scrutiny of Bills, which could in turn lead to stronger rights outcomes. In addition, adding structure

[3] This recommendation is consistent with that made in the 2010 'Agreement for a Better Parliament' made between the Australian Labor Party and the independent members Mr. Tony Windsor and Mr. Rob Oakeshott on 7 September 2010 (Windsor and Oakshott 2010 para [5]). The proposals in the agreement, together with some proposals from the Greens and Mr. Wilkie, formed the basis of the procedural changes in the House of Representatives in the 43rd Parliament. Most of these changes were implemented via amendments to the Standing Orders on 29 September 2010 (the second sitting day of the 43rd Parliament) and on 19 and 20 October 2010.

to the process of multi-committee collaboration would also provide incentives for other key participants in the system - including submission makers, media commentators and public servants - to capitalise on the benefits of multi-committee scrutiny documented in my research. For example, it would enable sophisticated submission makers to plan ways of engaging efficiently and effectively with multiple committees in the system. As set out below, it would also provide opportunities and incentives for the technical scrutiny committees and the inquiry committees to work together to develop guidance materials that speak directly to policy makers and legislative drafters, increasing their potential to have a rights-enhancing 'hidden' impact on the shape and content of the law.

Some of the practical measures that could be introduced to help consolidate and formalise multi-committee scrutiny and collaboration include facilitating and coordinating Bill references to multiple inquiry-based committees (in addition to the technical scrutiny committees), particularly when the Bill attracts broad public interest or gives rise to rights concerns. This includes utilising existing forums for committee Chairs to meet and help coordinate multi-committee inquiries into the same Bill and amending the Standing Orders to make it clear that, when examining Bills or draft Bills, all committees should consider any past or concurrent reports on the Bill published by any other relevant committee. As discussed in further detail below, I also recommend amending the Standing Orders for both Houses to make it clear that, as a general rule, the second reading debate on a Bill should not proceed unless all relevant committee reports on the Bill have been tabled.

The evidence in Part II also demonstrates that facilitating parliamentary committee scrutiny of proposed legislation at the draft Bill or discussion paper stage can have important rights-enhancing results. For this reason, I recommend strategies to encourage proponent Ministers and departments to utilise relevant inquiry-based committees when developing significant, rights-engaging legislative proposals. These strategies received specific support from a number of submission makers that regularly engage with counter-terrorism Bills and who are looking for further opportunities to engage at the policy development stage. For example, Civil Liberties Australia has made its own recommendation to facilitate what it considers to be more effective public scrutiny of counter-terrorism policy, centred on the idea of a National Security Blue Paper, akin to a Defence 'White Paper' (Civil Liberties Australia 2015). As Civil Liberties Australia explains, the 'Blue Paper' approach would allow for parliamentary committee scrutiny of national security legislation at the pre-introduction stage, with the potential to improve the deliberative quality of law making in this area. A number of scholars have also recommended engaging parliamentary committees more regularly in the scrutiny of proposed Bills, including Marsh (2004) and Halligan (2008), who argue that committees involving members from both houses provide meaningful forums for the routine review of strategic issues and create a safe space for new or different views to be voiced and debated.

When recommending changes that foresee *more* committee scrutiny of rights-engaging laws and policies, I acknowledge the need to address concerns expressed by some key participants who consider the committee system to be already overstretched (Childs 1992). Some have observed, for example, that large numbers of committee inquiries leads to 'exhaustion from submitters', fatigue among industry and community bodies and 'exhaustion from the secretariats who are run off their feet trying to write reports' (Crossin et al. 2010 at p. 134). These concerns are shared by former Clerk of the Senate Rosemary Laing who told journalists that workload pressures for committee secretariat staff have become worse as the number of independent and minor party Senators have increased (Thompson 2016). The interview material also points to difficulties associated with ensuring a quorum of committee members are present for key committee meetings and public hearings, particularly when individual parliamentarians may be involved in multiple committees at the same time.

These concerns are addressed by my recommendations in two ways. First, as discussed above, I recommend a range of strategies to increase the resources available to committee secretariats, committee members and submission makers to support the system to respond effectively and efficiently to increases in workload. Secondly, I recommend the formalisation of a range of strategies already employed on an ad hoc basis to improve the process of making referrals to committees and to encourage effective collaboration between committees working on the same Bill. For example, like ALP Senator Patricia Crossin (Crossin et al. 2010 at p. 138–9) and former Australian Greens Senator Christine Milne (at p. 134), I recommend utilising existing forums for committee Chairs (e.g Senate Standing Order 25(10)) to meet and help coordinate multi-committee inquiries into the same Bill. I further recommend that this practice be supported by changes to the Standing Orders to make it clear that, when examining Bills or draft Bills, all committees should take into account any past or concurrent reports on the Bill published by any other relevant committee. Senate Standing Order 40, which governs meetings with House committees, could also be amended to facilitate more flexible opportunities for Senate committees to discuss inquiries with their House and joint committee counterparts. This could be based on existing Senate Standing Order 25(2A). These changes would help target the 'submission-maker fatigue' described above by providing transparent options for individual committees to draw upon submissions made to other committees, or by facilitating shared committee hearings, where members from two committees would be permitted to attend the same public hearing and question witnesses.

In addition to these strategies, I support efforts to review the number of individual committees across both Houses of Parliament with a view to rationalising this number if it is shown to be unworkably large. When taken together, these strategies have the potential to capitalise on the rights-enhancing impact and other benefits that flow from multi-committee scrutiny of rights-engaging laws, whilst at the same time guarding against adding unnecessarily to the heavy workload experienced by committee members and secretariat staff.

8.4.4 Documenting and Acknowledging the Contribution Parliamentary Committees Make to a Common Rights-Scrutiny Culture Within the Australian Parliament

One of the most unexpected outcomes of my research was the preliminary finding that there may be an emerging rights-scrutiny culture at the federal level. By examining the way Parliament undertakes its rights scrutiny task in the form of committee work, and by reflecting on the way the Parliament discusses its rights scrutiny functions when debating proposed laws, it is possible to suggest that the federal Parliament may already be in the process of developing its own set of scrutiny principles that can be built upon and enhanced when seeking to improve the existing parliamentary model of rights protection. This finding is preliminary in nature only - a flag for further research, rather than a concrete conclusion - but nevertheless, an important starting point for others to explore.

The evidence presented in Chaps. 5 and 6 describes the rights and scrutiny principles that were most commonly discussed when Parliament debated the case study Acts, suggesting that it may be possible to identify a common set of scrutiny principles that a wide range of parliamentarians, public servants and submission makers consider to be important when evaluating the merits of a proposed law. I have summarised these principles as follows:

- The proposed provisions and Explanatory Memorandum should be clearly drafted so the meaning and policy aim is clear to Parliament.
- The expansion of executive power must come with procedural fairness guarantees including access to legal representation, preservation of common law privileges and access to judicial review.
- Parliament should have access to information about how government departments and agencies are using their powers.
- If the law is designed to respond to an extraordinary set of circumstances, Parliament should be required to revisit the law to determine whether it is still needed.
- New criminal offences should have clearly defined physical and mental elements, allocate the burden of proof to the prosecution, ensure access to legal representation, and not apply retrospectively.
- Any restriction of free speech should be accompanied by exceptions to promote robust debate on matters of public interest.
- Freedom of association and the right to privacy should not be unduly burdened and any restriction should be subject to independent oversight.
- The proposed law should not infringe freedom of religion, and should respect Australia's ethnic and cultural diversity.
- The rights of children require special protection.

These scrutiny principles feature prominently in the work of parliamentary committees, have a particularly strong connection to the scrutiny criteria applied by the

SSCSB, and align closely with the features and functions of the Australian Parliament and the common law 'bill of rights' as well as established constitutional doctrines (as described in Chap. 1). For example, many of the principles listed above, such as the need to ensure parliamentary oversight of executive powers and the use of sunset clauses for extraordinary laws, are drawn directly from Parliament's constitutional role in holding the executive government to account, and reflect the doctrine of parliamentary sovereignty. For example, by focusing on increasing parliamentary oversight of elective powers and mandating parliamentary review of proposed provisions, for example through the use of sunset clauses. The scrutiny principles identified above also reflect the doctrine of separation of powers reflected in Chap. 3 of the *Constitution*, such as those concerning access to meaningful judicial review of executive action, and limitations on the use of executive power (see further Gray 2016; Foley 2012).

Taken together, this material suggests that there is a positive relationship between the features and functions of the Parliament discussed in Chap. 3 and the emerging rights-scrutiny culture discussed in Chap. 6. This may seem like an obvious conclusion to draw; however, it is important to keep these findings in mind when developing and evaluating options for improving the parliamentary model of rights protection in Australia. This is because, when viewed optimistically, this emerging rights-scrutiny culture may provide fertile ground on which to establish a more concrete statement of Australian rights that resonate across political lines and can be readily incorporated into parliamentary discourse. Such an approach aligns with the 2006 (pre-PJCHR) recommendations made by Evans and Evans (2006a, b, c, 2007), who saw benefits in developing a 'home-grown' set of rights at the federal level rather than adopting a human rights Act approach (2007), and with the 'democratic bill of rights' model advocated by Campbell (2006) and discussed further below. The recommendations made following the National Consultation also supported the development of an 'Australian statement of human rights', as an alternative to replicating the provisions of the international human rights conventions when enacting a federal human rights Act or other legal statement of rights (Australian Government 2010). More recently, Rice (2020) has considered the benefits of taking a more 'contestable' approach to determining the contours of the rights standards that should be applied by the PJCHR, acknowledging the need to broaden the range of key participants who are involved in or see the benefit of rights scrutiny in the Australian context. As noted above and discussed further below, building upon this emerging rights-scrutiny culture may also hold advantages over other approaches to articulating and promoting a lists of rights, as it feeds into rather than disturbs the existing institutional framework for resolving rights disagreements that exists at the federal level.

The significance of this emerging rights-scrutiny culture for future evaluations of Australia's parliamentary model of rights protection is discussed in Chap. 10. However, it must also be emphasised that the rights-scrutiny principles described above were derived from the experience of four committees considering 15 counter-terrorism Acts and may not illuminate the true nature of the rights-scrutiny culture within the federal Parliament. As noted in Chap. 1, the counter-terrorism case study concerns a highly dynamic area of law making that is responsive to unpredictable international and domestic events, and formal parliamentary scrutiny of other areas of law by other committees may generate different results. As noted above, this case study also tends to focus on civil and political rights (as opposed to economic, social and cultural rights). This further emphasises the need to undertake additional research to investigate whether this emerging rights-scrutiny culture applies in other contexts (see e.g. Moulds 2019, 2020), particularly in the context of laws and committees that engage more closely with economic, social and cultural rights (Byrnes 2020; Goldblatt 2017). Because of this, I recommend further research to document the rights-scrutiny culture across a range of different subject areas, and across the full range of parliamentary committees. In line with the key findings of my research, I recommend that, when conducting this further research, scholars focus on the contribution of the *system* of committees working together, rather than evaluating individual committees within the system.

This system-wide approach to investigating Australia's parliamentary rights scrutiny culture may also provide the space to re-evaluate the relevance of alternative rights scrutiny models in other jurisdictions, and for the unique aspects of the Australian approach to be considered by other parliamentary democracies. For example, the Australian multi-faceted, sometimes 'ad hoc' approach to post enactment review of rights engaging laws (that regularly involves a combination of parliamentary and non-parliamentary actors and can include a wide range of scrutiny criteria) may hold deliberative benefits over more structured, systematic approaches to post-legislative scrutiny such as those employed by some European Parliaments (see Moulds 2019, 2020; Evans 1993 at pp. 17–19; Prat 2012). Similarly, the more prescribed, holistic pre-introduction, post-introduction and post-enactment rights scrutiny processes employed in Sweden, the Netherlands and the UK (described in Fletcher 2018 at pp. 203; De Vrieze and Hasson 2018; see also Bull and Cameron 2015; Kuijer 2015) that may have at first seemed too daunting for any single Australian parliamentary committee to undertake, appears eminently possible to achieve across a range of different committees working together as a system, particularly if the strengths of the existing Australian parliamentary committee system are preserved and enhanced in the process.

In summary, the changes to the system of parliamentary committees I recommend aim to make modest adjustments to the way individual committees work together to maximise the opportunities for committees to have a rights-enhancing influence on proposed federal laws. When taken together, and supported by the committee-specific recommendations set out in Chap. 9, these changes respond to the findings in Part II about the rights-enhancing impact parliamentary committees had on the case study Acts, and also recognise the place parliamentary committees hold in the broader parliamentary system, as considered in Part I. The next chapter completes this picture by setting out the committee-specific changes recommended in this research. These recommendations are also set out in Table form in Tables 9.1–9.4.

Table 8.1 Reform options for the system of committees

Aim	Recommendation	Implementation
Improve communication between committees and key participants	Improve communication between inquiry-based committees and the media (including through adopting the committee-specific recommendations set out in Tables 9.1, 9.2, 9.3 and 9.4).	Committee Chairs, committee members, secretariat
	Improve communication between committees and regular submission makers (including through adopting the committee-specific recommendations set out in Tables 9.1, 9.2, 9.3 and 9.4).	Committee Chairs, committee members, secretariat
	Improve communication between individual committees (including through adopting the committee-specific recommendations set out in Tables 9.1, 9.2, 9.3 and 9.4).	Committee Chairs, committee members, secretariat staff
	Ensure all committees prepare timely annual reports that document the full range of impact (legislative, public and hidden) the committee has on the development of new laws.	Parliamentary offices, committee Chairs
	Improve communication between committees and those responsible for developing and drafting legislative proposals. This could involve committee secretariat staff liaising with public servants to develop subject-specific Guidance Notes and Drafting Directions. It could also include committee Chairs providing feedback on high-quality SoCs and EMs, or publicly praising helpful responses to committee requests for information from departments or Ministers.	Committee Chairs, committee members, secretariat, senior public servants
	Undertake specific training to assist in the facilitation of respectful, deliberative public hearings. For example, specific training could be provided to inquiry-based committee Chairs and members to develop strategies to promote a culture of respect and support for a diverse range of witnesses and processes to update and expand 'invited submission maker' lists.	Committee Chairs, committee members, secretariat
	Require government responses to all Legislation Committee reports before the conclusion of second reading debate on the Bill, and to all Reference Committee reports within six months of tabling.	Parliament
Increase committee resources and address high workloads to ensure timely tabling of reports	Provide additional funding for to the Senate Office and House of Representatives Office to apply to the general staffing pool that services parliamentary committees. The amount of additional funding should be determined following a work analysis to determine the nature and level of secretariat support necessary for future demands on the committee system.	Parliament

(continued)

Table 8.1 (continued)

Aim	Recommendation	Implementation
	Encourage the use of responsive staffing practices, such as shared secretariats and flexible staffing pools, which enable parliamentary staff to move between committees in response to changing workloads.	Committee Chairs
	Encourage the appointment of high-quality, politically independent, part-time specialist advisors to support parliamentary committees over a fixed period, or for particularly complex or lengthy inquiries. This could take the form of a 'pool' or 'panel' of experts that are available to a range of committees on short notice, for discrete periods.	Committee Chairs
	Encourage the use of departmental or agency secondee arrangements to support parliamentary committees over a fixed period, or for particularly complex or lengthy inquiries (accompanied by the transparency arrangements recommended for the PJCIS in Table 9.2).	Committee Chairs
Encourage multi-committee scrutiny of rights-engaging Bills	Facilitate and coordinate Bill references to multiple inquiry-based committees (in addition to the technical scrutiny committees), particularly when the Bill attracts broad public interest or gives rise to rights concerns. This includes utilising existing forums for committee Chairs to meet and help coordinate multi-committee inquiries into the same Bill and amending the Standing Orders to make it clear that, when examining Bills or draft Bills, all committees should take into account any past or concurrent reports on the Bill published by any other relevant committee.	Selection of Bills Committee, committee Chairs, secretariat staff, Ministers and senior public servants, Parliament
	Encourage proponent Ministers and relevant departments to refer draft Bills and discussion papers to inquiry-based committees for report prior to formally introducing the Bill into Parliament. This could be facilitated by adopting the 'Blue Paper' strategy recommended by Civil Liberties Australia in 2016.	Relevant Ministers and senior public servants
	Support parliamentarians in their involvement in parliamentary committees, including through improving training programs for parliamentarians' staff, and profiling high-quality contributions from individual committee members.	Parliamentary offices

(continued)

Table 8.1 (continued)

Aim	Recommendation	Implementation
	Promote parliamentary committees as part of the policy and legislative development process amongst the broader public service, including by pointing out the efficiency gains to be made by anticipating and addressing parliamentary scrutiny issues at the pre-introduction stage. This should be supported by training for all policy officers in the scrutiny criteria applied by the technical scrutiny committees. This could take the form of the targeted, departmental-level human rights training package that was implemented in 2012 as part of the Rudd Government's Australian Human Rights Framework.	Parliamentary offices, senior public servants
	Amend the Standing Orders for both Houses to make it clear that, as a general rule, the second reading debate on a Bill should not proceed unless all relevant committee reports on the Bill have been tabled.	Parliament
Document committees' contribution to establishing a common rights-scrutiny culture within the Parliament	Invest in research to track the rights language used in parliamentary debates and parliamentary committee reports across a wide range of subject areas to evaluate the level of acceptance of the rights and scrutiny principles listed in Chap. 6.	Rights advocates, academics, commentators, parliamentarians
	Encourage individual committees to more clearly and specifically document the impact they have on the development and debate of proposed new laws, particularly those committees with specific rights-scrutiny mandates.	Rights advocates, academics, commentators, parliamentarians
	Facilitate workshops and forums to discuss, document and debate the contribution of parliamentary committees to rights protection in Australia, for example by adopting a similar format to the public forum conducted to celebrate the tenth anniversary of the SSCSB.	Rights advocates, academics, commentators, parliamentarians

References

Standing Orders

House of Representatives, Parliament of Australia, *Standing Order*, Chapter 16, Order 222. https://www.aph.gov.au/About_Parliament/House_of_Representatives/Powers_practice_and_procedure/House_of_Representatives_Standing_Orders

Senate, Parliament of Australia, *Standing Order*, Chapter 5, Order 25. (2000a). https://www.aph.gov.au/Parliamentary_Business/Chamber_documents/Senate_chamber_documents/standingorders/b00/b05

Senate, Parliament of Australia, *Standing Order*, Chapter 5, Order 25A (2000b). https://www.aph.gov.au/Parliamentary_Business/Chamber_documents/Senate_chamber_documents/standingorders/b00/b05

Parliamentary Committee Reports

House of Representatives Standing Committee on Procedure. (2010). *Building a modern committee system: An inquiry into the effectiveness of the house committee system*. Canberra: Parliament of Australia. https://www.aph.gov.au/Parliamentary_Business/Committees/House_of_Representatives_Committees?url=proc/committees2/report/fullreport.pdf

Parliamentary Joint Committee on Intelligence and Security. (2015). *Advisory report on the provisions of the Australian citizenship amendment (allegiance to Australia) bill 2015*. Canberra: Parliament of Australia. http://www.aph.gov.au/~/media/02%20Parliamentary%20Business/24%20Committees/244%20Joint%20Committees/PJCIS/Citizenship/FullReport.pdf?la=en.

Senate Standing Committee on Legal and Constitutional Affairs Legislation Committee. (2002). *Inquiry into the security legislation amendment (terrorism) bill 2002 [no 2] and related bills*. Canberra: Parliament of Australia. https://www.aph.gov.au/Parliamentary_Business/Committees/Senate/Legal_and_Constitutional_Affairs/Completed_inquiries/2002-04/terrorism/index.

Senate Standing Committee for Scrutiny of Bills. (2012). *Inquiry into the future direction and role of the scrutiny of bills committee*. Canberra: Parliament of Australia. https://www.aph.gov.au/Parliamentary_Business/Committees/Senate/Scrutiny_of_Bills/Completed_inquiries/futuredirection2011/index.

Books/Articles/Reports/Speeches

Argument, S. (2011, July 21–22). *Of parliament, pigs and lipstick (Slight Return): A defence of the work of legislative scrutiny committees in human rights protection*. Paper presented at the Australian Institute of Administrative Law Forum, Canberra.

Australian Government. (2010). National consultation on human rights. Commonwealth of Australia, *Australia's Human Rights Framework* (2010) https://www.ag.gov.au/Consultations/Documents/Publicsubmissionsonthedraftbaselinestudy/AustraliasHumanRightsFramework.pdf

Bergin, A., & Trood, R. (2015). *Creative tension: Parliament and national security*. Canberra: Australian Strategic Policy Institute (online). Retrieved from https://www.aspi.org.au/report/creative-tension-parliament-and-national-security. Accessed 17 Jan 2020.

Bull, T. & Cameron, I. (2015) Legislative review for human rights compatibility: A view from Sweden. In Hunt, M. Hooper, H.J & Yowell, P. (Eds.), Parliaments and human rights: Redressing the democratic deficit (p. 279). Oxford: Hart Publishing.

Byrnes, A. (2020). Economic and social rights in the Australian parliamentary human rights scrutiny process. In J. Debeljak & L. Grenfell (Eds.), *Law-making and human rights* (pp. 135–171). Sydney: Thompson Reuters.

Campbell, T. (2006). Human rights strategies: An Australian alternative. In T. Campbell, J. Goldsworthy, & A. Stone (Eds.), *Protecting rights without a bill of rights* (pp. 319–334). London: Ashgate.

Childs, B. (1992). *The truth about parliamentary committees* (Parl Paper No 18). Parliament of Australia. Retrieved from https://www.aph.gov.au/~/~/~/link.aspx?_id=DD64348A4FEC4F94A3332033C6003F64. Accessed 10 Jan 2020.

Civil Liberties Australia. (2015). Blue paper for police and spooks. *CLArion No 1511* (online), 1 November 2015 http://www.cla.asn.au/clarion/1511CLArion(1col).pdf.

Crossin, P., Milne, C., & Humphries, G. (2010). The future of senate committees: Challenges and opportunities' in commonwealth. *Senate committees and government accountability* (Parl Paper No 54 of 2010). Canberra: Parliament of Australia. Retrieved from https://www.aph.gov.au/About_Parliament/Senate/Powers_practice_n_procedures/~/~/link.aspx?_id=E0F46C0A16C743148BA988A0B316DDD9&_z=z. Accessed 17 Jan 2020.

Dalla-Pozza, D. (2006). *The conscience of democracy? The role of Australian parliamentary committees in enacting counter-terrorism laws*. Paper presented at the Australasian law and society conference. Retrieved from http://unsworks.unsw.edu.au/fapi/datastream/unsworks:8439/SOURCE02. Accesssed 6 Jan 2020.

Dalla-Pozza, D. (2016). Refining the Australian counter-terrorism legislative framework: How deliberative has parliament been? *Public Law Review, 27*(4), 271.

De Vrieze, F., & Hasson, V. (2018). *Post legislative scrutiny: Comparative practices of post-legislative scrutiny in selected parliaments and the rationale for its place in democracy assistance*. London: Westminster Foundation for Democracy.

Department of the House of Representatives. (2014). *Annual report 2013–14*. Canberra: Parliament of Australia. https://www.aph.gov.au/About_Parliament/Parliamentary_Departments/Department_of_the_House_of_Representatives/Annual_Reports/2013-14_Annual_Report

Department of the Prime Minister and Cabinet. (2017). *Legislation handbook*. Canberra: Government of Australia. Retrieved from https://www.dpmc.gov.au/resource-centre/government/legislation-handbook. Accessed 7 Jan 2020.

Department of the Senate. (2014). *Annual report 2013–14*. Canberra: Parliament of Australia. https://www.aph.gov.au/About_Parliament/Parliamentary_Departments/Department_of_the_Senate/Annual_Reports/Annual_Report_2013-2014

Department of the Senate. (2015). *Annual report 2014–15*. Canberra: Parliament of Australia. https://www.aph.gov.au/About_Parliament/Parliamentary_Departments/Department_of_the_Senate/Annual_Reports/Annual_Report_2014-2015

Department of the Senate. (2016). *Annual report 2015–16*. Canberra: Parliament of Australia. https://www.aph.gov.au/About_Parliament/Parliamentary_Departments/Department_of_the_Senate/Annual_Reports/Annual_Report_2015-2016

Evans, H. (1993). Parliamentary committees and the public interest. *Legislative Studies, 1*, 15–23.

Evans, C., & Evans, S. (2006a). *Australian parliaments and the protection of human rights*. Paper presented in the Department of the Senate Occasional Lecture Series, Canberra, 8 December 2006.

Evans, C., & Evans, S. (2006b). Evaluating the human rights performance of legislatures. *Human Rights Law Review, 6*, 545–569. https://doi.org/10.1093/hrlr/ngl012.

Evans, C., & Evans, S. (2006c). Legislative scrutiny committees and parliamentary conceptions of human rights. In *Public Law* (Vol. 785). London: Sweet & Maxwell.

Evans, C., & Evans, S. (2007). *Australian parliaments and the protection of human rights* (Parl Paper No 47). Canberra: Parliament of Australia. https://www.aph.gov.au/About_Parliament/

Senate/Powers_practice_n_procedures/~/~/link.aspx?_id=8B6C280930C4453C92CA146B8 2B01CE6&_z=z
Fletcher, A. (2018). *Australia's human rights scrutiny regime*. Melbourne: Melbourne University Press.
Foley, E. P. (2012). Judicial engagement, written constitutions, and the value of preservation: The case of individual rights. *George Mason Law Review, 19*(4), 909. http://georgemasonlawreview.org/archives/vol-19-no-4-special-issue/.
Goldblatt, G. (2017). Social (in) security and inequality in Australia: The limited role of human rights in the policy debate. In A. Durbach & B. Edgeworth (Eds.), *Law and poverty in Australia: 40 years after the poverty commission* (pp. 183–198). Sydney: Federation Press.
Gray, A. (2016). *Criminal due process and chapter III of the Australian constitution*. Sydney: Federation Press.
Halligan, J. (2008). Parliamentary committee roles in facilitating public policy at the commonwealth level. *Australasian Parliamentary Review, 23*(2), 135–156.
Hiebert, J. L. (2015). Legislative rights review: Addressing the gap between ideals and constraints. In M. Hunt, H. J. Hooper, & P. Yowell (Eds.), *Parliaments and human rights: Redressing the democratic deficit* (pp. 39–56). Oxford: Hart Publishing.
Hunt, M., Hooper, H. J., & Yowell, P. (Eds.). *Parliaments and human rights: Redressing the democratic deficit* (p. 295). Oxford: Hart Publishing.
Kuijer, M. (2015). *Guaranteeing international human rights standards in the Netherlands: Parliamentary dimensions*.
Larkin, P. (2009). Transcript of evidence, 22 October 2009 as cited in house of representatives standing committee on procedure. In *Building a modern committee system: An inquiry into the effectiveness of the House committee system (2010)*. Canberra: Parliament of Australia. https://www.aph.gov.au/Parliamentary_Business/Committees/House_of_Representatives_Committees?url=proc/committees2/report/fullreport.pdf
Levy, R., & Orr, G. (2016). *The law of deliberative democracy*. London: Routledge.
Marinac, A. (2003). *The usual suspects? Civil society and senate committees*. Paper submitted for the senate baker prize. Retrieved from https://www.aph.gov.au/About_Parliament/Senate/Powers_practice_n_procedures/pops/~/link.aspx?_id=1AF5557C98A84D45A0ACCB0E6C36945D&_z=z. Accessed 10 Jan 2020.
Marsh, I. (2004, November 26). Australia's representation gap: A role for parliamentary committees?. In *Speech delivered at the Department of the Senate Occasional Lecture Series*. Canberra: Parliament House.
Meagher, D. (2014). The human rights (parliamentary scrutiny) Act 2011 (Cth) and the courts. *Federal Law Review, 42*(1), 1–25. https://doi.org/10.22145/flr.42.1.1.
Moulds, S. P. (2018). *The rights protecting role of parliamentary committees: The case of Australia's counter-terrorism laws*. Doctoral thesis, University of Adelaide, Adelaide, South Australia, Australia. https://digital.library.adelaide.edu.au/dspace/handle/2440/115212
Moulds, S. P. (2019). Parliamentary rights scrutiny and counter-terrorism lawmaking in Australia. *Journal of South East Asian Human Rights, 3*(2), 185–230. https://doi.org/10.19184/jseahr.v3i2.13461.
Moulds, S. P. (2020). Parliamentary committees facilitating parliamentary deliberation: A case study of marriage equality reform. In J. Debeljak & L. Grenfell (Eds.), *Law making and human rights* (pp. 745–786). Sydney: Thompson Reuters.
Prat, L. (2012). Political protections of fundamental rights. *Macquarie Law Journal, 10*, 77–96.
Rajanayagam, S. (2015). Does parliament do enough? Evaluating statements of compatibility under the human rights (parliamentary scrutiny) act. *University of New South Wales Law Journal, 38*(3), 1046–1077.
Rice, S. (2020). Allowing for dissent: Opening up human rights dialogue in the Australian parliament. In J. Debeljak & L. Grenfell (Eds.), *Law-making and human rights* (pp. 99–134). Sydney: Thompson Reuters.

Russell, M., & Benton, M. (2009, June 24). *Assessing the policy impact of parliament: Methodological challenges and possible future approaches*. Paper presented at the Public Service Association Legislative Studies Specialist Group Conference, London. Retrieved from https://www.academia.edu/2069151/Assessing_the_policy_impact_of_Parliament_Methodological_challenges_and_possible_future_approaches. Accessed 7 Jan 2020.

Thompson, P. (2016, February 7). Department of the Senate dealing with too many inquiries. *The Canberra Times* (Canberra). http://www.canberratimes.com.au/national/public-service/department-of-the-senate-dealing-with-too-many-inquiries-20160207-gmo4pj.html

Uhr, J. (1995). *Keeping government honest: Preconditions of parliamentary effectiveness* (Parl Paper No 29). Canberra: Parliament of Australia. https://www.aph.gov.au/About_Parliament/Senate/Powers_practice_n_procedures/~/~/link.aspx?_id=54B15879D3FA4BFE84D1A1885AE7950C&_z=z

Uhr, J. (1998). *Deliberative democracy in Australia: The changing place of parliament*. Cambridge: Cambridge University Press.

Willams, G., & Reynolds, D. (2016). The operation and impact of Australia's parliamentary scrutiny regime for human rights. *Monash University Law Review, 41*(2), 469–508.

Williams, G., & Burton, L. (2015). Australia's parliamentary scrutiny act: An exclusive parliamentary model of rights protection. In M. Hunt, H. J. Hooper, & P. Yowell (Eds.), *Parliaments and human rights: Redressing the democratic deficit* (pp. 258–279). Oxford: Hart Publishing.

Windsor, T., & Oakshott, R. (2010). *Agreement for a better parliament*. Made in Canberra on 7 September 2010 exerted in Department of Parliamentary Services (2013) *The hung parliament: Procedural changes in the house of representatives*. Parliamentary Research Papers 2013–2014 Parliamentary library, Canberra: Parliament of Australia, 2013. Retrieved from https://www.aph.gov.au/About_Parliament/Parliamentary_Departments/Parliamentary_Library/pubs/rp/rp1314/HungParliament. Accessed on 17 Jan 2020.

Websites

Parliament of Australia. (2016). *Commonwealth legislative scrutiny unit*. https://www.aph.gov.au/Parliamentary_Business/Committees/Legislative_Scrutiny_Unit. Accessed 7 Jan 2020.

Chapter 9
Refining the Roles and Promoting the Strengths of Individual Committees within the System

Abstract This chapter focuses on the ways in which the functions and powers of particular parliamentary committees could be enhanced or adjusted to support the rights-protecting capacity of the overall committee system. Building on the conclusions and recommendations explored in Chap. 8, this chapter reflects on the particular strengths and weaknesses of the committees studied in this book to propose practical reforms to both how these committees work, and how they interact within the broader system. This chapter reflects upon the past recommendations made by other studies of parliamentary committees, and the interview material obtained from those with direct experience working with the committees studied. While these recommendations focus on the four committees featuring the case study, they have relevance beyond this small sample. This is because they highlight, invest in and build upon features of individual committees that are shared by other committees within the system.

9.1 Implications for Individual Committees Within the System

The conclusions and recommendations explored in Chap. 8 focus on improving the capacity of the system of parliamentary committees to contribute to rights protection in Australia, having regard to the particular strengths and weaknesses of the committees studied in this book. This next chapter explores what implications these changes may have for the individual committees within the system. It reflects upon the past recommendations made by other studies of parliamentary committees, and the interview material obtained from those with direct experience working with the committees studied. While these recommendations focus on the four committees featuring the case study, they have relevance beyond this small sample. This is because they highlight, invest in and build upon features of individual committees that are shared by other committees within the system. For example, the recommendations made with respect to the LCA Committees apply to all Senate Legislative Committees tasked with inquiring into Bills (established under Senate Standing

S. Moulds, *Committees of Influence*, https://doi.org/10.1007/978-981-15-4350-0_9

Order 25), and those made with respect to the SSCSB are also relevant to the work of the SSCRO. The recommendations made with respect to the PJCIS also have relevance to other joint or single-house committees established by statute with subject-specific mandates. While the recommendations directed at the PJCHR are less readily transferrable to the other more established committees in the system, they too have relevance beyond this case study as they offer guidance to those tasked with evaluating options for the introduction of new committees into the system in the future. Taken together with Chap. 8, the changes suggested in the chapter present a new vision for the role parliamentary committees play in the current parliamentary model of rights protection. The recommendations are discussed in this Chapter are summarised in Tables 9.1–9.4.

9.2 LCA Committees and Other Senate Legislation Committees

As noted above, the key strength of the Senate Legislation Committees, such as the LCA Committees, is their capacity to provide a meaningful deliberative forum by attracting a large number of diverse submission makers and witnesses to public inquiries, and by involving a diverse range of parliamentarians as members (see also Sibraa 1990 and Halligan 2008). These strengths help committees like the LCA Committee to attract attention to the key rights issues arising from the Bills they scrutinise through their public inquiry function and exhibit the decision-making characteristics that Levy and Orr (2016) and Halligan (2008) have described as central to meaningful deliberation. The evidence in Chap. 6 also suggests that these committees can have a long-term impact on the shape of future legislative reforms by preparing reports that include alternative policy proposals that are subsequently adopted and reflected in new policy proposals or draft Bills.

In light of these strengths, I recommend changes that enhance the deliberative quality of the Senate Legislation Committees' inquiries and increase these committees' engagement with draft Bills and discussion papers. These changes reflect suggestions made in the course of interviews with past LCA Committees members, secretariat staff and key submission makers.[1] They include formalising processes for selecting witnesses to inquiries to ensure a broad range of interested parties are consistently involved; improving feedback processes between submission makers and the committee's secretariat staff; and encouraging the referral of draft Bills or discussion papers to the committees for consideration.

My recommendations also call for improved reporting by the Senate Legislation Committees on government responses to their reports and legislative implementation of their key recommendations. This would allow key participants to have a stronger sense of the overall impact of these committees on proposed laws, and

[1] Further information about the interviews conducted for this research is available at Moulds 2018 Appendix A.

further support and encourage high-quality participation among parliamentarians, public servants and submission makers. Currently, outside of academic analysis such as this book, it is difficult to access this type of information, particularly for the many Senate Legislation Committees, including the LCA Committees, which do not publish their own annual reports.

The evidence in Part II also highlights that in some areas the LCA Committees are struggling to have a consistently strong impact. In particular, since 2013, the LCA Committees have not been engaged in any public inquiries relating to counter-terrorism Bills, with government members of the LCA Committee deferring consideration of these Bills to the PJCIS. Some may consider this a sensible approach, given the very high workload facing the LCA Committees and the general demands placed on committee members and secretariat staff to respond to the increasing number of references parliamentary committees receive (see e.g. Jennett 2016). However, this book argues that, at least when it comes to rights-engaging Bills, the LCA Committees' complete deference to the PJCIS is a worrying trend. This is because the evidence in Part II clearly shows that the most substantial, rights-enhancing impacts occur when multiple parliamentary committees consider a Bill. As discussed in Chap. 5, this was the case for the SLAT Bills, the ASIO Bills and the Control Order Bills, which were reviewed by at least two inquiry-based committees, in addition to the regular scrutiny conducted by the SSCSB and later the PJCHR. For this reason, I recommend that reforms be implemented to encourage the Senate Legislation Committees to continue to accept and act upon subject-specific references, including counter-terrorism related references, and desist the recent practice of deferring inquiries into such Bills to the PJCIS or other subject-specific committees with statutorily prescribed mandates. This recommendation is also supported by interviews conducted with a range of submission makers who preferred the experience of appearing before the LCA Committees to that of the PJCIS.

In other words, my findings suggest that concurrent inquiries into the same Bill by different committees can have important rights-enhancing results, despite any perceived duplication in scrutiny functions or roles. As discussed in Chap. 8, this is because the different attributes of different committees work to minimise any potential weaknesses or threats to legitimacy posed by any single committee in the system. As the findings in Part II demonstrate, the potential benefits of multi-committee scrutiny are particularly pronounced when the committees involved exhibit authoritative attributes (such as those demonstrated by the PJCIS) and deliberative attributes (such as those demonstrated by the Senate Legislation Committees). As discussed further in Chap. 10, this approach also builds upon the findings of Dalla-Pozza (2016) in her examination of parliamentary committee and counter-terrorism laws, and aligns with the analytical framework for multi-stage scrutiny proposed by Stephenson (2016).

It is important to note that multi-committee scrutiny need not lead to a full duplication of scrutiny roles by different committees in the system. Rather, as discussed in Chap. 8, my recommendations aim to facilitate efficient collaboration between committees, particularly those inquiring into the same Bill. However, in recognition of the need to address the demanding workload faced by less-specialised committees such as the Senate Legislation Committees, I also recommend the introduction of strategies to provide practical support for these committees and their secretariats. For example, I recommend that the LCA Committees adopt the secondee approach utilised so effectively by the PJCIS and available to the LCA Committees under existing Standing Orders. This includes Senate, Standing Order 25(17) currently provides that committees shall be provided with 'all necessary staff, facilities and resources' and have the power to 'appoint persons with specialist knowledge for the purposes of the committee' – which could be utilised to facilitate the appointment of expert advisors or departmental secondees in line with changes proposed in Chap. 8. As discussed in Chap. 4, the use of secondees can help build relationships of trust between a committee and the executive, which can in turn increase the likelihood of the committee's recommendations being reflected in legislative amendments.

In addition to addressing workload issues, my recommendations above also seek to improve the Senate Legislation Committees' capacity to collaborate with other committees, particularly those that are able to provide the Senate Legislation Committees and their submission makers with timely rights-specific analysis. For example, I recommend that the LCA Committees (or at least their secretariat staff) liaise regularly with SSCSB and PJCHR to develop specific Guidance Notes on rights issues that commonly arise in their work, such as parliamentary oversight of the use of executive power to prescribe places or organisations, and the type of safeguards necessary to ensure those suspected of engagement in terrorist activity have access to procedural fairness and natural justice. This would help ensure that the materials published by the SSCSB and the PJCHR are well tailored to the work of inquiry-based committees and their submission makers, which would in turn increase the rights-enhancing capacity of the committee system. These recommendations are summarised in Table 9.1.

Table 9.1 Reform options for the LCA committees and other Senate legislation committees

Aim	Recommendation	Implementation
Enhance the deliberative quality of the inquiry process	Formalise and actively build upon existing databases of potential submission makers so that direct invitations to be involved in committee work are distributed more consistently to a broader range of potentially interested parties.	Committee Chair, secretariat staff
	Formalise processes for selecting witnesses for public inquiries to guard against unconscious bias or preference for 'usual suspects'.	Committee Chair, secretariat staff
	Invest in online materials and secretariat staff capacity to support submission makers and witnesses, particularly new witnesses, for example by:	Senate Office, committee Chair, secretariat staff
	utilising the LCA Committees' existing website to provide:	
	examples of high quality submissions;	
	video content to convey the 'typical' witness experience;	

(continued)

Table 9.1 (continued)

Aim	Recommendation	Implementation
	lists of tips for what committee members find useful in submissions and oral hearings; and/or	
	a FAQ page for new submission makers and witnesses with links to more experienced organisations to help establish mentor relationships;	
	facilitating regular workshops for regular and new submission makers and witnesses; and	
	establishing a modest hardship fund to support non-government witnesses travelling from regional or remote locations to attend public hearings in person.	
	Invest in reliable video communication technologies in capital cities and regional centres to facilitate remote access public hearings. This could be supported by the interim use of video conferencing facilities provided by 'host' organisations, such as local councils or public libraries.	
Increase LCA Committee engagement with draft Bills and discussion papers	Liaise with proponent Ministers and the AGD to encourage the referral of draft Bills or discussion papers to the LCA Committees for consideration.	Committee Chair
Encourage and support the LCA Committees to continue to engage with counter-terrorism related Bills	Demonstrate the impact of LCA Committee inquiries by documenting and reporting on the government response to and legislative implementation of the committees' recommendations, for example through annual report and more instantaneous platforms including social media and direct email through a subscription alert service.	Committee Chair, secretariat staff
	Proactively engage with regular submission makers, for example through a biannual workshop, to convey the importance of multiple committee scrutiny of rights-engaging Bills.	Committee Chair, secretariat staff, submission makers
	When receiving a reference into a Bill that has also been referred to the PJCIS, require the Chairs and Secretaries of both committees to discuss options for appropriate collaboration, which could include:	Committee Chair (LCA and PJCIS), secretariat staff (LCA and PJCIS)
	(a) coordinating submission deadlines to ease pressure on submission makers;	
	(b) 'sharing' public submissions in an open and transparent way – for example by alerting all submission makers that their submissions will be considered by the other committee;	
	(c) coordinating public hearings – which could include holding 'joint hearings' – to ensure a wide range of witnesses can be heard; and/or	
	(d) agreeing that only one committee will hold public hearings, but that both committees will have access to hearing transcripts and will table substantive reports.	

(continued)

Table 9.1 (continued)

Aim	Recommendation	Implementation
Address workload pressures	Increase the overall staffing levels of the Senate Office to support the existing practice of allocating additional staff to the LCA Committees when dealing with multiple or complex references (see also recommendations in Chap. 9).	Senate Office
	Appoint a part-time specialist advisor to assist the LCA Committees, in a similar way as the Legal Advisor assists the SSCSB and PJCHR.	Committee Chair, Senate Office
	Liaise with government departments, particularly the AGD and DIPB, to facilitate transparent secondee relationships for particularly large or complex Bills inquiries or references.	Committee Chair, secretariat, AGD, DIPB and related departments
	Continue to utilise the LCA Committees' existing subcommittee power to ensure sufficient members are able attend public hearings.	Committee Chair, secretariat
Encourage collaboration with committees with rights-specific mandates	Encourage early and explicit consideration of PJCHR and SSCSB and structure reports to highlight key rights issues.	Committee Chair (LCA, PJCHR, SSCSB), secretariat staff (LCA, PJCHR, SSCSB)
	Liaise with SSCSB and PJCHR to develop and publish specific Guidance Notes on the rights issues commonly arising from the LCA Committees' work.	Committee Chairs, secretariat staff
	Explicitly acknowledge reliance on PJCHR and SSCSB reports in PJCIS reports and encourage committee members to use these sources as the basis for questions for witnesses at public hearings.	Committee Chair, committee members
	Incorporate the PJCHR's analytical approach into training and induction processes for secretariat staff and new committee members and secondees.	Committee Chair, secretariat staff

9.3 PJCIS and Other Statutory Based, Subject-Specialist Committees

My research suggests that those committees within the system who hold subject-specific scrutiny mandates that are prescribed by statute have unique opportunities to have a strong, rights-enhancing legislative impact on federal law. For example, Part II of this book highlighted the many comparative strengths of the PJCIS, including its particularly strong legislative impact on the case study Acts since 2013 (see also Dalla-Pozza 2020). It highlighted the PJCIS's strong, positive working relationships with government departments, key law enforcement and intelligence agencies, sophisticated submission makers and oversight bodies. It also explained how the majority-party-controlled membership of the PJCIS can help facilitate the effective negotiation of recommended legislative reforms to address rights concerns. Part II also documented the PJCIS's expanding statutory oversight and legislative review role, and explained why the PJCIS may have replaced the LCA Committees as a forum of choice for review of counter-terrorism Bills. Chap. 8 explained how these features combine to give the PJCIS a number of advantages when it comes to rights-enhancing impact.

However, the evidence presented in Part II also suggests that the PJCIS may suffer from shortcomings and potential threats to its future legitimacy, often precisely because of the unique character of its relationship with government and its agencies. The PJCIS's secondee arrangements, for example, have attracted negative feedback from some submission makers and oversight bodies, despite contributing significantly to the committee's strong legislative impact. For this reason, I recommend changes to improve the transparency of secondee arrangements, such as ensuring that the secondee has *not* been involved in the development of the legislative proposal or legislative proposal approval process[2] and disclosing the secondee as the source of any information relied upon by the committee when making findings or recommendations in its report.

Like the LCA Committees, the PJCIS also lacks a clear rights-scrutiny mandate, meaning that it is often reliant upon submission makers, and the work of the SSCSB and the PJCHR, for consistent and detailed rights-specific analysis. As discussed in Chaps. 7 and 8, I do not see this as inappropriate and do not recommend that it be changed, rather it is a characteristic of the PJCIS to which my recommendations are attuned. For this reason, a number of changes to the PJCIS's processes and practices are recommended to encourage a more diverse range of participants to the PJCIS inquiries and to ensure that the PJCIS and its submission makers have timely access to high-quality human rights analysis from the technical scrutiny committees. For example, I recommend changes to promote liaison between the PJCIS and the technical scrutiny committees to ensure that Guidance Notes and scrutiny reports are well tailored to the needs of the PJCIS. These recommendations share features in common with those made by other commentators, including former PJCIS member, former Senator John Faulkner (2014) and the Australian Strategic Policy Institute (Bergin and Trood 2015). They also align with recommendations made by the Department of Prime Minister and Cabinet's 2017 Independent Intelligence Review (at pp. 8–9, 118–25 and Recommendations 21 and 23).[3]

The practical changes I recommend aim to minimise the tensions between the PJCIS's authoritative and deliberative role discussed in Chap. 4, without compromising the PJCIS's unique strengths. Designed to preserve specialist expertise and relationships while also encouraging meaningful external deliberation, they have

---

[2] See discussion in Chap. 4; see also Interview with a former senior member of an oversight body (telephone, 8 November 2016).

[3] For example, this review recommended that the PJCIS be empowered to: review all proposed reforms to counter-terrorism and national security legislation and review all such expiring legislation (recommendation 23(b)); initiate its own inquiries into proposed or existing counter-terrorism and national security laws (recommendation 23(c); request briefings from the INSLM and ask the INSLM to provide the PJCIS with a report on matters referred by the PJCIS and to coordinate reports on national security legislation (recommendation 23(d)).

application beyond the PJCIS and are relevant to term subject-specific committees within the system. The changes I recommend, set out in detail in Table 9.2, centre on the following themes: improving transparency of relationships with Government agencies, and in particular secondee arrangements; encouraging a diverse range of submission makers to public inquiries; and encouraging collaboration with committees with rights specific mandates.

Table 9.2 Reform options for the PJCIS and other specialist committees

Aim	Recommendation	Implementation
Enhance and document strong legislative impact	Continue to document and report on government responses to and legislative implementation of Committee recommendations in Annual Reports and more immediate means such as social media and subscription based email alert system.	Committee Chair, secretariat staff
	Encourage committee members to explicitly refer to the work of the PJCIS and the contribution of submission makers and witnesses in parliamentary debates.	Committee Chair, committee members
	Continue to invest in additional resources for Secretariat Staff and committee members faced with significant increases in statutorily prescribed workloads.	Senate Office
	Maintain and strengthen the development of legal and counter-terrorism expertise within PJCIS, particularly for new members and new Secretariat staff, for example through training, liaison with international counter-parts and regular formal and informal meetings with OIL and relevant intelligence and law enforcement agencies.	Committee Chair, secretariat staff, law enforcement and intelligence agencies
Improve transparency of relationships with Government agencies	Continue to utilise secondee arrangements, and expand to include a broader range of policy and operational experts, including human rights experts and constitutional law experts where appropriate.	Committee Chair, secretariat staff, AGD
	Improve the transparency of secondee arrangements by:	Committee Chair, secretariat staff, committee members
	Publicly confirming that the secondee is not answerable to the proponent Minister at any time when seconded to the committee;	
	Acknowledging in each report and before each public hearing that the Committee is utilising the expertise of a secondee from X agency or Department;	
	Ensuring that the secondee has *not* been involved in the development of the legislative proposal or legislative proposal approval process, prior to being seconded to the committee;	

(continued)

Table 9.2 (continued)

Aim	Recommendation	Implementation
	Disclosing the secondee as the source of any information relied upon by the Committee when making findings or recommendations in its report;	
	Excluding the secondee from private meetings conducted by the Committee; and	
	Seeking feedback from non-government submission makers and witnesses about the use of secondees.	
	Continue to enhance the PJCIS's working relationships with oversight bodies by:	Committee Chair, secretariat staff, oversight bodies
	Coordinating statutory mandated reviews and reporting requirements where possible	
	Inviting the IGIS, INSLM, and Ombudsman to give evidence at public inquiries into Bills as a matter of course, and ensuring evidence is given as part of a public inquiry (even if a closed hearing is also required)	
	Requesting additional briefings from the IGIS, INSLM, or Ombudsman when seeking to give effect to or depart from the specific recommendations for legislative change made by these oversight bodies.	
Encourage a diverse range of submission makers to public inquiries	Formalise and actively build upon existing databases of potential submission makers so that invitations to be involved in committee work are distributed more consistently to a diverse range of potentially interested parties.	Committee Chair, secretariat staff
	Formalise processes for selecting witnesses for public inquiries to guard against unconscious bias or preference for 'usual suspects'.	Committee Chair, secretariat staff
	Invest in materials and Secretariat staff capacity to support submission makers and witnesses, particularly new witnesses, for example by adopting the strategies recommended with respect to the LCA Committees above.	Senate Office
Encourage collaboration with committees with rights specific mandates	Encourage early and explicit consideration of PJCHR and SSCSB reports to help structure draft PJCIS Reports and isolate key rights issues.	Committee Chairs (PJCIS, PJCHR, SSCSB), secretariat staff (PJCIS PJCHR, SSCSB)
	Liaise with SSCSB and PJCHR to develop specific Guidance Notes on the rights issues commonly arising from the work of the PJCIS.	Committee Chairs (PJCIS, PJCHR, SSCSB), secretariat staff (PJCIS PJCHR, SSCSB)

(continued)

Table 9.2 (continued)

Aim	Recommendation	Implementation
	Explicitly acknowledge reliance on PJCHR and SSCSB reports in PJCIS reports and encourage committee members to use these reports as the basis for questions for witnesses at public hearings.	Committee Chair, committee members
	Incorporate the PJCHR's analytical approach into training and induction processes for Secretariat staff and new committee members and secondees	Committee Chair, secretariat staff

9.4 SSCSB and the SSCRO

As discussed in Chap. 8, the SSCSB's strengths lie in its strong hidden impact on the case study Acts, and in the high levels of legitimacy it attracts across key participants in the parliamentary scrutiny system. As an interviewee said, the SSCSB is 'part of the Senate furniture' (Canberra 23 May 2016). Similar comments have been made with respect to the SSCRO, the oldest committee in the system (Grenfell 2015), which like the SSCSB is well placed to build upon its existing high levels of legitimacy to influence law-making at the pre-introduction phase (see also Debeljak and Grenfell 2020, pp. 2–23).

These strengths are preserved and enhanced by the above recommendations, which aim to further enhance the role of the SSCSB and the SSCRO in policy development and legislative drafting, including by developing new, rights-focused guidance material that provides clear legislative options for public servants seeking to avoid negative scrutiny by the SSCSB.[4] For example, Guidance Notes could be prepared on topics including access to meaningful judicial review of executive decisions or the type of safeguards necessary to protect against undue interference with individual privacy by law enforcement or intelligence officers.[5] I also recommend that the SSCSB take better advantage of its power in Senate Standing Order 24(1)(b) to scrutinise exposure drafts of proposed legislation. This would amplify the committee's existing strong behind-the-scenes impact by providing specific rights-scrutiny advice to departments at the pre-introduction stage.

Other practical changes to the work practices of the SSCSB supported by my research include:

- Liaising more frequently with the inquiry-based committees to identify what SSCSB publications are most useful to these committees when undertaking inquiries into rights-engaging Bills and prioritise the development of Guidance

[4] This is supported by evidence from public servants and parliamentary counsel about the utility of previous SSCSB guidance materials, and the documentary evidence showing how these notes were used in Drafting Directions and policy guidance materials for the AGD. These matters were discussed in detail in Chap. 7.

[5] These issues arise regularly in SSCSB reports, but also in inquiry-based committee reports on counter-terrorism laws. For examples, see Chaps. 3 and 5.

Notes that address any needs of the inquiry-based committees for reliable, 'technical' analysis of commonly arising rights or scrutiny concerns.
- Compiling a database of SSCSB's findings and recommendations that allows the SSCSB's Alert Digests and reports to be searched thematically or by key word to improve access to key elements of the SSCSB's reports, and allow analysis of the SSCSB's findings on particular rights issues over time. This could include a link from the Bill's homepage to any relevant Alert Digest or report which comments on that Bill.
- Being explicit about the connection between the SSCSB scrutiny criteria and that of the PJCHR in all SSCSB publications, including Scrutiny Reports, Guidance Notes and Annual Reports.
- Liaising regularly with the Chair and secretariat staff of the PJCHR with a view to preparing joint (or at least complementary) Guidance Notes on areas of common concern, such as retrospectivity, access to judicial review and procedural guarantees.
- Utilising Senate Standing Order 24(7) to actively encourage public input into the development of Guidance Notes and other SSCSB publications.

These recommendations are focused on increasing the SSCSB's opportunities to interact meaningfully with other parliamentary committees in the system. They echo those made above for the LCA Committees and the PJCIS, and encourage the SSCSB to work with these inquiry-based committees to identify what Guidance Notes are most useful when undertaking public inquiries into rights-engaging Bills. It is further recommended that the SSCSB keep a 'running record' of the instances when the SSCSB has been quoted in an inquiry-based committee report as means of highlighting the existing rights-enhancing contribution made by the SSCSB and improving the relevance of the SSCSB's publications. This recommendation builds upon existing Senate Standing Order 25.2A which requires legislative and general purpose committees to take into account any SSCSB or SCSRO reports.

Despite its many strengths, the evidence in Part II demonstrates that the SSCSB's engagement with non-government participants, and in particular with the broader community and the media, is limited compared to the other committees studied. Chap. 5 also documents the challenges the SSCSB faces when it comes to tabling its final reports prior to the resumption of the second reading debate on a Bill, particularly when responses from Ministers are delayed or inadequate. In light of these comparative 'weaknesses', it is tempting to recommend a raft of changes that reframe the 'technical' character of the SSCSB and bring it closer to that of the PJCIS or LCA Committees. However, as the earlier discussion in this chapter warns, making such changes to the SSCSB could jeopardise the precise features of the committee that give it its comparative strengths as a 'non-political', 'technical' committee.

For this reason, my recommendations stop short of calling for the SSCSB to hold more public inquiries into Bills, or encouraging the committee to publicise its findings in media releases. Instead, my recommendations focus on increasing the SSCSB's opportunities to interact meaningfully with other parliamentary committees, as well as identifying new opportunities for the SSCSB to improve its engagement with the broader community. For example, I recommend that the SSCSB actively seek public feedback on existing and proposed Guidance Notes or other statements that seek to flesh out aspects of its scrutiny criteria in more detail. This could be easily managed by the committee without disturbing its 'technical' character, for example by drawing upon its already strong relationships with the legal profession and public servants. It could also allow the SSCSB to proactively engage with other community groups on general principles without holding public hearings into particular Bills or impinging on tight time frames for completing scrutiny reports.

The publication of more targeted Guidance Notes would also provide a practical opportunity for the SSCSB to liaise with the PJCHR. For example, the two committees (which are already supported by a combined secretariat structure that also includes the SSCRO) could develop joint Guidance Notes on rights issues of common concern. Such joint Guidance Notes could explicitly identify the different ways the SSCSB and the PJCHR approaches the rights issue or evaluates the appropriateness of safeguards or limitations on rights, whilst at the same time demonstrating the commonality in analytical approaches between the two committees. This in turn would help improve the relevance of these materials for a wider range of key participants, as well as public servants and parliamentary counsel who rely upon consistency and clarity when it comes to providing advice on the rights-compliance of legislative options for government.

While my research challenges the assumption that short time frames lead to poor scrutiny outcomes, Part II of this book also describes the clear benefit of technical scrutiny committees tabling at least their initial scrutiny reports as soon as possible, so that they can be considered by all members of parliament and be used by other committees in the system, including submission makers to inquiry-based committees. For this reason, I strongly support the changes recommended by the SSCSB in its 2012 report on the future directions of the Committee. In particular, I support changes that would require the SSCSB to:

- consider and publish its scrutiny reports during non-sitting periods in appropriate cases;
- notify the Senate of any instance of a Minister's failure to respond to a request for information from the SSCSB (after a reasonable time and with notice to the Minister);
- include a link from the Parliament's homepage for a Bill to any relevant *Alert Digest or report* which comments on that Bill; and
- establish an internal database to capture the committee's comments on Bills from 2000 onwards (SSCSB 2012 at paras [7.16]–[7.22]).

If implemented, these changes would increase the timeliness and accessibility of the SSCSB's reports without jeopardising its 'technical scrutiny' character, and strong legitimacy within the committee system. From the interview material obtained for this book, it appears that moves are already underway to implement some of these strategies in practice. For example, an interviewee said that the committee has been:

> producing a quarterly responsiveness table, which provides the opportunity to [identify] people for a lack of response. [The previous committee] put in a notice of motion for a

temporary order where any senator could take note of a lack of response before debate. … [I]t will be up to the next committee whether it proceeds with that (Canberra 23 May 2016).

As noted in Chap. 3, since November 2017 this has been reflected in Standing Order 24(1)(d) which provides that the SSCSB shall 'maintain on its website a list of bills in relation to which the committee has sought advice from the responsible minister and not yet received a response'. The amended Standing Order also provides that, where the SSCSB has not been able to complete a final report on the Bill because a ministerial response has not been received, then 'any senator may ask the minister for an explanation of why the minister has not provided a response to the committee' (Senate Standing Order 24(1)(e)). This can be followed by a motion without notice asking that the 'Senate take note of the explanation' or that the Senate note the Minister's 'failure to provide an explanation' (Senate Standing Order 24(1)(f)-(g). Similar strategies are also recommended with respect to the PJCHR and are discussed below. My recommendations with respect to the SSCSB and the SSCR are summarised in Table 9.3.

Table 9.3 Reform options for the SSCSB and SSCRO

Aim	Recommendation	Implementation
Enhance and document strong hidden impact	Document and report on the extent to which SSCSB publications have been incorporated into formal guidance materials for public servants and parliamentary counsel, including in the *Legislation Handbook*, Drafting Directions and the Guide to Framing Commonwealth Offences.	Secretariat
	Prioritise the development of targeted Guidance Notes, focusing on the most common rights-related concerns that arise in the SSCSB's reports. This guidance material should be developed in close consultation with parliamentary counsel and instructing departments and be subject to public review.	Committee Chair, secretariat
	Proactively utilise the power in Senate Standing Order 24(1)(b) to scrutinise exposure drafts of proposed legislation and provide specific rights-scrutiny advice to departments at the pre-introduction stage.	Committee Chair, relevant Ministers and departments
Encourage collaboration with other committees	Liaise with the inquiry-based committees to identify what SSCSB publications are most useful to these committees when undertaking inquiries into rights-engaging Bills and prioritise the development of Guidance Notes that address any needs of the inquiry-based committees for reliable, 'technical' analysis of commonly arising rights or scrutiny concerns.	Committee Chair, secretariat
	Document and report on instances when the SSCSB has been quoted in an inquiry-based committee report.	Secretariat
	Continue to issue timely Alert Digests in short, accessible format. The tabling of Bill-specific Alert Digests should be encouraged for particularly complex or rights-concerning Bills.	Committee Chair, secretariat

(continued)

Table 9.3 (continued)

Aim	Recommendation	Implementation
	Compile a database of SSCSB's findings and recommendations that allows the SSCSB's Alert Digests and reports to be searched thematically or by key word to improve access to key elements of the SSCSB's reports, and allow analysis of the SSCSB's findings on particular rights issues over time. This could include a link from the Bill's homepage to any relevant Alert Digest or report which comments on that Bill.	Secretariat
	Be explicit about the connection between the SSCSB scrutiny criteria and that of the PJCHR in all SSCSB publications.	Committee Chair, secretariat
	Liaise regularly with the Chair and secretariat staff of the PJCHR with a view to preparing joint (or at least complementary) Guidance Notes on areas of common concern, such as retrospectivity, access to judicial review and procedural guarantees.	Committee Chair, secretariat
	Utilise Senate Standing Order 24(7) to actively encourage public input into the development of Guidance Notes and other SSCSB publications.	Committee Chair, secretariat
Encourage timely ministerial responses	'Name and shame' delayed responses from proponent Ministers to reasonable requests for information by the committee, for example by utilising recently amended Standing Order 24(1)(d)–(g) to publicise late responses to requests for information and to demand an explanation from the proponent Minister in Parliament.	Committee Chair
	Publish Alert Digests and reports during non-sitting periods in appropriate cases, for example by adopting a provision similar to Standing Order 38(7) that currently permits this approach for other Senate committees.	Committee Chair, secretariat

9.5 PJCHR

As observed in Part II and Chap. 8, of all the committees studied in this book, the PJCHR struggled to demonstrate high impact on the case study Acts. The relatively short lifespan of the committee, coupled with its complex mandate, contribute to its comparatively lower status among key participants, and its relative lack of direct legislative and public impact. This is further exacerbated by the confusion that appears to exist about the true goal or purpose of the committee. As discussed in Chap. 3 and highlighted in the interview material included in Part II, for many key participants it is either not clear exactly what the PJCHR's goal is, or whether the PJCHR is capable of living up to the high expectations held at the time of its establishment. Is it a technical scrutiny committee, or a committee designed to actively promote human rights compliance? Is the committee comfortable working largely on the papers, or should it facilitate human rights discussions among the broader

Australian community? These are some of the persistent questions that have plagued the PJCHR's early history. They lead, in turn, to more practical questions relating to timing of tabling of reports, how dissenting views should be dealt with, and the content and quality of SoCs.

This book argues that, by focusing on the PJCHR's emerging strengths, and its potential capacity to collaborate with other parliamentary committees in the system, it is possible to resolve at least some of the existential questions confronting the PJCHR, and to improve its rights-enhancing impact. As Part II documented, the PJCHR's emerging strengths centre on the following practices and outputs:

- the provision of high-quality and detailed rights analysis that often involves reference to comparative international sources, common law rights, High Court decisions and findings by other oversight bodies such as the AHRC and the INSLM. The evidence in Part II suggests that it is increasingly relied upon and referred to by other parliamentary committees and in submissions to inquiry-based committees;
- the high degree of cross-over between the findings of the PJCHR on a narrow range of 'legal process' related rights and the recommendations made by inquiry-based committees, which are regularly reflected in successful amendments to proposed laws;
- the articulation and application of the 'proportionality test' (PJCHR Guidance Note 1 2014; cf. Chordia 2016) as a framework for balancing competing rights and interests arising from a particular law; and
- a small but growing awareness of the value of the analysis provided by the PJCHR by a handful of parliamentarians, and among some government departments, particularly the AGD.

These strengths suggest that the PJCHR is performing relatively well as a 'technical scrutiny' committee, at least for a committee of its age. As explored in Chaps. 4 and 7, these are also the features of the PJCHR that appear to attract the most legitimacy among the broadest range of key participants, suggesting that investing in the PJCHR's technical scrutiny role may also help to improve the committee's political authority.

One way to invest in the PJCHR's technical scrutiny function is to ensure that the committee's reports are targeted to those responsible for developing and drafting proposed legislation. For example, I recommend that the PJCHR allocate time and resources to the preparation of Guidance Notes that focus on commonly arising rights issues, and specifically identify examples of the types of safeguards that should be included in proposed provisions that seek to interfere with or limit a protected right. This would serve the dual purpose of (1) clearly acknowledging that it may be permissible for the executive to limit a right, provided certain criteria are met; and (2) providing clear, prospective guidance to policy makers and parliamentary counsel about the types of provisions and safeguards that would be considered rights compliant by the PJCHR.

These types of more targeted Guidance Notes could be developed in active consultation with key submission makers, the SSCSB and the inquiry-based committees. Indeed, this type of successful public engagement occurred at the beginning of the PJCHR's life, when the processes and practices of the committee were still being finalised. The PJCHR has also been proactive in providing its own submissions to the inquiry-based committees on occasion, and this practice could be further supported and encouraged as a way of adding value to the multi-committee scrutiny process (PJCHR Annual Report 2012–13 at paras [1.34]–[1.35]). This approach also shares similarities with the shift towards a more 'contestable' conception of human rights standards explored by Rice (2020). Rice, a former legal advisor to the PJCHR, suggest that consideration should be given to moving away from an approach where the PJCHR appears to be the sole authority on human rights in Australia (and human rights standards are considered to be relatively static) towards an approach where a range of key participants can be involved in articulating the contours of the wide range of human rights that fall within the PJCHR's scrutiny mandate. For Rice (2020), it is important to recognise that there can be legitimate differing views on whether or not a proposed law is compatible or incompatible with human rights. He encourages the PJCHR to play a facilitative role in establishing a meaningful conversation about what international human rights mean in an Australian context, rather than 'telling off' government departments or Ministers for failing to understand the technical intricacies of international human rights law. From a different perspective Byrnes (2020) arrives at a similar conclusion – highlighting the need for the PJCHR to develop its own contextualised approach to the application of economic and social rights in the Australian context, guided by (rather than dictated to) international human rights bodies and comparative jurisprudence. By opening up space for a meaningful, deliberative conversation about the human rights standards to be applied by the PJCHR my recommendations build upon these themes whilst also recognising the value of preserving the PJCHR's character as a 'technical scrutiny' committee rather than an inquiry-based committee. They aim to facilitate more open community engagement with the rights scrutiny standards being applied, whilst protecting the PJCHR from the criticism of engaging in a pseudo political critique of the merits of government policy. In this way, my recommendations both align with and depart from the findings made by Rice and Byrnes.

The utility of the reports prepared by the PJCHR could be further enhanced by making it easier to access and understand the PJCHR's views on particular rights issues over time. While efforts are currently made in the PJCHR's annual report to list those rights most commonly considered by the committee, it remains a slow and cumbersome task to distil the key principles applied by the committee on commonly considered rights such as the right to a fair trial. This could be addressed by compiling a database of PJCHR reports that could be searched thematically or by 'key word' to enable submission makers, parliamentary committee staff, parliamentary counsel and others to quickly access what the PJCHR has said on a particular rights issue across a range of different Bills. This would in turn improve the likelihood that submission makers to inquiry-based committees, and parliamentarians themselves, would draw upon the work of the PJCHR in their public advocacy on particular rights issues or Bills.

My research suggests that the PJCHR could also improve its legitimacy among public servants and government parliamentarians by regularly and publicly acknowledging positive efforts by the executive to have regard to the rights implications of proposed laws at an early stage. This could include, for example, publishing examples of high-quality SoCs on the PJCHR website. It could also involve the PJCHR explicitly recognising that, very often, the policy driver behind proposed laws is at least in part rights promoting, even if the provisions of the proposed law are not rights compliant. Like the former INSLM Bret Walker SC, I recommend that these rights-promoting aims be consistently and explicitly acknowledged in PJCHR reports, before descending into a more critical analysis of the overall rights compliance of the Bill. Fletcher (2018 at Chapter 3 and pp. 289–296) also has a range of practical suggestions for improving the quality of SoC's and for encouraging a greater 'behind the scenes' rights literacy for public servants involved in drafting and preparing SoCs and responses to the PJCHR's requests for further information. For example, Fletcher (2018) suggests that the type of investment in public sector training in the area of human rights that occurred in the 2012–13 'golden era' be resumed with a view to encouraging policy makers across all departments to explore how human rights standards relate to their respective portfolios and to reflect on the range of options available to government that may achieve the requisite policy ends with less rights intrusive results. For Fletcher (2018) this involves exposure to both international human rights law concepts, but also to policy making processes in comparative jurisdictions such as the UK, and could take the form of additional or updated guidance notes or handbooks, including the incorporation of additional information in the *Legislation Handbook* (Fletcher 2018 at p. 290).

When public servants' knowledge of human rights concepts is contextualised and practical, it can in turn lead to the type of 'back office' (Fletcher 2018 p. 290) rights scrutiny processes that have been documented in Chap. 7, where public servants can be relied upon to triage legislative proposals for rights compliance well before the formal parliamentary rights scrutiny process occurs. Like Fletcher, I also support an increased role for the PJCHR in scrutinising draft legislation or discussion papers for rights compliance as a means of encouraging a genuine exchange of views on the rights compatibility of a range of legislative options outside of the glare of the political commitment that comes from introducing a Government Bill. This would give the PJCHR and the SoC process a much more explicitly *preventative* rights function, whilst maintaining its particular strengths within the broader committee system (Fletcher 2018 at p. 290; see also Weston 2015).

Like Fletcher (2018), my recommendations aim to create a safe space for public servants to contest the boundaries of the rights standards being applied by the PJCHR and to acknowledge and explain 'incompatibilities' between the Government's legislative choices and relevant human rights standards, either 'behind the scenes' (for example by providing submissions in response to consultation on the contents of the PJCHR's scrutiny mandate) or in public view (through the use of more contextualised, detailed SoCs). As Fletcher explains, this would ensure that Parliament has a clearer impression of both the policy and legislative goals of the proposed law, and of its rights compatibility. In this way, Fletcher's suggestions on improving the quality of SoCs align with Rice's (2020) thoughts on broadening the space for dissent and discussion within the PJCHR. My recommendations build upon these ideas by recognising the PJCHR's place within the broader system of committees, and provide opportunities for the scrutiny standards being applied by the PJCHR to be articulated in a way that is more directly applicable and relevant to the work of policy makers and public servants, and open to contestation through community consultation processes.

Of course, the efficacy of these recommendations depends in large part upon key participants receiving the reports of the PJCHR in adequate time to make use of their contents before the passage of the particular Bill. As a result I support recommendations made by other scholars designed to improve the timeliness of the tabling of PJCHR reports. For example, I support the recommendation made by Williams and Reynolds (2016 at p. 479) that a 'guaranteed minimum time period' be provided between the introduction of a Bill and the completion of the second reading debate on the Bill to ensure that the PJCHR can consider and report on any proposed Bill (see also Reynolds and Williams 2020). This recommendation is also supported by Fletcher (2018, 2020 at pp. 291) and Rajanayagam (2020). This could be achieved by the adoption of a Standing Order, applicable in both Houses, that provides that, as a general rule, the second reading debate on a Bill should not resume until the reports of all relevant committees have been tabled (Williams and Reynolds 2016 at p. 502; ALRC 2016 at p. 52). However, in recognition that such a reform would demand strong executive leadership and majority parliamentary support across both Houses, I also recommend reforms that can be implemented by the PJCHR itself. Chief among these is the recommendation that the PJCHR adopt the Alert Digest style[6] reporting practices of the SSCSB to ensure its initial views on the human rights compatibility of a Bill are available *prior* to the resumption of the second reading debate. These Alert Digests could be drafted in a similar style and structure to the SSCSB's Alert Digests (more recently known as Initial Scrutiny Reports), leaving the more detailed analysis and response from the proponent Minister to be discussed in subsequent final reports (more recently known as 'Commentary on Ministerial Responses').

Recent experience suggests that the PJCHR is already experimenting with tabling multiple reports on particularly complex or rights-engaging Bills and issuing scrutiny reports which include consideration of 'matters where a response is required' as well as 'concluded matters' (see e.g. PJCHR Report No 6 of 2017). This appears to be supported by the recent practice of sharing secretariat staff between the SSCSB and the PJCHR. This type of initial scrutiny reporting allows the PJCHR's preliminary views to be made available to Parliament prior to the completion of the second reading debate on the Bill, while their concluded views are

[6]As noted in Chap. 3, since 2017, the SSCSB began publishing its scrutiny comments on recently introduced Bills (including responses received on matters previously considered by the committee) in one report, the *Scrutiny Digest*. However, the *Scrutiny Digest* continues to be divided into initial reports on the Bill (previously called 'Alert Digests', now called 'Initial Scrutiny') and concluded reports on the Bill (previously called 'Reports' now called 'Commentary on Ministerial Responses'). Similar language could be adopted by the PJCHR.

presented some time later, following the receipt of a response from the relevant Minister. My recommendation to adopt a more consistent Alert Digest or Initial Scrutiny approach would formalise this process, without undermining the PJCHR's commitment to engaging in a meaningful 'dialogue' with the executive about the rights compliance of proposed laws.[7]

The interview material gathered for this book suggests that the use of Alert Digest and Bill-specific reporting would also greatly improve the chances of the views of the PJCHR being considered by a wide range of key participants prior to decisions being made on the content and merits of the Bill. Alert Digest style reports could be supported by the development of Guidance Notes on commonly occurring rights issues, as discussed above, and by the establishment of a searchable database of PJCHR comments, to enable public servants who are involved in the legislation development process to quickly and easily access past PJCHR comments on relevant provisions or rights issues.

Alert Digest style reporting could also assist the PJCHR to experiment with ways of expressing a concluded view on a proposed law when a response from the proponent minister is not provided, as recommended by Williams and Reynolds (2016 at p. 479), and help to diffuse the tensions surrounding the handling of dissent within the PJCHR. For example, it would enable the committee to express preliminary rights compatibility concerns in the form of questions, or 'leaving matters to the Parliament as a whole to consider', in the style of the SSCSB, rather than requiring PJCHR members to directly criticise an aspect of government policy on human rights grounds.

Alert Digest style reporting by the PJCHR could also help the committee experiment with new ways to present dissenting views on rights compatibility in its reports. For example, the PJCHR could follow a practice of raising rights compatibility questions at the Alert Digest stage, along with information about how such questions are resolved under international human rights law. This would allow the rights issue to be brought to the early attention of the Parliament and could provide a useful analytical framework to inform the public debate on the rights question. If dissenting views are still held within the committee, they could be set out at the final report stage in a similar style to the 'dissenting comments' or 'additional comments' frequently included in the LCA Committees' reports (similar to that proposed by Williams and Reynolds 2016 at p. 503 and Rice 2020).

Alert Digest style reporting would also provide a strong basis for the PJCHR to adopt the type of strategies currently being implemented by the SSCSB to address the lack of timely response by Ministers to requests for further information and demand that Ministers be held to account for their failure to respond through a motion in Parliament. For example, like the SSCSB, the PJCHR could take steps to publicise instances of delayed responses from proponent Ministers to reasonable

[7] The commitment of committee Chairs, members and staff to the preservation of this dialogue – which hinges on the proponent Minister having the opportunity to provide further written information to the PJCHR –appears to have thwarted efforts to ensure speedy tabling of PJCHR reports in the past.

requests for information (facilitated by powers similar to those contained in Senate Standing Order 24(1)(d)-(g) described above).

Should the recommendations above relating to Alert Digest style reporting be adopted by the PJCHR, similar procedural consequences could follow. For example, a Bill could be barred from the 'non-controversial' list if it receives criticism from the PJCHR in its initial scrutiny report on the Bill. While most Bills dealing with national security or counter-terrorism would automatically be categorised as 'controversial', this procedural change could provide an additional incentive for proponent Ministers to take the initial scrutiny findings of the PJCHR seriously and implement practices for responding to PJCHR requests for information in a timely way.

Taken together, these recommendations are designed to improve the utility and effectiveness of the PJCHR as a 'technical scrutiny' body, rather than an inquiry-based committee, on the basis that this is the best way for the committee to improve its rights-enhancing impact within the broader committee system. While at first blush it may be tempting to recommend more radical reforms, the evidence gathered in Part II warns against this approach. For example, the evidence presented in Chaps. 4 and 7 suggests that encouraging the PJCHR to conduct more public hearings and more proactively publicise its findings of non-compliance could put the legitimacy of the PJCHR at risk. By more proactively entering the public debate on a Bill, the PJCHR could be *more* susceptible to perceptions of illegitimately engaging in policy evaluation, at greater risk of alienating parliamentarians and submission makers, and face larger challenges when it comes to dealing with dissent (Inglis 2017; Crowe 2017). The findings and conclusions of the PJCHR may also be harder to predict, putting at risk its emerging hidden impact among public servants and parliamentary counsel who rely upon consistency and clarity when it comes to articulating and applying human rights principles.

My recommendations are also consistent with the views of a number of key participants interviewed, including a former Chair of the PJCHR Dean Smith, who rejected the idea of increasing the deliberative role of the PJCHR when it comes to Bills scrutiny on the basis that it would undermine the 'technical' scrutiny role of the committee and bring it into conflict with the Parliament's role as the final adjudicator on rights issues. Senator Smith said:

> there should not be a deliberative role for committees with a scrutiny function. The scrutiny undertaken by the committee is expert based, prepared with the assistance of an expert legal advisor. The onus is on the government to demonstrate compliance with the human rights standards. The debate on balancing human rights and the public interests is up to Parliament (telephone 22 September 2016).

By focusing on the PJCHR's technical scrutiny role, my recommendations also acknowledge what Stephenson describes as Australia's system of multi-stage rights review (Stephenson 2016 at p. 8), and seek to maximise the PJCHR's ability to contribute positively to resolving institutional disagreements on rights, rather than exacerbating those disagreements by investing the committee with a more proactive rights-adjudicating role. My recommendations concerning the PJCHR are summarised in Table 9.4.

Table 9.4 Reform options for the PJCHR

Aim	Recommendation	Implementation
Enhance relevance and accessibility of analysis	Use reports to highlight rights-*protecting* as well as rights-infringing qualities of proposed laws.	Committee Chair, secretariat
	Continue to explicitly acknowledge instances where international human rights law concepts overlap with or intersect with SSCSB criteria, common law principles or other established principles of Australian law.	Committee Chair, secretariat
	Build capacity within the committee's membership to articulate and apply a consistent approach to 'balancing' rights and public interests. This could be assisted by the publication of more Guidance Notes (see below).	Committee Chair, secretariat
	Publicly acknowledge high-quality SoCs including through the Chair's Tabling Statement, the annual report and by informal means such as posting on PJCHR's website	Committee members, secretariat
	Compile a database of PJCHR reports and SoCs that can be searched thematically and/or by 'rights issue'.	secretariat
	Prioritise the development of rights-specific Guidance Notes that focus on rights issues commonly emerging from the committee's work, and include specific examples of the types of safeguards necessary if the Parliament intends to permissibly limit a protected right. These Guidance Notes should be developed in close consultation with the SSCSB, OIL, other relevant departments and parliamentary counsel. Public input should also be sought, for example, by requesting comments on draft Guidance Notes.	Committee Chair, secretariat
	Liaise with parliamentary counsel to distil commonly applied human rights principles into a drafting check list that can be readily incorporated in Drafting Directions and the *Legislation Handbook*.	Secretariat
	Prepare and table regular annual reports that document the impact of the PJCHR on the content and development of proposed laws.	Committee Chair, secretariat
Improve timeliness of reporting, including through Alert Digests	Adopt Alert Digest style reporting practices to ensure that the PJCHR's initial views on human rights compatibility are available prior to the resumption of the second reading debate on a Bill. These Alert Digests could be drafted in a similar style and structure to the SSCSB's Alert Digests, leaving the more detailed analysis and response from the proponent Minister to be discussed in the subsequent final report	Committee Chair, secretariat
	'Name and shame' delayed responses from proponent Ministers to reasonable requests for information by the committee, for example by publicising late responses to requests for information and demanding an explanation from the proponent Minister in Parliament, in line with recently amended Standing Order 24(1)(d)–(g).	Committee Chair

(continued)

Table 9.4 (continued)

Aim	Recommendation	Implementation
Encourage collaboration with other committees	Liaise regularly with the Chair and secretariat staff of the SSCSB with the view to preparing joint Guidance Notes on areas of common concern, such as retrospectivity, access to judicial review, and procedural fairness guarantees.	Committee Chair, secretariat
	Amend Senate Standing Order 25.2A to require inquiry-based committees to have regard to reports of the PJCHR as well as the SSCSB.	Parliament
	Liaise with the inquiry-based committees to identify what resources and reports prepared by the PJCHR are most useful to these committees when undertaking inquiries into rights-engaging Bills. Prioritise the development of Guidance Notes that address the needs of the inquiry-based committees for reliable, 'technical' analysis of common rights concerns.	Committee Chair, secretariat

9.6 Summary of Committee-Specific Reforms

The recommendations discussed above build upon the work of a number of scholars discussed in Part I, particularly those interested in exploring how parliamentary mechanisms can facilitate deliberative law making (see e.g. Halligan 2008; Dalla-Pozza 2016; Levy and Orr 2016), and those keen to identify, articulate and build upon an organically emerging culture of rights scrutiny at the federal level (Evans and Evans 2006a, b, c, 2007; Australian Government 2010). These recommendations also align with the analytical framework set out by Stephenson (2016), which focuses on multi-stage rights scrutiny, by looking to invest in those existing features of the committee system that help diffuse or resolve rights disputes between institutions, rather than exacerbating any potential rights-conflicts between branches of government. My recommendations also descend into the practical detail necessary to ensure that the individual committees in the committee system capitalise on their particular strengths as identified in Part II of my research. They aim to equip each committee with new tools and strategies to ensure that their already rights-enhancing work is seen and relied upon by key decision makers in the system. They also provide opportunities and incentives for individual committees to work collaboratively and include a strong focus on responding to the needs of public servants and sophisticated submission makers, who are at the front line when it comes to influencing the content of rights-engaging laws and policies.

My recommendations also resist the temptation to look to one particular committee to carry the lion's share of rights-scrutiny work, or to create a 'super committee' with extensive powers and wide-ranging functions. Instead, the reforms I advocate listen to the views obtained from those working closely in the committee system and reflect on the features of Australia's multi-stage approach to rights review discussed in Part I of this research. For this reason, my recommendations allow each individual committee to continue to perform the role that attracts the most legitimacy in the eyes of key participants, whilst ensuring that other committees in the system have the capacity to perform some of the functions necessary for meaningful rights protection. This reflects the broader theme of this research by encouraging investment in the way committees work together as a system. In this way, my work offers a new standpoint from which to view the parliamentary committee system's role in Australia's parliamentary model of rights protection, which is discussed further detail in the final chapter below.

References

Standing Orders

Senate, Parliament of Australia, *Standing order*, Chapter 5, Orders 17 to 39. (17 November 2017). https://www.aph.gov.au/Parliamentary_Business/Chamber_documents/Senate_chamber_documents/standingorders/b00/b05

Parliamentary Committee Reports

Parliamentary Joint Committee on Human Rights. (2017, June 20). *Report no 6 of 2017*. Canberra: Parliament of Australia. https://www.aph.gov.au/Parliamentary_Business/Committees/Joint/Human_Rights/Scrutiny_reports/2017/Report_6_of_2017

Parliamentary Joint Committee on Human Rights. (2013). *Annual report 2012–13*. Canberra: Parliament of Australia. https://www.aph.gov.au/Parliamentary_Business/Committees/Joint/Human_Rights/Scrutiny_reports/Annual_Reports/Annual_report_2012-13/index.

Parliamentary Joint Committee on Human Rights. (2014, December). *Guidance note 1: Drafting statements of compatibility*. Canberra: Parliament of Australia. http://www.aph.gov.au/Parliamentary_Business/Committees/Joint/Human_Rights/Guidance_Notes_and_Resources

Senate Standing Committee for Scrutiny of Bills. (2012). *Inquiry into the future direction and role of the scrutiny of bills committee*. Canberra: Parliament of Australia. https://www.aph.gov.au/Parliamentary_Business/Committees/Senate/Scrutiny_of_Bills/Completed_inquiries/futuredirection2011/index.

Books/Articles/Reports/Speeches

Australian Government, (2010). Budget measures: Budget paper no 2: 2010–11: Attorney-General's portfolio.. Canberra.

Australian Law Reform Commission. (2016). *Traditional rights and freedoms – Encroachments by commonwealth laws*. Report No 129 (2016). Retrieved from https://www.alrc.gov.au/publication/traditional-rights-and-freedoms-encroachments-by-commonwealth-laws-alrc-report-129/. Accessed 7 Jan 2020.

Bergin, A., & Trood, R. (2015). Creative tension: Parliament and National Security. *Canberra: Australian Strategic Policy Institute.*, (6 August 2015). Retrieved from https://www.aspi.org.au/report/creative-tension-parliament-and-national-security. Accessed 17 Jan 2020.

Byrnes, A. (2020). Economic and social rights in the Australian parliamentary human rights scrutiny process. In J. Debeljak & L. Grenfell (Eds.), *Law- making and human rights* (pp. 135–171). Sydney: Thompson Reuters.

Chordia, S. (2016, November 30). *The problem of balancing: Structured proportionality and tiered scrutiny* (Harvard law school visiting scholar colloquium series). Harvard Law School, Cambridge.

Department of Prime Minister and Cabinet. (2017). *Independent intelligence review*. Canberra: Government of Australia. Retrieved from https://pmc.gov.au/national-security/2017-independent-intelligence-review. Accessed 7 Jan 2020.

Crowe, D. (2017, February 28). Malcolm Turnbull urged to overhaul HRC as review splits on 18C. *The Australian* (online), 28 February 2017. http://www.theaustralian.com.au/national-affairs/malcolm-turnbull-urged-to-overhaul-hrc-as-review-recommends-no-changes-to-18c/news-story/e8fbbcd2f0163f4a3dfbc7cd6770066d.

Dalla-Pozza, D. (2016). Refining the Australian counter-terrorism legislative framework: How deliberative has parliament been? *Public Law Review, 27*(4), 271.

Dalla-Pozza, D. (2020). A dual scrutiny mechanism for Australia's counter- terrorism law landscape: The INSLM and the PJCIS. In J. Debeljak & L. Grenfell (Eds.), *Law making and human rights* (pp. 673–700). Sydney: Thompson Reuters.

Debeljak, J., & Grenfell, L. (2020). Contextualising law- making and human rights. In J. Debeljak & L. Grenfell (Eds.), *Law-making and human rights* (pp. 2–28). Sydney: Thompson Reuters.

Evans, C. & Evans, S. (2006a). *Australian parliaments and the protection of human rights.* Paper presented in the Department of the Senate Occasional Lecture Series, Canberra, 8 December 2006.

Evans, C., & Evans, S. (2006b). Evaluating the human rights performance of legislatures. *Human Rights Law Review, 6*, 545–569. https://doi.org/10.1093/hrlr/ngl012.

Evans, C., & Evans, S. (2006c). Legislative scrutiny committees and parliamentary conceptions of human rights. *Public Law, 785.*

Evans, C. & Evans, S. (2007). *Australian Parliaments and the protection of human rights*, Parl Paper No 47. Canberra: Parliament of Australia. https://www.aph.gov.au/About_Parliament/Senate/Powers_practice_n_procedures/~/~/link.aspx?_id=8B6C280930C4453C92CA146B82B01CE6&_z=z

Faulkner, J. (2014). *Surveillance, intelligence and accountability: An Australia story.* Senate Occasional Paper, Parliamentary Library, Canberra: Parliament of Australia. Retrieved from https://apo.org.au/node/41934. Accessed 17 Jan 2020.

Fletcher, A. (2018). *Australia's human rights scrutiny regime*. Melbourne: Melbourne University Press.

Fletcher, A. (2020). Human rights scrutiny in the Federal Parliament: Smokescreen or democratic solution? In J. Debeljak & L. Grenfell (Eds.), *Law making and human rights: Executive and parliamentary scrutiny across Australian jurisdictions* (pp. 31–66). Sydney: Thompson Reuters.

Grenfell, L. (2015). An Australian spectrum of political rights scrutiny: Continuing to lead by example? *Public Law Review, 26*(1), 19–32.

Halligan, J. (2008). Parliamentary committee roles in facilitating public policy at the commonwealth level. *Australasian Parliamentary Review, 23*(2), 135–156.

Inglis, R. (2017, February 28). Parliamentary joint committee on human rights releases freedom of speech report, *The Examiner* (Hobart), 28 February 2017 http://www.examiner.com.au/story/4498392/free-speech-report-tabled/.

Jennett, G. (2016, August 2016). Record crossbench a headache for stressed senate budget, workload. *ABC Online*, 22 August 2016 http://www.abc.net.au/news/2016-08-22/jennett-senate-committee-inquiries/7765838.

Levy, R., & Orr, G. (2016). *The law of deliberative democracy*. London: Routledge.
Moulds, S. P. (2018). *The rights protecting role of parliamentary committees: The case of Australia's counter-terrorism laws* (Doctoral thesis). University of Adelaide, Adelaide, South Australia, Australia. https://digital.library.adelaide.edu.au/dspace/handle/2440/115212
Rajanayagam, S. (2020). Urgent law-making and the human rights (parliamentary scrutiny) act. In J. Debeljak & L. Grenfell (Eds.), *Law-making and human rights* (pp. 647–672). Sydney: Thompson Reuters.
Reynolds, D., & Williams, G. (2020). Evaluating the impact of Australia's Federal Human Rights Scrutiny Regime. In J. Debeljak & L. Grenfell (Eds.), *Law- Making and Human Rights* (pp. 67–96). Sydney: Thompson Reuters.
Rice, S. (2020). Allowing for dissent: Opening up human rights dialogue in the Australian parliament. In J. Debeljak & L. Grenfell (Eds.), *Law making and human rights* (pp. 99–134). Sydney: Thompson Reuters.
Sibraa, K. (1990). *Session one: The revolutionary proposals of the 1970s*. Keynote address at conference to mark the twentieth anniversary of Senate Legislative and General Purpose Standing Committees and Senate Estimates Committees, Canberra, Parliament of Australia, 3 October 1990. Retrieved from https://www.aph.gov.au/binaries/senate/pubs/pops/pop12/s01.pdf. Accessed 17 Jan 2020.
Stephenson, S. (2016). *From dialogue to disagreement in comparative rights constitutionalism*. Sydney: Federation Press.
Williams, G., & Reynolds, D. (2016). The operation and impact of Australia's parliamentary scrutiny regime for human rights. *Monash University Law Review, 41*(2), 469–508.
Weston, E. (2015). The Human Rights Act 1998 and the effectiveness of parliamentary scrutiny. *King's Law Journal, 26*(2), 266–284.

Chapter 10
Conclusion

Abstract This chapter concludes by reflecting on the central theme of this book, and argues that understanding parliamentary committees working together as a *system* provides the most fertile opportunity to identify options to improve Australia's parliamentary model of rights protection. It also explains that the findings made in Part II and the recommendations made in Part III are of particular relevance to rights advocates because they provide a persuasive counterpoint to those who have expressed scepticism about the capacity of the parliamentary committee system to deliver meaningful rights protection. In this way, this chapter brings a new perspective to the broader discussion on how rights should be protected in Australia, whilst reflecting on the particular contribution these committees of influence have made to the content and contours of counter-terrorism laws in Australia.

10.1 Understanding Australia's Committees of Influence

At the heart of this research is a determination to get a clearer understanding of how Australia's parliamentary model of rights protection works in practice, and to evaluate the role and impact of the system of parliamentary committees within that model. The key purpose of this work is to identify the legislative, public and hidden impact parliamentary committees can have on federal laws, and having documented that impact, reflect on how to improve the capacity of the parliamentary committee system to contribute to Australia's parliamentary model of rights protection.

While many other rights scholars have offered views as to why and how this parliamentary model of rights protection should be *replaced*, my work is focused on what we can do with the model that is *in place now*. My findings, particularly those that suggest that scrutiny by parliamentary committees is rights-enhancing, provide new perspectives on how to make the most of the existing features of Australia's parliamentary model of rights protection. My work also provides a useful check list of relevant considerations for those scholars advocating for structural reform, and a contextual basis from which to evaluate reform options. This makes my work both modest in scope, but optimistic in character. I have argued that the current model is worth investing in, and that it can deliver meaningful rights outcomes, but I have

S. Moulds, *Committees of Influence*, https://doi.org/10.1007/978-981-15-4350-0_10

also flagged areas where further structural reform may be needed to ensure comprehensive rights protection in Australia.

This book has explored the role and function of parliamentary committees and how they contribute to rights protection at the federal level through the lens of the counter-terrorism case study. Part II of this book collated evidence of three tiers of impact (legislative, public and hidden) attributable to the work of the four parliamentary committees, elucidating with new clarity the rights-enhancing role parliamentary committees can play. The material in Part II also highlighted that different parliamentary committees have different strengths and weaknesses and therefore impact proposed laws in different ways. Part II revealed that it is when different committees work together to scrutinise a law that the biggest rights impact is felt. These findings provide the basis for the recommendations discussed in Chaps. 8 and 9 and detailed in Appendix A, which are designed to lay out a new, practical pathway for improving the contribution parliamentary committees can make to rights protection in Australia.

In this concluding chapter, I reflect on the central theme of this book, and argue that understanding parliamentary committees working together as a *system* provides the most fertile opportunity to identify options to improve Australia's parliamentary model of rights protection. I also argue that the findings made in Part II and the recommendations made in Part III are of particular relevance to rights advocates as they provide a persuasive counterpoint to those who have expressed scepticism about the capacity of the parliamentary committee system to deliver meaningful rights protection. In this way, my research brings a new perspective to the broader discussion on how rights should be protected in Australia, which is considered in further detail below.

10.2 Understanding Parliamentary Committees as a System Is the Key to Improving Their Rights-Protecting Capacity

Many of the rights advocates discussed in Chap. 1, including Evans and Evans (2006a, b, c, 2007), Williams and Burton (2015) and Charlesworth (2002), have argued that the parliamentary model of rights protection operating at the federal level is fundamentally flawed and that significant structural change is needed to ensure meaningful and comprehensive protection of rights in Australia. They have pointed out, for example, that the rights of minorities can often be overlooked or overridden in a system that leaves open multiple opportunities for executive dominance and popularist policy making (eg. Fletcher 2018; Williams and Burton 2015). Some have cited rights-abrogating features of Australia's counter-terrorism laws as examples of the failure of the parliamentary model of rights protection to guard against unjustified intrusion into individual rights (Carne 2015). While initially hopeful that the establishment of the PJCHR would help to 'fill the gaps' in rights protection at the federal level, many have since lamented the inability of the PJCHR to have a strong rights-protecting impact on legislation (e.g Fletcher 2018; Williams and Burton 2015).

As noted in Chap. 1, prior to commencing my research I shared the views expressed above; however, the substantial list of rights-enhancing changes attributable to the work of parliamentary committees uncovered in Part II persuaded me to reassess my previous scepticism. It also led me to engage in a different way with the arguments of those who had previously sought to evaluate the role of parliamentary committees in rights protection.

As I conducted my research, it became clear that previous analysis of the role of parliamentary committees in rights protection in Australia and elsewhere had been focused on individual committees achieving (or struggling to achieve) their prescribed scrutiny mandates. It had not included a sustained focus on how different committees in a parliamentary system work together, the impact such a system might have on the behind-the-scenes development of legislation, or how such a system of committees might work to generate its own dynamic rights-scrutiny culture. This leaves open the possibility that past analysis of Australia's parliamentary model of rights protection has underestimated the contribution made by parliamentary committees working as a *system*, and the potential for this system to be improved.

By focusing on how parliamentary committees work together, my research uncovers new opportunities for improving the rights-enhancing role of parliamentary committees that build upon the particular strengths and weaknesses of particular committees and encourage system-level collaboration and coordination. My research suggests that relatively minor changes could be made to the practices and processes of individual committees, which would allow them to maximise their rights-enhancing contribution to the committee system, without changing their character or diluting the respect they enjoy in the eyes of key participants. For example, my recommendations strengthen the capacity of the inquiry-based committees to attract a broader and more diverse range of submission makers and introduce practical strategies to improve the experience for first-time inquiry witnesses. My recommendations also encourage the scrutiny committees to prioritise the development of the type of materials and publications that the other key participants in the committee system find most useful.

My recommendations also seek to address a number of structural and resource-related shortcomings within the committee system that may present barriers to individual committees working more effectively with other committees in the system. For example, my recommendations encourage the expanded use of transparent secondee arrangements to support the high performing but under-resourced pool of secretariat staff that support parliamentary committees. I also recommend changes to the Standing Orders to set out clear expectations around response times to committee requests for information, and for the timely tabling of committee reports. Specific changes are also recommended to the tabling of PJCHR reports – centred around the adoption of Alert Digest style reporting – to give key participants greater opportunity to access and understand the PJCHR's rights analysis prior to making decisions about the merits of a proposed Bill. These changes are designed to be implemented primarily by public servants, parliamentary committee staff and committee Chairs and are generally not dependent on legislative change. It is hoped, therefore, that they could be adopted swiftly, and their veracity quickly tested by monitoring whether the rights-enhancing impact of the individual committees studied – and the system more broadly – improves.

My research also highlights the value in understanding and investing in the rights-scrutiny culture that currently exists among the system of committees at the federal level, rather than relying upon one particular committee to hold the executive to account for its compliance with human rights obligations. While this may initially sound like a 'weak' approach to rights protection or an uncritical endorsement of the status quo, my research suggests that investing in the existing committee system has a number of advantages over other more radical models of rights reform.

These advantages derive from the fact that the parliamentary committee system emulates and reinforces the existing institutional culture of the Australian Parliament described in Chap. 3, including the way institutions of government instinctively seek to resolve disagreements on rights. As Stephenson (2016) explains, this institutional culture can have a particularly powerful behind-the-scenes impact and is difficult to shift, even when structural reforms are implemented that seek to give explicit rights-protecting roles to other branches of government (at pp. 8, 211). Stephenson's work suggests that building upon the parliamentary committee system as a way to improve rights protection at the federal level may be an easier cultural fit – and therefore more readily accepted and more likely to be sustainable – than adopting more radical structural change, such as the introduction of a constitutionally entrenched bill of rights, that would significantly alter the way federal institutions 'disagree' with each other on rights. This is supported by the contextual material presented in Chap. 3, which demonstrates that the non-rights-protecting roles parliamentary committees play (such as providing the opportunity for parliamentarians to build their public profile and influence policy development, make connections with sophisticated submission makers and generate media interest) encourage a broad range of parliamentarians to be involved in committee processes. This in turn provides a broad and powerful base of parliamentarians who can then potentially go on to utilise this committee system to protect and promote the rights they consider to be important and shared by the Australian community, such as those principles set that appear to be forming part of the emerging rights scrutiny culture discussed above.

Human rights advocates such as Carne may be correct to point out the shortcomings in any attempt to articulate a list of commonly acknowledged individual rights from a parliamentary setting, warning that such lists rarely cover the full range of internationally protected rights and risks ignoring rights of unpopular or politically isolated minorities (Carne 2015; Charlesworth 2002; Williams 2016). However, my research (particularly Chap. 5 documenting legislative impact) suggests that the emerging rights-scrutiny culture within the federal Parliament may be more robust than first imagined, at least in the context of the case study Acts, and could be the key to improving the capacity of Australia's parliamentary model of rights protection. For this reason, I recommend changes to the parliamentary committee system that seek to legitimise and acknowledge all meaningful efforts to undertake rights scrutiny, regardless of the language used or the scope of the rights criteria applied. The recommendations I propose seek to do this by supporting *both* the SSCSB and the PJCHR to continue to produce timely and accessible analysis of Bills using their own separate 'rights criteria', whilst at the same time looking for opportunities for the two committees to collaborate where appropriate. This approach aims to welcome rights advocates from all political persuasions by emphasising the shared and dynamic nature of the emerging rights-scrutiny culture at the federal level, rather than alienating those parliamentarians who may be reluctant to embrace international human rights law, either due to lack of knowledge or political positioning. This recommendation feeds into and is supported by my broader recommendation to undertake further research to test and document the emerging rights-scrutiny culture identified in this case study in other areas of law. These considerations also inform the new perspective I now bring to bear on Australia's model of rights protection and the ways it can be improved in the future.

I argue that understanding the ways different committees work together as a system – and exploring the committee system's place with Australia's broader parliamentary rights scrutiny culture - provides new opportunities to engage with the ideas and recommendations explored by Debeljak and Grenfell (2020a, b), Rice (2020), Byrnes (2020), Fletcher (2018, 2020), Williams and Reynolds (2016) and Reynolds and Williams (2020). For example, a system-wide approach reveals new sites for experimentation when it comes to developing more 'contestable' approaches to rights scrutiny that can accommodate dissenting or differing views (Rice 2020), provides new incentives for public servants and others working behind the scenes to document and reflect on their scrutiny impacts (Fletcher 2020) and creates the space needed for the federal Parliament to reflect upon the Australian approach to protecting and promoting economic and social rights (Byrnes 2020). A system-wide approach also eases the pressure on any one committee to issue urgent scrutiny reports (Rajanayagam 2020) and provides avenues for productive 'dual scrutiny' relationships to be forged between parliamentary committees and non-parliamentary actors (Dalla-Pozza 2020). A system-wide approach also gives rise to new opportunities to experiment with new technologies and new deliberative techniques that have the potential to speak to a new generation of Australians, some of whom have exhibited apathy when it comes to engaging with traditional parliamentary processes (Moulds 2019, 2020).

As these and many other authors (e.g Hiebert 2015; Reynolds and Williams 2017, 2020) have emphasised, even when changes are made to the way parliamentary committees undertake their work and how they work together, the quality of parliamentary scrutiny hinges heavily on access to resources and political will. These are not factors that a system-wide approach can remedy alone. However, a system-wide approach can encourage a broader range of actors – across political spectrums and within and outside of government – to recognise and value the impact parliamentary committees can have on the way laws are made and the extent to which they adhere to rights standards. It can broaden the potential investors and beneficiaries of a parliamentary model of rights protection that derives its legitimacy from its democratic characteristics and dynamic, responsive nature. For these reasons, the system-wide approach to evaluating the impact and influence of parliamentary committees aims to supplement and support related scholarship in the field of law making and rights protection, and has relevance across state boundaries. It suggests, for example, that there is value investing in committee systems with deliberative and authoritative attributes (as well as specialist human rights committees) and it highlights the value of adopting a broad, inclusive approach to post-legislative scrutiny that engages with a wide range of parliamentary and non-parliamentary actors (as a supplement or alternative to prescribed or periodic legislative review through the use of sunset clauses or judicial review). In this way, my research may provide new opportunities for participants and scholars in other Westminster-inspired parliaments to develop and build upon their own scrutiny cultures in an organic, inclusive way - maximising the potential for a broader range of actors to engage in rights protection and to participate actively in the law making process.

10.3 New Perspectives on Australia's Parliamentary Model of Rights Protection

By focusing on parliamentary committees working together as a system, my research also offers important new perspectives on the work of other rights advocates who have considered the role parliamentary committees play (or could play) in Australia's parliamentary model of rights protection. For example, my findings help provide a broader context in which to assess the performance of the PJCHR, building upon the qualitative work undertaken by Fletcher (2018, 2020), Campbell and Morris (2015), Williams and Reynolds (2016), Reynolds and Williams (2020), and Williams and Burton (2015), and offering alternative options for enhancing the PJCHR's capacity to contribute to Australia's parliamentary model of rights protection. While my research confirms many of the findings of these scholars on the PJCHR's limited legislative and public impact, I argue that the high-quality rights analysis provided by the PJCHR is making an important contribution to the rights-enhancing work of other committees and their submission makers. Moreover, I argue that this analysis is the source of the PJCHR's current and future legitimacy among key participants, and that this more 'technical scrutiny' role should be the future focus of the committee. For this reason, I recommend strategies to maximise the quality, timeliness and accessibility of the rights-scrutiny analysis of proposed laws, but warn against changing the character of the committee to resemble that of the inquiry-based committees.

My findings also build upon and update the 2006 evaluation of rights protection in the Australian Parliament undertaken by Evans and Evans, by highlighting a broader spectrum of rights-enhancing impacts made by the parliamentary committee system during the period 2001–15 (see Evans and Evans 2006a, b, c). The emergence of the PJCIS as a committee with a strong legislative impact, and the considerable behind-the-scenes influence of the SSCSB revealed in my research, challenge the conclusion reached by these scholars during their 2006 study that the rights protection offered by committees was severely limited in scope and ad hoc. My analysis of the strengths and weaknesses of the PJCHR, which was created after the Evans and Evans study, also provides a fresh perspective to test some of the recommendations made by these scholars to fill what they saw to be the gaps in rights protection within the parliamentary model.

From a deliberative democracy perspective, my research substantiates past findings made by Dalla-Pozza (2016), Uhr (1998) and Halligan (2008) and suggests that the inquiry-based committees considered in my research not only provide meaningful deliberative forums but also deliver rights-enhancing results. For example, I argue that the particular strengths of the LCA Committees, such as their diverse membership and capacity to attract a diverse range of submission makers, should be considered when evaluating the contribution committees can make to Australia's parliamentary model of rights protection. As Secretary to the LCA Committee Sophie Dunstone said in an interview in 2016:

> I really fundamentally believe that one of the real strengths of the, particularly the Senate committee system, is that you are facilitating a process that enables anyone from Jo Bloggs on the street through to some academic who's an expert in the field to provide their view and for Senators to have access to that information (Canberra 23 May 2016).

By focusing directly on the ways in which key participants and community members engage with the parliamentary committee system, my recommendations also share themes with international efforts to articulate the appropriate 'democratic' role of parliaments in rights protection, including the draft *Principles and Guidelines on the Role of Parliaments in the Protection and Realisation of the Rule of Law and Human Rights* reproduced in Hunt et al. (2015, pp. 485–99) and discussed in detail by Fletcher (2018, particularly pp. 294–6). This is because, as discussed in Chaps. 9 and 10, a system-wide focus creates space for a more dynamic, contestable approach to human rights scrutiny to emerge that aligns with, rather than pulls against, the existing rights scrutiny culture identified in Chap. 6 and considered from different perspectives by many other rights scholars including Byrnes (2020) and Rice (2020). It does this by recognising that no single component of the rights scrutiny system operating at the federal level in Australia should be relied upon to single-handed deliver robust and democratic rights protection. Instead, when considered as a part of a broader system, it is possible to invest different committees with different functions and attributes that together maximise the potential for rights-enhancing results. My recommendations also recognise the important role those working behind the scenes play within the Australia parliamentary model of rights protection, and aim to support what Fletcher (2018) has described as 'back office' rights scrutiny or a culture of justification (Debeljak and Grenfell 2020a, b) when it comes to integrating human rights standards in policy development and legislative drafting.

By focusing on the system of parliamentary committees working together it is also possible to evaluate the rights impact of committees such as the PJCIS which, despite its lack of specific rights mandate and close relationship with the executive, remains a powerful rights scrutiny body within the counter-terrorism context. In fact, as discussed in Chap. 8, my research suggests that the strong relationships the PJCIS has been able to forge with key law enforcement and intelligence agencies and national security experts, and the strong legislative impact that has followed, offer important new opportunities to improve the deliberative quality of law making at the federal level, potentially with rights-enhancing results.

Like Marsh (2004), Monk (2010) and Uhr (1998 at p. 219), my research also supports the finding that parliamentary committees have much to offer in improving the quality of law making at the federal level, including at the pre-introduction stage. By documenting the influence of the SSCSB on the work of parliamentary counsel and policy makers, for example, it is possible to see how those responsible for drafting and developing federal laws pre-empt committee scrutiny with rights-enacting results. As Byrnes (2014), and Campbell and Morris (2015) predicted, this trend is also beginning to emerge with respect to the PJCHR, but could be considerably enhanced by adopting reforms to support the PJCHR's 'technical scrutiny' role and looking for ways to support the PJCHR working more closely with other committees in the system.

Finally, my research provides the basis for the further investigation of an emerging rights-scrutiny culture within the federal Parliament, with important implications for future options for reforming or replacing Australia's current model of rights protection. At its highest, this emerging rights-scrutiny culture could have the potential to deliver the type of outcomes Campbell was looking for in his 2006 proposal for the establishment of a 'democratic Bill of Rights' to be developed and applied exclusively by a parliamentary committee (Campbell 2006 at p. 333). For Campbell (2006), there was a need to improve upon Australia's pre-PJCHR model of parliamentary protection by investing a specific parliamentary committee with the power to generate a list of rights standards itself, and then scrutinise proposed laws for compliance with these rights standards (at pp. 333–6). That is, in effect, what I have observed occurring organically among the four committees studied in my book. In other words, it is possible to compile a list of common rights and scrutiny principles from the work of the PJCHR, SSCSB, PJCIS and LCA Committees in the context of their scrutiny of counter-terrorism laws that appear to resonate across political lines and attract public interest and submission maker support. Moreover, my research suggests that, when the committees make recommendations to improve a law's compliance with these rights-scrutiny principles, these recommendations are frequently reflected in legislative amendments.

As noted above, the nature of the case study chosen, and the character of the particular committees studied, naturally favour a focus on civil and political rights (as opposed to economic, social and cultural rights which are considered by Byrnes 2020). This makes my findings on the emergence of a rights scrutiny culture within the Australian Parliament preliminary in nature. Further research is required to investigate whether this emerging rights-scrutiny culture applies in other contexts, and in particular in the context of laws and committees that engage more closely with economic, social and cultural rights. It may be that the rights scrutiny culture within Parliament has a clear preference for civil and political rights over other forms of rights. If this is the case, it again tells us something important about our parliamentary model of rights protection, and what types of investments may need to be made to improve the depth and breadth of rights protection within this system. Further research may also help confirm my preliminary view that the emerging rights scrutiny culture that I have documented appears to have the type of democratically articulated and dynamic character that scholars such as Kinley (1999), Kinley and Ernst (2012), Campbell and Morris (2015) considered to be integral for developing a model of rights protection that transcend the criticisms levelled at statutory or constitutionally entrenched bills of rights. Of course, my findings and recommendations depart in important respects from those of Campbell. Unlike Campbell, I do not recommend providing a constitutional backing for parliamentary committees, or a more proactive legislative development role for the PJCHR. However, like Campbell, my research suggests that parliamentary committees should play a central role in any future reforms to improve rights protection in Australia.

In addition, my research suggests that understanding this emerging rights-scrutiny culture could help identify opportunities to move the Australian Parliament away from what Levy and Orr (2016) describe as 'conceptual balancing' approaches to determining rights disputes, and towards 'deliberative accommodation' approaches, by highlighting the potential for parliamentary committees to encourage a broader range of views to be heard and evaluated in a meaningful way (at pp. 76–80).

When exploring these issues, I emphasise again that my research finds that parliamentary committees have had an important rights-*enhancing* impact on Australia's counter-terrorism laws, but have rarely been able to completely remedy all of the rights-abrogating features of these laws (Williams 2011, 2015; Appleby 2015; Lynch and McGarrity 2008). These rights-abrogating features are so significant that, even if the changes recommended in this book were fully implemented, Australia's counter-terrorism laws would still fail to comply with the full range of internationally recognised human rights and common law rights to which Australia subscribes. For this reason, I do not argue that improving the parliamentary committee system is *enough* when it comes to rights protection at the federal level. Rather I argue that understanding how the parliamentary committee system works and the overall impact it has on our laws is critical to improving the model of rights protection that is in place *now*, and should be carefully considered when thinking about introducing different models of rights protection in the future. By engaging with key participants in the system and gathering views on how laws should be scrutinised for rights compliance, my research may point to the most sustainable and pragmatic pathway towards the development of further legislative or judicial protections for commonly respected human rights.

10.4 Conclusion

The goal of my research was to evaluate the role played by parliamentary committees in Australia's parliamentary model of rights protection and identify practical options for improvement. This goal was pursued against a background of scepticism amongst rights advocates about the capacity of the parliamentary committee system to make a meaningful contribution to rights protection and in the face of more than a decade of rights-abrogating counter-terrorism related legislative activity. The outcome of my research has been the articulation of a new perspective on the role played by parliamentary committees in rights protection in Australia, informed by a three-tiered analysis of their impact on 15 case study Acts, and in particular by insights obtained from key participants working closely within the committee system.

As a rights advocate who previously shared the conventional view about the inability of the parliamentary model to provide robust rights protection in Australia, the findings made in this book have been surprising and encouraging. The material presented in Part II suggests that parliamentary committees are having a rights-enhancing impact on Australia's counter-terrorism laws, and that in some cases this impact is quite profound. In particular, my research suggests that, when individual parliamentary committees work together as a system, they can effect rights-enhancing change at the policy development level, right through to the content of enacted provisions. They can smooth off rough edges of proposed laws that seek to extend executive power at the expense of individual rights, introduce safeguards to ensure access to review of executive decisions, and significantly limit the scope of proposed new law-enforcement and intelligence-gathering powers and new criminal offences. They can also work to focus the minds of public servants, parliamentary counsel and parliamentarians on the type of principles that should be observed when making laws that broaden the powers of the executive branch of government at the expense of individual rights, and offer analytical frameworks for balancing competing rights or interests. When the scrutiny approaches of these committees are well entrenched and respected, they can also lay the foundations for a rights-scrutiny culture to emerge within the Parliament, and provide meaningful deliberative forums for those directly affected by these laws to express their views and concerns. They can also empower backbenchers and non-government members to push for amendments to proposed or existing laws that reflect the documented concerns of the Australian community, or the considered views of independent oversight bodies.

My research does not find that parliamentary committees alone are well placed to *remedy* unjustified or disproportionate intrusions into individual rights, or that they can singlehandedly sustain the type of rights culture that may be thought necessary for a country like Australia. Studies of the content of Australian laws, including counter-terrorism laws, consistently conclude that Australia trails behind its Western counter-parts when it comes to complying with international human rights standards, particularly when it comes to minority rights (see e.g. Roach 2015 at pp. 650–88; Williams et al. 2014; Williams 2012; Zifcak 2015; Foot 2007). However, the findings made in this book suggest that rights advocates would be wise to rethink their past scepticism about the rights-enhancing capacity of the existing parliamentary committee system when seeking to improve the current parliamentary model of rights protection, or when developing proposals for more radical structural reform. In particular, my research demonstrates that investment in the parliamentary committee *system*, as well as in individual parliamentary committees, would greatly enhance the overall rights-enhancing impact of the current model.

My research finds that reflecting on the role and function of the broader Australian Parliament helps identify the best opportunities to invest in the parliamentary committee system's rights-enhancing capacity. For this reason, my recommendations are about making sure that the work of committees – which is already highly valued and respected – is readily available and accessible to those in a position to make decisions about the development and content of proposed laws. This means recognising the particular strengths and weaknesses of the different committees studied, while at the same time identifying ways to improve the quality of the interactions between different committees in the system. For example, my recommendations suggest that strengthening the behind-the-scenes impact of the technical scrutiny committees and promoting the deliberative opportunities provided by the inquiry-based committees could increase the rights-enhancing capacity of the system by ensuring that policy makers, legislative drafters and sophisticated submission makers have access to (1) the technical analysis they need to draw attention to the rights impact of a Bill and (2) a diverse range of views to generate less rights-abrogating policy alternatives at the public inquiry stage. This would in turn bring the parliamentary committee system closer to what Levy and Orr (2016) describe as the 'deliberative accommodation' approach to resolving rights-related disputes (at pp. 76–80), and enhance the quality of the multi-stage rights review identified by Stephenson (2016 at pp. 8 and 211). My recommendations also clarify the goals and objectives of newer committees such as the PJCHR, and encourage the use of innovative techniques such as the use of specialist secondees to preserve the already high legislative impact of committees such as the PJCIS.

While motivated by the findings of the counter-terrorism case study, I recognise that further research is needed to confirm that the observations made in this study apply to other subject areas and to other individual committees (see e.g. Moulds 2019 and 2020). In particular, further research is required to determine whether the emerging rights-scrutiny culture I identify is applicable in other contexts, such as with respect to laws and policies that more squarely engage economic and social rights (see e.g. Byrnes 2020). With these considerations in mind, the recommendations made in this book are not radical or profound, but rather pragmatic and incremental. They suggest investing in, rather than disrupting, the existing multi-stage rights review at the federal level. In developing these proposed changes, I have resisted my initial temptation to conclude that the rights-enhancing contribution of parliamentary committees is fatally flawed without significant structural change. I have been persuaded by the evidence collected during the case study, and in particular by the views and experiences of those interviewed. I am now of the view that the current parliamentary committee system has much to offer as a form of rights protection, because of, not in spite of, its central characteristics, which draw from the features and functions of the Parliament itself. For this reason, I look forward to future studies of how the *system* of parliamentary committees contributes to Australia's current model of rights protection, and how this system can be utilised in any alternative models of rights protection being considered at the federal level. I hope this book contributes in some small way to this important body of work.

References

Books/Articles/ Reports/Speeches

Appleby, G. (2015). The 2014 counter-terrorism reforms in review. *Public Law Review, 26*(1), 4–7.

Byrnes, A. (2014). *Human rights under the microscope: Reflections on parliamentary scrutiny*. Speech delivered at Law Society of South Australia Continuing Professional Development Program, Adelaide, 11 December 2014. http://www.ahrcentre.org/sites/ahrcentre.org/files/mdocs/Byrnes%20%2D%2D%20%20PJCHR%20-%20handout%20for%20Adelaide%20talk%20December%202014%20revised.pdf

Byrnes, A. (2020). Economic and social rights in the Australian parliamentary human rights scrutiny process. In J. Debeljak & L. Grenfell (Eds.), *Law making and human rights* (pp. 135–171). Sydney: Thompson Reuters.

Campbell, T. (2006). Human rights strategies: An Australian alternative. In T. Campbell, J. Goldsworthy, & A. Stone (Eds.), *Protecting rights without a bill of rights* (pp. 319–334). London: Ashgate.

Campbell, T., & Morris, S. (2015). Human rights for democracies: A provisional assessment of the Australian human rights (Parliamentary scrutiny) act 2011. *University of Queensland Law Journal, 34*(1), 7–27.

Carne, G. (2015). Re-orientating human rights meanings and understandings? Reviving and revisiting Australian human rights exceptionalism through a Liberal democratic rights agenda. *Flinders Law Review Journal, 17*, 1–67. http://www.austlii.edu.au/au/journals/FlinLawJl/2015/1.pdf.

Charlesworth, H. (2002). *Writing in rights: Australia and the protection of human rights*. Sydney: UNSW Press.

Dalla-Pozza, D. (2016). Refining the Australian counter-terrorism legislative framework: How deliberative has parliament been? Public Law Review, *27*(4), 271.

Dalla-Pozza, D. (2020). A dual scrutiny mechanism for Australia's counter- terrorism law landscape: The INSLM and the PJCIS. In J. Debeljak & L. Grenfell (Eds.), *Law making and human rights* (pp. 673–700). Sydney: Thompson Reuters.

Debeljak, J., & Grenfell, L. (2020a). Contextualising law making and human rights. In J. Debeljak & L. Grenfell (Eds.), *Law making and human rights* (pp. 2–28). Sydney: Thompson Reuters.

Debeljak, J., & Grenfell, L. (2020b). Future directions for engaging with human rights in law-making: Is a culture of justification emerging across Australian jurisdictions? In J. Debeljak & L. Grenfell (Eds.), *Law making and human rights* (pp. 789–818). Sydney: Thompson Reuters.

Evans, C. & Evans, S. (2006a). *Australian parliaments and the protection of human rights*. Paper presented in the Department of the Senate Occasional Lecture Series, Canberra, 8 December 2006.

Evans, C., & Evans, S. (2006b). Evaluating the human rights performance of legislatures. *Human Rights Law Review, 6*, 545–569. https://doi.org/10.1093/hrlr/ngl012.

Evans, C., & Evans, S. (2006c). Legislative scrutiny committees and parliamentary conceptions of human rights. *Public Law, 785*.

Evans, C. & Evans, S. (2007), *Australian Parliaments and the protection of human rights*, Parl Paper No 47. Canberra: Parliament of Australia. https://www.aph.gov.au/About_Parliament/Senate/Powers_practice_n_procedures/~/~/link.aspx?_id=8B6C280930C4453C92CA146B82B01CE6&_z=z

Fletcher, A. (2018). *Australia's human rights scrutiny regime*. Melbourne: Melbourne University Press.

Fletcher, A. (2020). Human rights scrutiny in the Federal Parliament: Smokescreen or democratic solution? In J. Debeljak & L. Grenfell (Eds.), *Law- making and human rights* (pp. 31–63). Sydney: Thompson Reuters.

Foot, R. (2007). The United Nations, counter terrorism and human rights: Institutional adaptation and embedded ideas. *Human Rights Quarterly, 29*(2), 489–514. https://doi.org/10.1353/hrq.2007.0018.

Halligan, J. (2008). Parliamentary committee roles in facilitating public policy at the commonwealth level. *Australasian Parliamentary Review, 23*(2), 135–156.

Hiebert, J. L. (2015). Legislative rights review: Addressing the gap between ideals and constraints. In Hunt, M. Hooper, H. J & Yowell, P. (Eds.), Parliaments and human rights: Redressing the democratic deficit (pp. 39–52). Oxford: Hart Publishing.

Hunt, M., Hooper, H. J., & Yowell, P. (Eds.). (2015). Parliaments and human rights: Redressing the democratic deficit. Oxford: Hart Publishing.

Kinley, D. (1999). Parliamentary scrutiny of human rights: A duty neglected. In P. Alston (Ed.), *Promoting human rights through bills of rights: Comparative perspectives* (pp. 158–172). Oxford: Oxford University Press.

Kinley, D., & Ernst, C. (2012). Exile on main street: Australia's legislative agenda for human rights. *European Human Rights Law Review, 1*, 58–70.

Levy, R. & Orr, G. (2016) *The law of deliberative democracy*. London: Routledge. pp. 4, 22-23.

Lynch, A., & McGarrity, N. (2008). Counter-terrorism laws: How neutral laws create fear and anxiety in Australia's Muslim communities. *Alternative Law Journal, 33*(4), 225–228.

Marsh, I. (2004, November 26). *Australia's representation gap: A role for parliamentary committees?* Speech delivered at the Department of the Senate Occasional Lecture Series, Parliament House, Canberra.

Monk, D. (2010). A framework for evaluating the performance of committees in Westminster parliaments. *Journal of Legislative Studies, 16*, 1–13. https://doi.org/10.1080/13572330903541904.

Moulds, S. P. (2019). Parliamentary rights scrutiny and counter-terrorism lawmaking in Australia. *Journal of South East Asian Human Rights, 3*(2), 185–230. https://doi.org/10.19184/jseahr.v3i2.13461.

Moulds, S. P. (2020). Parliamentary committees facilitating parliamentary deliberation: A case study of marriage equality reform. In J. Debeljak & L. Grenfell (Eds.), *Law making and human rights* (pp. 745–786). Sydney: Thompson Reuters.

Rajanayagam, S. (2020). Urgent Law-Making and the Human Rights (Parliamentary Scrutiny) Act. In J. Debeljak & L. Grenfell (Eds.), *Law-making and human rights* (pp. 647–672). Sydney: Thompson Reuters.

Reynolds, D., & Williams, G. (2017). *A charter of rights for Australia* (4th ed.). Sydney: NewSouth Books.

Reynolds, D., & Williams, G. (2020). Evaluating the impact of Australia's federal human rights scrutiny regime. In J. Debeljak & L. Grenfell (Eds.), *Law making and human rights* (pp. 67–96). Sydney: Thompson Reuters.

Rice, S. (2020). Allowing for dissent: Opening up human rights dialogue in the Australian parliament. In J. Debeljak & L. Grenfell (Eds.), *Law making and human rights* (pp. 99–134). Sydney: Thompson Reuters.

Roach, K. (Ed.). (2015). *Comparative counter-terrorism law* (pp. 650–688). Cambridge: Cambridge University Press.

Stephenson, S. (2016). *From dialogue to disagreement in comparative rights constitutionalism*. Sydney: Federation Press.
Uhr, J. (1998). *Deliberative democracy in Australia: The changing place of parliament*. Cambridge: Cambridge University Press.
Williams, G. (2011). A decade of Australian anti-terror laws. *Melbourne University Law Review, 35*(3), 1136. http://classic.austlii.edu.au/au/journals/MelbULawRw/2011/38.html.
Williams, G. (2012). Anti-terror legislation in Australia and New Zealand. In V. Ramraj, M. Hor, K. Roach, & G. Williams (Eds.), *Global anti-terrorism law and policy* (p. 541). Cambridge: Cambridge University Press.
Williams, G. (2015). The legal assault on Australian democracy: The annual Blackburn lecture. *Ethos, 236*, 18–23.
Williams, G. (2016). *Scrutiny of primary legislation principles and challenges: Where are we now and where are we headed?* Speech delivered at the Australia-New Zealand Scrutiny of Legislation Conference, Parliament House, Perth, 12 July 2016. http://www.parliament.wa.gov.au/WebCMS/WebCMS.nsf/resources/file-anzslc-provisional-conference-program/$file/ANZSLC%20Provisional%20Conference%20Program%20V5.pdf
Williams, G., & Burton, L. (2015). Australia's parliamentary scrutiny act: An exclusive parliamentary model of rights protection. In M. Hunt, H. J. Hooper, & P. Yowell (Eds.), *Parliaments and human rights: Redressing the democratic deficit* (pp. 258–279). Oxford: Hart Publishing.
Williams, G., & Reynolds, D. (2016). The operation and impact of Australia's parliamentary scrutiny regime for human rights. *Monash University Law Review, 41*(2), 469–508.
Williams, G., Davis, F., & McGarrity, N. (Eds.). (2014). *Surveillance, counter-terrorism and comparative constitutionalism*. London: Routledge.
Zifcak, S. (2015). Counter-terrorism and human rights. In J. Menadue & M. Keating (Eds.), *Fairness, opportunity and security*. Adelaide: ATF Press.

The manufacturer's authorised representative in the EU is Springer Nature Customer Service Centre GmbH, Europaplatz 3, 69115 Heidelberg, Germany. If you have any concerns regarding our products, please contact ProductSafety@springernature.com

Printed and bound by CPI Group (UK) Ltd, Croydon, CR0 4YY

30/09/2026

02225510-0011